The Best of Me

A
Gerontius
Centenary
Companion

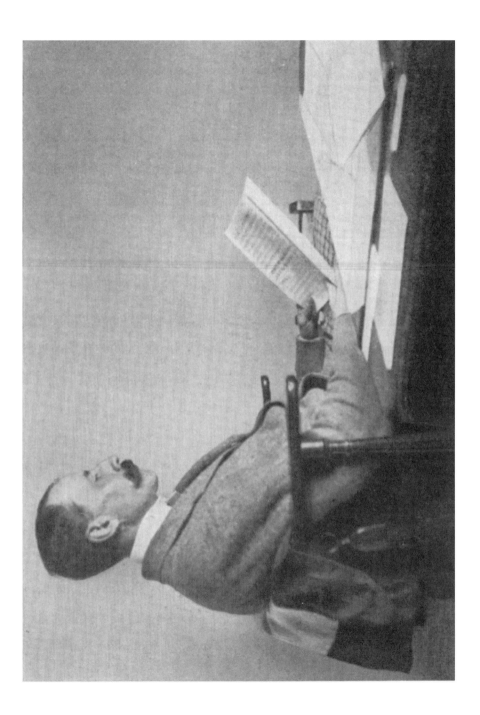

The Best of Me

A Gerontius Centenary Companion

edited by
Geoffrey Hodgkins

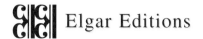 Elgar Editions

Published in Great Britain by

Elgar Editions

the publishing imprint of

Elgar Enterprises
20 High Street, Rickmansworth, Herts WD3 1ER
(e-mail : editions@elgar.org)

First Published : October 1999
Reprinted with corrections : March 2000

British Library Cataloguing in Publication Data
A Catalogue record of this book
is available from the British Library

ISBN 0 9537082 0 9 (Elgar Editions)

Printed and bound in Great Britain by Antony Rowe Ltd,
Bumper's Farm, Chippenham, Wiltshire

*Frontispiece : Edward Elgar in his study at Birchwood in August 1900,
shortly after completing the score of* The Dream of Gerontius

This is the best of me;
for the rest, I ate, and drank, and slept,
loved and hated, like another:
my life was as the vapour and is not;
but this I saw and knew;
this, if anything of mine, is worth your memory.

- **John Ruskin** : *Sesame and Lilies*

Contents

Part IV - The Intervening Years

Part V - The Recorded Legacy

Part VI - Performing Gerontius Today

Acknowledgements

The Elgar Society is extremely grateful to those authors who have permitted their original work to appear in this book : David Bury, Walter Essex, Lewis Foreman, John and Ann Kelly, Michael Kennedy, Charles McGuire, Carl Newton, John Norris, and Alan Tongue. The piece by the late Gareth Lewis appears by kind permission of Mrs Gina Lewis. I am particularly grateful to John Knowles, author of *An Elgar Discography*, for producing the list of *Gerontius* recordings. Gratitude is also expressed to the proprietors of those journals who have allowed us to publish material originally found in their pages. The piece by E A Baughan from the November 1900 issue of *Musical Opinion* appears by kind permission of the Editor. Sir John Barbirolli's thoughts on *Gerontius* are reprinted by kind permission of EMI Records (UK) Ltd. Permission to quote from *Edward Elgar : memories of a variation* by Dora Powell (published by Scolar Press) has been kindly granted by Mr Claud Powell. Robert Carballo's article on Cardinal Newman's poem is provided courtesy of the Eternal Word Television Network, PO Box 3610, Manassas, VA 22110, USA. The review by Sir Neville Cardus was published in *Cardus on Music*, edited by Donald Wright, and published by Hamish Hamilton in 1988 and Sphere in 1990; it is © copyright Sir Neville Cardus Estate. Thanks are due to Malcolm Burrows and Christopher Fifield for help in the translation of material, and to Martin Bird for willingly providing additional assistance at short notice. Every effort has been made to trace current copyright owners; any infringement is deeply regretted and will be corrected in subsequent editions.

Lewis Foreman writes: I wish to acknowledge the assistance of various expert helpers without whom the original presentation and its recasting here would not have been possible. To Julia Chandler, who despite flu and bronchitis translated the German cuttings I have reproduced and to David Michell, David Mason and Eliot Levin for locating and dubbing for me many of the 78s that were played then. The Elgar Birthplace for allowing me to photograph pages from the scrapbooks. Finally to Garry Humphreys who took the voice of Jaeger and read the bulk of the extracts, and to my wife Susan, who portrayed the voice of Rosa Burley.

David Mason kindly translated the extensive German verbatim reports and reviews of the Düsseldorf performances, from difficult Gothic script originals. We are all greatly in his debt. To librarians and archivists at the Elgar Birthplace, and at Westminster, Worcester, Birmingham, the Barbican, Washington, New York, Chicago and Sydney, very many thanks. To Susanne Meusel of Vienna for locating for me a postcard portrait of Wüllner and to the many dealers and book sellers who over the years have provided me with a considerable library of material used in this article. To Max Keogh in Sydney and Erik Johnson in New York. To Dr Percy M Young for his kind agreement that I might expand the tables first quoted in his *Elgar OM*. To the copyright owners of all material quoted still in copyright, and especially to Wulstan Atkins, my thanks. The material reproduced is all from my personal archive with the exception of those few illustrations taken from the Elgar scrapbooks at the Elgar Birthplace, and from other archives, which are acknowledged in the text.

Carl Newton would like to express his thanks to the following, without whose co-operation the research for his article would not have been possible:

> Bob Steedman, Head of Office Services, British Council : Monica Scott, Records Manager, British Council; Jacqueline Kavanagh, Written Archivist, British Broadcasting Corporation, who identified several important documents in the BBC files on my behalf; Antony Lewis-Crosby, Chief Executive, and Vincent Tyndall, Archivist, Liverpool Philharmonic Society; Robert Edwards, Archivist, Royal Huddersfield Choral Society, who personally acted as a guide to the archives in Huddersfield; Suzanne Lewis, Senior Archive Assistant, EMI Archives; and Nicholas Cox, Director of Modern Records, Public Record Office, who drew my attention to the 'Sargent File'.

Many other people have been of great help in the production of this book. Thanks are due to the President of the Elgar Society, Richard Hickox, for writing the Foreword. The staff at the Elgar Birthplace Museum at Broadheath have provided invaluable assistance, especially Chris Bennett. So too has Robert Tucker at the Barbican Music Library, London. Robert Anderson, Ronald Taylor and Raymond Monk have been helpful and encouraging as ever. Lewis Foreman, apart from contributing a major piece on *Gerontius* itself, has generously allowed us to use illustrations from his extensive collection of contemporary photographs, as well as giving us the benefit of his vast experience of publishing. Other illustrations are reproduced courtesy of The Elgar Foundation, David Bury, John Knowles, John Kelly, Raymond Monk, Monsignor George Stack, Ann Vernau, and the Fathers of the Birmingham Oratory.

Finally, thanks are due to John Norris and Ann Vernau. John was instrumental in the formation of Elgar Enterprises, and had the original idea for this volume. His enthusiasm, initiative, professionalism and persistence - as well as his original written contributions - have taken much of the drudgery out of editing the book, and any credit in its production is due to him. Ann's photographs, proof-reading and helpful comments have been similarly invaluable. When Elgar conducted *King Olaf* at Morecambe in 1905, the chorus was trained by Henry Coward, and the performance was a great success. In a speech following the concert, Elgar said: "Dr Coward loaded the gun, and I came and let it off". If the contents of this particular "firearm" reach its target, we have two other expert "loaders" - John Norris and Ann Vernau - to thank for it.

Geoffrey Hodgkins
September 1999

Foreword

Richard Hickox

As a young boy I was given a set of LPs of *The Dream of Gerontius*, conducted by Sir Malcolm Sargent. I found it intriguing but at the age of 11 difficult to comprehend. When I went up to Cambridge in 1967 I joined the CUMS Choir specifically to have the experience (and pleasure) of singing under Sir David Willcocks. In our first term we performed the *Dream of Gerontius* in King's College Chapel and it was an experience I will never forget. Not only did Sir David conduct and work marvellously, but he also had many anecdotes about Elgar and Worcester which made it feel an incredibly authentic experience.

Five years later I was able to conduct an amateur performance and it has remained close to my heart, and firmly in my repertoire, ever since. Two occasions that particularly stick in my memory were preparing the London Symphony Chorus when they gave the work's first performance in Russia with Svetlanov, and then in 1998 conducting the first ever performances in Czechoslovakia with the Prague Symphony Orchestra. Another milestone was my recording for Chandos which was really the start of my close relationship with them. I will never forget the London Symphony Chorus crowding into the control room in Watford Town Hall and marvelling at the sound that Chandos had got - for the first time in many many recordings it really sounded like 'us'. For the centenary I will be conducting the *Dream of Gerontius* with the Royal Scottish National Orchestra in Glasgow and Edinburgh, with the Bamberg Symphony, the City of London Sinfonia at the Royal Concert Hall Nottingham, and, most excitingly, in Westminster Cathedral, the home of Cardinal Newman.

As President of the Elgar Society, I am delighted to welcome this book on *Gerontius*, and hope it will be the first of many successful ventures of this kind.

About the Editor

Geoffrey Hodgkins has been an active member of the Elgar Society for over twenty-five years, during which time he has published numerous articles on all aspects of Elgar's music. His definitive Elgar bibliography appeared in The Music Review (volume 54, no 1) and he has also written booklet notes to accompany a CD recording of Elgar's part-songs, for him a particular passion. A further claim to fame of particular relevance to this volume was his participation as a member of the London Philharmonic Choir in the 1975 Boult recording of the work. Geoffrey has edited the Elgar Society Journal since 1991, a period which has seen sustained growth in the authority and influence of the Journal. He became editorial director of Elgar Enterprises on its formation in 1999.

INTRODUCTION

Geoffrey Hodgkins

Was there ever a composer apart from Elgar about whom so many legends and enigmas exist? We are all familiar with the *Variations*, of course, and no doubt solutions will continue to appear in the future; the 'soul' of the Violin Concerto is another; and the "single short remark about himself" made to Ernest Newman shortly before his death "... only five words, but... too tragic for the ear of the mob". If the mysteries surrounding *The Dream of Gerontius* are on a lower level, they are still intriguing.

The first relates to the date Elgar was approached by the Birmingham Festival Committee. On 17 November 1898 Elgar wrote to Alfred Littleton of Novello : "I saw Mr Beale on Tuesday in last week & we settled, verbally, that I am to have the principal place in the Birmingham Festival - *Wedy* morning... " It has been assumed by some that this was the commission itself, but in a letter of 20 October to Jaeger it is clear that Elgar has already talked to Novello about it, and in May he had written to the critic Joseph Bennett : "The Birmingham people have more than hinted..." It would seem that Beale's November meeting was to confirm that Elgar's work would be the *principal* novelty at Birmingham, rather than the other new works - Parry's *De Profundis*, and the completion of Coleridge-Taylor's *Hiawatha*.The commission to write the chief new work for the 1900 Festival was final proof that Elgar had "arrived"; Birmingham was the most prestigious of the major festivals (more than Leeds or the Three Choirs, Elgar's previous commissions).

Then there is Elgar's choice of Newman's poem. His initial idea for Birmingham was a work on the life of St Augustine, but this was rejected by the Festival committee, and so instead he fell back on the idea of a scriptural oratorio on the life of Jesus. Elgar had hoped that Bennett might provide a libretto, but it was all rather vague and by the end of 1899 nothing had been decided. However, it seems that *Gerontius* was his own original preference. Rosa Burley tells us that :

... it was *Gerontius* which really appealed to him the more. He was afraid, however, that the strong Catholic flavour of the poem and its insistence on the doctrine of purgatory would be prejudicial to success in a Protestant community. He told me in fact that Dvořák, who had planned a setting of the work for the 1888 Festival, had been discouraged from making it for this very reason.[1]

Elgar was right to anticipate objections to the text; the opening line - 'Jesu, Maria, I am near to death' - not only contained a prayer to the Virgin Mary, but appeared to place her on the same level as Christ, more than enough to offend Protestants. But there were other problems with the choice of the poem. The church in general was approaching the end of a century during which it had taken a battering from many quarters. Biblical criticism, especially from German theologians, combined with scientific revelations concerning geology and biological evolution, had shaken or destroyed the faith of many, especially among the educated classes. Churchmen were reeling, unsure whether to confront or to try and accommodate the new ideas. And although the Roman Catholic Church in England had grown enormously since emancipation in 1829, there was now less of an emphasis on certain tenets of the faith. As Diana McVeagh has written:

> Cardinal Newman's poem... published in 1865, stood for the Church's authority and for the value of revelation in an age in which questioning intellectuals were turning towards free-thinking rationalism. Its beauty and originality were recognised in spite of the fact that in 1891 it was deemed among poems of the nineteenth century 'the least in sympathy with the temper of the present time'... For Elgar to choose it was a decision of moral force. He was born a Roman Catholic in a staunchly Protestant part of England. This was one of several elements that made him feel an outsider; he was convinced that his faith prejudiced his career. So for him to set such a text was an act of courage, almost of defiance; a personal identification.[2]

By the end of 1899 Elgar was beginning to panic and to consider pulling out of the commission. The situation was saved by G H Johnstone of the Birmingham Festival, who realised that the absence of an existing libretto meant that a Biblical oratorio was now out of the

---

[1]   Burley, Rosa and Carruthers, Frank C : *Edward Elgar : the record of a friendship* (Barrie & Jenkins, 1972) p 134

[2]   Sleeve notes to boxed set CRD 1026/7 (1977). Thomas Dunhill wrote that "... this poem... may well be disliked... by some of the more reticent Roman Catholics" (see *Edward Elgar* (Blackie & Son, 1938) p 58)

question. He took Elgar back to Newman's poem and, whilst recognising problems with the text, promised to square the decision with the Committee. Thus Elgar's greatest choral work came about almost by default.

Yet the composer insisted that the Festival commission was incidental:

> The book was a wedding present to me (in 1889) from the late Father Knight, of Worcester, at whose church I was organist. Before giving it to me he copied into its pages every mark inserted by General Gordon into his (Gordon's) copy, so that I have the advantage of knowing those portions of the poem that had specially attracted the attention of the great hero. It seems absurd to say that I have written the work to order for Birmingham. The poem has been soaking in my mind for at least eight years. All that time I have been gradually assimilating the thoughts of the author into my own musical promptings.[3]

In a sense, there is no contradiction, as Elgar is merely saying that he wanted to write a setting of *Gerontius*, and probably would have done at some stage; but as we know from Burley and elsewhere, he had earlier backed away from setting the poem for the reasons given. It is perhaps difficult to believe that he would have composed it without any external stimulation, such as a commission.

However, from now on Elgar's commitment to the work is fervent and complete. We are fortunate in being able to follow the course of its composition through the correspondence between Elgar and his publishers, especially with his great friend, August Johannes Jaeger, of Novello. This correspondence, surely unique for any major musical work, is essential reading for anyone with more than a passing interest in *The Dream of Gerontius*; and we are fortunate to be able to read it in full in Jerrold Northrop Moore's *Elgar and his Publishers : Letters of a Creative Life* (2 vols, Clarendon Press, 1987).

The next 'enigma' concerns the notorious first performance at Birmingham on 3 October 1900. That *Gerontius* received such an appalling première that it nearly killed off the work is admitted by all. Almost immediately blame was apportioned to those considered

---

[3]   *The Musical Times*, October 1900 p 648. The quotation is part of a biographical sketch of the composer (by the Editor, F G Edwards, based on an interview given on 7 September) to coincide with the premiere of *Gerontius*.

responsible. Actually there were faults almost everywhere, starting with the composer himself, as Dora Penny realised[4]. Elgar finished the composition on 6 June 1900 and the orchestration on 3 August, leaving exactly two months - nothing like long enough - to bring the work to fulfilment. Novello had taken on the engraving of several other scores for Birmingham and other festivals, and this caused delays. Printed vocal parts (ie, single vocal lines) were not ready until late August and the first chorus rehearsal was on 20 August, a mere six weeks before the première. As Lewis Foreman explains, ten other major choral works were to be given at Birmingham. So while the choir no doubt deserved the censure heaped upon it, in light of the above its dismal effort was only too predictable. Much blame has always been laid at the feet of William Stockley, called out of retirement to train the chorus after the death of Dr Swinnerton Heap on 11 June. He was old, it is said, out of sympathy with the theology of Newman and unable to cope with the modernity of the music. Certainly Jaeger was in no doubt as to his culpability, as he wrote to Dora Penny on 14 October : "Old St— the choir-mess-ter ought to be boiled & served on Toast for having had us in Purgatory for nigh 2 Hours".[5] Yet given the last-minute nature of the preparation, would even Heap have been able to save the day?[6]

---

[4]   See p 150 *et seq*

[5]   Powell, Mrs Richard : *Edward Elgar : memories of a variation* (4th edn., Scolar Press, 1994) p 44

[6]   Although Heap had been a close friend of Elgar's - he was the dedicatee of the Organ Sonata (1895) and *The Light of Life* (1896) - there is evidence that Elgar may have had doubts about his abilities to prepare the Birmingham choir, possibly due to declining health. In an unpublished letter to Bantock dated 3 January 1900 Elgar encouraged him to think seriously about applying for the Principal's position at the Birmingham and Midland Institute, and indicated some of the other musical opportunities : "Then: they don't like Heap as trainer of the Festl. Chorus - you wd. have that & some of the societies round about wd. naturally engage you to conduct : then the Festival wd. sooner or later want a new conductor... poor Heap seems to be failing & they have no man worth his salt in Bham & it can only be a question of a season or two. I *don't* think he will coach the Chorus for the Festival this year". Elgar's attitude towards Heap may still have been coloured by an altercation between the two men at the premiere of *King Olaf* in 1896. According to Rosa Burley "the breach was never healed" (Burley, *op cit*, pp 91-92.)

Richter almost certainly underestimated the difficulties presented by the work, but he only saw the full score ten days before the première. Finally the Festival authorities were taken to task about organising a major and prestigious event with such inadequate preparation.

One legend which died hard, but which has hopefully been laid to rest now, is the reception given to *Gerontius* by the critics. In the same letter as quoted above, Jaeger said : "It was lack of enthusiasm both in the performance & amongst the critics which riled me at B'ham & afterwards, when I read the critiques. Now you Englishers have a composer at last you might be excused if you waxed enthusiastic over him for once in a way. But oh dear no!"[7] Elgar expressed a similar view to the young Arnold Bax who visited him at Birchwood in August 1901.

> [Elgar] was still sore over the *Gerontius* fiasco at Birmingham in the previous autumn, and enlarged interestingly upon the subject. "The fact is", he said, "neither the choir nor Richter knew the score". "But I thought the critics said..." I started to interpose. "Critics!" snapped the composer with ferocity. "My dear boy, what do the critics know about anything?"[8]

Reading the press reports now, it is hard to justify such strong reactions. We must allow that Jaeger, being so enthusiastically committed to the work, was deeply disappointed with what he heard and thus probably inclined to over-react; whilst Elgar could be accused of posturing before an impressionable teenager.

Possibly the worst review came from Fuller Maitland in *The Times*. Most of his plaudits are countered by criticism; such praise as there is tends to be faint, and Elgar was compared unfavourably to Parry and Stanford. Further salt must have been rubbed into Elgar's wound by Fuller Maitland's comments on those works at the 1900 Festival written by some of Elgar's contemporaries. Dvořák's *The Spectre's Bride* was a "beautiful cantata... a work which represents the Bohemian master in his best and most spontaneous mood"; Glazunov's Sixth Symphony was "splendid - the highest point of attainment of the younger Russian school of music"; while of Coleridge-Taylor's *Hiawatha* the critic wrote: "The success which the piece has

---

[7]   Powell, *ibid.*

[8]   Bax, Arnold: *Farewell, My Youth* (Longmans, Green, 1943) p 30

enjoyed in all parts of the country was fully confirmed, and a fitting tribute was paid to the gifted composer of a work full of poetic imagination, charm and genuine distinction". By comparison, his *Gerontius* review ended with the comment "... a remarkable, and in some ways a beautiful work".

Joseph Bennett of the *Daily Telegraph* was another critic not totally at ease with 'modern' music, but he too recognised the work's greatness. The rest of the critics were much more positive; and the truth is surely nearer to Foreman, who writes: "[The critics] all sent the same message: a masterpiece recognised in spite of a less than perfect performance".

Yet in this recognition by the critics of "a masterpiece" one still senses in many of them a lack of total commitment, of effusive and unqualified welcome (for instance, E A Baughan). This could be partly explained by a reluctance to commit oneself completely to a new work on a single hearing; and for some, distaste at its Catholicism. But I believe there is another explanation, hinted at by Basil Maine: "It is difficult for the ordinary English concert-goer... to realise the effect that Elgar's oratorio made when first produced. Even those who were present at that production... are frequently unable to convey the nature of their reaction except in very broad and vague terms".[9] In other words, what the audience heard that Wednesday morning overwhelmed them, bemused them, stupefied them; in modern parlance, we might say it "blew them away". Having come to hear an English oratorio, divided into neatly packaged solos, choruses and ensembles (which as usual they would be able to buy separately in due course) they were unprepared for a music-drama which seemed more like the first act of an opera - almost forty minutes of music before a break. What they were hearing might well be great music, but it was beyond them, and they did not know how to respond. Was this how English composers were meant to write? In June Elgar had written to Jaeger : "... every ass I meet says:- 'I suppose' or 'I hope you're going to keep to the old A[ncient] & M[odern] Tune for 'Praise to the Holiest'!!!!!' Blast the B[ritish] P[ublic] - they have no souls, hearts or minds worth a thought".[10] Such folk

---

[9]   Maine, Basil: *Elgar - His Life and Works* (2 vols., Bell & Sons, 1933) Vol 1, p 98.

[10]   Moore, *Elgar and his Publishers*, p 201. The same thing was said by others to Dora Penny (Powell, *op cit*, p 42)

must have found the modernity of the music, with its echoes of Wagner, and the overt Catholicism of the words a potent and disturbing mixture. Certainly Elgar picked this up, as he told Jaeger six days later : "It is curious to be treated by the old-fashioned people as a criminal because my thoughts & ways are beyond them".[11]

I think it significant that the greatest acclamation awarded to *Gerontius* at its première was by such people as Jaeger, Richter, Herman Klein, Otto Lessmann, Julius Buths, and Arthur Johnstone, who were all born into or educated in the European musical tradition. They felt completely comfortable speaking of Elgar and his music in the same breath as Wagner or Richard Strauss, recognising a comparable genius. The great American conductor, Theodore Thomas, was born in Germany in 1835. He was considered avant-garde, introducing music by such composers as Schumann, Liszt and Wagner to North America. Interviewed in 1902, he said : "Elgar has abilities that make him the superior as an orchestral writer of any man the world knows now, or ever has known for that matter". When asked specifically about *Gerontius*, he replied : "Its orchestral score is tremendous. As a choral work I consider it the greatest the last century has produced - I except none..." (One hundred years on it is pertinent to note Alan Tongue's remarks about *Gerontius'* recent reception in Budapest : "One great thing about Elgar is how well he travels... he seems to fit into the continental Romantic tradition very easily".)

But Elgar's disappointment at the atrocious sounds he heard in Birmingham Town Hall on 3 October was immense. He had invested too much of himself in *Gerontius* - "the best of me" - to allow him to shrug it off and forget it. In the letter to Jaeger quoted above he wrote:

I have worked hard for forty years &, at the last, Providence denies me a decent hearing of my work ; so I submit - I always said God was against art & I still believe it... I have allowed my heart to open once - it is now shut against every religious feeling & every soft, gentle impulse *for ever*.[12]

---

[11]   Moore, *op cit*, p 244

[12]   Michael De-la-Noy (*Elgar : The Man*, (London: Allen Lane, 1983) pp 92-3) makes the point that this letter contains many inconsistencies on Elgar's part.

No doubt the work's ultimate approval, and the success of *The Apostles* and *The Kingdom* gave a measure of healing; but it does seem that there was long term damage to his sensitive psyche.

All the sense of discouragement that had pursued him in the early years came back with redoubled force when he saw his greatest work languishing in disrepute and neglect. It is said by those who long had access to his private mind that he was always ready to see himself as slighted and unwanted; on such a disposition the episode of *The Dream of Gerontius* left a scar that never healed.[13]

The work certainly went into a kind of limbo immediately after Birmingham, and although there were a few tentative plans for further performances, August Manns - possibly influenced by reports of the choral difficulties - decided on only the prelude instead of the full work at the Crystal Palace. At this point we must not overlook Jaeger's part in the story, and understand that the ultimate acceptance of *Gerontius* must in a considerable measure be put down to him. As well as trying to get a second performance in England,[14] it was he who had brought Buths over to Birmingham for the première. And it was Buths' subsequent enthusiasm which led to the two Düsseldorf performances, the success of which set up the work for acceptance in Britain.

One outcome of the first performance of *Gerontius*, if Elgar is to be believed, was that he stopped reading criticism of his works. In later years he often states that he no longer reads the critics, and the date 1900 is specifically mentioned, or at least implied. For instance, on 18 September 1920 he wrote to Ivor Atkins: "I shall be glad to hear any news of the [Three Choirs] festl. I have read no press notices but, for the first time in twenty years, am anxious to know how the reptiles

---

[13]   McNaught, W : *Elgar* (Novello, n.d. [1937]) p 10

[14]   "I'm still trying hard to get *Gerontius* performed in London, but it is almost hopeless. I still hope Wood will do it..." (Letter to Dora Penny, 27 December 1900; in Powell, *op cit,* p 45). H A Chambers of Novello wrote : "It is largely due to [Jaeger's] efforts that *Gerontius* has secured an established place in the repertory of oratorio" ('Publishing Office Memories', in *Edward Elgar : Centenary Sketches* (Novello & Co, 1957) p 12).

viewed it all".[15] Then, in a letter of 24 October 1932 to the Belfast musician E Godfrey Brown just after a performance of *Gerontius* in that city, Elgar writes: "I have seen nothing & heard nothing except a sentence or two at the luncheon, so I (as usual) am entirely ignorant of the effect as recorded in the press - I have read nothing since 1900 & have got so into the way of it that I resent - or something like that - any knowledge".[16]

Elgar later befriended the *Manchester Guardian* critic Arthur Johnstone (they had a mutual friend in Canon Charles Gorton of Morecambe), and as can be seen from his writings, Johnstone was a fervent advocate of *Gerontius* from the outset. Yet in his lecture 'Critics' given at Birmingham University on 6 December 1905, Elgar said :

> I do not agree with all the views, held by the late Arthur Johnstone, and I have never read a word of criticism on my own works; but referring only to his writings on the classics and large works produced in Manchester, I should place him very high. His training at Cologne Conservatorium gave him great distinction and his knowledge of things outside music - things and forces which go to make human beings of men - assisted his judgement in literature, art and music in a wonderful way. A collection of his criticisms is about to be published and if any student here is going to devote himself to literature, I advise him to study the clear and incisive English, the absolute correct use of every word, without I may add, adopting all the opinions expressed by the writer.[17]

Yet the thrust of the lecture was that good criticism was necessary and healthy. "It has been my happiness and I trust may continue to be, to receive advice from [the critics]".[18] He was unhappy with what he called the "journalistic side" of criticism, which focused on "some sensation of the moment" or the amount of applause, or the dress of the audience, instead of reporting on "matters musical". In his introduction to the lecture Elgar said:

---

[15]   Atkins, E Wulstan: *The Elgar-Atkins Friendship* (David & Charles, 1984) p 319

[16]   Quoted in Greer, David : 'Elgar in Belfast', *Elgar Society Journal* vol 10, no 4 (March 1998) p 173

[17]   Young, Percy M (ed): *A Future for English Music and other lectures* (Dobson, 1968) pp 183-5.

[18]   *op cit,* p 163

We who are criticised feel the differing value of written criticism, and, that most read, that of the daily journal is from the very fact of its hasty production frequently of less value than the opinions more slowly evolved. The hurried criticism may be of value to the composer as showing the effect of a single performance of his work on a trained mind; but such an opinion may be reversed or modified on a second hearing, and all our good critics - unless a work is hopelessly bad or immature - make a reservation in this way. But the real, lasting educational good is gained from the mature slowly-wrought opinion.[19]

If those remarks truly represented Elgar's views, it makes his reaction to the critics' reception of *Gerontius* another enigma, for that is surely what happened after the première. Even the most hesitant reviewer was completely won over in due course, especially after the Düsseldorf performances; "reservations" gave place to "mature slowly-wrought" approval. So maybe the critics were a useful public scapegoat for the real cause of Elgar's dissatisfaction over the 'failure' of the première - God, or more often, 'Providence'. Yet the intensity of personal feeling and expression which Elgar put into *Gerontius*, which was borne out by the Ruskin quote, and which was noted immediately by Baughan and others, remained with him. During a performance of the work at the 1908 Norwich Festival, a young Worcestershire composer named Julius Harrison found himself sitting next to Elgar behind a curtain near the platform. "Obviously he was very much moved by the performance, for from time to time he would brush the tears from his cheeks".[20]

Lewis Foreman's article charting the early history of *Gerontius* ends around 1904, and of course from then on it is established, its reputation assured, and it is given everywhere. During the next few years one of the most pleasing performances to the self-taught Elgar - although he was out of the country at the time - must have been that in King's College, Cambridge on 15 June 1909. The King's' organist, A H ('Daddy') Mann, had become something of an Elgar devotee, and this performance completed an Elgar trilogy at King's, *The Apostles* and *The Kingdom* having been given there in 1906 and 1907 respectively.

---

[19]   *ibid.*

[20]   From a radio broadcast, 27 October 1960. I am grateful to Michael Trott for making a transcript available to me.

Within a few years *The Dream of Gerontius* had certainly broken the long domination of the seemingly unassailable triumvirate of choral works - *Messiah, Elijah,* and *The Creation.* In 1916 Thomas Dunhill wrote :

> It was not until it became known that [*Gerontius*] was being performed and applauded in Germany that the slow-moving mind of the English people began to realise that an injustice had been done. *Gerontius* was reconsidered and performed again... Ultimately it came to pass that no existing choral work, not even Elijah or The Messiah, made such a wide appeal or drew such a huge audience. Such is a brief history of the conquest of the public by this remarkable composition![21]

Now, on the verge of its centenary, *Gerontius* still possesses tremendous drawing power and, along with Messiah, is unchallenged in the choral repertoire of this country; this in spite of the unfashionable nature of its text. Yet, as is pointed out in several places in this volume, its theme - the ultimate destiny of the individual after physical death - is of universal interest; and this, plus the wondrous fusion of words and music, and the "white-hot inspiration" of Elgar's genius, will I believe guarantee its immortality. Michael Kennedy calls it "an impassioned human document".[22] Like Walter Essex, I find it impossible to be objective about *Gerontius*; I am too close to it emotionally. I know its faults, and love them too. We are in good company; Percy Young has written : "I have often set out deliberately to refuse to allow *Gerontius* to overpower me. Yet invariably it does".[23] Diana McVeagh calls it "... Elgar's greatest work... The magnitude of its subject is matched by the beauty and perception of its music... Even those whose temperament is alien to the thought and mood of the work cannot fail to admit its greatness... A performance of *Gerontius* is a profound and moving experience."[24] Michael Kennedy wrote : "In *Gerontius* we find the fullest expression of all Elgar's many-sided gifts. It is his finest work... From his deepest experience, Elgar created the

---

[21] 'Elgar's Choral Music' by Thomas Dunhill in *The Music Student* August 1916, pp 339-340

[22] Kennedy, Michael: *Portrait of Elgar* (2nd edn., OUP, 1982) p 138

[23] Young, Percy : *The Choral Tradition* (London : Hutchinson & Co, 1962) p 257

[24] McVeagh, Diana : *Edward Elgar - his life and music* (Dent, 1955) p 129

last great artistic monument of the reign of Queen Victoria and the last of the nineteenth century".[25]

It is the kind of work that lends itself to great performances, to memories and anecdotes. I remember the first time I sang it, as a member of a suburban choral society; the soloists were Sybil Michelow, Kenneth Bowen, and Bryan Drake, no mean team. I remember a similarly strong trio at the first Albert Hall *Gerontius* I sang - Alfreda Hodgson, Alexander Young, and Stafford Dean; and at the first I did at the Festival Hall - Anna Reynolds, Richard Lewis, and John Shirley Quirk. I remember an emotional evening twenty years ago in south-east London at a concert in aid of the Vietnamese boat children, when the local amateur symphony orchestra joined forces with the Dutch Handel Society Chorus under that great Dutch Elgarian, Jack P Loorij. The choir needed extra singers for the semi-chorus and contacted the Elgar Society; I volunteered. The choir were superb, but had minor problems with the English - it had to be pointed out to them that the first letter of "psalm" is silent! My only problem was learning the words for the Dutch national anthem! The Angel that evening was a brilliant young Dutch mezzo, now internationally known, Jard van Nes. And I certainly remember recording the work in July 1975 for Sir Adrian Boult; how could I forget, when the final recording session was scheduled for the day after my wedding! If the tenors sound a little thin in "Praise to the Holiest", it may be because they were one short!

The nature of *Gerontius*'s subject matter often makes for special memories at time of loss. The 1958 Proms performance, conducted by Sargent, was dedicated to the memory of Vaughan Williams, who had just died. The audience stood in silent tribute, after listening to a work which had greatly influenced VW, especially in his *Sea Symphony*. Michael Kennedy tells of the memorial concert to Barbirolli on 27 September 1970, when the Hallé under Maurice Handford gave the *Dream*. "At the end, where the Angel sings 'Farewell but not for ever! Brother dear/ Be brave and patient on thy bed of sorrow;/ Swiftly shall pass thy night of trial here/ And I will come and wake thee on the morrow', Janet Baker's voice broke and she stood, head bowed, the tears streaming down her cheeks, while the orchestra continued until

---

[25]   Kennedy, *ibid.*

she whispered her last words. He would have been so proud".[26] And on the day my own father died (one Good Friday, incidentally) my brother-in-law, a gifted amateur musician, who had played in the National Youth Orchestra under Boult in the 1950s, was playing in a performance of *Gerontius* in the evening. He said it was one of the most difficult concerts he has ever done; concentration and self-control were well-nigh impossible, and he forgot about the monumental pause before the **fffz** at cue 120, and his flute pierced the silence. Never, he said, did a musician so completely identify with the soloist's 'Take me away' which follows immediately after.

———————————

The Dream of Gerontius has acquired a substantial literature over the years. A systematic account of the composition and a detailed analysis of the work itself can be found in all the major biographies. The Elgar-Jaeger correspondence has already been referred to, and is fundamental to an appreciation of *Gerontius*. So too is the book of Analytical Notes written by Jaeger and published by Novello. Dr Percy Young's recent book, published by Scolar - *Elgar, Newman, and The Dream of Gerontius* - fills in a lot of the background, particularly on the growth of Catholicism in nineteenth-century Britain.

The aim of this centenary companion is to present the origins and subsequent history of this remarkable work by drawing together articles and extracts already published, as well as new material. Many of the pieces originally appeared in The Elgar Society Journal and its predecessor The Elgar Society Newsletter, and some of these have been amended or enlarged for inclusion here. The opening section deals with Cardinal Newman and his poem, with a scholarly analysis. The text is printed in full, and the lines that Elgar actually set have been differentiated. Also included, for the first time in a work on Elgar, are the markings made by General Gordon which it was such an "advantage" to know, according to Elgar.

We then move on to *Gerontius*'s composition, beginning with the places associated with the work. Elgar was always inspired by landscape and

———————————

[26] Kennedy, Michael : *Barbirolli - Conductor Laureate* (McGibbon & Kee, 1971) p 327

the natural world, and the close association of *Gerontius* with Birchwood, the tiny cottage some three miles north of Malvern, is enshrined on the title page of the work. The most evocative description of the Elgars at Birchwood at this time is given by Dora Powell, and we include that as well as photographs of the cottage and other locations familiar to Elgar at that time. Charles McGuire then analyses the way Elgar adapted Newman's text to fit his own ideas about the work. Also included, for the benefit of scholars, is a list of what remains of Elgar's manuscripts, sketches and proofs, and their current location.

Section III is entitled 'The Struggle for Survival', and looks at the way in which *Gerontius* established itself in the repertoire. In many ways the centrepiece of the book is Lewis Foreman's in-depth look at the first four years of *Gerontius*, from its Birmingham première to its performance at the 1904 Covent Garden Elgar Festival, with particular emphasis on those artists who performed the work. Not the least of its fascinations is the translation of reviews of the two Düsseldorf performances in the German press, and premières in America and Australia. It also seemed sensible to cover the first performance from several viewpoints : a singer in the choir (William Bennett), a member of the audience (Dora Powell again), and three of the most prominent critics - Fuller Maitland in The Times; E A Baughan in The Musical Standard and Musical Opinion; and Arthur Johnstone in the Manchester Guardian. Johnstone's reviews also include the 1902 Düsseldorf performance, and the 1903 Manchester première, when Richter made amends for Birmingham. The late Gareth Lewis looks at Richter's career as a conductor, which helps us to see the *Gerontius* première in greater perspective. Finally, David Bury gives an account of the London première in Westminster Cathedral in June 1903.

Memorable performances since then could fill another book, and we have confined ourselves to a unique event which took place during the First World War, when Clara Butt organised six performances on consecutive days, all conducted by Elgar in aid of war charities. Critical reaction in later years comes from A J Sheldon, Harvey Grace, Neville Cardus and Ferruccio Bonavia. Also included in this section is a series of cartoons drawn in 1913 by T Martin Jones. They preserve in a wonderful way the Edwardian atmosphere, with suffragettes, avuncular policemen, and crooked bookmakers. These drawings prove that *Gerontius* was sufficiently well-known and well-loved to be treated in this way only thirteen short years after its composition. There must have been some at that time who found these drawings offensive, as they appear at face value to mock a sacred theme, but to me they speak rather of affection for the work. They are to be found in the archives of the Elgar Society, but no one seems to know how they got there, and I have been unable to discover anything about Mr Jones. Information which would throw more light on this fascinating collection and its artist would be most welcome.

Given the reputation quickly achieved by *Gerontius*, it is perhaps surprising that it took nearly fifty years to be recorded in full, during the final stages of the Second World War, in circumstances that have only recently come to light after painstaking research by Carl Newton. It seems that we may have to thank another composer, William Walton, for causing the recording to be made. Walter Essex looks at the twelve complete recordings to date, plus a video of the 1997 performance in St Paul's Cathedral, and the two sets of extracts from performances conducted by Elgar himself in 1927. John Knowles, author of an Elgar discography, provides the complete listing of recordings, including extracts; and Sir John Barbirolli gives his thoughts on *Gerontius*, which were included in the notes with his recording of the work in 1965.

The final section looks at *Gerontius* after one hundred years. For those wishing to perform the work the advice of Elgar as given to Nicholas Kilburn and Gregory Hast will be of considerable interest, as will the unique memories of Edgar Day, who accompanied the Worcester Festival Chorus at a time when they sang the work regularly under Elgar himself.

Gerontius is still winning new devotees wherever it is given, and there are accounts of latter-day first performances in Istanbul and Budapest. These suggest that we might expect its fame to continue to grow well into its second century, and a list of recent performances from many places would seem to confirm this. Finally, Michael Kennedy reviews the first hundred years and leaves us with some food for thought.

Part One

Before Elgar

Previous page :   *John Henry Newman, photographed in 1863,*
                      two years before the publication of The Dream of Gerontius

JOHN HENRY NEWMAN
A Short Biography

by John Norris

What makes a successful partnership? A meeting of minds, or an attraction of opposites. Born in London, into an established middle class family with a solid background in banking; early indications of precocity leading effortlessly to a privileged Oxford education; developing religious convictions that moved from Non-Conformism through Establishment Protestantism to Catholicism; an increasing rejection of material comforts in favour of a semi-monastic life - what could be further from Elgar, the provincial tradesman's son without formal musical education whose religious beliefs weakened as he climbed the Establishment ladder. Where there were parallels, they were somewhat superficial - a mutual dexterity on the violin, a shared love of the countryside, and a lasting affection for a particular childhood home. Yet this was John Henry Newman - Cardinal Newman - the man who, despite other notable achievements, is today best known to music lovers as the author of the poem which inspired Elgar to compose some of his greatest music : *The Dream of Gerontius*.

To understand Newman, it is first necessary to understand the times in which he grew up. In early nineteenth century England, a university education remained the privilege of the few able to gain acceptance by one of the loosely associated colleges of Oxford and Cambridge. These offered a rather unstructured education, with no formal teaching and tutors whose responsibilities were directed as much toward policing their flock as to guiding their intellectual development. A university education was intended to expand the mind rather than to prepare for a chosen career. But, as a concentration of many of the most brilliant minds in the country, the universities provided a reckonable seat of power, able to challenge the government effectively on the issues of the day.

The Church of England occupied a similar position but, as the century progressed, it felt its position increasingly threatened. Unrest in Ireland made continued suppression of, and discrimination against, Catholics there increasingly unsustainable. Politicians who previously were firmly opposed to any compromise now saw concessions as inevitable, leading to the Catholic Emancipation Act of 1829 which applied throughout the United Kingdom. Realistically, this presented no great threat to the established church, but the leadership lacked confidence. Minor setbacks assumed an unreasonable significance; a paralysed hierarchy made matters worse.

Add to this the poor communications of the time. Not only was there no radio or television to bring news instantly to a large audience; newspapers were generally local affairs, with national debate largely conducted through the publication of pamphlets. The penny post was still some way off and postal deliveries depended on slow stagecoaches. Conditions were ripe for intrigue and misunderstanding, even within the confines of an Oxford college.

Childhood and Youth

These conditions changed during Newman's long life, with Newman himself playing an incisive part in changing some of them. But this was the world into which Newman was born, at 80 Old Broad Street in the City of London, on 21 February 1801. He was the eldest of six children, his father a partner in the Kentish Bank, a small provincial bank based in Maidstone, his mother devoting her life to the needs of the family. Early life was divided between houses in Southampton Street (now Southampton Row) in Bloomsbury and Grey Court House in Ham, now well within the London conurbation but then deep in the Middlesex countryside close to the Thames. In 1807, when Newman was six, the family gave up Grey Court House and settled permanently in Southampton Street, but Ham left a lasting impression on Newman in much the same way as Elgar never lost his deep affection for Broadheath.

On 1 May 1808, John Henry was sent off to Dr Nicholas' School in Ealing. He adapted well to his new surroundings, becoming what most would nowadays regard as a parent's dream: he preferred studying, particularly in the academic subjects, to sport and more frivolous pastimes and, not surprisingly, got on well with his teachers. He wrote his first poem in Latin at the age of eleven, practised his French in letters to his parents and took up the violin. But Newman Senior encouraged his son to follow a broader curriculum and insisted that he develop his horse-riding skills.

Grey Court House, Ham, with (below) the plaque commemorating Newman's early residence there.

Newman had received a religious education from an early age. Both parents were religious, although his father not greatly so. It was the stronger religious convictions of his mother, and her encouragement that he should read the bible, that provided Newman with a Calvanist upbringing and the foundation for his early leaning towards Evangelicalism. But it was to The Reverend Walter Mayers, a teacher at Ealing, that Newman later attributed his discovery of certain Christian belief, what he later referred to as "this beginning of divine faith in me". Newman dated his "inner conversion" to 1816, aged fifteen years, at which tender age he also committed himself to a life of celibacy. It is clear that he had the intellect and personal qualities to lead a prominent life in a number of fields. The path he followed was of his own choosing.

At the age of fifteen, he sought entry to Oxford. In those days, admission was a far more casual affair than today, with no formal entrance examination procedures. Success depended to a great extent on personal contacts. His father's inclination was that he should continue his studies at Cambridge but Reverend Mullins, curate at St James' Church in Piccadilly, London, persuaded Newman's father to consider Oxford. Mullins himself visited Oxford with Newman in December 1816. He first tried to find the boy a place in his own former college, Exeter, but without success. A place was found at Trinity College, however, where Newman eventually took up residence in June 1817.

Newman quickly gained the impression that many of his fellow students were more interested in the energetic social life of the University than in bettering themselves academically. In contrast, with little formal tuition at the University in general and at Trinity in particular, Newman pestered his tutors to be set more work. Not that Newman did not find time for extra-curricular activities. With another student by the name of Bowden, whom he had befriended during his first days at Trinity, he edited a rather stuffy magazine named *The Undergraduate*. This sold well, although its success perhaps owed as much to a mischievous interest in the views of Newman once he was known to be its editor as to any particular literary or journalistic merits of the magazine. And with Bowden he also wrote an epic poem, *St Bartholomew's Eve*, whose anti-Catholic sentiments found favour with Newman's parents. But these were no more than distractions from the rigorous regime of intense study to which he subjected himself.

Naturally, it was expected that his efforts would lead to excellent examination results. A double first was widely predicted. But these expectations were not to be fulfilled. When in November 1820 he sat his finals, he gained only a lower second in Classics and failed completely in Mathematics. His disappointment was intense. Today, such results would severely curtail the options for continuing at Oxford. But not in Newman's day. In the Spring of 1818, Newman had sat for, and obtained, a Trinity scholarship carrying an entitlement to a grant of £60 a year for a period of nine years. At the time of his finals, the scholarship still had seven years to run, enabling Newman to return to Trinity at the start of 1821 to continue his studies.

But his poor examination results no doubt still rankled, particularly as he and close friends knew that they bore little relationship to his true capabilities. In February 1822, therefore, he determined on the audacious step of seeking a fellowship at Oriel College. At this time, Oriel was considered the pre-eminent Oxford college and it may have appeared over-optimistic, even foolhardy, for a Trinity failure to make the attempt. His papers so impressed the Oriel authorities, however, that in April 1822 Newman was elected a Fellow of Oriel.

In his writings, Newman admitted to some difficulty in maintaining his earlier commitment to a life of chastity. Despite this, and under pressure from his father not to let matters drift, in January 1822 he finally determined to follow his religious vocation. Oriel provided a far more conducive environment than Trinity in which to develop his theological position and three associates proved to be particularly important in this respect. The first was Richard Whately. He had recently resigned his Oriel Fellowship on marriage but was nevertheless appointed to act as Newman's mentor during his probationary year at Oriel. He maintained an interest in Newman's career over the next ten years, by which time their theological differences made a close friendship unsustainable. The second of the three, Edward Pusey, was elected to Oriel a year after Newman. Temperamentally similar, the two would take long walks together, engaging in discussions on all manner of theological topics which helped both to refine their religious standpoints. Pusey followed Newman into the Church of England but not into the Roman Catholic Church. The two nevertheless remained on friendly terms until Pusey's death in 1882. The trio was completed by Edward Hawkins, also a fellow of Oriel, who in 1823 became Vicar of the University Church of St Mary. When Newman first took on preaching commitments, Hawkins offered to cast a critical eye over Newman's early sermons. Hawkins took Newman to task for their extreme evangelical tone and persuaded him to adopt a more balanced position. This shift can be presented as the origins of Newman's journey from Canterbury to Rome, and from Oxford to Birmingham.

A Name in Oxford

The following few years saw rapid advancement for Newman. In May 1824, he was appointed curate of St Clement's Church, Oxford; in June, he was ordained Deacon, being admitted to the priesthood the following May; and in March 1828, he succeeded Hawkins as Vicar of St Mary's.

Not that these years were without worries for Newman. In September 1824, his father had died after a short illness, leaving John Henry as the head of the family. As in all things, Newman took his new responsibility seriously. The job of curate, though demanding, was not well rewarded and he sought various means of increasing his income so as to provide his mother and sisters with the necessary financial support. He took on additional responsibilities within the university, becoming junior treasurer of Oriel in October 1824 and accepting Whately's offer in March 1825 to serve as his vice-principal at the university's Alban Hall. His financial anxieties were eventually solved in 1826 when he was appointed a tutor at Oriel, with a salary in excess of £600 a year. In the same year, his brother Frank gained the double first degree that had eluded his elder brother. John Henry gave up his positions as curate and vice-principal and the following year moved his mother and sisters to more suitable accommodation in Brighton. He was now considerably freer to pursue matters that concerned him.

As Newman himself recognised, he was becoming something of a figure at Oxford. Well liked by his students, he had published essays which attracted a measure of attention and his position as a preacher gave him a platform from which to advance his theological position. But, whether through a lack of foresight or a disregard for the consequences, Newman's incautious approach to so many matters meant that controversy was never far away.

In November 1827, a vacancy for the provostship of Oriel College resulted in a contest between Hawkins and John Keble. Although Newman could count both men among his friends, he came out decisively in support of Hawkins and, by so doing, persuaded Keble to withdraw his candidature. One consequence of this was that Newman succeeded to Hawkins' former position as Vicar of St Mary's.

Newman's next courtship with controversy came the following year. Ironically, at the heart of the matter lay the issue of Catholic emancipation. Sir Robert Peel, at that time the Member of Parliament for Oxford University, had long opposed Catholic emancipation but, eventually coming to the view that a degree of reform was essential to the national interest, he had felt honour-bound to offer himself for re-election. Despite his shift of position, Peel retained a good degree of support at Oxford and, led by Hawkins and Whately, Oriel had come out in support of him. But Newman and Froude organised an effective and ultimately decisive campaign in favour of his opponent Sir Robert Inglis, who still rejected the notion that Catholics should be admitted to Parliament. It was not that Newman opposed Catholic emancipation in principle but he did not wish to see Catholics admitted to Parliament where they could vote on issues directly affecting the Church of England.

Newman's support for Hawkins had thus proved to be short-lived. But, whereas their relationship might have survived their different positions over the re-election of Peel, Newman's next initiative developed into a direct challenge to Hawkins' authority as Provost. Newman had long held the view that a tutor's role should extend to the pastoral care and spiritual development of his students. Hawkins' predecessor, Copleston, had refused to countenance the idea and Hawkins harboured concerns that Newman's wishes would lead to the preferential treatment of students whose views and demeanour coincided with his own. Newman and two of his three fellow tutors recognised that they stood little chance of persuading Hawkins and, without reference to him, began to organise their teaching responsibilities as they considered appropriate. For a while, Hawkins let matters run but, in April 1830, adopted a subtle ploy that would give Newman time to retract without loss of face. He allowed Newman to continue as a tutor but refused to assign further students to his care. Newman did not back down and, as those already under his tuition completed their studies, he found his duties at Oriel gradually evaporating. In 1830, he relinquished his position as tutor.

This was to prove to be a watershed in Newman's life, a time of change. In 1831, Whately was appointed Archbishop of Dublin. Newman hoped that Whately might offer him a position in Dublin but Whately offered him no more than a return to his old position as Vice-Principal in Alban Hall; Newman, hoping for better things, declined. It is interesting to ponder the path Newman's career might have followed, and the consequences for Catholicism in England, had Whately offered Newman a position in Ireland. Instead, Newman put his energies over the next year into the writing of a book on *The Arians of the Fourth Century*, but the book failed to find favour with his editors, in part because they considered it to be written from too 'Romanist' a perspective.

Towards the end of 1832, Newman was invited by Froude to join him and his father on an extended journey around the Mediterranean. Setting sail on 8 December, they visited Greece, Malta and Sicily before landing at Naples, from where they travelled on to Rome. Italy delighted Newman. Amid intensive sightseeing, he found the inspiration to write his first two religious poems, the Lyra Apostolica, and time to meet Nicholas Wiseman, then Rector of the English College in Rome but later to become Archbishop of Westminster. At the end of their stay in Rome, the Froudes decided to travel home by an overland route but Newman determined to return to Sicily. Sicily held unexpected dangers for him, however. He contracted a fever which took him close to death and it was a full two weeks before he had recovered sufficiently to face the journey home.

Predictably, he saw God's hand in his illness, believing it to be a warning against his impetuousness or perhaps his temporary neglect of duties at home. On his return journey, the boat taking him from Palermo to Marseilles became becalmed for a week. Newman occupied himself by writing poetry. This included verses which he entitled *The Pillar of the Cloud*, now better known as the hymn *Lead, Kindly Light*.

While in Rome, news had reached Newman of the Church Temporalities Bill which legislated to abolish ten Church of England sees in Ireland. He saw this as further unjustified State interference in the established Church, as did a number of his friends. On 14 July 1833, only days after Newman's return to England, John Keble delivered a sermon in St Mary's Church on 'National Apostasy'. The sermon was later published but, in itself, made little national impact. Its greater significance was to act as a call for action to the many churchmen anxious at the failure of the Church authorities to mount an active defence to the continuing attack on the Church's position from Parliament and elsewhere.

Not that there was a general consensus on how best to respond. Some favoured a campaigning organisation that would challenge Parliament directly but Newman and Keble opposed the establishment of any formal association, fearing that such a body would undermine the authority of the Church leaders. Their preference was for a loosely bound movement that would alert a wider population to the perceived dangers, and re-emphasise the essential beliefs of the Church, through the publication of tracts. After some debate and manoeuvring, the views of Newman, Keble and their supporters in Oxford gathered strength. Newman set about writing the first tract, a call to the Anglican clergy published in September 1833, and organised others to write for the series, to be called *Tracts for our Times*.

The tracts achieved an immediate measure of popularity and the influence of the movement grew. Other initiatives followed, including a petition to the Archbishop of Canterbury signed by 7,000 members of the clergy. Such were the origins of what was to become known as the Oxford Movement. But the movement had its detractors, both in Parliament and closer to home. Prominent among the latter was Renn Dickson Hampden who had taken over many of Newman's tutorial duties at Oriel. Newman had continued to play an active role in Oriel affairs after his resignation as a tutor in 1830 and was elected Dean of the college in Autumn 1833. During his year in office, he had sought the Moral Philosophy Professorship but his former sponsor Edward Hawkins threw his support behind Hampden, who was appointed to the professorship. Worse was to follow.

In the 1830s, Oxford remained a strictly Anglican University : to gain admission, it was necessary for a student to 'assent' to the *Thirty-Nine Articles of Faith of the Church of England*. There were those who considered this an unreasonable restriction and a Parliamentary Bill was drafted to admit dissenters to the University. The lobby of Oxford theologians held firm against the Bill and it was defeated in the House of

Lords. Hampden then broke ranks, publishing a pamphlet in August 1834 entitled *Observations on Religious Dissent with Particular Reference to the Use of Religious Tests in the University*. It was not enough to sway the issue - a proposal to replace assent to the Thirty-Nine Articles by a simpler Declaration of Conformity to the Church of England was brought before the House of Convocation at Oxford but was roundly defeated. But it singled out Hampden as the leader of the Liberal opposition within the Church and therefore as a target for the Oxford Movement.

In early 1836, Hampden was made Regius Professor of Divinity. Following his appointment, Newman published a forty-seven page pamphlet criticising his theological position, and further attacks on Hampden continued over the ensuing years. But Hampden, like Newman, was a doughty opponent and took the positive view that such controversy was an inevitable part of the process of change, an indication that the arguments were being heard and were having the desired effect. Meanwhile, Newman had himself attracted a measure of national opprobrium in 1834 when, in his role as Vicar of St Mary's, he refused to marry a woman who had not been baptised. The row blew over but it signalled a hardening of attitudes.

Newman continued to write vigorously but he and his fellow Tractarians came increasingly under suspicion for propounding views considered to be too close to those of the Roman Catholic church. Pusey persuaded Newman to defend the Movement in print by publishing a series of books promoting Anglo-Catholicism as the *Via Media* - the middle way between what Newman considered to be the twin extremes of Roman Catholicism and 'popular' (for which read 'increasingly lax') Protestantism. In essence the transcripts of sermons delivered at St Mary's, the books were published over a period of fifteen months in 1837 and 1838. Newman subsequently recognised the importance of the four volumes in first setting the Movement apart from the main body of the Anglican church.

From 1838 to 1841, Newman acted as editor of a periodical called *British Critic* and used its columns to further advance the views of the Movement. But while Newman and his supporters responded in kind to attacks from Hampden and his kind, some criticisms could not be so easily brushed aside. In 1838, Richard Bagot, Bishop of Oxford, admonished Newman over the tone of certain *Tracts*. Newman immediately offered to stop the series but Bagot considered the warning sufficient. In retrospect, this proved to be unfortunate, for the following year Nicholas Wiseman published an attack on the Church of England in the *Dublin Review*. The attack drew parallels between Anglicans and Donatists, a fourth century movement which had broken away from the Roman Catholic church. It caused Newman further to question his own position.

Despite his intensive publishing schedule, Newman still found time for periods of detailed theological reading and analysis. At the time Wiseman's article appeared, Newman had recently completed a study of the fifth century doctrinal differences between the Roman Catholic and Greek Orthodox churches. In all significant respects, the Anglican church still adhered to the doctrinal principles which defined the fifth century Roman church. Newman's realisation of this, coupled with the underlying subtext of Wiseman's attack - the futility of schisms - caused Newman grave doubts about the path along which he was leading the Oxford Movement. Instead of aggressively promoting the *Via Media* as the preferred path between irreconcilable extremes, Newman now saw the way ahead as one of increasing convergence between two essentially similar wings of a Universal Church. Newman's public response was to write *Tract 90'* eventually published in 1841, which sought to show the compatibility of the *Thirty Nine Articles of Faith* with current Catholic teaching.

Newman's motive in writing the tract was to defend the position of the Anglican church, but few others saw it that way. Oxford, fearing a revolt against the Anglican establishment, led the way in roundly condemning the tract; the rest of the country soon followed. Newman was broken. He gave up the editorship of the *British Critic* and surrendered to Pusey his *de facto* role as leader of the Oxford Movement. Anglican bishops lined up to add their voices to the criticism; Bagot initially adopted a more moderate position but, recognising that the wider interests of the church demanded a united front, he eventually joined in the condemnation of *Tract 90*. Newman's humiliation was complete. He agreed not to publish further tracts and to limit his public participation in church matters to his responsibilities at St Mary's and the associated duties at the church at Littlemore. Within two years he was to relinquish these also.

An outcast at Oxford, in 1842 Newman moved to Littlemore, where he had bought a small L- shaped block of cottages, to live a semi-reclusive life. But even this did not halt the attacks on him. He was not without his supporters, young men from Oxford and further afield such as John Dalgairns and Ambrose St John who shared his religious convictions and, unprompted, followed him to Littlemore. This led to accusations, supported by exaggerated and fanciful descriptions, that he had established an Anglican monastery at Littlemore. Newman firmly refuted the accusations but his voice went unheard.

The cottages at Littlemore with
(right) the bust of Newman
which stands in the grounds and
(below) the plaque to Newman
on the external wall

Despite the attacks and his own personal doubts, at the time of his arrival at Littlemore Newman remained a firm adherent to the Anglican church. But the regime at Littlemore and the loss of his external responsibilities left Newman with far more time for reflection and study. This led him entirely, if slowly, in one direction : he reached the point where he could see no reason for remaining an Anglican yet he still lacked the conviction to commit himself to Rome. But, for once, others were beating a path ahead of him. William Lockhart, another who had followed him to Littlemore, converted to the Roman Catholic Church, then Tom Mozley, Newman's brother-in-law, informed him of his own plans to convert. Newman now resigned his remaining duties at St Mary's; he called his last sermon at Littlemore 'The Parting of Friends'.

In early 1845, he began a historical analysis which he called *Essay on the Development of Christian Doctrine*. He was never to complete it. As his study progressed, his remaining concerns resolved themselves. He could now accept the Roman Church as the true path and the Anglican way as an abberation. At last, he determined to seek admittance to the Catholic Church and, to prepare the way, resigned his Fellowship of Oriel on 3 October 1845. St John and Dalgairns had by now already converted to Rome, and Dalgairns was sent to arrange for Father Dominic Barberi of the Passionist Congregation to visit Newman at Littlemore. On 8 October, Newman wrote to various close friends to inform them of his intention. Few were surprised. That evening, Father Dominic arrived at Littlemore, heard Newman's confession and admitted him into the church.

From Outcast to Cardinal

It is difficult today to appreciate the turmoil in British society that Newman's defection caused. Despite his loss of formal status in the Anglican church, he retained an influence well beyond his immediate circle, both within and outside the church. Even Gladstone, then President of the Board of Trade, asked to be kept informed of developments and predicted serious consequences for the established church.

The immediate consequence was that a significant body of other Anglo-Catholics followed Newman into the Roman church. They were not numerically great, but they were largely individuals of standing, from established and influential families. Among the clergy who now made the transition, the most significant in the light of subsequent developments was Frederick Faber, an Oxford don who had taken the position of vicar of Elton in Huntingdonshire. But Keble and Pusey stood firm. Keble, anticipating Newman's defection, had attempted to organise the brightest Anglican theologians to develop arguments in defence of the church's position. But, with its leadership in disarray, the Oxford Movement effectively folded.

Not that his conversion opened up clear new opportunities for Newman. Despite the long transitional period, his lack of conviction until the very last stages had left him with little time to consider the future and he had given little thought to the role he might now take on. His options appeared limited. Many Catholics remained suspicious towards him, but fortunately he found a champion in Nicholas Wiseman. Wiseman had returned from the English College in Rome to become President of the recently rehoused Oscott College, a few miles north of Birmingham. He was also Vicar Apostolic of the Midland district, which extended to include Oxford. Wiseman invited Newman and his companions from Littlemore to Oscott to be confirmed and, having done so on 1 November, he offered Newman the use of the old college buildings.

Newman was reluctant to accept. He had no wish to leave his beloved university at Oxford, but the strong Anglican dominance made any kind of meaningful role for him impossible there. Birmingham held no attraction - if not Oxford, he would have preferred London - but he recognised his responsibilities towards his followers. Oscott offered prospects for a community not unlike Littlemore that would combine devotional studies with missionary work among the local population. By the end of the year, plans for the establishment at Oscott had been agreed. To avoid confusion with the newer college site, Newman chose the name Maryvale. Some work was needed to adapt the old buildings to their new function. Newman passed much of the intervening period travelling around England visiting various religious establishments, meeting and making friends, and gathering ideas for Maryvale. At last all was ready. He completed the final preparations and left Littlemore for good on 22 February 1846.

Wiseman was keen that Newman should seek ordination as a Roman Catholic priest. He persuaded Newman to receive instruction at the College of Propaganda in Rome, the body that administered Catholic institutions not under the direct control of the church. Accompanied by St John, Newman left the UK on 7 September 1846, spending five weeks in Milan before eventually reaching Rome on 28 October. Two matters of lasting importance took place during their stay. The first was an audience with the Pope, Pius IX; the second, the development of an idea by Newman that he should establish an Oratory in England.

The Oratorian tradition had been established in 1564 by St Philip Neri, who had founded the Oratory in Rome. In contrast to the cloistered lives of many religious communities, Oratorians considered their responsibilities to include[1] the education of the local population, and not

---

[1] "The chief task of Oratorians is to lead men to God by prayer, popular preaching - they have a daily evening sermon in all their churches - and the Sacraments... In conformity with the intentions of their founder, St Philip Neri, they lay great stress on attractive services and especially on good music; the modern "oratorio" grew out of the *laudi spirituali* singing in their devotional exercises..."
The Oxford Dictionary of the Christian Church (OUP, 1958), p986

just in religious matters. In many respects, therefore, an Oratorian's role was not greatly dissimilar from that which Newman had envisaged for the tutors at Oriel some twenty years earlier. To pursue his ambition, he now needed the approval of the necessary church authorities : the Propaganda, the Roman Oratory and, not least, the Pope. Approval was speedily obtained in February, the Pope proving to be particularly supportive of the plan. But Newman and St John were to spend much of the remaining months of 1847 in Rome, being ordained into the priesthood at the end of May before receiving instruction in the Oratorian tradition.

Newman and St John eventually left Rome on 6 December 1847, arriving back at Maryvale at the end of the month. Newman was keen to set to work to establish the Oratory but news of his plans had preceded him. Following his own conversion, Faber, under the sponsorship of the Earl of Shrewsbury, had established a religious community at Cheadle in Staffordshire which he called St Wilfrid's. This he also planned to develop on Oratorian lines. The Pope's ready acceptance of Newman's parallel plans irritated Faber, but Newman was able to persuade him that their mutual interests were best served by Faber and his followers joining Newman's English Oratory. The first nine members, including St John and Dalgairns, were admitted to the Congregation on 1 February 1848; Faber and other Wilfridians followed on 14 February.

A dispute then arose regarding the intended location of the Oratory. To succeed in its aims, it was axiomatic that an Oratory must be situated in a centre of population, but the Earl of Shrewsbury, having spent a considerable amount on the foundation at Cheadle, was unwilling to stand back and see Wilfridians desert him for Maryvale. Yet the maintenance of separate centres at Maryvale and Cheadle was clearly beyond the resources of the Oratorians. A compromise was agreed whereby the Oratorians moved to Cheadle, allowing the premises at Maryvale to be sold while Newman continued the search for suitable buildings in which to establish Oratories in the urban centres of Birmingham and London.

In Birmingham, he soon settled on a former gin distillery in Alcester Street. Conversion of the buildings proceeded quickly; Newman moved his personal possessions to Birmingham in late January and the Oratory chapel opened on 2 February 1848. But London proved to be more problematic and it was not until April 1849 that Newman committed to premises close to the Strand for the London Oratory. The Oratory was founded on 31 May under Faber's immediate control, with members of the Birmingham Oratory, including Dalgairns, moving to

London to assist him. Newman retained overall responsibility for the Oratorian Congregation in England.

Problems with Faber continued, however. Although a notably charismatic figure and in some respects Newman's intellectual equal, Faber lacked Newman's strategic perspective. He coupled energy and enthusiasm with an impulsive and somewhat irascible temperament; his lack of forethought often caused friction. In partnership, Newman's more temperate personality and political acumen provided an adequate balance to the weaknesses in Faber's psychological make-up, but the separation led to predictable difficulties. Eventually, recognising the impossibility of controlling Faber from a distance, Newman agreed to London becoming an autonomous Oratory on an equal footing with Birmingham. The decree from Rome became effective in October 1850 with Faber being elected Superior.

Earlier the same year, Rome had announced plans to establish a geographically-based church hierarchy in Britain, with Wiseman being elevated to Cardinal and becoming Archbishop of Westminster. The establishment was outraged, seeing it as a direct and deliberate attack on the position of the Church of England. Newspapers denounced the move as a Papist plot; mobs took to the streets. Oratorians, with their distinctive style of address, became a particular target for abuse. The Evangelical Alliance located a discredited former Dominican monk, Giacinto Achilli, and organised a lecture tour for Achilli to incite anti-Catholic passions with lurid tales of his treatment at the hands of a Roman Inquisition.

Achilli's sins had been well documented by Wiseman in an article in the Dublin Review. After Achilli had lectured in Birmingham, Newman used the article as the basis of a sermon intended to set the record straight. Backed by the Evangelical Alliance, Achilli sued for libel. Newman asked Wiseman to provide the documentary evidence on which he had based his article, and also sought an accurate record from Rome of the proceedings of the Inquisition into Achilli's activities, but neither quarter recognised the urgency attached to Newman's request. When, in June 1852, the case came to trial, Newman still lacked the crucial evidence with which to defend himself. The jury found for Achilli.

Newman sensed an anti-Catholic bias throughout the proceedings and The Times took a similar view, publishing a censorious article arguing that British justice was the real loser. The damages awarded against

Newman were slight - £100 - but his expenses, at £14,000, considerably greater. A public subscription organised by his friends quickly raised enough to cover the expenses, and more besides.

These were not happy years for Newman. Faber's erratic behaviour continued to trouble his subordinates who, despite the separation of the two Oratories, still looked to Newman for help. Attempts to send Faber away on extended leave brought relief only for the period of his absence. In 1855, Newman belatedly discovered that Faber had petitioned Rome for changes to the rules governing the London Oratory, giving Rome the impression that Newman had sanctioned the proposal. Newman's response was to press for a complete separation of the two establishments, so that the changes would not also apply to the Birmingham Oratory. This was agreed with the proviso that no other Oratory should be established in London, a condition sought by Faber to thwart Newman's plans for an Oratory in the East End. The whole affair caused considerable resentment between the two Oratories, for which Newman, generally the innocent party, attracted a large measure of the blame.

Another venture which occupied much of Newman's time from 1851 to 1857 was the ultimately successful attempt to establish a Catholic University in Ireland. Newman had been asked to take this on by Archbishop Cullen of Armagh and, later, Dublin. Newman, while sympathetic, felt that his prime responsibilities remained with the Birmingham Oratory; the Irish bishops did not wholly support Newman's candidature; and there was uncertainty over his precise role and title. Newman nevertheless persuaded the organising sub-committee to move the proposed site of the University from Thurles to Dublin where, in 1854, Newman found suitable premises. He put surplus funds from the public subscription following the Achilli trial towards the building of a University church. But his efforts remained divided between Birmingham and Dublin and progress was therefore slow. In late 1856, Newman tendered his resignation, to take effect the following November. Only now did the Irish bishops appear to value their impending loss. Attempts were made to persuade Newman to stay on; he agreed to continue to assist as best he could from Birmingham but played no active part after November 1858.

Despite his considerable efforts in Dublin, his involvement with the Catholic University, ending shortly after the formal separation of the two Oratories in England, further reduced his standing with the Catholic authorities. A brief involvement as editor with The Rambler, a periodical for and by the Catholic laity which the church distrusted because of its independence of spirit, caused further anxieties; the loss of the Papal territories on the unification of Italy in 1860 caused a further long-running schism in which Newman became deeply involved.

The years saw some positive developments, notably in Birmingham where the Oratory continued to prosper : a move to superior, purpose-built premises in Edgbaston in 1852; the purchase of land at Rednal, to the south-west of the city, for a rest-house and cemetery in 1854; and the establishment of an Oratory school on the Edgbaston site in 1859. And in London, the Oratorians purchased a spacious site in Brompton on which to build the magnificent church where, in 1889, the Elgars were to marry. But even the positive developments brought their own problems. Father Nicholas Darnell, appointed to head the Oratory school, developed authoritarian tendencies not unlike Faber's. When, in December 1861, his demands for unfettered control over all school affairs were not met, Darnell resigned, as did all his staff. Recognising the need to act quickly if the school were not to close, Newman asked Ambrose St John to become headmaster and turned to two close friends, James Hope-Scott, a relative by marriage of Sir Walter Scott, and Edward Bellasis, a fellow convert, for help in appointing new staff. It was the same Father Bellasis that Elgar turned to almost forty years later when he was considering setting *Gerontius* for the 1900 Birmingham Festival.

The early 1860s saw Newman rebuilding bridges with a number of old friends who had remained Anglicans. Rumours were put about that

The buildings of the Birmingham Oratory at Edgbaston

Newman was dissatisfied with the Roman church and was considering reconverting to Anglicanism. The rumours were without foundation but, perhaps sensing a vulnerability, a number of Protestants launched attacks on his integrity through the columns of popular journals. Although not untroubled by the attacks, Newman for the most part ignored them and continued re-establishing old friendships, but one attack in particular could not go unanswered.

Charles Kingsley, today known primarily as the author of *The Water Babies*, was a prominent member of the Christian Socialist movement. The January 1864 issue of MacMillan's Magazine carried a review by Kingsley of Froude's *History*, in which Kingsley insinuated that Catholics did not place great value in truth and quoted Newman in support of this. Newman saw the need to respond in order to defend not just his own reputation but that of his church. He did so by means of a reasoned pamphlet entitled *Mr Kingsley and Mr Newman*. Fellow Catholics were delighted by Newman's stance and rallied round, but Kingsley in turn responded with his own, more aggressive pamphlet, *What then does Mr Newman mean?*. This made plain the thrust of his complaint : that, to support his own ambitions, Newman had for many years remained an Anglican while sustaining Catholic beliefs.

The charge could not be ignored. Newman determined that the best response was an essentially factual account of his life and religious belief from his discovery of faith in 1816 up to his conversion to Catholicism in 1845. His account, *Apologia Pro Vita Sua*, was published in seven weekly instalments during the Spring of 1864, and later in book form under the name *History of my Religious Opinions*. The *Apologia* was written with an honesty and candour that left the reader in no doubt : Newman provided a clear and detailed statement of the development of his religious beliefs and Kingsley's charge was unambiguously refuted. The work sold exceptionally well and his reputation was considerably enhanced. But the work was not written without much effort : there was an urgency in replying to Kingsley's charge and Newman's diary records the long hours he worked on the project. He claimed at one point that the pressures he applied to himself led to a sense of approaching death.

This was perhaps the germ of an idea which resulted the following year in the writing of *The Dream of Gerontius*. He claims to have written the poem in a single night, 17 January 1865, committing it to numerous scraps of paper before making a fair copy over the following three weeks. This hardly seems credible, given the length and complexity of the poem.

It is more likely that ideas had been forming in his head for some time; indeed, the central idea of a soul's journey through the afterlife was a recurrent theme in sermons delivered in Oxford before his conversion. Newman offered the completed poem to the Catholic periodical *The Month*, which published it in two parts in its issues for May and June 1865. Much is said elsewhere in this book about the literary merits of the poem. Suffice to say here that it achieved an immediate and widespread measure of success, being reprinted numerous times during Newman's life, with translations appearing in French and German.

Gerontius firmly established Newman at the forefront of moderate Catholics in England. His reputation could not have been higher, a complete transformation from the nadir of only two years before. Moreover, the success of *Gerontius* persuaded Newman of the power he could exercise through his writings. But he was no longer a young man. It is easy to be misled by the fact that he was to live on for another twenty-five years. Although only sixty-four years old when *Gerontius* was published, the effect of the years and their battles were becoming apparent. Faber had commented as long ago as 1852 that Newman was looking old and Newman had acknowledged signs of advancing frailty in a letter written in 1860. He had only one substantial battle still to fight, a battle against extreme views within his own church.

Reference has already been made to the loss of the Papal territories on the unification of Italy in 1860. Newman considered this of no lasting importance, recognising that it did not impact on the Pope's spiritual authority. Others took a different view. Prominent among the latter were the Ultramontanes, a faction within the Roman church that believed in the Pope's infallibility on all matters of religion. Within England, the Ultramontanes were led by H E Manning, a former Archdeacon of Chichester, who in 1850 had followed Newman from the Anglican to the Roman church. Oxford University's abolition of religious tests in 1854 had opened up admission to the University to Catholics and this had led to plans to establish firstly a Catholic college and later a Catholic mission in the city, but the Ultramontanes had opposed both, believing that the education of all Catholics should be confined to institutions under the direct control of the church. The Ultramontanes distrusted Newman for his involvement in such projects and for his liberal views. This would have been of little consequence had Cardinal Wiseman not died in 1865, opening the way for Manning to succeed him as Archbishop of Westminster.

This placed the Ultramontanes firmly in the ascendency. Newman saw the damage to the Catholic church that their extremist actions and attitudes could cause, but also recognised that he could use his persuasive writing skills to present an alternative, more moderate view. His greatest literary achievement in his remaining years was the book *The Grammar of Assent*, published in 1870, which presented a detailed and reasoned argument on the nature of religious belief, that it is perfectly reasonable to have an unshakable faith in something with no logical explanation or physical manifestation. His two most influential pieces during this period were in response to attacks by, in 1865, his old friend Edward Pusey and, in 1875, William Gladstone, who by now had served three terms as Prime Minister. In his responses to both, Newman sought to distance moderate Catholics from the extremist views Pusey and Gladstone attacked. Gladstone in particular responded warmly to Newman's measured response and the two remained on good terms.

Ultimately, Newman's efforts achieved only a limited effect. Manning developed a hostility towards Newman which the latter unsuccessfully attempted to overcome; the two accepted that their differences could not be resolved. In December 1869, the Ultramontane-inspired First Vatican Council ruled on Papal infallibility. Again, Newman saw the ruling as unnecessary and divisive, laying Catholics open to accusations of subservience to a foreign power, charges which Gladstone was later to exploit. Manning continued to seek to undermine Newman's influence whenever the opportunity presented itself, but Newman's position was secure. Fellow Oratorians intervened on his behalf to ensure that Manning's manoeuvrings were exposed and their effectiveness nullified.

In 1878, the Duke of Norfolk and the Marquis of Ripon, lay friends of Newman, proposed to the Pope that Newman's work should be recognised by his elevation to Cardinal. Manning sought to block the move by putting it about that Newman had been offered and had declined the Cardinalate, but Newman's acceptance was conditional only on his being allowed to remain at Birmingham. His elevation was announced on 18 March 1879.

The last ten years of his life were troubled by recurrent periods of illness. Failing eyesight and increasing physical frailty placed limitations on his continuing intellectual alertness and he became increasingly reclusive. He eventually died in his room at the Oratory on 11 August 1890. He was buried in the grounds of the Oratory rest-house at Rednal, next to Ambrose St John who had died some fifteen years earlier.

Retrospective

What then does Dr Newman mean .... to us, today? To many Elgarians, the received image does not stretch much beyond the convert to Catholicism who rose to become a Cardinal and, somewhere along the way, wrote *The Dream of Gerontius*. The clichéd impression is of a saintly man; those who know more of his constant quarrels with authority may choose to qualify this characteristic with words such as difficult, argumentative, even cantankerous. But all caricatures are inevitably superficial and subjective.

Certain of Newman's essential characteristics are not open to question: a biting intellect and unswerving honesty, supported by a way with words and an appetite for new challenges that frequently led him to take on more than he could reasonably handle. While he did not court controversy, neither did he avoid it; his integrity would not allow him to shirk issues that required his intervention. This, coupled with an early naïvety and stubbornness, often led him to confront head on opponents who would have been more susceptible to a subtler approach and a willingness to compromise. But for these characteristics, and with greater personal ambition, he could undoubtedly have advanced further within the Anglican church .... again with what consequences for the Roman church in Britain, and for Elgar?

Newman's reputation obviously survives, but on what? Both the *Apologia* and *Gerontius* captured the public imagination through the clarity of expression and on a literary merit that Newman displayed throughout his life. Their immediate and immense success reversed Newman's reputation at a point when it was in sharp decline. A direct line can be drawn from their publication to Newman's eventual elevation to Cardinal and thence to the position in the public imagination that he holds today.

A similar causal relationship can be established for Elgar. *Gerontius* certainly captured Elgar's imagination, firing him to write the work which is arguably as important in defining his public image. It may not be as popular as some of his orchestral works (although the listing of recent performances in Part 6 of this book suggests that the difference may not be great) but it is the work that tags Elgar as a 'Catholic' composer. Yet, given Elgar's later loss of faith and his willingness to meddle with Newman's words in order to increase the acceptability of the work for performance in Protestant venues, who can doubt that Elgar was attracted by the dramatic impact of the story-line rather than by the theological imagery. And the public interest in the poem created by General Gordon's markings on his copy, all at a time when Elgar was toying with the composition of a symphony in honour of the man, probably provided a commercial incentive which is lost on us today.

Would *Gerontius* have survived without Elgar? Many think not. It is a period piece, in accord with the attitudes and superstitions of the time but whose popularity, like that of the poem *The Music Makers*, many now find hard to understand. It is Elgar's music that now gives life to both works. So 'Cardinal' Newman, the Catholic convert who wrote *Gerontius*, he may be to many, but this overlooks two more significant and lasting achievements.

The first of these is his continuing influence on both churches. The paradox here is that, as an Anglican, he strove to protect his church against external liberal forces seeking to reduce the standing of the church in matters of state whereas, as a Catholic, he was a liberal seeking to limit damage to the church from extreme conservative forces operating within it. He was only partially successful in both roles during his lifetime but his legacy is two churches which remained closer to each other than they might otherwise have become. His quiet demeanour concealed revolutionary thinking; ahead of his time, his views initially fell on barren ground but eventually grew to gain acceptance at the second Vatican Council which sat from 1962 to 1965. He did not convert to Catholicism enthusiastically; it became the least worst option once a continuing active role in the Anglican church had become untenable. But, while the Catholic church may not have met all his aspirations, he did not expect better and so was content.

His second lasting achievement originated in his views on the role of a tutor, first espoused at Oriel College and leading to his split with Hawkins and his distancing from Oxford. He refined and developed these views over the years until they eventually found full public expression in a series of lectures he gave during his short tenure of office at the Catholic University in Dublin. The lectures, subsequently published as *Discourses on the Scope and Nature of University Education* and subsequently retitled *The Idea of a University* were influential in the development of further education. While *Gerontius* may be the perception of Newman's legacy, today's universities are the true benefactors.

The COMPLETE WORDS
including General Gordon's Marking of the Text

Cardinal Newman's poem *The Dream of Gerontius* first appeared in a Catholic magazine, *The Month*, in 1865. The May edition carried the poem as far as the beginning of the Demons' Chorus, ending with the well-known lines, "But hark! Upon my sense... could I be frighted". The June edition began by repeating these three lines, and then continued to the end. The following year, the poem was published separately, and its popularity can be gauged from the fact that General Gordon's 1884 copy was the eighteenth edition; while Alice Elgar's copy is the twenty-second edition from 1886. It is clear that a few minor revisions were carried out by Newman prior to its publication as a separate work in 1866. For instance, the word "Amen" after each litany ("Noe from the waters", etc) now appears in brackets, where there were none originally. In Part II, the Angel's words ".. For thee the bitterness of death is past", had "passed" in the original (and for some reason "passed" is used in Jaeger's analysis). The First Choir of Angelicals sing of "His Viceroy in the world", and this was "Vice-roy" originally. More importantly, there were two word changes from the original; "But hark! a deep mysterious harmony", where "deep" was replaced by "grand"; and the first line of the Angel's Farewell, initially "Softly and gently, dearest, sweetest soul", which became the more familiar, "dearly-ransomed soul".

Newman made one or two further slight revisions after the first edition, but these do not occur in the lines Elgar set. However, the last line of Part I exists in *three* versions. In *The Month* and in the first edition it read; "through the Same, through Christ, our Lord". (These are the words Elgar set, showing that he had access to the first edition.) By the eighteenth edition, it had become; "through the Name of Christ, our Lord", whilst modern editions read "in the Name of Christ, our Lord".

General Charles Gordon was given a copy of Newman's poem just before he left for the Sudan in 1884, and after his death the following January he quickly became a national hero. His copy of the poem, complete with sidelinings and underlinings he had added to it, found its way back to England. Due to Gordon's popularity, the markings were widely copied and re-copied. Elgar was quoted as having received a copy of *Gerontius* with the markings as a wedding present, ie. in May

1889; but Jerrold Northrop Moore has pointed out that Alice's copy, dated 12 June 1887, indicates that the markings she made were taken from Elgar's copy, implying that he already owned the book.

The words here follow Newman's layout and punctuation as faithfully as possible, except that lines which Elgar omitted from his libretto are shown in italics. Gordon's markings are also included.

---

§1

GERONTIUS

JESU, MARIA - I am near to death,
  And Thou art calling me; I know it now -
Not by the token of this faltering breath,
  This chill at heart, this dampness on my brow,
(Jesu, have mercy! Mary, pray for me!) -
  'Tis this new feeling, never felt before,
(Be with me, Lord, in my extremity!)
  That I am going, that I am no more.
'Tis this strange innermost abandonment,
  (Lover of souls! great God! I look to Thee,)
This emptying out of each constituent
  And natural force, by which I come to be.
| Pray for me, O my friends; a visitant
  Is knocking his dire summons at my door,
The like of whom, to scare me and to daunt,
  Has never, never come to me before ;
| *Tis death, - O loving friends, your prayers!* ‑|||
  'tis he ! . . . .
As though my very being had given way,
As though I was no more a substance now,
And could fall back on nought to be my stay, ||
  (Help, loving Lord! Thou my sole
    Refuge, Thou,)
And turn no whither, but must needs decay
  And drop from out the universal frame
Into that shapeless, scopeless, blank abyss,
  That utter nothingness, of which I came:
This is it that has come to pass in me;
O horror! this it is, my dearest, this;
So pray for me, my friends, who have not
  strength to pray.

ASSISTANTS

Kyrie eleïson, Christe eleïson, Kyrie eleïson.
Holy Mary, pray for him.
All holy Angels, pray for him
Choirs of the righteous, pray for him.
Holy Abraham, pray for him.
St. John Baptist, St. Joseph, pray for him.
St. Peter, St. Paul, St. Andrew, St. John,
All Apostles, all Evangelists, pray for him.
All holy Disciples of the Lord, pray for him,
All holy Innocents, pray for him.
All holy Martyrs, all holy Confessors,
All holy Hermits, all holy Virgins,
All ye Saints of God, pray for him.

GERONTIUS

Rouse thee, my fainting soul, and play the man;
  And through such waning span
Of life and thought as still has to be trod,
  Prepare to meet thy God.
And while the storm of that bewilderment
  Is for a season spent,
And, ere afresh the ruin on thee fall, ||
  Use well the interval.

ASSISTANTS

Be merciful, be gracious; spare him, Lord.
Be merciful, be gracious; Lord, deliver him.
From the sins that are past;
  From Thy frown and Thine ire;
    From the perils of dying;
    From any complying
    With sin, or denying

His God, or relying
On self, at the last;
From the nethermost fire;
From all that is evil;
From power of the devil;
Thy servant deliver,
For once and for ever.

By Thy birth, and by Thy Cross,
Rescue him from endless loss;
By Thy death and burial,
Save him from a final fall ;
By Thy rising from the tomb,
By Thy mounting up above,
By the Spirit's gracious love,
Save him in the day of doom.

GERONTIUS

Sanctus fortis, Sanctus Deus,
    De profundis oro te,
Miserere, Judex meus,
    Parce mihi, Domine.
Firmly I believe and truly
    God is Three, and God is One ;
And I next acknowledge duly
    Manhood taken by the Son.
And I trust and hope most fully
    In that Manhood crucified ;
And each thought and deed unruly
    Do to death, as He has died.
Simply to His grace and wholly
    Light and life and strength belong,
And I love, supremely, solely,
    Him the holy, Him the strong.
Sanctus fortis, Sanctus Deus,
    De profundis oro te,
Miserere, Judex meus,
    Parce mihi, Domine.
And I hold in veneration,
    For the love of Him alone,
Holy Church, as His creation,
    And her teachings, as His own.
And I take with joy whatever
    Now besets me, pain or fear,

And with a strong will I sever
    All the ties which bind me here.
Adoration aye be given,
    With and through the angelic host,
To the God of earth and heaven,
    Father, Son, and Holy Ghost.
Sanctus fortis, Sanctus Deus,
    De profundis oro te,
Miserere, Judex meus,
    Mortis in discrimine.

I can no more ; for now it comes again,
That sense of ruin, which is worse than pain,
That masterful negation and collapse
Of all that makes me man ; *as though I bent*
Over the dizzy brink
Of some sheer infinite descent;
Or worse, as though
Down, down for ever I was falling through
The solid framework of created things,
And needs must sink and sink
Into the vast abyss. And, crueller still,
A fierce and restless fright begins to fill
The mansion of my soul. And, worse and worse,
Some bodily form of ill
Floats on the wind, with many a loathsome curse
Tainting the hallowed air, and laughs, and flaps
Its hideous wings,
And makes me wild with horror and dismay
O Jesu, help ! pray for me, Mary, pray !
Some angel, Jesu ! such as came to Thee
In Thine own agony. . . .
Mary, pray for me. Joseph, pray for me.
    Mary, pray for me.

ASSISTANTS

Rescue him, O Lord, in this his evil hour,
As of old so many by Thy gracious power :-
                    (Amen.)
Enoch and Elias from the common doom ;
                    (Amen.)
Noe from the waters in a saving home ;
                    (Amen.)
Abraham from th' abounding guilt of

Heathenesse ;   *(Amen.)*
Job from all his multiform and fell distress ;
          (Amen.)
Isaac, when his father's knife was raised to
*   slay;*   *(Amen.)*
Lot from burning Sodom on its judgment-
*   day ;*   *(Amen.)*
Moses from the land of bondage and despair ;
          (Amen.)
Daniel from the hungry lions in their lair ;
          (Amen.)
And the Children Three amid the furnace-
*   flame;*   *(Amen.)*
Chaste Susanna from the slander and the
*   shame;*   *(Amen.)*
David from Golia and the wrath of Saul ;
          (Amen.)
And the two Apostles from their prison-
*   thrall ;*   *(Amen.)*
Thecla from her torments ;   *(Amen.)*
          -so, to show Thy power,
Rescue this Thy servant in his evil hour.

GERONTIUS

Novissima hora est ; and I fain would sleep,
The pain has wearied me. . . . Into Thy hands,
O Lord, into Thy hands . . . .

THE PRIEST

Proficiscere, anima Christiana, de hoc mundo !
Go forth upon thy journey, Christian soul !
Go from this world ! Go, in the name of God
The omnipotent Father, who created thee !
Go, in the name of Jesus Christ, our Lord,
Son of the living God, who bled for thee !
Go, in the Name of the Holy Spirit, who
Hath been poured out on thee ! Go, in the name
Of Angels and Archangels ; in the name
Of Thrones and Dominations ; in the name
Of Princedoms and of Powers; and in the name
Of Cherubim and Seraphim, go forth !
Go, in the name of Patriarchs and Prophets ;
And of Apostles and Evangelists,

Of Martyrs and Confessors ; in the name
Of holy Monks and Hermits ; in the name
Of holy Virgins ; and all Saints of God,
Both men and women, go ! Go on thy course ;
And may thy place to-day be found in peace,
And may thy dwelling be the Holy Mount
Of Sion : -in the Name of Christ, our Lord.

§2

SOUL OF GERONTIUS

I went to sleep ; and now I am refreshed.
A strange refreshment : for I feel in me
An inexpressive lightness, and a sense
Of freedom, as I were at length myself,
And ne'er had been before. How still it is !
I hear no more the busy beat of time,
No, nor my fluttering breath, nor struggling
          pulse;
Nor does one moment differ from the next.
I had a dream ; yes :- some one softly said
"He's gone" ; and then a sigh went round
*   the room.*
And then I surely heard a priestly voice
Cry " Subvenite " ; and they knelt in prayer.
I seem to hear him still ; but thin and low,
And fainter and more faint the accents come,
As at an ever-widening interval.
Ah ! whence is this ? What is this severance ?
This silence pours a solitariness
Into the very essence of my soul ;
And the deep rest, so soothing and so sweet,
Hath something too of sternness and of pain,
For it drives back my thoughts upon their spring
By a strange introversion, and perforce
I now begin to feed upon myself,
Because I have nought else to feed upon.

Am I alive or dead ? I am not dead,
But in the body still ; for I possess
A sort of confidence which clings to me,
That each particular organ holds its place
As heretofore, combining with the rest
Into one symmetry, that wraps me round,

And makes me man ; and surely I could move,
Did I but will it, every part of me.
And yet I cannot to my sense bring home,
By very trial, that I have the power.
'Tis strange ; I cannot stir a hand or foot,
I cannot make my fingers or my lips
By mutual pressure witness each to each,
Nor by the eyelid's instantaneous stroke
Assure myself I have a body still.
Nor do I know my very attitude,
Nor if I stand, or lie, or sit, or kneel.

So much I know, not knowing how I know,
That the vast universe, where I have dwelt,
Is quitting me, or I am quitting it.
Or I or it is rushing on the wings
Of light or lightning on an onward course,
And we e'en now are million miles apart.
Yet . . is this peremptory severance
Wrought out in lengthening measurements
*   of space,*
Which grow and multiply by speed and me ?
Or am I traversing infinity
By endless subdivision, hurrying back
From finite towards infinitesimal,
Thus dying out of the expansed world ?

Another marvel ; some one has me fast
Within his ample palm ; *'tis not a grasp*
Such as they use on earth, but all around
Over the surface of my subtle being,
As though I were a sphere, and capable
To be accosted thus, a uniform
And gentle pressure tells me I am not
Self-moving, but borne forward on my way.
And hark ! I hear a singing ; yet in sooth
I cannot of that music rightly say
Whether I hear or touch or taste the tones.
Oh what a heart-subduing melody !

ANGEL

My work is done,
My task is o'er,

And so I come,
   Taking it home.
For the crown is won,
   Alleluia,
For evermore.

My Father gave
   In charge to me
This child of earth
   E'en from its birth,
To serve and save,
   Alleluia,
And saved is he.

This child of clay
   To me was given,
To rear and train
   By sorrow and pain
In the narrow way,
   Alleluia.
From earth to heaven.

SOUL

It is a member of that family
Of wondrous beings, who, ere the worlds
   were made,
Millions of ages back, have stood around
The throne of God : - *he never has known sin ;*
But through those cycles all but infinite,
Has had a strong and pure celestial life
And bore to gaze on th' unveiled face of God
And drank from the eternal Fount of truth,
And served Him with a keen ecstatic love.
Hark ! he begins again.

ANGEL

O Lord, how wonderful in depth and height,
*   But most in man, how wonderful*
*   Thou art!*
With what a love, what soft persuasive might
Victorious o'er the stubborn fleshly
*   heart,*

Thy tale complete of saints Thou dost
provide,
To fill the thrones which angels lost
through pride !
He lay a grovelling babe upon the ground,
Polluted in the blood of his first sire,
With his whole essence shattered and unsound,
And, coiled around his heart, a demon
dire.
Which was not of his nature, but had skill
To bind and form his opening mind to ill.

Then was I sent from heaven to set right
The balance in his soul of truth and sin,
And I have waged a long relentless fight,
Resolved that death-environed spirit to
win,
Which from its fallen state, when all was lost,
Had been repurchased at so dread a cost.

Oh what a shifting parti-coloured scene
Of hope and fear, of triumph and dismay,
Of recklessness and penitence, has been
The history of that dreary, lifelong fray !
And oh the grace to nerve him and to lead,
How patient, prompt, and lavish at his need !

O man, strange composite of heaven and earth !
Majesty dwarfed to baseness ! fragrant
flower
Running to poisonous seed ! and seeming worth
Cloking corruption ! weakness mastering
power !
Who never art so near to crime and shame,
As when thou hast achieved some deed of
name : -

How should ethereal natures comprehend
A thing made up of spirit and of clay,
Were we not tasked to nurse it and to tend,
Linked one to one throughout its mortal day
More than the Seraph in his height of place,
The Angel-guardian knows and loves the
ransomed race.

SOUL

Now know I surely that I am at length
Out of the body : had I part with earth,
I never could have drunk those accents in,
And not have worshipped as a god the voice
That was so musical ; but now I am
So whole of heart, so calm, so self-possessed,
With such a full content, and with a sense
So apprehensive and discriminant,
As no temptation can intoxicate.
Nor have I even terror at the thought
That I am clasped by such a saintliness.

ANGEL

All praise to Him, at whose sublime decree
The last are first, the first become the last;
By whom the suppliant prisoner is set free,
By whom proud first-borns from their
thrones are cast;
Who raises Mary to be Queen of heaven,
While Lucifer is left, condemned and
unforgiven

§3

SOUL

I will address him. Mighty one, my Lord,
My Guardian Spirit, all hail !

ANGEL

All hail, my child !
My child and brother, hail! what wouldest thou ?

SOUL

I would have nothing but to speak with thee
For speaking's sake. I wish to hold with thee
Conscious communion; though I fain would know
A maze of things, were it but meet to ask,
And not a curiousness.

ANGEL

You cannot now
Cherish a wish which ought not to be wished.

SOUL

Then I will speak. I ever had believed
That on the moment when the struggling soul
Quitted its mortal case, forthwith it fell
Under the awful Presence of its God,
There to be judged and sent to its own place.
What lets me now from going to my Lord ?

ANGEL

Thou art not let ; but with extremest speed
Art hurrying to the Just and Holy Judge :
For scarcely art thou disembodied yet.
Divide a moment, as men measure time,
Into its million-million-millionth part,
Yet even less than that the interval
Since thou didst leave the body ; and the priest
Cried " Subvenite," and they fell to prayer ;
Nay, scarcely yet have they begun to pray.
For spirits and men by different standards mete
The less and greater in the flow of time.
By sun and moon, primeval ordinances -
By stars which rise and set harmoniously -
By the recurring seasons, and the swing,
This way and that, of the suspended rod
Precise and punctual, men divide the hours,
Equal, continuous, for their common use.
Not so with us in the immaterial world ;
But intervals in their succession
Are measured by the living thought alone,
And grow or wane with its intensity.
And time is not a common property ;
But what is long is short, and swift is slow,
And near is distant, as received and grasped
By this mind and by that, and every one
Is standard of his own chronology.
And memory lacks its natural resting-points
Of years, and centuries, and periods.

It is thy very energy of thought
Which keeps thee from thy God.

SOUL

Dear Angel, say,
Why have I now no fear at meeting Him ?
Along my earthly life, the thought of death
And judgment was to me most terrible.
I had it aye before me, and I saw
The Judge severe e'en in the crucifix.
Now that the hour is come, my fear is fled ;
And at this balance of my destiny,
Now close upon me, I can forward look
With a serenest joy.

ANGEL

It is because
Then thou didst fear, that now thou dost not fear.
Thou hast forestalled the agony, and so
For thee the bitterness of death is past.
Also, because already in thy soul
The judgment is begun. *That day of doom,*
One and the same for the collected world-
That solemn consummation for all flesh,
Is, in the case of each, anticipate
Upon his death ; and, as the last great day
In the particular judgment is rehearsed,
So now too, ere thou comest to the Throne.
A presage falls upon thee, as a ray
Straight from the Judge, expressive of thy lot.
That calm and joy uprising in thy soul
Is first-fruit to thee of thy recompense,
And heaven begun.

§4

SOUL

But hark ! upon my sense
Comes a fierce hubbub, which would make
me fear,
Could I be frighted.

ANGEL

We are now arrived
Close on the judgment court ; that sullen howl
Is from the demons who assemble there.
It is the middle region, where of old
Satan appeared among the sons of God,
To cast his jibes and scoffs at holy Job.
So now his legions throng the vestibule,
Hungry and wild, to claim their property,
And gather souls for hell. Hist to their cry.

SOUL

How sour and how uncouth a dissonance !

DEMONS

Low-born clods
    Of brute earth,
        They aspire
To become gods,
    By a new birth,
And an extra grace,
    And a score of merits.
        As if aught
Could stand in place
    Of the high thought,
    And the glance of fire
Of the great spirits,
    The powers blest,
    The lords by right,
        The primal owners,
        Of the proud dwelling
And realm of light,-
Dispossessed,
Aside thrust.
        Chucked down,
By the sheer might
Of a despot's will,
    Of a tyrant's frown,
Who after expelling
    Their hosts, gave,
Triumphant still,
And still unjust,

Each forfeit crown
To psalm-droners,
And canting groaners,
    To every slave,
And pious cheat,
And crawling knave,
Who licked the dust
    Under his feet

ANGEL

It is the restless panting of their being ;
Like beasts of prey, who, caged within their
        bars,
In a deep hideous purring have their life,
And an incessant pacing to and fro.

DEMONS

The mind bold
    And independent,
        The purpose free,
So we are told,
Must not think
    To have the ascendant.
        What's a saint ?
One whose breath
    Doth the air taint
Before his death ;
    A bundle of bones,
Which fools adore,
        Ha ! ha !
When life is o'er,
Which rattle and stink,
    E'en in the flesh.
We cry his pardon !
    No flesh hath he ;
        Ha ! ha !
    For it hath died,
    'Tis crucified
    Day by day,
Afresh, afresh,
    Ha ! ha !
    That holy clay,
        Ha ! ha !

This gains guerdon,
  So priestlings prate,
    Ha ! ha !
Before the Judge,
  And pleads and atones
For spite and grudge,
  And bigot mood,
And envy and hate,
  And greed of blood.

SOUL

How impotent they are ! and yet on earth
They have repute for wondrous power and skill ;
And books describe, how that the very face
Of the Evil One, if seen, would have a force
Even to freeze the blood, and choke the life
Of him who saw it.

ANGEL

In thy trial-state
Thou hadst a traitor nestling close at home,
Connatural, who with the powers of hell
Was leagued, and of thy senses kept the keys,
And to that deadliest foe unlocked thy heart.
And therefore is it, in respect of man,
Those fallen ones show so majestical.
But, when some child of grace, angel or saint,
Pure and upright in his integrity
Of nature, meets the demons on their raid,
They scud away as cowards from the fight.
Nay, oft hath holy hermit in his cell,
Not yet disburdened of mortality,
Mocked at their threats and warlike overtures;
Or, dying, when they swarmed, like flies, around,
Defied them, and departed to his Judge.

DEMONS

Virtue and vice,
  A knave's pretence,
    'Tis all the same;
      Ha ! ha !
Dread of hell-fire,

Of the venomous flame,
  A coward's plea.
Give him his price,
  Saint though he be,
Ha ! ha !
  From shrewd good sense
    He'll slave for hire ;
      Ha ! ha !
    And does but aspire
To the heaven above
    With sordid aim,
And not from love.
      Ha ! ha !

SOUL

I see not those false spirits ; shall I see
My dearest Master, when I reach His throne ;
Or hear, at least, His awful judgment-word
With personal intonation, as I now
Hear thee, not see thee, Angel ? Hitherto
All has been darkness since I left the earth ;
Shall I remain thus sight bereft all through
My penance time ? If so, how comes it then
That I have hearing still, and taste, and touch,
Yet not a glimmer of that princely sense
Which binds ideas in one, and makes them live ?

ANGEL

Nor touch, nor taste, nor hearing hast thou now;
Thou livest in a world of signs and types,
The presentations of most holy truths,
Living and strong, which now encompass thee.
A disembodied soul, thou hast by right
No converse with aught else beside thyself ;
But, lest so stern a solitude should load
And break thy being, in mercy are vouchsafed
Some lower measures of perception,
Which seem to thee, as though through
    channels brought,
Through ear, or nerves, or palate, which are gone.
And thou art wrapped and swathed around in
    dreams,
Dreams that are true, yet enigmatical ;

For the belongings of thy present state,
Save through such symbols, come not home
*   to thee.*
And thus thou tell'st of space, and time, and size,
Of fragrant, solid, bitter, musical,
Of fire, and of refreshment after fire ;
As (let me use similitude of earth,
To aid thee in the knowledge thou dost ask) -
As ice which blisters may be said to burn.
Nor hast thou now extension, with its parts
Correlative, - long habit cozens thee, -
Nor power to move thyself, nor limbs to move.
Hast thou not heard of those, who, after loss
Of hand or foot, still cried that they had pains
In hand or foot, as though they had it still !
So is it now with thee, who hast not lost
Thy hand or foot, but all which made up man ;
So will it be, until the joyous day
Of resurrection, when thou wilt regain
All thou hast lost, new-made and glorified.
How, even now, the consummated Saints
See God in heaven, I may not explicate.
Meanwhile let it suffice thee to possess
Such means of converse as are granted thee,
Though, till that Beatific Vision thou art blind ;
For e'en thy purgatory, which comes like fire ,
Is fire without its light.

SOUL

His will be done !
I am not worthy e'er to see again
The face of day ; far less His countenance
Who is the very sun. Nathless, in life,
When I looked forward to my purgatory,
It ever was my solace to believe
That, ere I plunged amid th' avenging flame,
I had one sight of Him to strengthen me.

ANGEL

Nor rash nor vain is that presentiment ;
Yes, - for one moment thou shalt see thy Lord.
Thus will it be : what time thou art arraigned
Before the dread tribunal, and thy lot

Is cast for ever, should it be to sit
On His right hand among His pure elect,
Then sight, or that which to the soul is sight,
As by a lightning-flash, will come to thee,
And thou shalt see, amid the dark profound,
Whom thy soul loveth, and would fain approach,
One moment ; but thou knowest not, my child,
What thou dost ask : that sight of the Most Fair
Will gladden thee, but it will pierce thee too.

SOUL

Thou speakest darkly, Angel ! and an awe
Falls on me, and a fear lest I be rash.

ANGEL

There was a mortal, who is now above
In the mid glory : he, when near to die,
Was given communion with the Crucified; -
Such, that the Master's very wounds were
    stamped
Upon his flesh ; and, from the agony
Which thrilled through body and soul in that
    embrace
Learn that the flame of [the[1]] Everlasting Love
Doth burn ere it transform.

§5

. . . Hark to those sounds !
They come of tender beings angelical,
Least and most childlike of the sons of God.

FIRST CHOIR OF ANGELICALS

Praise to the Holiest in the height,
    And in the depth be praise :
In all His words most wonderful ;
    Most sure in all His ways !

To us His elder race He gave
    To battle and to win,
Without the chastisement of pain,
    Without the soil of sin.

---

[1]   Added by Elgar to Newman's original

The younger son He willed to be
   A marvel in his birth :
Spirit and flesh his parents were ;
   His home was heaven and earth,

The Eternal blessed His child, and armed,
   And sent him hence afar,
To serve as champion in the field
   Of elemental war.

To be His Viceroy in the world
   Of matter, and of sense ;
Upon the frontier, towards the foe,
   A resolute defence.

ANGEL

We now have passed the gate, and are within
The House of Judgment ; *and whereas on earth*
Temples and palaces are formed of parts
Costly and rare, but all material,
So in the world of spirits nought is found,
To mould withal and form into a whole,
But what is immaterial ; and thus
The smallest portions of this edifice,
Cornice, or frieze, or balustrade, or stair,
The very pavement is made up of life-
Of holy, blessed, and immortal beings,
Who hymn their Maker's praise continually.

SECOND CHOIR OF ANGELICALS

Praise to the Holiest in the height,
   And in the depth be praise :
In all His words most wonderful ;
   Most sure in all His ways !

Woe to thee, man ! for he was found
   A recreant in the fight ;
And lost his heritage of heaven,
   And fellowship with light.

Above him now the angry sky,
   Around the tempest's din ;
Who once had angels for his friends,
   Had but the brutes for kin.

O man ! a savage kindred they ;
   To flee that monster brood
He scaled the seaside cave, and clomb
   The giants of the wood.

With now a fear, and now a hope,
   With aids which chance supplied,
From youth to eld, from sire to son,
   He lived, and toiled, and died.

He dreed his penance age by age ;
   And step by step began
Slowly to doff his savage garb,
   And be again a man.

And quickened by the Almighty's breath,
   And chastened by His rod,
And taught by Angel-visitings,
   At length he sought his God :

And learned to call upon His name,
   And in His faith create
A household and a fatherland,
   A city and a state.

Glory to Him who from the mire,
   In patient length of days,
Elaborated into life
   A people to His praise !

SOUL

The sound is like the rushing of the wind -
The summer wind among the lofty pines ;
Swelling and dying, echoing round about,
Now here, now distant, wild and beautiful ;
While, scattered from the branches it has stirred,
Descend ecstatic odours.

THIRD CHOIR OF ANGELICALS

Praise to the Holiest in the height,
   And in the depth be praise :
In all His words most wonderful ;
   Most sure in all His ways !

The Angels, as beseemingly
    To spirit-kind was given,
At once were tried and perfected,
    And took their seats in heaven.

For them no twilight or eclipse ;
    No growth and no decay :
'Twas hopeless, all-ingulfing night,
    Or beatific day.

But to the younger race there rose
    A hope upon its fall ;
And slowly, surely, gracefully,
    The morning dawned on all.

And ages, opening out, divide
    The precious and the base,
And from the hard and sullen mass,
    Mature the heirs of grace.

O man ! albeit the quickening ray,
    Lit from his second birth,
Makes him at length what once he was,
    And heaven grows out of earth ;

Yet still between that earth and heaven -
    His journey and his goal -
A double agony awaits
    His body and his soul.

A double debt he has to pay -
    The forfeit of his sins,
The chill of death is past, and now
    The penance-fire begins.

Glory to Him, who evermore
    By truth and justice reigns ;
Who tears the soul from out its case
    And burns away its stains !

ANGEL

They sing of thy approaching agony,
Which thou so eagerly didst question of :
It is the face of the Incarnate God
Shall smite thee with that keen and subtle pain ;

And yet the memory which it leaves will be
A sovereign febrifuge to heal the wound ;
And yet withal it will the wound provoke,
And aggravate and widen it the more.

SOUL

Thou speakest mysteries; still methinks I know
To disengage the tangle of thy words :
Yet rather would I hear thy angel voice,
Than for myself be thy interpreter.

ANGEL

When then - if such thy lot - thou seest thy Judge,
The sight of Him will kindle in thy heart,
All tender, gracious, reverential thoughts.
Thou wilt be sick with love, and yearn for Him,
And feel as though thou couldst but pity Him,
That one so sweet should e'er have placed
    Himself
At disadvantage such, as to be used
So vilely by a being so vile as thee.
There is a pleading in His pensive eyes
Will pierce thee to the quick, and trouble thee.
And thou wilt hate and loathe thyself ; for,
    though
Now sinless, thou wilt feel that thou hast sinned,
As never thou didst feel ; and wilt desire
To slink away, and hide thee from His sight
And yet wilt have a longing aye to dwell
Within the beauty of His countenance.
And these two pains, so counter and so keen,-
The longing for Him, when thou seest Him not;
The shame of self at thought of seeing Him,-
Will be thy veriest, sharpest purgatory.

SOUL

My soul is in my hand : I have no fear, -
In His dear might prepared for weal or woe.
But hark ! a grand mysterious harmony :
It floods me, like the deep and solemn sound
Of many waters.

ANGEL

We have gained the stairs
Which rise towards the Presence-chamber; there
A band of mighty Angels keep the way
On either side, and hymn the Incarnate God.

ANGELS OF THE SACRED STAIR

Father, whose goodness none can know, but they
    Who see Thee face to face,
By man hath come the infinite display
    Of Thy victorious grace ;
But fallen man - the creature of a day-
    Skills not that love to trace.
It needs, to tell the triumph Thou hast wrought,
An Angel's deathless fire, an Angel's reach
    of thought.

It needs that very Angel, who with awe,
    Amid the garden shade,
The great Creator in His sickness saw,
    Soothed by a creature's aid,
And agonised, as victim of the Law
    Which He Himself had made ;
For who can praise Him in His depth and height,
But he who saw Him reel amid that solitary
    fight?

SOUL

Hark ! for the lintels of the presence-gate
Are vibrating and echoing back the strain.

FOURTH CHOIR OF ANGELICALS

Praise to the Holiest in the height,
    And in the depth be praise :
In all His words most wonderful ;
    Most sure in all His ways !

The foe blasphemed the Holy Lord,
    As if He reckoned ill,
In that He placed His puppet man:
    The frontier place to fill.

For even in his best estate,
    With amplest gifts endued,
A sorry sentinel was he,
    A being of flesh and blood.

As though a thing, who for his help
    Must needs possess a wife,
Could cope with those proud rebel hosts,
    Who had angelic life.

And when, by blandishment of Eve,
    That earth-born Adam fell,
He shrieked in triumph, and he cried,
    A sorry sentinel ;

The Maker by His word is bound,
    Escape or cure is none ;
He must abandon to his doom,
    And slay His darling son."

ANGEL

And now the threshold, as we traverse it,
Utters aloud its glad responsive chant.

FIFTH CHOIR OF ANGELICALS

Praise to the Holiest in the height,
    And in the depth be praise :
In all His words most wonderful ;
    Most sure in all His ways !

O loving wisdom of our God !
    When all was sin and shame,
A second Adam to the fight
    And to the rescue came.

O wisest love ! that flesh and blood
    Which did in Adam fail,
Should strive afresh against the foe,
    Should strive and should prevail ;

And that a higher gift than grace
    Should flesh and blood refine,
God's Presence and His very Self,
    And Essence all divine.

O generous love ! that He who smote
   In man for man the foe,
The double agony in man
   For man should undergo ;

And in the garden secretly,
   And on the cross on high,
Should teach His brethren and inspire
   To suffer and to die.

§6

ANGEL

Thy judgment now is near, for we are come
Into the veiled presence of our God.

SOUL

I hear the voices that I left on earth.

ANGEL

It is the voice of friends around thy bed,
Who say the " Subvenite" with the priest.
Hither the echoes come ; before the Throne
Stands the great Angel of the Agony,
The same who strengthened Him, what time
   He knelt
Lone in the garden shade, bedewed with blood.
That Angel best can plead with Him for all
Tormented souls, the dying and the dead.

ANGEL OF THE AGONY

Jesu ! by that shuddering dread which fell on
   Thee;
Jesu ! by that cold dismay which sickened
   Thee;
Jesu ! by that pang of heart which thrilled in
   Thee;
Jesu ! by that mount of sins which crippled
   Thee;
Jesu ! by that sense of guilt which stifled Thee;
Jesu ! by that innocence which girdled Thee;
Jesu ! by that sanctity which reigned in Thee;

Jesu ! by that Godhead which was one with
   Thee;
Jesu ! spare these souls which are so dear to
   Thee,
Who in prison, calm and patient, wait for Thee ;
Hasten, Lord, their hour, and bid them come
   to Thee,
To that glorious Home, where they shall ever
   gaze on Thee.

SOUL

I go before my Judge. Ah ! . . . .

ANGEL

    . . . . Praise to His Name !
The eager spirit has darted from my hold,
And, with the intemperate energy of love,
Flies to the dear feet of Emmanuel ;
But, ere it reach them, the keen sanctity,
Which with its effluence, like a glory, clothes
And circles round the Crucified, has seized,
And scorched, and shrivelled it ; and now it lies
Passive and still before the awful Throne.
O happy, suffering soul ! for it is safe,
Consumed, yet quickened, by the glance of God.

SOUL

Take me away, and in the lowest deep
   There let me be,
And there in hope the lone night-watches keep,
   Told out for me.
There, motionless and happy in my pain,
   Lone, not forlorn,-
There will I sing my sad perpetual strain,
   Until the morn.
There will I sing, and soothe my stricken breast,
   Which ne'er can cease
To throb, and pine, and languish, till possest
   Of its Sole Peace.
There will I sing my absent Lord and Love : -
   Take me away
That sooner I may rise, and go above,
And see Him in the truth of everlasting day.

§7

ANGEL

Now let the golden prison ope its gates,
Making sweet music, as each fold revolves
Upon its ready hinge. And ye great powers,
Angels of Purgatory, receive from me
My charge, a precious soul, until the day,
When, from all bond and forfeiture released,
I shall reclaim it for the courts of light.

SOULS IN PURGATORY

1. Lord, Thou hast been our refuge: in every generation ;
2. Before the hills were born, and the world was : from age to age thou art God.
3. Bring us not, Lord, very low : for Thou hast said, Come back again, ye sons of Adam.
4. *A thousand years before Thine eyes are but as yesterday : and as a watch of the night which is come and gone.*
5. *The grass springs up in the morning : at evening-tide it shrivels up and dies.*
6. *So we fail in Thine anger : and in Thy wrath we are troubled.*
7. *Thou hast set our sins in Thy sight : and our round of days in the light of Thy countenance.*
8. Come back, O Lord ! how long : and be entreated for Thy servants.
9. *In Thy morning we shall be filled with Thy mercy : we shall rejoice and be in pleasure all our days.*

10. *We shall be glad according to the days of our humiliation : and the years in which we have seen evil.*
11. *Look, O Lord, upon Thy servants and on Thy work : and direct their children.*
12. *And let the beauty of the Lord our God be upon us: and the work of our hands, establish Thou it.*
Glory be to the Father, and to the Son, and to the Holy Ghost.
As it was in the beginning, is now, and ever shall be : world without end. Amen.

ANGEL

Softly and gently, dearly-ransomed soul,
In my most loving arms I now enfold thee,
And, o'er the penal waters, as they roll,
I poise thee, and I lower thee, and hold thee

And carefully I dip thee in the lake,
And thou, without a sob or a resistance,
Dost through the flood thy rapid passage take,
Sinking deep, deeper, into the dim distance.

Angels, to whom the willing task is given,
Shall tend, and nurse, and lull thee, as
thou liest ;
And Masses on the earth, and prayers in heaven,
Shall aid thee at the Throne of the Most Highest.

Farewell, but not for ever ! brother dear,
Be brave and patient on thy bed of sorrow ;
Swiftly shall pass thy night of trial here,
And I will come and wake thee on the morrow.

NEWMAN as LIBRETTIST :
Towards A Non-Didactic Poetry of Dogma

Robert Carballo

By the mid-1830s, at the beginning of the Victorian Era and during his most active years in the Oxford Movement, John Henry Newman had written most of his poetry. Many of these poems are devotional or meditative and are grouped in the *Lyra Apostolica*, a work marked by a decidedly Tractarian flavour similar to John Keble's better known *The Christian Year*. They are also informed by the moralistic poetic theory of Newman's critical essay 'Poetry with Reference to Aristotle's Poetics[1] which may account for the preachiness of their general tone and which justifies this unflattering judgment of Newman's poetic abilities by his great admirer C F Harrold : "... in Newman, the moralist was fiercely at war with the poet. And the moralist won".[2]

However, in the intervening decades, up to the time of the publication of *The Dream of Gerontius* in 1865, Newman's poetic theory must have matured because in this poem we find evidence of a less didactic conception of the nature and function of poetry. But the absence of didacticism in tone and diction does not mean that Newman abandoned the theological frame of mind so integral to his nature to become suddenly the Christian poet envisioned by T S Eliot, one who writes "unconsciously, rather than deliberately and defiantly, Christian" literature.[3] The *Dream* is intrinsically a theological poem which dramatizes a recurrent theme of Newman's sermons : that in this world we mortals have no lasting city. What makes it different from much religious poetry in the nineteenth

---

[1]   Pick, John : 'Newman the Poet', in *Renascence* 8, (1956), p 133

[2]   Harrold, C F : *John Henry Newman : an expository and critical study of his mind, thought and art* (Hamden, Conn.: Archon Books, 1966) p 270

[3]   Eliot, T S : 'Religion and Literature'; in *Selected Prose of T S Eliot*, ed. Frank Kermode (New York : Harcourt, Brace, Jovanovich, 1975) p 100

century is the artistry with which a subject of the highest didactic nature is handled without the trappings of didacticism so offensive to the modern critical taste. Newman does not preach in the *Dream*; rather, he contemplates through the poetic imagination the eternal verities of his faith by dramatising one man's metaphysical transformation. In fact, the *Dream* should be read as an epic journey rather than as a sermon in verse. The poet seems to have heeded the advice of his agnostic brother, Francis, that he try after the unexpected success of the *Apologia* his hand at a religious poem of dramatic proportions in the tradition of Aeschylean tragedy but free of religious propaganda.[4]

The Dream of Gerontius dramatises the passage of the central character, a dying, old Christian man, from mortality to immortality through the interaction of four elements : time, the senses, music, and dogma. The first three undergo radical metamorphoses inherent in Gerontius's changed existence. Dogma alone, as the limited formulation of immutable truths, remains permanent. The *Dream*, as a compendium of Newman's basic beliefs about man's nature, his purpose on earth, and the higher reality of the unseen spiritual world is what chiefly interests us in this study : not just as a credal statement, but rather as a unique poetic genre which Helen G Hole has called a "poetry of dogma which conceives of dogma as a mystery appealing to the imagination as well as the reason".[5]

One of the underlying doctrines of the *Dream* is Platonic rather than Christian. Its philosophical frame is suggested by the title and refers to Newman's long-held conviction, elucidated in the sermon 'On the Greatness and Littleness of Human Life,' that all mortal life is but "a serious dream." The title also suggests a certain ambiguity in the dream frame of the poem, for it could be said that the dream is, as in Coleridge's *Kubla Khan*, the total context of the poem and that it "should be read as a dream, a dream of supersensible things".[6] In fact, Esther Pese has found in the *Dream* affinities with the medieval genre of eschatological dream visions, especially with St Peter Damian's eleventh-century hymn

---

[4]   Mulcahy, Daniel J : 'Source of an "Inspiration": Francis Newman's influence on the form of The Dream of Gerontius', in *The Victorian Newsletter* 19, (1961), pp 21-22

[5]   Helen G Hole : *A New Look at Newman's Dream of Gerontius* (dissertation, Indiana University, 1970) p i

[6]   Harrold, *op cit*, p 278

De Die Mortis.[7] One can also argue that the dream only begins when Gerontius falls into a comatose state and slowly ceases to hear the suppliant voices of his congregated friends and priest; in which case the dream would begin with line 171, when Gerontius's dramatic parts are spoken to the end by his Soul. But Newman's philosophical scepticism about materiality (openly admitted in the first chapter of the *Apologia Pro Vita Sua*) rather suggests that the dream stops with line 170, when Gerontius actually dies and when the transcendent realities of the spiritual world begin. If this is the author's intention, then the dream of Gerontius actually occupies the first fourth of the poem when the old man is still amid the shadows of this world and burdened with physical existence. Gerontius's own words seem to support this thesis :

I went to sleep; and now I am refreshed,
A strange refreshment : for I feel in me
An inexpressive lightness, and a sense
Of freedom, as I were at length myself,
And ne'er had been before...
I had a dream; ... (171-179)

This interpretation fits well with the "doctrine of economy" that Newman espouses in the *Apologia,* or the notion that "the visible things of the creation exist primarily as symbols, 'economies', of the invisible".[8] The *Dream*'s Platonism accounts for more than its view of this world as illusory, as an unreal city; it may very well also account for its singular dearth of natural imagery and for its reliance on sound and hearing.

The philosophical content of the *Dream* furthers its basic premise that in this world we have no lasting city. The poem does not deviate from its theological orientation. Geoffrey Wamsley, for example, says that the best commentary on the *Dream* is to be found in the Oxford sermons of Newman's Anglican period.[9] Certainly the notion of life as a dream, as a deceptive shadow, is found in an early Anglican sermon collected in *Plain*

---

[7]   Pese, Esther R B : 'A Suggested Background for Newman's Dream of Gerontius', in *Modern Philology* 47, (November 1949) pp 108-116

[8]   Weatherby, H L : 'Newman and Victorian Liberalism : a study in the failure of influence', in *Critical Quarterly* 13 (1971), p 208

[9]   Wamsley, Geoffrey : 'Newman's Dream of Gerontius', in *Downside Review* 91 (1973) p 174

and *Parochial Sermons*. 'On the Greatness and Littleness of Human Life',
mentioned earlier in this study, contains the doctrinal roots of the
Dream, as the following passage shows :

> We should remember that [this life] is scarcely more than an accident of our being -
> that it is no part of ourselves, who are immortal spirits, independent of time and space,
> and that this life is but a sort of outward stage, on which we act for a time... We should
> consider ourselves to be in this world in no fuller sense than players in any game are
> in the game; and life to be a sort of dream, as detached and as different from our real
> external existence, as a dream differs from waking; a serious dream, indeed, as
> affording a means of judging us, yet in itself a kind of shadow without substance...[10]

To the extent that the general doctrine embodied in the poem is
traditionally Christian, Wamsley's thesis about the Anglican roots of the
Dream is acceptable. But apart from the belief that this world is a
transitory stage where our souls are tried, common indeed to various
Christian and non-Christian traditions, the pivotal doctrine of expiation
or purgation is too distinctly Roman to warrant fully Wamsley's assertion.

Doctrine informs more than the *Dream*'s content, however. It influences
its tone and technique as well. The artistry of the poem consists mainly of
a dramatic contrast between the transformations attendant on Gerontius's
death and the immutable religious truths which Newman unfolds through
dramatic narrations and litanies. The principal of these are the nature of
angelic existence, the importance of intercessory prayer, the ineffable triune
Godhead, the sufferings of the damned, and the need for the particular
judgment and purgatorial expiation before entering the Beatific Vision.

Closely related to the *Dream*'s dogma are certain insights into the
spiritual life that render it less abstract. For example, the poem opens
with a consideration of the experience of dying and the temptation to
despair as death becomes imminent.   Gerontius expresses a "new
feeling, never felt before" (line 6), and in a "strange innermost
abandonment" (9) beseeches Jesus and Mary to help him in his
extremity. Besides undergoing the traumatic separation of body and
soul, "This emptying out of each constituent/ And natural force, by which
I come to be" (11-12), he succumbs, even if only momentarily, to the sin
of despair, the most serious sin against the Holy Ghost. His last
moments on earth, ostensibly the most decisive of his mortal existence,

---

[10]   *Newman, John Henry : A Newman Treasury*, ed. C F Harrold (New
York: Longmans, Green & Co, 1943) p 148

are fraught with spiritual perils, with the temptation to a nihilistic loss of faith. At one point Gerontius declares :

> ... but must needs decay
> And drop from out the universal frame
> Into that shapeless, scopeless, blank abyss,
> That utter nothingness, of which I came... (22-25)

Gerontius' desolation, however, is only a bitter part of his necessary transition to judgment and ultimately to blessedness. He soon recovers his former Christian perspective with the aid of his earthly friends and of his Guardian Angel. The Catholic doctrine of the communion of the saints is thus dramatised as the members of the Church Militant, gathered around the dying man, intone a somewhat shortened and modified litany of the saints in one of the many liturgical moments of this poem: "Kyrie eleison, Christe eleison, Kyrie eleison./ Holy Mary pray for him./ All holy angels, pray for him" (29-31). In fact, liturgical elements function in the *Dream*, together with description and narration, as an artistic medium for the non-didactic exposition of dogma. There are many other instances of intercessory prayer in this poem (particularly in the case of the Angel of the Agony at the Judgment), typically in the form of highly musical litanies. So dependent is the *Dream* on cadence, rhythm and harmony that Sir Edward Elgar found it ideally suited for an oratorio and Fernand Laloux used its text for a musical dramatic poem first performed in London in 1951.[11]

However, the various litanies of the *Dream* serve other than musical and rhetorical functions. The 'Sanctus fortis, Sanctus Deus' (72-107), taken from the Good Friday liturgy, is an example of Newman's harmonious blending of the confessional and the Liturgical. It is Gerontius' creed and final affirmation of the faith that is to bring him to salvation. Here he gives assent to belief in the Trinity: "God is three, and God is One"; in the incarnation and the hypostatic union : "And I next acknowledge duly/ Manhood taken by the Son"; in redemptive grace: "And I trust and hope most fully/ In that Manhood crucified"; in the divine institution of the church :   "And I hold in veneration,/ For the love of Him alone, Holy Church, as His Creation,/ And her teachings, as His own"; and finally in angelic creation and intercessory prayer : "Adoration aye be given,/ With and through the angelic host."

---

[11]   Pick, *op cit*, p 129

The *Dream* has other musical elements besides the litanies of the first part. These are the hymns of the angelic choirs - five in all - which recount, after the invariable antiphon of praise, the trajectory of mankind's fall, its redemption through the incarnation and passion of Christ, its regeneration by sanctifying grace, and the justice of purgatorial expiation for forgiven sins. As in the litanies, in the angelic hymns musical and doctrinal elements function harmoniously in Gerontius' transition. But the rhetoric of divine truth in the second part is narrative rather than confessional. The hymns become biblical in tone rather than liturgical and contain a very brief history of salvation. Ina Rae Hark has observed that the angelic accounts differ further from the static, earlier litanies in their progressive notion of time and history, reflective of "the Christian view of history as having a beginning, a middle, and an end - a progression from Creation to Judgment".[12] But the artistic continuity between the two is to be found in the combination of religious truth and lyrical intensity, which Newman considered indispensable in good poetry.[13]

In dramatic contrast to the lofty and harmonious poetry of the litanies, hymns, and antiphons (most of evident ecclesiastical origins) is the dissonance of the demonic choirs Gerontius encounters as he approaches the seat of judgment. Here, too, poetic form reflects doctrinal truth. The demons' incoherent diction and syntax reflect the traditional Christian teaching about infernal chaos, but occasionally Newman allows their parts some lucidity in order to reveal their hatred of Christian piety and their cynical free-thinking. They appear in this drama as eloquent exponents of the anti-dogmatic principle which Newman tells us in the *Apologia* was the real enemy of the Puseyites during the years of the Tractarian Movement. Their subjectivism and irreverence become the unmistakable mark of the damned :

> The mind bold/ And independent,
> The purpose free,/ So we are told,
> Must not think/ To have the ascendant.
> What's a saint?/ One whose breath
> Doth the air taint/ Before his death;
> A bundle of bones, / Which fools adore... (447-458)

---

[12] Hark, Ina Rae : 'Newman's Dream of Gerontius : beyond time and sense', in *Renascence* 28 (1975) p 20

[13] Watson, Edward A : 'Newman and Aristotle's Poetics', in *Renascence* 20 (1968) p 179

The inclusion of the fallen angels serves a double purpose here : to offer in their blasphemous songs of irregular and harsh rhythms a dramatic contrast to the harmony of the angels' hymns recounting the interaction of God and man, and to portray vividly the doctrine of free will so pivotal in this poem. Like man, like Gerontius, the fallen angels once had a choice between God and hell. Now, however, there is no merciful second chance for them through redemption and purgation. In just proportion to their superior angelic intelligence, their choice is final.

Newman presents the scriptural and ecclesiastical teaching on angelic existence without preaching, although, as Wamsley points out, they were for him "not mythical figures or... figments of the human mind but... objects of belief".[14] The angels in this poem serve both as dramatic chorus and as a poetic response, however subtle, to Victorian materialism and scepticism regarding the supernatural order. For Newman the angels are emblematic of that unseen, real world that his Christian Platonism suggests.

The second section of the *Dream* is an extensive expostulation of the nature and mission of guardian angels. Gerontius is accompanied in his journey to the judgment by his Guardian Angel, always by his side on earth but now made manifest and accompanied by music. He instructs Gerontius and guides him in the sensory and psychological adaptations he must make after the severance of death. Gerontius' former confusion about time and space ("I hear no more the busy beat of time, ... Nor does one moment differ from the next" [176, 178]) begins to dispel with the angelic aid as he perceives the qualities of subtlety and agility which theologians traditionally attribute to incorporeal existence :

> Over the surface of my subtle being,
> As though I were a sphere... a uniform
> And gentle pressure tells me I am not
> Self-moving, but borne forward... (228-232)

But Gerontius' angel does more than coach his expanded understanding; he serves a catechetical function as well.

As the angel concludes the task of guiding his charge to judgment, he leaves Gerontius with a final catechesis - uttered in rather Miltonic tones - concerning the grandeur of God and all His creation, the significance of

---

14   Wamsley, *op cit*, p 177

the Fall, the effects of original sin, man's dual nature, the immense gulf between human and angelic existence, the relationship of the guardian angels to their charges, the mystery of redemption, the particular and general judgments, and, most important to Gerontius' imminent experience, the nature of purgatory as a state of being outside time and space. But the Guardian Angel is unable, somewhat like Virgil in his inability to guide Dante through Paradise, to explain the ineffable mystery of God. The failure of analysis with reference to God is a significant reminder by Newman of the ultimate limitations of dogma as linguistic attempts to express transcendent truths. Therefore, the Guardian Angel impresses upon Gerontius the decorum of purgation as a requisite for enjoying the Beatific Vision.

The Guardian Angel is Gerontius' co-protagonist, and their relationship must be understood within the larger context of the doctrine of the communion of the saints which is, in fact, the infrastructure of the *Dream*. The mutual charity of the members of the Church in her three dimensions - the Church Militant on earth, the Church Suffering in purgatory, and the Church Triumphant in heaven - is central to both the plot and the theme. Intercessory prayer sets Gerontius' passage in motion as his friends and priest pray by his death-bed; the Guardian Angel conducts him and entrusts him to the Angels of Purgatory until the end of his purgation, when he will return to lead him to the 'mysterium tremendum'[15] in Paradise; and the spiritual drama closes with echoes of the intercession of the members of the Church Militant : "I hear the voices that I left on earth" (827). The *Dream's* vision has, in short, the specific context of Newman's ecclesiology and theology.

Despite its specific doctrinal content, however, the *Dream* has the universal appeal of a spiritual epic, complete with the epic agon and the epic journey. Its doctrines serve as the means to moral truths about the human soul and its destiny. It reflects the advice of Newman's free-thinking brother Francis in a letter dated 15 October 1864 which suggested its form and purpose as "merely Catholic as coming from the heart without conscious object [of propaganda]" and hence no more offensive to a non-Catholic audience than "the paganism of Aeschylus or Sophocles".[16] Even men radically different from Newman in creed and

---

[15]   Wamsley, *op cit*, p 178

[16]   Mulcahy, *op cit*, p 23

temperament could accept the spiritual vision of the *Dream*. Gladstone, Swinburne, and Newman's public enemy, Charles Kingsley, for example, were among those who read and praised it. Swinburne admired "the force, the fervour, the tense energy"[17] in the poem and Kingsley had this to say in a letter to Sir William Cope dated May 1868:

> I read the *Dream* with awe and admiration. However utterly I may differ from the entourage in which Dr Newman's present creed surrounds the central idea, I must feel that the central idea is as true as it is noble, and it, as I suppose, is this : The longing of the soul to behold the Deity... that the soul is ready, even glad, to be hurled back to any depth, to endure any pain, from the moment it becomes aware of God's actual perfection and its own impurity and meanness.[18]

Newman's epitaph summarises the trajectory in the *Dream* : 'Ex umbris et imaginibus in veritatem'; or in the words of Charles Reading, the hero of Newman's novel *Loss and Gain*, "Coming out of the shadows into realities".[19] Its power lies in its ability to excite in the reader, especially in the Christian reader, that "poetical view of things" which Newman considered the duty of Christians.[20] Its appeal stems from its majestic portrayal of a spiritual drama, or what Louis Martz calls "an interior drama of the mind",[21] which sustains without didacticism or propaganda a frank colloquium between the soul and supersensible realities.

Faith & Reason, Summer 1993

---

[17]   Harrold, *op cit*, p 278

[18]   *Kingsley, Charles : His Letters and Memoirs of His Life*, ed. F E Kingsley, 2 vols, (London : Henry S King & Co, 1877) p 270

[19]   Barry, William : *Newman* (New York : Charles Scribner's Sons, 1904) pp 170-171

[20]   Wamsley, *op cit*, p 185

[21]   Martz, Louis : *The Poetry of Meditation* (New Haven : Yale University Press, 1962) p 330

Part Two

The Composition
of a Masterpiece

Previous page :   A *further study of Edward Elgar at Birchwood in August 1900,*
shortly after completing the score of The Dream of Gerontius

The PLACES that INSPIRED

by John Norris
with original photographs by Ann Vernau

It was in the Summer of 1898 that Mr Beale of the Birmingham Triennial Festival Committee approached Elgar to see if he would write a major new work for the 1900 festival. Elgar accepted. It was agreed from the start that it should be a choral work with a religious theme, but Elgar's initial choice of Saint Augustine as the subject was thought to be too controversial. Elgar was asked to reconsider.

During the first months of 1899, Elgar was still hard at work on the *Enigma Variations*. He orchestrated the whole of the work during a two-week period in February 1899 but much still remained to be done in correcting proofs, persuading Hans Richter to conduct the first performance and other activities directed towards ensuring a successful première. Moreover, the Elgars began the year at Forli, a solid semi-detached property at Malvern Link, one mile to the north of the centre of Malvern, but sought a larger house which matched Elgar's growing standing as a composer. On 21 March, they moved to a far more imposing detached property which Elgar promptly named Craeg Lea, situated overlooking the Wells Road some way south of the town centre. Elgar detested the disruption that inevitably accompanied such a move and left as much as possible of the administrative arrangements to Alice, but it would have been impossible to avoid being distracted by the move.

In short, Elgar had more pressing matters than the Birmingham commission on his mind during the first half of 1899. He was not encouraged by Novello, to whom he wrote to see if they would be prepared to publish the new work but received no reply. Nor did these preoccupations end with the first successful performance of the *Variations* on 19 June 1899. His friend August Jaeger felt the original ending to be somewhat perfunctory and with some difficulty persuaded Elgar to compose the extended ending with which we are familiar today. Elgar worked on the new ending during the Summer and the revised work was first performed on 13 September 1899 at that year's Three Choirs Festival, held in Worcester. During the same period, he also composed *Sea Pictures*, his setting for contralto and orchestra of five poems with a maritime theme. The work occupied him from 11 July until 18 August and received its première on 5 October at that year's Norwich Festival, with Clara Butt singing. It is therefore not surprising that Elgar appears to have given little further thought to the work for Birmingham until the Autumn of 1899.

Elgar had owned a copy of Newman's poem since at least 1885; he had been given a further copy by Father Knight of St George's Church, Worcester as a present on his marriage to Alice in May 1889. It is not recorded whether Father Knight's choice of gift was prompted by the venue for the wedding, the Brompton Oratory, the church in whose foundation Newman had played a pivotal role. By his own admission, Elgar had been considering setting Newman's poem for at least eight years, so it would not have been surprising if, on rejection of his suggestion of St Augustine by the Birmingham committee, his thoughts had turned to *Gerontius*. And Alice's diary for September 1899 records that, in the margins of a 'Three Choirs concert, 'E. walked with Father Bellasis', a priest from the Birmingham Oratory who had known Newman personally. But the implication that Elgar was at this point considering setting Newman's poem for the Birmingham festival is not borne out by subsequent events.

In November 1899, Elgar sent Jaeger his first sketches for the new work, thus beginning a correspondence providing arguably the most comprehensive record of the composition of any musical work. Elgar's comments accompanying the sketches suggest that they were intended for a work based on the scriptures. Although this and other sketches sent to Jaeger over ensuing weeks eventually found their way into *Gerontius*, the concept Elgar was toying with eventually matured into *The Apostles* and, when in Spring 1903 Elgar recast that work, *The Kingdom* as well.

Time was passing, the work drifting, no doubt much to the consternation of the festival committee. The commission was discussed when G H Johnstone, the committee's Chairman, and his wife visited the Elgars for lunch on New Year's Day 1900. This may have induced a sense of urgency in Elgar, or more likely of despair, for on 10 January he wrote to Jaeger in familiar terms of self pity,

Elgar's first sketch for Gerontius, sent to Jaeger in November 1899

bemoaning his choice of subject, the fact he had accepted the commission or indeed had ever chosen to pursue a career as a composer. His realisation that he could not complete the work he planned in time for the festival was now near.

Later the same month, Elgar wrote to Jaeger hinting at a radical change to his choice of subject which, for contractual reasons, he could not divulge. To enable Elgar to concentrate on composing, Johnstone had offered to take on the task of finding a publisher and this may have lain behind Elgar's unusual reticence with Jaeger. But by 5 February Johnstone had agreed terms with Novello and Elgar wrote to Jaeger revealing his choice of subject. Not that Novello was enthusiastic about the subject: its chairman Alfred Littleton expressed reservations about the work's limited appeal, based on both the theology it espoused and its failure to provide a leading soprano solo role. Aware that Dvořák had been dissuaded from setting Newman's poem for the 1888 Birmingham Festival, Elgar shared these reservations to some extent. But, conforming to his familiar psychological pattern of deep melancholy quickly followed by unbounded enthusiasm, it was not long before Elgar was fully engrossed in his new endeavour and the work developed quickly. After further discussion with Father Bellasis on 12 January, Elgar began to adapt the poem to provide a more satisfactory libretto; on 2 March, he sent Jaeger the first forty-four pages of the score; and the remainder of Part I followed on 20 March.

Like his contemporaries Sibelius and Mahler and other great composers before and since, Elgar drew much inspiration from the countryside. This is perhaps most evident in *Caractacus*, which is largely set at British Camp in the Malvern Hills, close to where he is now buried; and Kevin Allen, in his book *Elgar the Cyclist*, has drawn parallels between Elgar's cycling expeditions in the lanes of Worcestershire and Herefordshire and the composition of some of his greatest works. But, at the time of the composition of *Gerontius*, such excitements still lay in the future, since Elgar did not purchase his first bicycle, Mr Phoebus, until the Summer of 1900. To meet his own inspirational needs, Sibelius built Ainola, a large house deep in the Finnish countryside close to Jarvenpåa, some 30 miles north of Helsinki, in which he lived out the last fifty years of his life. For psychological as much as financial reasons, Elgar never achieved that level of domestic stability, moving through a succession of rented houses until eventually purchasing Severn House in Hampstead in 1912. Of all the houses, only Craeg Lea, with its panoramic views over the Severn Valley, could lay claim to providing the inspirational values Elgar sought, yet even here it was Elgar's sensitivity to the encroaching urban environment that eventually caused him to flee to Hereford.

In May 1898, while still living at Forli, the Elgars acquired the use of Birchwood, a cottage near Storridge on the border of Worcestershire and Herefordshire. Despite its comparative proximity to Malvern, the atmosphere was a world apart. The immediate surroundings of the property were far more wooded than today, although views of the Malvern Hills to the south and of Worcester to the east were possible from the first floor windows. The cottage provided the freedom from the pressures of everyday life that Elgar needed for composition. In his letters to Jaeger, he would note in favourable terms his impending departure for Birchwood and the rural activities he indulged in whilst there.

Although he completed much of the orchestration of *Caractacus* at Birchwood, continuing teaching commitments tied Elgar to Malvern during the working week so that Forli is more closely associated with the composition of the *Enigma Variations*. But it was to Birchwood that Elgar fled to find the peace, quiet and inspiration he needed to complete *Gerontius* against the tight deadlines he now faced. He used a south-facing room on the first floor at the front of the property as his

Birchwood : Elgar's study (below) lay
behind the left-hand first floor
window in the above photograph.

The view of the Malverns from Birchwood

---

study, with views along the length of the Malvern Hills towards British Camp. He had an 1844 Broadwood piano installed on which to try out his musical ideas; the piano, now owned by the Royal Academy of Music, can be seen today in the Cobbe Foundation collection at Hatchlands Park, Surrey and heard on Anthony Goldstone's recording of Elgar's own piano arrangement of the *Variations* (CD number MRCD94001). And when he failed to find the stimulus he sought from the view from his study window, he would take to the fields and lanes around Birchwood.

His letters to Jaeger tell of time spent felling and sawing trees, and watching birds and rabbits. Alice's diaries record frequent rounds of golf, where the long intervals between bursts of concentration on the game gave time to mull over a particular theme or setting. A favoured walk at this time took Elgar north along the lane passing Birchwood. After five miles or so of delightful undulating scenery, he would reach the village of Knightwick and his beloved River Teme. Here, the small village church is overshadowed by Ankerdine Common whose vast panorama includes views towards Broadheath, Worcester and beyond. Some believe Knightwick to be the 'secret spot' to which Elgar alluded but whose location he revealed only to a few close friends. The entry in Alice's diary for 2 May is of particular interest. It reads :

"E. for walk from Bransford to Powyke *[sic]*. Writing *lovely* part."

Elgar enjoys a round of golf

From Birchwood to Knightwick

Above : The lane from Birchwood leading to Longley Green and Knightwick;
Below : The road to Knightwick between Longley Green and Alfrick Pound

Right : The view
from the banks of
the River Teme
towards
Knightwick village
and the heights of
Ankerdine
Common;

Below :
Knightwick
Church

And on 27 June Elgar included the following passage in a letter to his friend Nicholas Kilburn :

> My work is good to me & I think you will find Gerontius far beyond anything I've yet done - I *like* it - I am not suggesting that I have risen to the heights of the poem for one moment - but on our hillside night after night looking across our 'illimitable' horizon (pleonasm!) I've seen in thought the Soul go up & have written my own heart's blood into the score.

With the necessary preconditions in place, Elgar converted fragmentary ideas into a complex and fully worked out vocal score with surprising rapidity. As has already been noted, he completed Part I in a two-month period between January and March 1900. Part II occupied a similar timespan despite the distraction of proofs of Part I requiring correction which began to arrive at Craeg Lea in early April. During this period, if Rosa Burley's account is to be believed, Elgar would frequently try out passages on her between lessons at The Mount, her school in Malvern. By late May, the vocal score was complete apart from the final "great chorus" ('Praise to the Holiest'). Alice's diary records Edward hard at work on this chorus during the last ten days of May, a concentrated burst of heightened compositional activity leading to completion on 6 June.

At this stage, of course, Elgar still had to orchestrate the work, but the priority was to provide the choir with copies of the vocal score with which to start rehearsing the work. The next month was therefore taken up with a protracted and detailed correspondence between Elgar and Jaeger discussing the finer points of the work as Elgar corrected and returned to Novello the remaining proofs.

Elgar's prickly reaction to even the mildest of criticisms is well recorded. He would take offence where none was intended and often gave offence by his boorish and ill-considered remarks to people he barely knew. Yet such was the strength and closeness of his friendship with Jaeger that he reacted positively to the latter's blunt comments on the most intimate aspects of his endeavour. Jaeger tore into the work, dissecting it section by section, page by page. He mixed messages of strong encouragement with demands for changes to what he considered the weaker passages. To all this, Elgar responded with surprising equanimity. Readers wishing to see this remarkable correspondence in full are referred to Jerrold Northrop Moore's book *Elgar and his Publishers*. Not that Elgar accepted all of Jaeger's suggestions : the meanings of Newman's text, the moods and attitudes of his characters, and the likely reaction of the audience to Elgar's interpretation were all debated and, in some cases, a consensus reached.

But on one passage - p159 of the vocal score, in which the Soul, having briefly glimpsed the Almighty, sings "Take me away ..." - they could not agree. Jaeger felt that Elgar's passive setting underplayed Newman's words. The Soul, Jaeger argued, would here be experiencing "an awful, overwhelming agitation" ... "a bewilderment of fear, excitation, crushing, overmastering hopelessness"; the music conveyed none of this. Jaeger called it the weakest page of the score. Elgar disagreed, telling Jaeger that he had misread the situation. In Elgar's view, the momentary glance of God would render the Soul "shrivelled, parched and effete, powerless and finished ... condemned to purgatory for punishment or purging". This was what the music was intended to convey, leading Elgar to conclude "No, I can't alter that". Jaeger persisted, referring to the music as a "whine", a description with which Elgar was happy to concur. Jaeger resorted to insult and intimidation, and at last Elgar began to give some ground. A letter to Jaeger dated 1 July details some re-ordering of sections around the contentious passage and, more particularly, the reinstatement of a theme which Elgar had originally composed for this point but had subsequently discarded. It is this theme, described by Elgar as "biggity-big", which we hear today at the words "Take me away ...".

The dialogue between Elgar and Jaeger consumed valuable time. The last proofs were not returned to Novello until 11 July and it was not until 17 July that Elgar made clear to Jaeger that further debate was futile. On several occasions, Elgar had chivvied Jaeger about Novello's tardiness in providing him with proofs but now he could have no complaint : copies of the vocal parts began to appear on 21 July and were in the hands of the choir by early August. Much still remained to be done, however, including the bulk of the orchestration. This Elgar completed on 3 August, but correction of the full score continued throughout the following month and there were still the orchestral parts to write out. Added to this, the appeal of the countryside in the now hot summer months proved strong. Persuaded by Rosa Burley, he learnt to ride a bicycle, taking his first lesson on 10 July. After extensive practice in the lanes around Birchwood, in early August he and Alice ventured forth on the two mile ride to Sherridge, home of the family of the eighth *Variation*, Winifred Norbury.

From Bransford

Views up (above) and downstream from Bransford Bridge. While the lower photograph was being taken, three kingfishers flew from under the bridge.

To Powick

Above : Harvesting between Bransford and Powick;
Below : The inspirational view of the Malverns from Powick

At last, all was complete. Elgar knew that he had created a work of outstanding merit, and not just by the standards of English music of the time. On completing the full score, he added to it the now famous quotation from John Ruskin's *Sesame and Lilies* : 'This is the best of me...'

Time was short although not impossibly so, even for as original and complex a work as this. But, Elgar and Jaeger apart, few could at this point have appreciated the work's complexity and, to turn a difficult situation into an impending disaster, the choirmaster, Charles Swinnerton Heap, who was already familiar with Elgar's style and had prepared the choir for a successful première of *King Olaf* some four years earlier, died unexpectedly in June 1900.

The consequences of this and the subsequent early history of the work are covered by Lewis Foreman later in this book. But it is tantalising to ponder from this distance what might have become of *Gerontius* without Jaeger. The choir would have received their vocal scores somewhat earlier and, with more time for rehearsal, may have given a more creditable performance at the Birmingham première. A more favourable critical reception might not have cast initial doubts over the work's survival. But the work would undoubtedly have been that little bit poorer. If so, would it still have grown in popularity and critical acclaim to achieve the position of respect it commands today?

Sherridge, home of the Norbury family

BIRCHWOOD, in SUMMER, 1900

Mrs Richard Powell

Dora Powell nee Penny (1874-1964) was the daughter of the Rector of Wolverhampton. Her stepmother was a friend of Alice Elgar, and she became a close family friend, immortalised by Elgar as 'Dorabella' in the Enigma Variations. *She put her experiences into a book* Edward Elgar : memories of a variation, *and the following is an extract relating to the composition of* Gerontius. *She dates it in 1899, but Dr Moore has pointed out this and some other inaccuracies in dating (the book was first published in 1937). 'The Lady' was her name for Alice, whilst 'H.E.' stood for 'His Excellency', her nickname for Elgar. Mrs Powell later wrote about her impressions of the* Gerontius *premiere (see page 150).*

I remember a visit to Birchwood, on a very hot summer day. I had bicycled from Wolverhampton, 40 miles, and arrived, rather warm and dusty, at the cart-track leading up through the wood to the house. When I was nearly there I thought I would rest, out of sight, and get cool. I heard the piano in the distance and, not wishing to lose more of it than I need, I soon went on. In a moment I came in sight of the Lady sitting on a fallen tree just below the windows. She had a red parasol. I think she sat there partly to warn people off - particularly people who had been known to commit the awful crime of ringing a bell to announce their arrival. Leaning the bicycle against a tree, I went and sat down by her without speaking. He was playing the opening of Part II, and those who know the music well will understand what it was like to hear that strangely aloof, ethereal music for the first time in such surroundings. Each time I hear it I think of that beautiful place and that glorious day with the sunshine coming through the lace-work of greenery and branches and the deep-blue sky over all.

Soon, however, the music ceased and a voice behind us remarked : "Are you two going to have your photographs taken, or what?"

That afternoon the Lady said she was busy, and we went into the woods and sat down on the ground. After a bit E.E. said : "If we are perfectly quiet perhaps someone will come and talk to us."

In a few minutes a robin came, and then a little love of a field-mouse. It ran towards us in jerks and came quite close, within touching distance, without a sign of fear. Later on E.E. lay down and went to sleep, and I felt very like dozing, what with the effect of my 40-mile ride, the hum of the bees, and the sheer beauty of it all.

"Tank-y-tank-tank", said the sheep-bell distantly. Lo! it was tea-time.

We went back to the house and had tea, and afterwards he settled down to the piano and I to my usual work of turning over. The music was in manuscript, but 'Praise to the Holiest' was, as far as I can remember, nearly completed in vocal score form. He went straight through it, and after the nine bars tied chord passage at the end, he stopped, sat back in his chair and got a pipe out of a pocket. I had been so absorbed, so amazed and overwhelmed by the music that I could say nothing, and there was silence. At last I murmured :

"How perfectly wonderful!" More silence. Then he said :

"How does that strike you?"

What a question! What *could* I say? An idea had come into my mind while he was playing; should I tell him? I summoned up my courage.

"It gives me the impression of great doors opening and shutting." He turned round in his chair and looked at me.

"Does it? That's exactly what I mean." (But it was not until I had heard a really good performance that my 'vision' was realised completely. The impression of an immense crowd of singers in that Region beyond the great doors, and the idea that separate sets of singers added their tributes, like asides to one another - "and in the Garden", "O generous Love", and in the latter, two groups in conversation, as it were.)

Then we had some of 'Praise to the Holiest' over again and then I asked for the Introduction to Part II which I had heard when I arrived in the morning. That particular bit of *Gerontius* is inextricably bound up with Birchwood in my mind; every time I hear it the scene comes vividly back to me.

At last I came down to earth and realized with dismay that my time was up and that I had a train to catch at Worcester - and a seven-mile bicycle ride. How the time had flown! I collected my things, said good-bye to the Lady and tore myself away. H.E. walked with me to the lane which led down to the main road. It had clouded over and had become very sultry; it was pretty obvious that a storm was coming up.

"I wish you hadn't to go off like this," he said, looking rather anxiously at the sky; "come again soon." I looked back when I got to the bottom of the hill. He was still standing there; I threw up an arm and got an answer. I rode as fast as I could into Worcester, the storm coming up behind me, but I got to the shelter of the station just in time. The first huge drops of rain were falling and the lightning lit up the dark staircase as I carried my bicycle up to the platform. I bought a postcard at the bookstall and wrote three words on it : "High and Dry" - and posted it, as the train came in, water pouring off it like a cascade. *What a day!* How the music sang in my head all the way home. We out-distanced the storm and left it behind us. I bought an evening paper at Birmingham (my people would have thought it odd if I had not done so), but found it unopened by my side when I reached my journey's end.

Birchwood Lodge, 1900

ONE STORY, TWO VISIONS
Textual Differences between Elgar's and Newman's The Dream of Gerontius

Charles E McGuire

Charles McGuire is active as a teacher, performer and scholar. In 1998, he completed his Ph.D. in musicology at Harvard University, where he has since taught musicology as a visiting lecturer. A member of the Elgar Society, he currently resides in Washington DC, where he continues to conduct and perform in area ensembles. He is working on a book on the British Sight-Singing movement.

Hailed as "the finest oratorio by an Englishman,"[1] Edward Elgar's *The Dream of Gerontius* signalled a departure from compositional tradition. In choosing to portray a fictional old man's final hours on earth and his soul's subsequent passage to heavenly judgment, Elgar cast away the usual subjects of an episode from the Bible or the exploits of an historical religious figure, such as Joan of Arc or Saint Cecilia. Furthermore, *Gerontius* stands alone among Elgar's four complete oratorios in springing from a finished text, a mystical and devotional poem by Cardinal John Henry Newman.[2]

Yet the importance of *Gerontius'* text transcends the uniqueness of its subject. Although several scholars have observed Elgar's success in

---

[1]   Diana Mcveagh : 'Edward Elgar' in the *New Grove Dictionary of Music and Musicians* (ed Stanley Sadie; London, 1980)

[2]   Elgar edited some of the Rev Edward Capel Cure's texts for *Lux Christi* during its composition (Robert Anderson : *Elgar* (New York, 1993)* pp 207-208). Elgar compiled his own texts for *The Apostles* and *The Kingdom*, continually refining them and even recasting the entire scenario while in the midst of composition. Christopher Grogan provides a description of this process in 'A Study of Elgar's Creative Process in The Apostles (Op 49), with Particular Reference to Sc II, "By the Wayside"' (Ph D dissertation, University of London, Royal Holloway & Bedford New College, 1989), esp vol 1, pp 19-48.

setting Newman's text,[3] a careful comparison of the original poem and the finished libretto reveals that Elgar radically altered the philosophical thrust of the poem, shifting the focus of the oratorio away from Newman's vision of the afterlife towards Gerontius as a suffering human figure.[4] Thus, Elgar downplayed Newman's interpretation of Heaven in favour of foregrounding the poignancy of Gerontius' physical experience. Cardinal Newman's poem was published in 1865 in two instalments in the Catholic magazine *The Month*, gaining immediate popularity. Not only did the poem run through twenty-seven editions in England before Newman's death in 1890, but it found admirers on the Continent, where it was translated into French by 1869 and German by 1885.[5] In the latter part of the 1880s, the poem gained romantic currency when General Charles Gordon read and annotated a copy of it before his death at Khartoum in January 1886.[6] Two years later, when Elgar married Alice Roberts, Father Thomas Knight presented the couple with a copy

---

[3]   See, for instance, Elizabeth Jay's 'Newman's Mid-Victorian Dream' in *John Henry Newman : Reason, Rhetoric and Romanticism*, edited by David Nicholls and Fergus Kerr, OP (Carbondale and Edwardsville, 1991) p 229; and Percy Young: *Elgar, Newman and The Dream of Gerontius in the Tradition of English Catholicism* (Aldershot and Brookfield, 1995) p 97.

[4]   Within musicological literature, only a short article by John Stasny and Byron Nelson mentions the differences between Elgar's and Newman's texts, tersely stating that Elgar made alterations to avoid "the theological animus of the primarily Protestant audience in Birmingham". However, this article only lists a few changes and does not discuss them in any detail. See Stasny and Nelson's 'From Dream to Drama : The Dream of Gerontius by John Henry Newman and Edward Elgar' in *Renascence*, vol 43, no 1-2 (Fall 1990/Winter 1991) p 125.

[5]   Young, *op cit*, p 97.

[6]   Robert Anderson's foreword to *The Dream of Gerontius, Op 38* (London, 1992) p iii. A copy with Gordon's annotations was released in 1889, edited by William Axon, who believed the annotations were made the night before Gordon's death. See the introduction to Axon's *On General Gordon's Copy of Newman's 'Dream of Gerontius'* (Manchester, 1889).

of the poem which included General Gordon's annotations.[7] It was therefore natural for Elgar to turn to the poem for inspiration when he decided not to compose an oratorio about the Apostles for the 1900 Birmingham Music Festival.

While Elgar's oratorio did not become immediately popular, it survived its disastrous English premiere to find success at the 1901 Lower Rhine Festival in Düsseldorf, and subsequently gained acceptance across England during the next few years. By 1910, *Gerontius* had secured its place as part of the English festival repertory, and was frequently heard throughout the world, with regular performances in Germany and North America.[8] August Jaeger, Elgar's friend and an agent of the publishing firm Novello, was instrumental in first introducing *Gerontius* to the public, writing an analysis for it that adopted Hans von Wolzogen's system of listing leitmotivs and their recurrences.[9]

Consequently, most discussions of *Gerontius* have limited themselves to two features of the composition's origin. First, many biographical studies have concentrated on the composition's initial failure to win public approval at Birmingham. Critiques of *Gerontius* have only recently addressed the wider issues of its context.[10] Second, while the

---

[7]   Percy Young : John Henry Newman, Edward Elgar and *The Dream of Gerontius*' (Occasional Paper No 1, The University of Birmingham Institute for Advanced Research in the Humanities, 1991) p 14.

[8]   By 1906, according to the cuttings files at the Elgar Birthplace (vols 6-9, ref. nos 1327-30), *Gerontius* was heard at least once in New York, Chicago, Cincinnati, San Francisco, Montreal and Minneapolis.

[9]   August Jaeger : *The Dream of Gerontius : Book of Words with Analytical and Descriptive Notes* (London, 1901; reprint, 1974). Jaeger also wrote analyses of both *The Apostles* and *The Kingdom*, published in 1903 and 1906 respectively. Wolzogen initially developed the system of naming leitmotivs as an analytic aid and guide to Wagner's later operas.

[10]   Even these studies deal predominantly with biographical issues, discussing the construction of *Gerontius* only briefly. See, for instance, Young 1995 and Young 1991, as well as Byron Adams' 'The Dark Saying of the Enigma : Homoeroticism and the Elgarian Paradox'. This paper was originally delivered at the 1995 meeting of the American Musicological Society in New York, and will be published shortly.

efficacy of Jaeger's thematic system is still debated, it continues to frame most of the analyses of *Gerontius*, as well as Elgar's later oratorios, *The Apostles* and *The Kingdom*.[11]

A similarly limited viewpoint has characterized studies of Newman's poem. Today, the poem is little known apart from its connection to Elgar's oratorio. Although its popularity persisted in England and America until the 1930s, the poem's hold on the public and scholarly imagination has sufficiently diminished in more recent years that major Newman biographies typically allude to it only in passing, if at all.[12] Hence, Newman's careful efforts with 'Gerontius' both to evoke a vivid vision of the afterworld as well as to convey the crucial elements of his theological beliefs are now generally overlooked. As a consequence, little attention has focused upon the differences between Newman's poem and Elgar's libretto.

---

[11]   To date, the most detailed critique concerning Jaeger's analyses of all three compositions occurs in Grogan 1989, esp Appendix ii, 'An assessment of the Elgar-Jaeger relationship during 1903 and 1906, and its bearing on Jaeger's Analytical Notes on *The Apostles* and *The Kingdom*', vol 2, pp 27-44, and his article '"My Dear Analyst": Some Observations on Elgar's Correspondence with A J Jaeger regarding the Apostles Project' in *Music & Letters* vol 72, no 1 (February 1991), pp 48-60. Grogan takes the position that Elgar did not use themes in the leitmotiv-like fashion which Jaeger describes in his analyses. The opposite position is briefly expressed by Michael Foster in *Elgar's Gigantic Worx : The Story of the Apostles Trilogy* (London, 1995) esp pp 46-47. For another view, see the present author's 'Epic Narration : The Oratorios of Edward Elgar' (Ph D thesis, Harvard University, 1998) esp pp 159-173, 202-209, and 255-273.

[12]   For instance, in Ian Ker's *John Henry Newman : A Biography* (Oxford, 1988), "Gerontius" is referred to three times. The most detailed passage (pp 574-576) briefly mentions its concern with Purgatory, and concentrates on its lasting popularity due to Elgar's setting. Such brief discussions of "Gerontius" are largely due to the fact that most think Newman's prose works overshadow his poetry (see John K Ryan's article 'Maker and Thinker' in *American Essays for the Newman Centennial*, edited by Ryan and Edmond Darvil Bernard; Washington DC, 1947, p 73) and that the poems are "for the most part... attached to passing moods and particular events" (Roger Sharrock, 'Newman's Poetry' in *Newman after a Hundred Years*, ed Ian Ker and Alan G Hill (Oxford, 1990) p 43).

To show the marked differences between Elgar's and Newman's versions of 'Gerontius', this essay will first briefly examine the themes and general construction of Newman's poem. A review of Elgar's libretto will then analyse the ways the composer altered the subject of the poem, discussing the wider implications of several of Elgar's detailed text alterations. This inquiry reveals that while Elgar did not intend to represent Newman's 'Gerontius' faithfully, his alterations left the libretto focused on the human character of Gerontius himself, rather than the overarching celestial framework of Newman's poem.

General characteristics of Newman's poem

'Gerontius' is a contemplative work. The poem concerns the feelings and impressions of a dying man and his introduction to Heaven. Newman may have written 'Gerontius' as a semi-autobiographical and self-comforting gesture, to allay fears of his own imminent demise.[13] Elizabeth Jay regards the poem as a conscious attempt to use prevalent contemporary death-bed imagery as an allegory for conversion from Protestantism to Catholicism, responding to a burgeoning Victorian interest in eschatology.[14] As a vision of the afterworld, 'Gerontius' presents the four last things - death, judgment, Hell and Heaven - in a way that makes them seem timeless, natural and even comforting, while incorporating a personalized interpretation of the Office for the Dead as well as a wholly Catholic vision of Purgatory.[15] Gerontius himself is an "Everyman," placed in an incredible situation but still easily identifiable by the reader.[16]

The poem is divided into seven sections, each with a central thematic

---

[13]   Sharrock, *op cit*, p 54.

[14]   Jay, *op cit*, pp 219-221.

[15]   See Sharrock, *op cit*, p 54 and Stasny and Nelson, *op cit*, p 121.

[16]   Gerontius' name is traditionally interpreted as a generic Greek word meaning "Old man". Jay, however, notes that since Newman was well-versed in the classics, he "would never have produced so hybrid a form. The source [of Gerontius' name] seems rather to have been the fourth-century Bishop Gerontius of Nicomedia whom the Church authorities attempted to depose on account of the scandal caused by his recounting the tales of his strange dreams" (Jay, *op cit*, pp 219-220).

idea, which Julius Gliebe termed paragraphs.[17] The first paragraph occurs on earth, portraying Gerontius' last hours of mortal life. Accompanying Gerontius in this paragraph are Assistants (perhaps minor clerics or servants) and a Priest. In paragraph 2, Gerontius awakes as a Soul, borne to Heaven by an Angel (presumably his Guardian Angel). Paragraph 3 continues with the first dialogue between the Soul and the Angel, revealing that Gerontius is speeding to his Judgment. Paragraph 4 introduces demons which threaten the Soul, but are shown as ineffectual. Paragraph 5 presents five choirs of Angelicals that surround God. Each choir articulates one mystery of the Catholic faith. In paragraph 6, God judges the Soul, following a plea from the Angel of the Agony, the angel present during Christ's Agony in the Garden of Gethsemane, who functions as a general representative for all souls. After the Judgment, the Soul is "Consumed, yet quickened by the glance of God" and cries for release to Purgatory. The Angel places the Soul in Purgatory in the seventh paragraph, and then bids it farewell, though promising a quick return to bear it to Heaven. Thus, each paragraph contains a separate subject that comments on one of the four last things, with the addition of Purgatory.

Newman's 900-line poem is constructed of lyrical and descriptive passages, providing for an easy musical setting.[18] The lyrical passages of 'Gerontius' contain rhymed couplets or paired rhymed couplets and lines of six, seven or eight syllables. The poem's descriptive texts are lines of mostly ten syllables (or sometimes pairs of lines alternating ten and six syllables), using iambic pentameter and not necessarily having any stable rhyme scheme at all.[19] Newman fashioned these texts to

---

[17]   Julius Gliebe : *Cardinal Newman's 'Dream of Gerontius' With Introduction and Commentary : For Use in High Schools, Academies and Colleges* (New York, 1916) p 14.

[18]   Young sees this as a manifestation of Newman's own musical abilities. See Young, 1991, p 8.

[19]   Portions of the ten-syllable "recitative" lines are arranged as rhymed couplets, such as Gerontius' first iteration in Paragraph 1, lines 1-28. Even here, though, the scheme is fractured slightly. Line 17 does not rhyme with line 19. A sense of cohesion is also added to these passages since some of the couplets overlap - the same ending rhyme used several times throughout the passage.

identify and distinguish characters, writing some texts for individuals and others for groups.

In Newman's hands, the first paragraph of the poem, which shows Gerontius' last hours on earth, offers a broad introduction to the remaining paragraphs. At 169 lines, this paragraph comprises almost a fifth of 'Gerontius'. The function of this paragraph is twofold. First, it presents Gerontius as an aged Everyman. His prayers show that he desires the expected release of death. But he also fears it: on two occasions in this paragraph, Gerontius specifically mentions his own visions of Hell (lines 17-27, 111-125). Only in retrospect (after ingesting paragraph 4) does the reader understand that Hell and its demons are wholly ineffectual. Consequently, the second function of this paragraph is to show that Gerontius cannot fully comprehend the afterworld. While Gerontius' prayers and those of his Assistants propel him towards Judgment, the realm of Heaven is so complex that his understanding requires the aid of an immortal, the Angel.[20]

During paragraphs 2-5, the Angel explains aspects of Heaven to Gerontius' Soul as a patient master instructs a student. These four paragraphs make up the bulk of the poem. In the two longest paragraphs of the poem, the demons deliver their curses and false statements and the Angelicals sing their choruses. Through these choruses, the Angel explains the history of religion to the Soul: the battle of good triumphing over evil; the religious education of humanity (who, "taught by angel-visitings... learn'd to call upon His name")[21]; why Judgment is essential for all souls; and the necessity of Christ's sacrifice. Such is the focus of Newman's poem: ultimately to allay the fear of death, revealing that God's love, as represented by the Angels, embraces all in mercy. The narrative frame of Gerontius' Soul moving through this realm towards its Judgment (in the final two paragraphs of the poem) is ultimately not as important as the lessons taught throughout the journey.

---

[20]   For a brief analysis of the comparison of 'Gerontius' to Dante's *Inferno*, see Jay, *op cit*, p 220.

[21]   John Henry Newman, *The Dream of Gerontius* (sixteenth edition; London, Burns & Oates, etc, 1865) lines 654 and 656.

Elgar's redaction of Newman's text

In contrast, Elgar constructed his libretto to avoid the lessons of paragraphs 2-5, centring instead on Gerontius' journey because it made a stronger characterization of the Everyman possible.[22] Although Elgar followed Newman's divisions between descriptive and lyric text[23] the broad architecture of their visions differs. Elgar devoted the entire first part of his oratorio to the earthly first paragraph of Newman's poem, while compressing paragraphs 2-7 into the second part. Elgar cut 470 lines from the poem, mostly Angelic descriptions of Heaven, and further shifted the balance of the original poem by selectively excising lines that dealt largely with Heaven and Gerontius' fear of Hell. Hence, *Gerontius'* first part sets 139.5 lines; the second 290.5. In the poem, there are about four lines in the paragraphs describing Heaven for every line devoted to earth. Elgar's redaction reduced the ratio to about two lines for Heaven for every line about earth, cutting only 29.5 of the lines from the first paragraph, while deleting 440.5 lines from those paragraphs set for the second part. For Elgar to have kept constant proportions between Heaven and earth, he would have had to cut about 67 more lines from the first part.

---

[22] Elgar certainly believed that Gerontius was a universal representation of humanity. In an oft-quoted letter to Jaeger, written approximately 28 August 1900, Elgar stated that he believed Gerontius "to be a man like us, not a Priest or a Saint, but a *sinner*, a repentant one of course but still no end of a *worldly man* in his life, & now brought to book". Letter transcribed in Jerrold Northrop Moore's *Elgar and His Publishers : Letters of a Creative Life* (Oxford and New York, 1987) vol 1, p 228. Underlined emphasis mine.

[23] Elgar sets most of the ten-syllable iambic pentameter lines in "Quasi Recit.", a common appellation throughout the last three oratorios. In *Gerontius*, Quasi Recit. sections are characterised by a continuously shifting rhythmic and orchestrational structure, supported at points by reminiscence themes. Elgar sets the lyrical sections as either arias or choruses, depending on how many characters state them. In the solo lyrical sections, the thematic structure shifts function and purpose : themes are periodic, repeated, sometimes curtailed and in differing orders, but continuously present. Elgar uses a variety of chordal means to portray the ensemble lyric sections, including imitative polyphony, homophony, and Anglican chant.

Similarly, Elgar deleted lines in the first part which detailed Gerontius' fear of Hell[24]:

> Pray for me, O my friends; a visitant
> Is knocking his dire summons at my door,
> The like of whom, to scare me and to daunt,
> Has never, never come to me before;
> ['Tis death,—O loving friends, your prayers! - 'tis he! ...
> As though my very being had given way,
> As though I was no more a substance now,
> And could fall back on naught to be my stay,
> (Help loving Lord! Thou sole Refuge, Thou,)
> And turn no whiter, but must needs decay
> And drop from out the universal frame
> Into that shapeless, scopeless, blank abyss,
> That utter nothingness, of which I came:
> This is it that has come to pass in me;
> O horror! this it is, my dearest, this;]
> So pray for me, my friends, who have not strength to pray.[25]

By removing these lines, Elgar centred the passage upon Gerontius' physical feelings ("as though my very being had given way"), de-emphasized the figure of Death, and removed completely a mention of Hell. While Death received a mention in the lines Elgar included from this passage ("a visitant/Is knocking his dire summons at my door"), Elgar eliminated the specific naming of the figure (line 16), as well as his powers (lines 17-19 and 21-24), since the audience does not hear Gerontius' twin fears of Death's negation and being installed in Hell. True, later in the part, Elgar included a passage that refers to negative images of Death - the demons heard in Part II. At the outset of the oratorio, however, Elgar's Gerontius thinks less of his spiritual health

---

[24]   Elgar made two excisions in this paragraph probably to avoid repetition. Both name saints and biblical personages to whom Gerontius and his Assistants pray, including Susanna, Abraham, Isaiah and Lot, as well as Saints Peter, Paul, and Andrew (Newman's lines 33-35 and parts of 132-144). These litanies are easily removed, since Elgar left similar ones intact in other parts of the movement.

[25]   Newman, *op cit*, lines 12-28. Square brackets - in this example and the remaining ones - indicate those lines Elgar omitted.

and more of his physical.[26]

Elgar's excisions from the second part further diminished the force of Newman's interpretation of Heaven, Purgatory and descriptions of the Soul's experience. For example, in one omitted section, the Angel outlines the construction of the Heavenly realm :

> We now have pass'd the gate, and are within
> The House of Judgment; [and whereas on earth
> Temples and palaces are form'd of parts
> Costly and rare, but are all material,
> So in the world of spirits naught is found,
> To mould withal and form into a whole,
> But what is immaterial; and thus
> The smallest portions of this edifice,
> Cornice, or frieze, or balustrade, or stair,
> The very pavement is made up of life -
> Of holy, blessed, and immortal beings,
> Who hymn their Maker's praise continually.][27]

Elgar retained the narrative section of the passage, which portrays the location of the Soul and Angel in Heaven ("within/The House of Judgment") as well as their motion. The deleted section illuminates Newman's interpretation of the inner workings of Heaven, presented through a binary difference between physical religion (rich, earthly temples) and the transcendent (Heaven). Newman's Heaven is constructed wholly of energy from life and music. Because of Elgar's omission, the audience concentrates more on the Soul and its questions during its passage, instead of noticing the beauty of Newman's carefully detailed Heaven itself.[28]

---

[26]   The second excision, Newman's lines 111-118, is much the same. It mentions a specific fear of Hell.

[27]   Newman, *op cit*, lines 616-627.

[28]   By removing this particular section, Elgar also avoided a possible avenue of theological attack. The passage vividly describes an opulent Heaven, which may have been insulting to some members of Elgar's predominantly Protestant audience. See Stasny and Nelson, *op cit*, pp 121-125.

Textual differences manifested within Elgar's musical structure

Such broad excisions abound in the compressed libretto of the second part, as Elgar omitted over 60% of the lines from these paragraphs. In each case, the omission focuses the narrative upon Gerontius' Soul, forgoing a discussion of the majesties of Heaven or an Angelic interpretation of history. *Gerontius'* musical structure further reflects Elgar's transformation of Newman's focus. In the new internal divisions Elgar laid on to paragraphs 2-7 of the poem, he rearranged certain texts and restructured the Soul's climactic Judgment.

First, Elgar condensed Newman's paragraphs 2-7 into four scenes of dialogue between the Angel and Soul, each of which culminates in a chorus or duet. Table 1, below, provides a list of these scenes. In the initial scene, the Angel introduces the Soul to some of the basic mysteries of Heaven. The remaining three scenes are *tableaux entendus*, or "heard pictures" : in a series of dialogues with the Soul, the Angel explains differing aspects of the afterlife.[29] The choruses of Angelicals and Demons become the scenery which the Angel describes to the Soul during the journey to Judgment. Although this mechanism appears in Newman's poem, Elgar's realization conveys two additional ideas : first, the motion of the Angel and Soul as they pass in review of the Heavenly scenes, and second, a finer sense of climax at the end of each division.

TABLE 1: Scenes in Elgar's *The Dream of Gerontius*, Part II.

SCENE NO.	CUE NOS:	TYPE
	1 - 4	Instrumental introduction
1.	4 - 28	Soul and Angel first speak
	29 - 32	Transition
2.	32 - 55	Demons' tableau
3.	55 - 101	Angelicals' tableau
	101 - 102	Transition
4.	102 - 137	Judgment tableau

[29]   For a more complete definition of *tableaux entendus* and their relation to the narrative structure of *Gerontius*, see McGuire, *op cit*, esp pp 177-187.

TABLE 2 : Newman's paragraphs 2-3
compared to Elgar's mvt II, scene 1 (excerpt)

LINE[30]	CHAR	NEWMAN'S TEXT	ELGAR'S TEXT
364 365 370	Soul	Dear Angel, say, Why have I now no fear of meeting Him? Along my earthly life, the thought of death And judgment was to me most terrible. I had it aye before me, and I saw The Judge severe e'en in the Crucifix. Now that the hour is come, my fear is fled; And at this balance of my destiny, Now close upon me, I can forward look With a serenest joy.	Dear Angel, say, Why have I now no fear of meeting Him? Along my earthly life, the thought of death And judgment was to me most terrible.
373 375 380 385	Angel	It is because Then thou didst fear, that now thou dost not fear, Thou hast forestalled the agony, and so For thee the bitterness of death is past. Also, because already in thy soul The judgment is begun. That day of doom, One and the same for the collected world That solemn consummation for all flesh, Is, in the case of each, anticipate Upon his death; and, as the last great day In the particular judgment is rehearsed, So now too, ere thou comest to the Throne, A presage falls upon thee, as a ray Straight from the Judge, expressive of thy lot. That calm and joy uprising in thy soul Is first-fruit to thee of thy recompense, And heaven begun.	It is because Then thou didst fear, that now thou dost not fear, Thou hast forestalled the agony, and so For thee the bitterness of death is past. Also, because already in thy soul The judgment is begun.
385 386 387 388 389 370 371 372 373	Angel with Soul		A presage falls upon thee, as a ray Straight from the Judge, expressive of thy lot. That calm and joy uprising in thy soul Is first-fruit to thee of thy recompense, And heaven begun. Now that the hour is come, my fear is fled; And at this balance of my destiny, Now close upon me, I can forward look With a serenest joy.

---

[30] The line numbers are taken from Newman's poem.

To accomplish this effect, Elgar condensed Newman's second and third paragraphs into the first scene of the second part (figs 4-28). In Newman's poem, paragraph 3 commenced with the Soul becoming conscious in Heaven, hearing the Angel for the first time. The Soul and the Angel do not speak until paragraph 3, when the Soul initially questions the Angel about Heaven's aspects. To compress these paragraphs into a single scene, Elgar omits 145.5 of Newman's 229 lines, setting only about a third of the original material.[31] In its place, Elgar adds a duet (figs 27-28) constructed from two passages Newman stated in a linear progression (Table 2), thereby producing a climactic moment. Elgar places the second half of the Soul's statement (lines 370-373) with the Angel's lines 385-389.[32] This changes the meaning of the Soul's words. Originally, lines 370-373 explained why the Soul asked the Angel about its Judgment, fleshing out lines 365-366 ("Dear Angel, say,/Why have I now no fear at meeting Him?"). In Elgar's version, the Soul's lines assert its freedom from fear. Again, the change shifts focus away from mechanics of explanation to Gerontius' character.

Second, Elgar gave the *tableaux entendus* a sense of immediacy and motion by rearranging several entrances of the Angelicals' choruses. At the opening of Newman's fifth paragraph, the Angel introduced the First Choir of Angelicals with the words "Hark to those sounds/They come of tender beings angelical,/Least and most childlike of the sons

---

[31]   The 145.5 excised lines include two lengthy passages (Newman's lines 178-185 and 190-223) of the Soul describing its feelings of confusion upon entering Heaven; a passage in which the Soul first notes the Angel's presence and the Angel describes the human condition (lines 260-319); and one where the Angel explains some of the mechanics of Heaven (337-364).

[32]   Elgar omits two of the Soul's lines and six and a half lines of the Angel's statement from the duet. The Angel's lines are problematic from a religious standpoint, as they provide a *deus ex machina* for the Soul's Judgment occurring at the present moment of the poem, rather than at Armageddon. Newman's reasoning, that Judgment occurs twice for all - first rehearsed "Upon his death" and then again on "That day of doom/ one and the same for the collected world" - would not sit well with most late nineteenth-century English Christians, who awaited a mass Judgment at the end of time.

Elgar, Gerontius : overlapping entrance of the Angel
and Angelicals - Part II, scene 3, fig 61.

of God."[33] Only after the Angel completed this introduction did
Newman's Angelicals speak. In contrast, Elgar juxtaposes the
entrances of the Angel and the Choir (figs 61-63; Example 1), a
construction that underlines the movement of the Angel and Soul
through Heaven. In Elgar's version, the Angel's narrative statement is

---

[33] Newman, *op cit*, lines 593-595

split into two sections. Initially, the Choir begins singing before the Angel describes its sound, as if the Angel and Soul approach it from a distance. After an intervening couplet from the Choir, the Angel finishes its narration. This overlap casts the entrance of the Angelicals as an introduction to the Angel's narrative, a shift of focus that the textural changes in this section also heighten. The Angelicals state their first two lines in a four-part texture, which decreases to two parts on a sustained third in the fifth bar of the example, so that the Angel's one-bar description is easily heard. After the Angel's first description, Elgar sets the second couplet of the Angelicals' verse in a full six-voice texture for five bars (not seen in the example). This, too, ends with only two parts on a sustained pitch (an A; bars 471-2), whereupon the Angel completes its narrative statement, while the Angelicals reiterate the first line of their verse. When the Angel ends the narration (fig 63), the Angelicals sing the remaining verses of the chorus uninterrupted. The main achievement of this juxtaposition is a detailed sonic picture: the Angel and Soul approach the Choir of Angelicals as if from afar, react to it, and finally hear it in full as they pass it. Such shifting of text to express motion is present throughout the entire tableau.[34]

In his final and most drastic complex of alterations, Elgar imported words from the first paragraph into the sixth, deleted the Angel's narration of the moment of Judgment, and shifted the moment of Judgment itself. Within the Judgment tableau, just as the Soul announces it will appear before its judge, the chorus of Assistants on earth is invoked ("Voices from Earth"), praying for the Lord's mercy (figs 114-115). The two lines the Assistants sing do not appear in Newman's poem, instead being drawn from lines 50-51 of the first paragraph. Earlier in both the libretto and the poem, the Soul referred to those voices, just before the Angel of the Agony began its plea (line 816 of Newman's poem; fig 103 in Elgar's score). Elgar's insertion of these lines makes the earlier reference explicit and provides the first moment of delay before the climax.

---

[34]   Another change Elgar made throughout this tableau is the naming of the Angelicals. In the vocal score libretto, Elgar refers to this body only as the Choir of Angelicals. In Newman's poem, there are five such choirs plus an additional chorus of Angels of the Sacred Stair - the last Elgar omitted entirely. See the vocal score of *The Dream of Gerontius* (London, 1900) p vii.

However, Newman did not return to the reference, as Elgar does. Instead, at the moment of Judgment, Newman's Soul stated a startled "Ah! ..." and then the poem turned immediately to the Angel's reaction, "Praise to His name" :

> Praise to His name!
> [The eager spirit has darted from my hold,
> And, with the intemperate energy of love,
> Flies to the dear feet of Emmanuel;
> But, ere it reach them, the keen sanctity,
> Which with its effluence, like a glory, clothes
> And circles round the Crucified, has seized,
> And scorch'd, and shrivell'd it; and now it lies
> Passive and still before the awful Throne.]
> O happy, suffering soul! for it is safe,
> Consumed, yet quickened, by the glance of God.[35]

Newman's Angel narrated the Soul's entire experience to the reader from the time that it moved away from the Angel's protection until God ("the keen sanctity"—the presence around Christ) caused it to shrivel and burn. This climax presumably occurred immediately before this speech: the Soul stated its amazed "Ah!," and the Angel narrated it either contemporaneously or immediately thereafter. Elgar, on the other hand, has his Angel state only selections of Newman's lines beginning with the same "Praise to His Name," and continuing with "O happy suffering soul! for it is safe,/Consumed, yet quicken'd, by the glance of God," excising eight lines.

From the correspondence between Elgar and Jaeger concerning this scene, it is obvious that both carefully considered its proper dramatic resolution. Jaeger asked Elgar to include a musical climax at the moment of the Soul's Judgment.[36] Elgar responded that such was impossible, since Newman did not include such a climax :

---

[35] Newman, *op cit,* lines 837-848

[36] Jaeger suggested the climax to Elgar in a letter written on 14-15 April 1900, before he had actually seen Elgar's first rendition of the scene. See the transcription in Moore, *op cit,* vol 1, p 174.

Please remember that none of the 'action' takes place in the presence of God: I would not have tried that neither did Newman[.] The Soul says 'I go before my God'-but we don't [—] we stand outside-I've thrown over all the 'machinery' for c[e]lestial music, harps, &c.[37]

After he saw the short-score draft of the scene, Jaeger again asked Elgar to consider some sort of a culmination.[38] Elgar at first refused, but eventually gave in, composing an orchestral climax based on the Prelude's "Judgment" theme.[39]

However, it is clear from Newman's poem, which includes both a climax and an explanation of it, that Elgar's initial refusal to provide one was poetic licence on his part. The lack of climax diffused the strict narrative of Newman's vision and ultimately worked to build a more character-driven dramatic moment. In Newman's poem, the Angel's account of the Soul's Judgement defined the Soul simply as another part of the structure of Heaven. Just as the Angel narrated Newman's vision of demons, angels and heavenly architecture to the Soul, the Angel's narration of the Judgement and its subsequent results inserts the Soul into that realm and detracts from the Soul's individual characterization. Consequently, by omitting the Angel's description, Elgar increases the emphasis on the Soul itself. Other details he changed in this scene underline Elgar's desire to forward this point. Elgar omits the Soul's startled "Ah," deleting a moment of surprise and instead leaves the audience only with the tremulous "I go before my judge" which builds a sense of final expectation. Rather than moving directly to the Angel's narrative statements as Newman did, Elgar instead incorporates the chorus of "Voices from Earth," singing lines from the poem's first paragraph, as a method of prolonging the dramatic moment. The moment is further extended as Elgar places the entire orchestral climax - the musical moment of the Soul's Judgment - only after the Angel states the lines "O happy suffering." This transforms the Angel's statement from a narrative about Judgement to

---

[37]   Letter from Elgar to Jaeger, 17 April 1900 (in Moore, *op cit*, vol 1, p 175). Editorial emendations Moore's.

[38]   Letter from Jaeger to Elgar, 15 June 1900 (in Moore, *op cit*, vol 1, p 198)

[39]   Moore, *op cit*, vol 1, pp 201-209.

an enigmatic utterance, which makes the moment of judgement more mysterious and dramatic.[40] Immediately after the thunderous orchestral climax, the Soul sings its final, pleading statement, "Take me away." The result of Elgar's changes in this scene is that the Soul's plea is much more poignant than if it had been mediated and explained by the Angel. The rearrangement of this section ultimately shows that Elgar was not afraid to change a number of basic elements of Newman's structure for the sake of his vision of the drama.[41]

The changes Elgar made to Newman's poem do not detract from *The Dream of Gerontius*. Rather, they present a different version of the events the poem described. By carefully excising and rearranging the poem's text, Elgar portrayed Gerontius' character much more directly and movingly than Newman did. Such a focus on the humanity of his characters is a hallmark of Elgar's oratorios, beginning with the Blind Man in *Lux Christi* and continuing through the presentations of Judas and Mary Magdalene in *The Apostles*. In Elgar's hands, therefore, the audience's vision shifted from contemplating Gerontius' celestial surroundings to his own death and Judgment. *The Dream of Gerontius* became the audience's dream about Gerontius.

---

[40]   Stasny and Nelson note the occurrence of this climax, but do not discuss the importance of Elgar's shifting it. See Stasny and Nelson, *op cit*, pp 125 and 132.

[41]   Elgar's first draft of the Judgment scene also contains some of these delaying elements. The original proofs are reproduced in Moore, *op cit*, pp 192-197. Instead of immediately moving to the Soul's statement of "Take me away" after the Angel finishes its abbreviated speech, Elgar postponed the Soul's reaction through the interpolation of a nineteen-bar Chorus of Souls taken from the later proclamations of Newman's "Souls in Purgatory", lines 871-874. Only after does the Soul react to its Judgment. In the final version of *Gerontius*, Elgar returned the chorus of "Souls in Purgatory" to Newman's original location.

An ENGLISH ORATORIO as PATHFINDER
Notes on the form and layout of
Edward Elgar's *The Dream of Gerontius*[1]

Andreas Friesenhagen

This article first appeared in the German language periodical Die Orchester, in the issue for August/September 1993. At the time of publication, Andreas Friesenhagen MA lived in Cologne and was working on his dissertation concerning Beethoven's *Missa Solemnis*.

Between January and August 1900, Edward Elgar composed the oratorio *The Dream of Gerontius*, op 38, to a text by Cardinal John Henry Newman. On 3 October of the same year it received its premiere at the music festival in the city of Birmingham. After two acclaimed performances in Düsseldorf in 1901 and 1902 under the city's music director Julius Buths, its popularity began to grow so strongly that it eventually became the second most popular work of its type after Handel's *Messiah*, at least in Anglo-Saxon countries. It remains a key work in the whole of Elgar's output.

Research on the work has long been confined almost exclusively to the English language.[2] The present investigation attempts, for the first time in the German language, a consideration of the basic structures of 'Gerontius' in the hope that this will contribute to an understanding of an oratorio often described as a masterpiece.

---

[1] This investigation is part of a study by the author of Elgar's *The Dream of Gerontius* which appears in volume 7 of the series *Handbooks on Music*, Studio Verlag, Cologne.

[2] A comprehensive introduction can be found in the fundamental biography by Jerrold Northrop Moore: *Edward Elgar, A Creative Life* (Oxford University Press, 1984) page 290 onwards; for a particularly detailed account of the genesis and reception of the work, see Michael Kennedy: *Portrait of Elgar* (London 1968) page 76 onwards.

On the Textual Basis

We shall later consider two over-riding and interrelated structural aspects of *The Dream of Gerontius*. The first is the layout of each of the work's two parts and the relationship between the different sections; the second is the basic key plan.   Each testifies to the composer's understanding and interpretation of the text. But firstly and briefly, let us consider the text and its treatment.

The basis of the libretto is the dramatic poem of the same title by Cardinal Newman, written in 1865. The choice of text is in sharp contrast to British oratorio practice in the nineteenth century: no saint or biblical figure stands at the central point, but a sketchily described Catholic Christian. It is not a setting of biblical history but rather the death and experience in the hereafter of an 'Everyman'. Compared to the expectations which Elgar's contemporaries had of an oratorio, this text meant a complete break with tradition, truly an innovation![3]

In the first part of the work a largely static scene is played out. Sensing his approaching death, Gerontius lies on his deathbed, surrounded by unfeeling watching 'assistants', friends and relatives who pray for him and remain with him in his final hours.   Solo passages, sung by Gerontius, alternate with the choral sections of the 'assistants'. At the end of Part I, Gerontius dies and a priest commends his soul to the mercy of God. The static nature of the scene is vividly depicted throughout by the poet and the composer. This Part presents, through prayers and appeals, the real and existing Catholic rites at the approach of death bracketed by freely composed verses, although some of the texts from the Catholic liturgy which Newman used, such as *Modus iuvandi morientes*,[4] were subsequently invalidated by the second Vatican Council.   Inasmuch as Elgar remains true to this restraint in his musical setting, he brings a further innovation to the

---

[3]   Frank Howes: *The English Musical Renaissance* (London 1966) page 43; Peter J. Pirie: *The English Musical Renaissance* (London 1979) page 30 and onwards.

[4]   *'Vade Mecum' for priests at the sick and death bed* (Regensburg 1959) page 41 and onwards; compare this with the more general pointer towards a liturgical orientation in Moore (*op cit*) page 113 onwards and page 127.

contemporary English oratorio: a liturgy set to music, facilitated through a fictional story, and realised in a near-perfect fashion.

Part II is set in the hereafter. Similar to journeys to the next world portrayed in medieval works such as Dante's 'Divina Comedia',[5] it portrays the soul of Gerontius as it meets its guardian angel (in the original only called 'angel') and, with him, undertakes a wandering through various regions of the supernatural world. The soul's wish, and thus the motivation for the journey, is to glimpse God. Before they can reach his throne, however, they must pass through the regions of the devils and the angels, experiencing both evil scorn and pious praise. The judgement of the Almighty, which the soul finally receives without God being introduced in person by the poet, means punishment by purgatorial fire. One can regard this as a contemporary, singularly Catholic manifestation of appropriate dogma, which is here characterised as a trait of the Oxford Movement.[6] The finale of the work is the farewell between the angel and the soul, whereby the latter finally meets punishment in purgatory with a feeling approaching happiness.

In contrast to Part I, Part II is characterised by movement. It largely abandons a close relationship with prescribed Catholic rituals, admittedly in part as a result of Elgar's radical abbreviation of the original text. This is also in constrast to Part I which Elgar left largely uncut.

On the Layout of Individual Movements

The foregoing short summary of the text helps us to understand two crucial points : firstly, that the development of both parts of the work - towards death in the first, towards purgatory in the second - was used by the composer as the motivation for his setting; and, secondly, the

---

[5]   On the genre of medieval journeys to the hereafter, see Aaron J. Gurjewitsch: *Medieval Folk Culture* (German translation, Munich, 1992).

[6]   The Oxford Movement strove for a union of the Anglican and Catholic rites: compare Nigel Barton : 'Oratorios and Cantatas' in *Music in Britain: The Romantic Age 1800-1914* (The *Athlone History of Music in Britain*, volume 5, Nicholas Temperley, London 1981) page 229.

Table No.1

Introduction	Prelude	to figure 21
Gerontius	'Jesu, Maria'	Figs.21-29
Assistants	'Kyrie Eleison'	Figs.29-33
Gerontius	'Rouse thee, my fainting soul'	Figs.33-35
Assistants	'Be merciful, be gracious'	Figs.35-40
Gerontius	'Sanctus Fortis'	Figs.40-57
Gerontius	'I can no more'	Figs.57-63
Assistants	'Rescue him'	Figs.63-66
Gerontius	'Novissima hora est'	Figs.66-68
Priest and Assistants	'Proficiscere anima'	Figs.68- end

importance of the relationship between the solo and choral movements which, in Part I, are integrated impressively into an overall plan constructed basically on principles of contrasts.

As will be seen, this results in an alternation of solo and choral settings which parallels the variation in the structure of juxtaposed sections. If one excludes the instrumental introduction (Prelude), Part I (in which the organisational principles can be seen most clearly) consists of nine identifiable movements. Elgar, through a partial elimination of their boundaries, allows these to flow together without a break; both parts of the work portray a 'through composed' entity. As table no.1 above shows, each pair of movements is grouped around the central axis of Gerontius' solo, 'Sanctus fortis'. Each pair of movements comprises a solo for Gerontius immediately followed by a choral movement for the 'assistants'.

How does the separation of 'Sanctus Fortis' come about? If one compares this solo for Gerontius with his other four in the first part, a basically different structure emerges. The four outer solos are 'recitative' in character, whereas the central movement shows, through its ordered, repeated phrases, a firmly constructed inner layout with similarities to a rondo form. Against this, the free flowing fugal form of the other solo movements, often built of short, changing sections, displays a structure built on a succession of *leitmotiven* in the orchestral accompaniment. This gives the vocal line of the soloist a constantly varying motion. Here the solo line and the accompaniment react to the varied moods of the text in a fashion which makes a strongly-based form impossible. In the score, Elgar marks these solos with the indication 'Recit' or 'Quasi Recit'.

The choral movements following the respective recitative passages, provide an additional contrast in form to those of the soloist. Compared to the solo 'Sanctus Fortis' they are thematically homogenous and, in their internal structure, built to a strong format.

The orchestral part is here subordinate to the choir voices, the latter expounding and carrying the motivic material. A simple ternary (A-B-A) or developed (A-B-A-B or A-B-A-B-A) form is present. In addition, the

---

Table No.2

The soul of Gerontius 'I went to sleep'	Figs. 1-11
Angel 'My work is done'	Figs.11-16
Soul 'It is a member' & Angel' All hail my child'	Figs.16-26
Soul/Angel: Duet 'A presage falls upon thee'	Figs.26-29
Soul 'But hark'	Figs.29-32
Demons 'Low born clods of brute earth'	Figs.32-55
Soul 'I see not' & Angel 'Yes, for one moment'	Figs.55-60
Angelicals 'Praise to the Holiest' (1)	Figs.60-74
Angelicals 'Praise to the Holiest' (2)	Figs.74-101
Angel 'Thy Judgement is now near'	Figs.101-106
Angel of the Agony 'Jesu: by that shuddring dread'	Figs.106-114
Soul 'I go before my judge'	Figs.114-120
Soul 'Take me away'	Figs.120-125
Souls in Purgatory 'Lord, thou hast been our refuge'	Figs.125-126
Angel 'Softly and Gently'	Figs.126-end

choral movements include imitative use of the voices as well as contrapuntal writing, showing them to be closely constructed forms. One could be allowed to presume, in these formalistic aspects, a relationship with the liturgical sources which form the basis of the choral movements. If one accepts the exclusion of the 'Prelude' and final movement of Part I by virtue of the theme which is heard only in these two movements, the balanced overall layout of the remainder of the Part underlines the assertion of the central movement, the dying man's avowal of belief being clearly delineated by this layout.

The second part of the work is seen to be basically different from the first: the static nature of the death scene is transformed into the movement of the journey in the hereafter, culminating in the judgment of the soul of Gerontius by God. Also, in the sequence of the individual movements, greater in number than in Part I, one no longer finds a balanced, centrally focused arrangement. This is a further reflection of the textual content. Part II begins with the second main character in the poem, the Angel, initiating the characteristic paired coupling of free recitative solo and strongly shaped choral movements. But the following division of the movements into six groups must be viewed differently.

While a similar, balanced layout can be seen (table 2), the coupling of pairs of groups here derives from the relationship between the content matter rather than from a movement structure. This is most clear in the contrasts of the two regions of, respectively, demonical and heavenly forms (Demons-Angelicals) which form the subject of the two central groups. The coupling arises from the antipathy of the regions of Evil and Good and their inhabitants, who are strikingly contrasted with each other. The textual editing by the composer heightens this contrast through the abbreviation of the proposition, but Elgar also separates each section by contrasting musical means. The principle of contrasted writing, which in Part I occurred between pairs of sections, can now be found within a section.

The similarity in content of the next-outermost groups can be clearly seen in the execution of the divine judgement. In the dialogue between the soul and the angel - figure 16 and onwards - a wish to see God is uttered. With the entry of the Angel of the Agony, introduced by Newman as an intercession before the throne of God (figure 102 and onwards), the fulfilment of this wish is in view. This is followed by a section ('I go before my judge') portraying the realisation of the presentiment described in the duet beginning at figure 26.

The outermost movement groups appear to be linked by thoughts of a pastoral idyll which begins the second part of the work and ends in the finale of the angel, 'Softly and gently'. Whereas in the final sections (figure 120 onwards) the judgement is already passed and the soul begins its sentence with the journey to the souls in the purgatorial flames, thoughts of judgement are still unmentioned in the first two solos at the beginning. These groups thus portray a 'before' and 'after' of the main action of divine judgement.

The first two groups, beginning at figure 1 and figure 16 respectively, differ not only in content but in their levels of communication. In the first pair of sections, the soul and the angel sing in successive monologues. Then a duologue for both characters brings them together and, in the duet 'A presage falls', finds its expression through the use of verbal imitation and musical devices. At this point, the characteristic idea of the first part - the coupling of free recitative with strong multiple forms - is taken up again. In both sectional pairs, the solo of the angel ('My work is done') and the duet is followed by dense 'aria' numbers in monologue and dialogue recitative, to which Elgar gives the marking 'Recit'.

In contrast to Part I, the chorus is now absent as a complementary partner in the recitative passages. Because of the enlarged dimensions of Part II, the chorus' entry as the army of demons and/or angels respectively is barely comparable with the principle of Part I. Moreover, the boundaries between the individual movements increasingly disappear. Thus the dialogue of the soul and the angel, for example, continues into the first part of the choral movement 'Praise to the Holiest' (figure 60 onwards), the two levels thus overlaying one another.

As a result, shorter episodes no longer corresponding to a numbered structure then appear with varying content and themes. The irregularities of the construction and the lack of a clear division of separate movements as the work nears its end are further demonstrated by Elgar's continuing use of the marking 'Recit' for the contrasting pairs of movements . Accordingly the two solo pieces in the final group are clearly separate 'arioso' movements. It can then be seen that the earlier recitative-like 'I go before my judge' forms not the introduction to the final group but the conclusion of the previous group.

The origin of this difference in structure is again to be found in the content of the libretto. The fate of Gerontius is decided in this part of the work, representing the point of highest drama. The arrangement of the sections, and above all the more frequent changes, reflect the factual content in a similar fashion, just as the balance of Part I exactly caught the motionless aura of the scene and its treatment. Nevertheless, one can find a brief foretaste in Part I of the separation of the movement schema if one looks at the solo 'Novissima hora' which introduces the passage toward death of Gerontius : here the appeal of the dying man (figure 66) is not treated as a recitative. The leitmotif structure at this point is also taken over by the vocal line, which introduces one of the work's most important motifs. The characteristic marking 'Recit.' is missing here and is only given seven bars later, when Gerontius continues the solo. In the non-recitative expression which follows of Gerontius' recognition that his final hour has come, we have before us a preview of the formation of the second part of the work.

The through-composition, abandoning a clear division between the sections of the composition, was a further innovation for the English oratorio. If, in the balanced form of Part I, Elgar adhered to the prevalent structure of larger vocal works - a structure which also holds for his first effort *The Light of Life* (1896) - he left behind the layout of a 'Mendelssohnian'[7] oratorio with the text and dynamic form of Part II. For the first time, a work of this form emerges in the British Isles which bears comparison with continental works exemplified by the music dramas of Wagner. Elgar's affinity with such music, shown in his great knowledge of the main works of the genre, is well known.[8]

---

[7]   The term ' Mendelssohnian' goes back to Arnold Schering: *History of the Oratorio* Handbooks on music history by genres, volume 3 (Leipzig 1911) page 552. In studying English oratorio composition, Schering divides the nineteenth century into the periods under the influence of Handel and, after 1846, of Mendelssohn.

[8]   Peter Dennison: *Elgar and Wagner* (*Music and Letters* 66, 1985) page 93 and onwards. One thinks also of Elgar's planned oratorio trilogy, following the example of Wagner's 'Ring', of which only the first two parts, *The Apostles* and *The Kingdom*, were completed, in 1903 and 1906 respectively.

Key Signature Plan

In parallel with the pairing of individual movements revealed by the foregoing examination of form and content, there is a further, linear structure to the material. Again particularly apparent in Part I, the work follows a key signature plan which mirrors the spiritual state of Gerontius by a musical device. To see this, it is necessary to list the movements of Part I alongside their respective basic key signatures.

Table No.3

Prelude	D minor (1♭)
Gerontius ' Jesu Maria'	Bb major (2♭)
Assistants 'Kyrie Eleison'	E flat major) (3♭)
Gerontius 'Rouse thee, my fainting soul'	E flat major (3♭)
Assistants 'Be merciful, be gracious'	A flat major (4♭)
Gerontius 'Sanctus fortis'	Bb minor (5♭)
Gerontius 'I can no more'	Bb major (2♭)
Assistants 'Rescue him, O Lord'	E flat minor (6♭)
Assistants 'Noe from the waters' (fig.64)	A flat minor (7♭)
Assistants 'Rescue this thy servant' (fig.65)	E major (4#)
Gerontius 'Novissima hora est'	C sharp minor (4#)
Priest & Assistants 'Proficiscere anima Christiana'	D major (2#)

From this table, it is interesting to note that, up to the litany 'Noe from the waters', an almost unbroken increase in the number of B flat dominants is recognisable. The only exception to this continuous descent in the cycle of fifths is the recitative solo of Gerontius, 'I can no more', which begins at first in B flat major but soon modulates into B flat minor. With this qualification, it fits into a general progression from the Prelude, which has a key signature with a single flat, to the chorus in seven flats.

An interpretation for this gradual progression is offered by the text : there is a relationship between the slow approach of Gerontius to his death and the progression of the dominants. The descent in the cycle of fifths which conditions Part II can be taken to symbolise the increasing approach of death, fixed by the composer at the furthest point from a 'neutral' C major. The sections with key signatures of E flat minor and A flat minor portray the end of the descending movement, although A flat minor strictly occurs somewhat before the lowest point in the soul's journey. Through an enharmonic interpolation of A flat, Elgar then reaches E major (Assistants 'Rescue this thy servant') with which the descent ends and a new, subconsciusly-felt direction is taken up. The continuation in C sharp minor (four-sharp) represents the change from fear before death to trusting acceptance and expectation. Although at this point the death of Gerontius has not yet taken place, it is hinted at by his composure, as indicated by the text and, in the music, by the use of the key signatures. In this way, Elgar interprets the text in his own fashion and unequivocally strengthens the essentially subconscious message of the text.

This is an example of Elgar's textual interpretation through compositional measures; other examples can be found elsewhere in the work. In this, Elgar goes considerably beyond the practice of his contemporaries and exposes the strongly personal affinity of the composer for his text.[9] The conclusion of the first part in D major can be seen as the outcome of the struggle with death, as a positive re-interpretation of the beginning of the Prelude in D minor.

The table in illustration no.4 (next page) shows the key signature progression in Part II. In this longer second Part, no direct parallels of a continuous, step-by-step progression in key signature can be established. Only after the chorus 'Praise to the Holiest' in C major can a structure be determined which parallels the model established in Part I, with a growing number of flat signatures through a succession of modulations to sharp keys. In the earlier sections of Part II, self-contained key signature constructions can be identified. Elgar frames the region of the demons with movements whose tonic is E flat major.

---

[9]   Elgar knew of Newman's poem at least eleven years before the composition of *Gerontius* and valued it greatly - see Diana McVeagh: *Edward Elgar, his life and music* (London 1955) page 130.

Table No.4

Soul of Gerontius 'I went to sleep'	F major (1♭)
Angel 'My work is done'	E minor (1#)
Soul 'It is a member'	C major
Soul & Angel 'A presage falls upon thee'	E flat major (3♭)
Soul 'But hark! upon my sense'	B♭ minor (5♭)
Demons 'Low born clods of brute earth'	D minor (1♭)
Demons 'Dispossessed, aside thrust' fig.35	G minor (2♭)
Demons 'The mind bold and independent' fig.43	G minor (2♭)
Soul 'I see not those false spirits'	E flat major (3♭)
Angelicals 'Praise to the Holiest' (1)	A flat major (4♭)
Angelicals 'Praise to the Holiest' (2)	C major
Angel 'Thy judgement now is near'	A flat major (4♭)
Angel of the Agony 'Jesu! by that shudd'ring dread'	D flat major (5♭)
Soul 'I go before my Judge'	A flat minor (7♭)
Voices on Earth 'Be merciful' (fig.115)	E major (4#)
Soul 'Take me away'	F sharp minor (3#)
Souls in Purgatory 'Lord, thou hast been our refuge'	D major (2#)
Angel 'Softly and gently'	D major (2#)

The second and third choruses of the demons are in G minor, the complimentary key to B flat major, which is the dominant of E flat major. The Demons' Chorus can thus be seen as depicting a dominating relationship over the two framing movements. This gives a closed construction of overlapping movements which mirrors the contrasting of individual movement groups seen elsewhere.

Nevertheless a significant analogy with Part I is found in the important key modulation from A flat minor to E major. If in Part I the moment of acceptance of death was the cause of the modulation, in Part II, in the solo 'I go before my Judge', it is the imminently approaching judgement of God that causes the same modulation. In both parts the modulation thus serves the same function, namely, to emphasize harmonically a crisis which represents the high point of the content. Like the ascending progression of the B flat key signatures in the first part, this can plainly be seen as a musical interpretation of the text by the composer. The contrasting of the two high points, Death and Judgement, is not cited in the poem; it is Elgar's own achievement. Consequently, both through his textual editing by employing the same harmonic operation, Elgar creates a direct parallel between, on the one hand, Gerontius' journey to, and calm acceptance of, death ('Novissima hora') and, on the other, his ascent to God and God's verdict. Appropriately, the ends of both parts are held in D major, a key signature which in Part II, as in Part I, is used to indicate the overcoming of the crisis of the hour of death and of judgement.

The particular key signatures Elgar uses to depict psychological events can be linked to a subjectively coloured key signature symbolism. There are parallels with the symbolic key signature usage of the classical-romantic tradition since the time of Bach. In Hermann Beckh's fundamental book on this subject,[10] in which he undertakes an exploration of the symbolic characterisation of the twelve keys of the chromatic scale, one finds an appropriate interpretation of the key signatures used by Elgar for *The Dream of Gerontius*. Beckh's evaluation of the key signatures A flat minor and E major coincides exactly with their use at respective points in Gerontius. The same can be said of the use of F major, E flat major and C major as basic key signatures for individual movements. Also D major is used in accordance with the traditional characteristics indicated by Beckh (contradicted however by examples of Elgar's use of D flat major or E minor).

The exploration of key signature symbolism does not carry with it any unequivocal results, so one cannot argue that Elgar was consciously following any assumed rule. Elgar was familiar with the music of the Continent, above all Germany, and Beckh similarly develops his symbolism with works of the German tradition, which for him began with Bach and has a clear focus in the music of Richard Wagner. Beckh's study also takes in the harmonic application of Beethoven, Schumann or Brahms, so it is possible that some of Elgar's parallel

---

[10]   Hermanh Beckh: *The language of the key signature in music from Bach to Bruckner* (First edition 1937, reprinted Stuttgart 1977).

use of key signature characteristics arises from his knowledge of the working methods of these composers. It is perhaps not therefore surprising to find in *Gerontius* a partial agreement with Beckh's key signature symbolism, probably less the result of a deliberate scheme than the subconscious influence of these composers on Elgar's work.

Closing Observation

In view of the influence on Elgar's music of German composers, we should perhaps also ask to what extent Elgar can be considered a representative of a national school, as is customarily the case with his Slavonic and Scandinavian counterparts. In contrast to the next generation of English composers, widely regarded as representatives of a British Musical Renaissance[11] - Vaughan Williams, Holst, Ireland, Bax, etc - in Elgar's work one finds only the scantiest evidence of a conscious relationship to English folk music roots. He valued the music of Brahms in particular because, in his opinion, it renounced a definite national idiom and, as a result, was more widely appreciated. To take Elgar as representative of an exclusively English national style is too limited.

The influence of Germany has a wider importance for *The Dream of Gerontius*, since the work only gained acceptance and understanding in Elgar's homeland after the performances in Dusseldorf. With good reason, one can speak here of a 'German midwife'. The calculated break with the English oratorio tradition, as seen in the choice of text and the compositional methods Elgar used in *Gerontius*, also speaks for the early international importance of Elgar. While composing the oratorio, he turned to, amongst others, the compositions of Franz Liszt, whose efforts as a composer attracted the disapproval of Elgar's contemporaries. Finally he studied Wagner intensively and, to an extent, adopted Wagner's techniques instead of following the reliable and, in England, accepted form going back to Mendelssohn's *Elijah*. Signs of both a traditional and progressive tendency by Elgar towards the Continent are then unmistakable.

---

[11]   For a history of English music in the twentieth century, see footnote 3.

The structural organisation of *Gerontius* I have attempted to portray here provides an insight into the textually-based conception of the music which, in its compositional construction and the structuring of its movements, demonstrates Elgar's radical innovation. If he lays out Part I in a balanced fashion, thereby remaining true to traditional schemes, only the textual linking of groups in Part II mirrors the layout of the model of Part I : ultimately, the dynamic of the text wins over customary concepts of musical form. In the harmonic layout, Elgar proves himself to be the interpreter of the poet. The contrast between two principal statements of the text, the death and judgment of Gerontius, both based on the same key signature artifice, is evidence of a really far-reaching conception.

Elgar thereby takes a stride into the twentieth century in the field of large-scale English vocal works. The new understanding of the form and message of the oratorio genre which he introduced can later be seen in works by Walton and Tippett. At the same time Elgar overcomes the stagnation of English musical thinking in the nineteenth century and we can see him to be the most significant figure in English music at the turn of the Century.

SOURCES of MANUSCRIPTS, SKETCHES and PROOFS

Elgarian students wishing to research the composition of The Dream of Gerontius *are likely to find the following sources of original reference material particularly helpful.*

A. Library of The Oratory, Edgbaston, Birmingham.

Full score (pp 1-304), including :
- Title page headed :
  'A.M.D.G.
  Birchwood.
  In Summer, 1900.
  Quae lucis miseris tam dira cupido?
  Virg: Whence doth so dyre desire of Light on wretches grow?
  (Montaigne - Florio)'
- At foot of title page :
  'Let drop the Chorus,
  let drop everybody -
  but let *not* drop the wings of your original
  Genius.
                        Hans Richter'
- The page also contains signatures of the soloists and of members of the Birmingham Festival executive.
- Comment on scoring of 'It is the restless panting of their being' :
  'Birchwood Lodge
  in thunder storm'
- Instruction for Part II cue 120 :
  'For the first chord at 120 (a crotchet/ staccato)
  any number of extra instruments
  & percussion may be employed' (p 271)
- Inscription at the end :
  FINE
  'This is the best of me; for the
  rest, I ate, and drank, and slept
  loved and hated, like another;
  my life was as the vapour, and
  is not; but *this* I saw and
  knew : this, if anything of
  mine is worth your memory' (p 301)

- Elgar's inscription when lodging the full score at the Oratory :
'I offer this M.S. to the Library of the Oratory,
with the deepest reverence to the memory of
Cardinal Newman whose poem I have
had the honour to attempt to set
to music.
Edward Elgar.
Malvern
Sept. 17: 1902'.

B. Elgar Birthplace Museum, Lower Broadheath, Worcester.

MSS 6-10. Manuscript vocal score, Part I complete, pp 1-83; pencil note at cue 64, 'Enquire as to words', because Elgar originally included 'Enoch and Elias from the common doom' and 'Abraham from the abounding guilt of Heathenesse', omitting Job and Moses. (See Jerrold Northrop Moore : *Elgar and his Publishers - Letters of a Creative Life* (Clarendon Press, 1987) pp 168-70,175; also Robert Anderson : *Elgar in Manuscript* (British Library, 1990) pp 49-51).

MSS 11. MS fair copy of Part II cue 11 to 16; dated 'March 1900', written out for Mrs Jaeger, and acknowledged by Jaeger on 30 March (see Moore, *op cit*, p 171).

MSS 12-15, Part II, cue 75 to 102, pp 1-34; cue 114 to end (without the alterations inspired by Jaeger), pp 1-28.

PR 23 (ref: 602d). Vocal score proofs, Part I complete, pp 1-10 used for making full score, with hints of instrumentation and timpani tuning, with 'Daniel from the hungry lions in their lair' at cue 64 and marginal note '? substitute/ David &c'; first proof date-stamped 2 April 1900.

PR 24. Vocal score proofs, Part II pp 55-81, used for making full score, with 'prosody' comment from Jaeger at 'Who after expelling'; revise, date-stamped 11 May 1900.

PR 25. Vocal score proofs. Part II, pp 109, 112-126, 147-149, used for making full score, with two lists of the orchestral instruments to be involved and pencil comment (p 147) 'psst.CAT.psst' and 'wopse' in right margin.

PR 26. Vocal score proofs. Part II pp 113-146

PR 27. Vocal score proofs. Part II pp 147-153; revise, date-stamped 7 June 1900.

MS 119. Sketch for Part I, cue 39. ?Part II, cues 58-59.

Photocopy of the manuscript full score.

British Library, Euston Road, London NW1 2DB

Add.MS 47902, fos 33-302. Sketches and drafts, including:
- 'I hate diminished 7ths' at the word 'dismay' on p 33 of the vocal score (f.88);
- references to Parry's oratorio *Job* and Stanford's *The Three Holy Children*, and the comment 'Rescue this Kyrie' in connection with 'Rescue him' at cue 63 (f.99);
- plan of end of Part I (f.115*v*);
- setting of four Newman lines near the start of Part II beginning 'I had a dream', later abandoned (fair copy, fos. 131-133);
- the word 'Jape' against the 5/8 section after cue 9 (f.135);
- pencil comment on 'The mind bold' sung by the Demons, 'some are bold' (f.160);
- version of 'And that a higher gift than grace' later used in *The Music Makers* (1912), bars 618-629 at the words 'With our dreaming and singing' (f.215);
- comment on 'wisest love' of vocal score p 125 top line '? 5ths/ hab Acht' (f.237);
- 'And now the threshold' of cue 73 linked with *The Music Makers* bars 241-254 and the words 'trample a kingdom down' (f.251);
- 'gargling duet' for Elgar and his wife entitled 'Duo.Garglione', with canto and basso trills (f.260*v*);
- idea used later for *In the South* bars 104-105 (f.268*v*);
- heading 'Canto fermo Souls' for 'Lord, Thou hast been our refuge' (f.43);
- plan for cue 126 to the end (f.292).

Add.MS 47904A f.120 : Sketch of 'Fear' motif dating from 1896 and found in material relating to *The Light of Life.*

Add.MS 49973B, f. 43 : Sketch for 'Praise' chorus idea.

Hereford Cathedral Library

'Prayer' motif in G R Sinclair's Visitors' Book (19-20 April 1898), 'The Moods of Dan, Illustrated No. III'.

In private collections

Sketches of Prelude to Part I, given by Elgar to Jaeger on 27 September 1900 and referred to in the covering letter as "these two *very first* sketches".

Sketches of Part I, cue 29-30, and Part II cue 9-10.

Sketch of a fragment of the Introduction to Part II, attached to a page of Alice Elgar's copy of the miniature score.

Jaeger's copy of the vocal score, containing :
- the 'Committal' motif pasted into it, originally intended for a 'Gordon' symphony, and dated 20 October 1898;
- the Angel of the Agony motif also pasted in, originally intended for Judas in *The Apostles*, and dated November 1899 (see Moore, *op cit*, pp 150-151);
- vocal score proofs pasted into it of the original pp 157-162, including the *piano* opening to 'Take me away' that so disappointed Jaeger (for facsimiles see Moore, *op cit*, pp 192-197, and the following pages for the ensuing correspondence which led to Elgar changing this section of the score).

Complete set of vocal score proofs as annotated by Jaeger for his Analysis.

Part Three

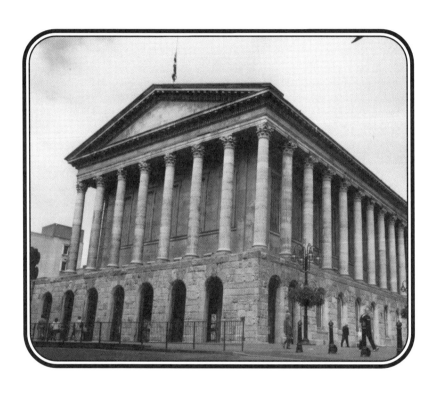

The Struggle
for Survival

Previous page :   *Birmingham Town Hall,*
venue for the premiere of Gerontius *on 3 October 1900*

The BIRMINGHAM PREMIÈRE
A Selection of Contemporary Reviews

In SOME WAYS a BEAUTIFUL WORK

J A Fuller Maitland

J A Fuller Maitland was chief music critic of The Times *from 1889 to 1911. He was at the forefront of the revival of interest in J S Bach, and was active in the English folk-song movement. With W B Squire he also edited the Fitzwilliam Virginal Book. It was perhaps inevitable that someone with a strict nonconformist upbringing, who had been a pupil of Stanford at Cambridge, and who found Debussy and Strauss difficult to accept, was always likely to be less than effusive about* Gerontius.

The attendance at the morning concert of today was unusually large, considering that the one principal novelty was given. As a rule the British public is so difficult to move from its accustomed ways that the new works receive scant recognition in comparison with the whole-hearted admiration bestowed on the familiar, not to say hackneyed, compositions. In choosing Cardinal Newman's *Dream of Gerontius* for musical treatment, Mr Elgar may have had in his mind the strong support which those connected with the Oratory can give to any part of the Birmingham Festival that appeals to them; and it is clear that no subject could appeal to them more strongly than that of Newman's justly admired poem, which, whether it deserves the name of masterpiece or not, is still sufficiently rich in musical suggestion to justify the choice. The poem has been set almost in its entirety, the most notable omissions being, strangely enough, the fine stanzas of the 'Angels of the Sacred Stair' and three out of the five long sections of the Angelicals' hymn, 'Praise to the Holiest in the height'. The composer has laid out his work in most grandiose style, with every orchestral resource, including the frequent division of the stringed instruments, sometimes into as many as 20 parts. In this connection may be mentioned the introduction of the little bells called 'Schellen' into the accompaniment of the chorus of demons; but it is not by out-of-the-way novelties like this that Mr Elgar's great effects are made, rather it is by his really remarkable instinct for orchestral colouring. The richest combinations are used, and the chief reproach to which the work as a whole is open is that there is so constant a succession of strange harmonies arranged, so to speak, in gorgeous clothing that the ear is a little apt to weary of these and to long for some passage of relief, some simple harmonic progression, some purely melodic theme, with only the slight support which the greatest masters of instrumentation, and only they, have used to heighten the effect of their richer passages. This want is satisfied, it is true, in the loveliest part of the work, the quiet introduction to the second part illustrating the disembodied soul's words, "How still it is!" The progressions, the pure three-part harmony, fall on the ear most gratefully, and are doubly effective from the contrast with what has gone before and what is to follow. In a work so elaborately disposed for voices and orchestra, it is impossible to do more than point out certain parts that call for special commendation. The choir is divided into semi-chorus and full chorus, and some of the concerted numbers in which these are used antiphonally or together are in the highest degree successful. A kind of litany sung by the 'assistants' at the death-bed, with the lovely recurrence of "Amen", is beautiful and impressive, and the commentatory utterance of the priest, 'Proficiscere, anima Christiana', is worked up into a really splendid climax. More ambitious but far less successful are the choral parts of the second section; the demons' chorus is strenuous and its rhythm, broken up into a bewildering maze of sound, outdoes in elaboration the similar passages in Berlioz's *Faust* or the impressive and dramatic chorus of devils in Dr Stanford's *Eden*, but it is not really convincing, partly, perhaps, as a result of too faithful an adhesion to the strange rhythms of the poem at this point. The treatment of the hymn 'Praise to the Holiest' is also far from being thoroughly successful, in spite of its extremely elaborate handling, in which various stanzas are sung simultaneously by the different choral bodies. An exception to the rule, as regards the later section of the work, is the closing scene, in which the mezzo-soprano role of the guardian angel is brought in with the semi-chorus of souls in Purgatory; this scene is marked by a beauty and a distinction which are rare in the rest of the composition. Of the three solo parts, that of Gerontius (tenor) is naturally the most important, yet it is seldom either grateful to the singer or very attractive to the average hearer. The dying utterances in the first part are very cleverly set, but the declamatory style is used almost too continuously, at all events for the listener of only moderate cultivation. How to write a long and mainly declamatory soliloquy with no lack of melodic beauty or affecting expression has been shown in Sir Hubert Parry's *Job*, and it is only necessary to allude to this in order to point the vast difference that exists between the two composers in this regard. For Sir Hubert Parry's wonderful power of building up a climax has evidently had an influence on the younger composer, and if we look back to the sugary inanities of the oratorios of Gounod, which nearly 20 years ago were so loudly admired in Birmingham, we may well be grateful for the solidity and the sincerity of feeling which are apparent on every page of Mr Elgar's score. If only he would more often yield to the instinct for melodic beauty, which many of his other works show him to possess, the new composition would merit very high rank indeed.

Its interpretation, under Dr Richter, was very good on the whole, though by no means perfect. The chorus had an exceedingly hard task before them, for, apart from the elaborate methods of division, the actual writing is of the very hardest, and it could hardly be expected that no faults of intonation should be noticed. Many of these there were, but it was clear from the accuracy with which the leads were attacked that enormous pains had been taken in preparing for the performance. Mr Lloyd's delivery of the tenor part was wonderfully beautiful in feeling, and must have fulfilled the composer's ideal as it will scarcely be fulfilled again. The cries of the dying man and the more peaceful passages of the second section were given with exactly the right expression. As the angel Miss Marie Brema made a great success, her performance was eminently sympathetic, tender, and often affecting. In the part of the priest a more definitely ecclesiastical style than that of Mr Plunket Greene might have been more impressive, but in the intercession of the 'Angel of the Agony' his delivery of the very difficult passage was admirable. The work was very warmly received, but the composer delayed to come before the public for an unusually long time. When he came he was heartily applauded. A minute analysis of the oratorio was as usual included in the book of words, but its style was so enthusiastic that it must have overshot its mark completely. Criticism, it should be remembered, is completely out of place in such a commentary, for where any hint of blame would obviously be unsuitable, it is evident that praise must be equally so; and the result of such an analysis can only be to endanger the ultimate success of what is after all a remarkable, and in some ways a beautiful work.

The Times, 4 October 1900, p 5

MUSIC that SPEAKS to the HEART

E A Baughan

E A Baughan was for many years Editor of the Musical Standard, *and wrote regularly for many other publications, including the* Daily News, Musical Opinion, *and the* Monthly Musical Record. *His article on* Caractacus *on 1 October 1898 was based on the London rehearsals for the Leeds Festival but pleased Elgar, who wrote to Troyte Griffith : "I will send you a M. Standard which is the first to give me the place I've fought for". Yet the review of the première itself on 8 October was much more qualified in its praise. Baughan's later critique of* The Apostles *was published in a collection of his writings,* Music and Musicians, *in 1906. His thoughts on* Gerontius *are included here as they represent his first reactions after the première, and two later reflections.*

Mr Edward Elgar is a composer on whom many of us have placed high hopes. The work he has hitherto given us has not been complete in its achievement. *Caractacus*, his last choral composition, was weak particularly in the writing for the voice, and in a more general way in the inadequate musical expression of a stirring subject. Since then he has given to the public his *Enigma Variations*, a great advance on any orchestral work he had composed. In the cantatas *King Olaf, The Light of Life* and *Caractacus*, there were Elgaresque mannerisms which to me, at least, proved wearisome after many hearings. All composers have mannerisms, it is true; but Mr Elgar's were of a peculiarly individual type, and they were introduced too frequently. In the *Enigma Variations*, however, he had to a great extent freed himself from them. And now in *The Dream of Gerontius* he is even less Elgaresque and yet has more marked an individuality. That may seem a paradox, but it is a genuine expression of the effect his work has had on me.

For one thing, I believe Mr Elgar has found a subject into which he can pour himself. The old Druids and Warriors of *Caractacus* are entertaining enough, but neither they nor their ideas touch the soul of a modern man. They but make good lay figures. The poem of Newman's, with its realistic description of a soul's release from life and introduction into Purgatory, would, perhaps, just as little appeal to many minds; but however little in sympathy you may be with Newman's poem it has the elements and spirituality and human feeling which place it among the real dramas of life. It represents at the least the release of a soul from suffering and the higher kindness and tenderness which are too absent in this world. Mr Elgar, a Catholic, has, however, thrown himself heart and soul into the realism of the poem, and in many ways he has achieved his greatest success in the depicting of the poem's environment. The note of his music apart from this is its peculiar tenderness which speaks straight to the heart. I have before accused Mr Elgar of sentimentality in his melody, and, in his earlier works, in the manner of scoring it so much for the strings. I do not note this defect in *The Dream of Gerontius*. There is a sadness of sentiment, of course; a certain whine which is inseparable, I suppose, from the human being when he regrets leaving this world, or is afraid of the ultimate destination of his soul. But it is genuine enough. Many strong men, some of the strongest, have felt it. In Mr Elgar's music it is not overdone. On the other hand, there is real beauty of tenderness in the solos of the Angel - this is where Mr Elgar has risen to his greatest height. And why? Because his effect is so simply obtained. There is no striving after effect by means of big climaxes of the orchestra with the voice poised on the top. It is music which could not be written by any man who had not felt the beauty of Newman's Angel and had not longed for a tender charity within which the bruised human soul could at last fold its wings and sleep. One is so glad of any simple musical poetry in these days when all is on the large scale that amazes but does not touch, that I must be excused for dwelling on this point. Besides, in a certain sense, the Angel gives the keynote of the work. There are choruses which have power, there is descriptive music which a modern Russian would have been glad to sign, there are climaxes of jubilation, and there is an Amfortas-like outburst of an Angel of the Agony - impressive enough in its semi-Wagnerian way. But where Mr Elgar has been most successful is in his illustration of a tenderness which (if one may say so without being accused of cant) wipes away the tears from the face of suffering. You find it in the utterances of the Angel, who guides the soul of Gerontius to the ante-chamber of the judgment seat, and you find it in many of the choruses, especially in the chorus 'Be merciful be gracious; spare him, Lord', and again, in the 'Rescue him, O Lord, in this his evil hour', with its ingeniously interpolated semi-chorus, and tenderly plaintive 'Amen'. The advance Mr Elgar has made in writing for the voice is remarkable. The long tenor solo with which the work opens, after the prelude (itself a tone-poem of singular beauty and simplicity), is, in spite of moments of vagueness, quite a masterpiece of emotional "endless melody", and often, in the rest of the work, the music assigned to Gerontius breaks into an unmistakable *cri du cœur*. When Death is upon him he cries out "O Jesu, help! Pray for me, Mary, pray!" No words will convey the sincerity of that outbreak, but my readers may see it for themselves on page 34 of the vocal score. Unfortunately Mr Lloyd is hardly the man for this type of music. He does all a singer can do by mere notes, but he cannot get that expression behind the voice which we admire so much in Jean de Reszke, and which even Clara Butt at her best sometimes gives us. Mere beauty of singing will not realise what Mr Elgar wants. Indeed the real difficulty of this work is not the contrapuntal devilment of the demon's chorus, difficult as that is, for an intelligent choir could easily be trained to sing it accurately; but in the demand Mr Elgar makes on his chorus, orchestra and soloists for expression. Of all, Miss Marie Brema, as the Angel, was alone satisfactory. The chorus, of which I will speak in the sequel, seemed quite devoid of any intelligence as to what the words meant. They are so used to straightforward blurting-out, or merely fussy and vigorous counterpoint, square-toed and unmistakeable, that the composer's demands worried them. Nor was Dr Richter much better, for the orchestra over and over again failed to give the right expression, and a real *pianissimo* seemed beyond their powers. (I say nothing of the blight of inaccurate intonation which settled on the first violins with cacophonous results.) The fact is that in *The Dream of Gerontius* Mr Elgar has written a choral work - and a very complicated choral work - which requires the intimate and plastic expression of a song. Through all its complex choruses and complex orchestra there is a thread of personal sentiment which must be realised in all its sensitive changes of mood. For the present I need only say that the sentiment was very far indeed from being realised - by the soloists (in a less degree), by the orchestra (in a greater), and by the chorus (in the greatest degree of all).

I have spoken of the advance in treating of the voice both in solos and chorus, and I have now to say a few words of the orchestra. It is, of course, symphonic throughout, and representative themes are largely used with the happiest effect. There are reminiscences (slight) of Wagner - *Die Walküre* and *Parsifal* - of Greig and Tchaikovsky, to whose use of the different groups of instruments Mr Elgar's score more nearly approximates; but in the main the harmony and scoring are the composer's own. He has shown a plastic gift in the use of the orchestra which none of his other compositions approaches, and though on the top of this orchestra stands many a complicated chorus it is always distinct and clear. In this respect as in the more important one of inspiration *The Dream of Gerontius* stands forth as the most complete example of the modern British school. It owes nothing to pedantic formation; it is no imitation of Bach or Brahms or Wagner; and from first bar to last it is MUSIC. If it has a weakness it is that a note of mysticism which somehow lies behind Newman's realistic and verbally clumsy poem is not quite realised.

Apologists for the performance of the Birmingham chorus in *Elijah* and *The Dream of Gerontius* lay much of the shortcomings of the singing to the fact that the death of Dr Swinnerton Heap changed the choirmasters in the very midst of the choir rehearsals. I am quite willing to admit that swopping horses in the middle of the stream is a dangerous practice, but it seems to me that the shortcomings are not wholly, or to any great extent, caused by the sudden death of Dr Heap. In such a case one might expect uncertainty, but in a familiar work such as the *Elijah* the singing of the chorus is practically the result of many years' training and tradition. And it was very bad indeed. Not only was it uncertain in attack but also totally wanting in expression. Again in Parry's *De Profundis* there was a scrambling roughness which we do not expect or pardon in the singers of our own Royal Choral Society. Things have not bettered since the opening day. *The Dream of Gerontius* is difficult, it is true. But let us distinguish between difficulties which are not completely vanquished and faults of expression. One might reasonably expect the chorus, 'Rescue him', with its semi-chorus, to go a little wrong. It is curiously instrumental in character - the one example in which Mr Elgar has written in his old manner of treating voices. Then again the contrapuntal complexities of the Demons' chorus, and the eight-part choruses of *Praise to the Holiest* might well tax the powers of any choir. But the mistakes were not by any means confined to these difficult parts of the works. If they had been I would have passed them over as leniently as possible. The mistakes, then, of the chorus were precisely those which it is least easy to forgive. They were unintelligent mistakes, and mistakes of bad intonation. The choir sang as if Mr Elgar's music meant nothing, as if when he had indicated a *ppp* he did not mean it; as if when he wrote *crescendo* he meant a sudden barking. There was never any tenderness of tone - never, in short, any expression.

The Musical Standard, 6 October 1900

My report of last week took us to the Wednesday night of the festival. Before going farther I would like to say a few words more on the subject of the choir's singing in general and its performance in Mr Edward Elgar's *The Dream of Gerontius* in particular. There have been apologists for the choir, of course, and to a certain extent some of the apologies put forward have weight. There is certainly something to be said for the disadvantage under which the chorus laboured in losing Dr Swinnerton Heap when the rehearsals were half through. Mr Stockley is an experienced choir-trainer, but his ideas necessarily clashed with those of his predecessor. Then it is held by the choristers themselves that Mr Elgar went the wrong way about to make known his criticism. A letter from a chorister, who must be nameless, speaks of the "gross insult" of which the composer was guilty in telling the choir that it was "all wrong" and that the Chorus of Demons was sung like a drawing-room ballad - and especially when, my correspondent naively remarks, "we had shouted ourselves hoarse." Mr Elgar's protest was possibly ill-timed and unnecessary : at any rate no good is ever done by making sweeping criticisms which leave no room for, and do not suggest, improvements. Doubtless Mr Elgar's protest took the spirit out of the chorus, and it seems to have so seriously injured the pride of many that it is quite a question if all did their loyal best with the composition on Wednesday morning. My correspondent speaks of the immense difficulty of the work, and thinks that some of the notes are almost impossible to sing. But then as I believe only some seven choral rehearsals of *The Dream of Gerontius* took place, it is not possible that a modern work of the calibre of Mr Elgar's could be adequately sung after so few rehearsals. As to the composer's irritation I can quite understand it. He has been working at the Birmingham composition for many years; it contains the best music he has ever written - in fact the best music of the modern English school, in spite of the absurd comparison made by a critic in *The Times* of Elgar with Parry and Stanford (to Elgar's detriment, of course); and, although difficult enough, it is not by any means impossible. As a fact the Birmingham chorus sang the music fairly well so far as accuracy went - at least one might have excused mere slips and unsteadiness - but the performance was lamentably poor in intelligent expression. Intelligence is not, I am sorry to say, a matter of rehearsal only. A semblance of it can be manufactured by mere careful preparation, but it is apt then to degenerate into mere virtuoso tricks of light and shade, such as Mr George Riseley can obtain from his Bristol chorus. The Birmingham choir was particularly unintelligent throughout the festival. It laboured to produce as much noise as possible, just like the least good of the brass bands of the North. It seemed to be impossible for it to sing *piano* for more than a couple of bars without rising quite unwarrantably to a *forte* and thence to a *fortissimo*. Its *crescendos* never swelled out gradually : its *diminuendos* were hardly marked at all. And very seldom did it give us the right tone colour. This was particularly noticeable in Coleridge-Taylor's *Hiawatha*. The performance was bright and vigorous to a degree - accurate, too. But point after point of fun and pathos was missed - especially the pathos. Although I say the chorus sang unintelligently I do not mean to infer that the enthusiastic ladies and gentlemen composing it have no sense of the fine shades of musical meaning. On the contrary I am sure they have, from one piece of evidence alone - the singing of Brahms's *Requiem* on the Friday morning. It was not by any means perfect; it was rough; the quality of voice (perhaps unavoidably at the end of a festival) was occasionally poor, especially among the tenors, who sometimes exhibited quite a German reediness; but the intelligence was there. It may be said that Bach's *St Matthew Passion* should also be bracketed with the *Requiem*, but the kind of intelligence I mean is not demanded by modern performances of Bach with their absence of emotional expression (which Bach experts hold is the right way to sing Bach) - for if you sing your parts accurately you will give a good performance of the work. And the Birmingham singers did sing fairly accurately. But why was the Brahms *Requiem* so much better performed than the *Elijah* or than even Dvořák's *The Spectre's Bride* on the Thursday evening? I may be wrong, but I believe the reason is to be found in the fact that Dr Richter himself was more in sympathy with the work than with any of the others, with the exception of the orchestral compositions, in the programme. How else is one to account for the expressiveness with which the chorus sang 'How lovely is thy dwelling-place' or 'Here on earth have we no continuing city'? And is it not possible that the rough-shod energy with which the chorus trampled out the fun and pathos of *The Song of Hiawatha* was a good deal due to Richter's want of sympathy with the score? Of course I do not know that he was really unsympathetic, but his straightforward conducting certainly looked as if he were. And that brings me to an important point to be considered with regard to these festivals in the future. I must ask my reader's patience while I give a few lines to its consideration, and leave for the present the few details that are required to make this notice of the Birmingham Festival complete.

It is perhaps necessary for the *éclat* of a festival that it should be conducted by a musician of eminence; but apart from the attraction of Dr Richter's name on the bill I think the Birmingham Festivals lose by retaining him as the conductor. He is not, except in one or two works, a great choral conductor. His sympathies do not lie that way. One might ask, perhaps, what conductor of modern mind could sympathise with *Elijah, Messiah, Israel in Egypt,* Sir Hubert Parry's mock Bach, and Dvořák's puerilely romantic *The Spectre's Bride*? But Dr Richter, I fancy, does not sympathise deeply with any choral music. He certainly does not conduct it well. That is one point. The other is common to all the festivals. The chorus at Birmingham is trained by one man and no less than fifty-five rehearsals were held of one sort or another. Dr Richter and the composers of the novelties attended at least one of the choral rehearsals at Birmingham. Then the whole force is put under the chief conductor's control for a Friday evening, the whole of a Saturday and part of a Monday. How, in the name of commonsense, are good results to be obtained? The chorus master is not a machine : he has his ideas ; the chief conductor is not a machine; he has his ideas. What is the chorus to do? At Birmingham it seemed to wait anxiously on Dr Richter, and the consequence was the performances were nothing more than rehearsals. I should not have been surprised if the conductor had stopped the choir and orchestra and bade them begin again at 'one, two, three, four, five - eight bars from forty-six.' The whole arrangement is absurd. There are two alternatives. First, the choir-trainer should conduct the choral works, and many a chorus-master is quite capable of doing so, the orchestral programme being left to the distinguished conductor, native or foreign. Secondly, the conductor-in-chief, if he is to conduct right through the festival, must be accustomed to choral as well as orchestral conducting, and he himself must direct a fair number of the choral rehearsals either with or without a local orchestra. As a matter of fact I believe Sir Arthur Sullivan did do so at Leeds, and at his own expense. Of course this would cost a deal of money. The net profit of the Birmingham Festival will, I hear, exceed £5,000. That sum goes to the General Hospital. Now, supposing my conductor-in-chief were obliged to give a month of these choral rehearsals previous to the festival, it would not cost (I suppose) more than £1,000 - I put the sum very high. The charity would still benefit to the extent of £4,000. Many people will make a clamour that I should advocate a course of action which would result in lessening the sum handed over to a doubtless deserving charity; but I think music has her claims, too, and she will persistently demand that they be paid in full or the festivals in time will cease to be. The outcry this year has been very general and has not been confined to a few confirmed grumblers. Some gentlemen of the Press, I see, have taken it for granted that the appointment of Dr Sinclair to the choirmastership of the Festival Choral Society will have a marked effect on future festivals. But the Festival Choral Society does not supply all the voices for the festival chorus, and, moreover, Dr Sinclair would never be able to give much time to the training of the festival chorus itself as his own Hereford Festival falls on the same year, and he is not free from it until the middle of September. As he is hardly likely to give up Hereford for the sake of the Birmingham Festival we cannot look to the energetic young conductor as the possible reformer of Birmingham. A change or reform, however, has got to be made if Birmingham desires to keep her position in the musical world.

The Musical Standard, 13 October 1900

The critics have seldom been so unanimous in anything as they have been in blaming the chorus at Birmingham. It certainly deserved all that has been said against its singing : but there are some extenuating circumstances. In the first place, the sudden death of Dr Swinnerton Heap, who had been training the choir, did not make for perfection; and, in the second, Mr Edward Elgar's *The Dream of Gerontius* is an exceedingly difficult work. There were fifty-five choral rehearsals, and ten choral compositions were performed, of which *The Messiah, Elijah*, a selection from *Israel in Egypt*, Dvořák's *The Spectre's Bride*, Brahms's *Requiem*, and Bach's *St Matthew Passion* were familiar; and *The Dream of Gerontius*, the last section of *The Song of Hiawatha*, Parry's *De Profundis*, and a selection from William Byrd's Mass were new. That is a good deal for a choir to take in hand; and when we learn that Elgar's new work had but seven rehearsals it is impossible to understand how it could be expected that justice would be done to it. And then the composer made matters worse at the final rehearsal by putting up the backs of the choir. He told them that their singing was "all wrong", and the Chorus of Demons was sung as if it were a drawing room ballad. The fact is that the choir were overworked, and they had not a conductor in Dr Richter who could inspire them with new life at the last moment...

On Wednesday morning came the principal novelty of the festival - Elgar's *The Dream of Gerontius*. I need not give details of the work, since it has been parsed and analysed by the critics of the daily press. It is by far the best work the composer has yet given to the world. There was a time when Mr Elgar could not write for the voice in his larger works. He was too fond of giving them music essentially instrumental in character, with the result that both for soloists and chorus it was extremely difficult to make an effect. There are still some choruses in *The Dream of Gerontius* which are a little too instrumental to be quite effective; but, as a whole, that defect is absent from the new composition. The feature of the music that struck me most was that it was so sincere in tone. The composer seemed to have found a subject which has called forth all that is best in him. He has, of course, conveyed into his music all the realism of Cardinal Newman's poem (such as the Chorus of Demons, to which I have already referred), but he has also caught its underlying tenderness. In spite of its technical cleverness and complexity, the music speaks to the heart, which is just what the modern clever young composer too often fails to do. The difficulty on the choral side is not that the part writing is so very complex, or that the intervals are a strain to the singers, but that the composer requires so much expression. It is not music that can be sung with straightforward energy, as much of Coleridge-Taylor's *Song of Hiawatha* can, for instance. And the Birmingham singers could not manage that expression. They did not know the music well enough, for one thing; and, for another, their great fault, exhibited throughout the festival, is that they pay but little attention to expression.

It may be that choral singing in general is in a backward state compared with that of other branches of the art, and that it will be a long while before our choirs can undertake music of the calibre of Mr Elgar's. It is no mere choral work designed to show off the ordinary capabilities of the choir; for the chorus takes its proper place in the scheme just as if the work were an opera and not a cantata. The orchestra is much more important than is usual in oratorios. The orchestral score makes a running commentary on the emotional drama, and is in itself full of ingenuity, striking themes, and happy instrumentation. As to the solo voices, the tenor has a deal to do. After the simple and poetic little prelude, there is a long monologue for the tenor which shows more than anything in the work that Mr Elgar has made great strides in his writing for the voice. And all through the work the tenor (Gerontius and his Soul) has much to do. Mr Lloyd sang very perfectly; and yet in a way he failed, only not in accuracy or intonation be it understood. His voice is not one in which sorrow or spiritual yearning finds a resting place. It is almost too musical a voice, and is not capable of sufficient change of tone colour for emotional music such as Mr Elgar has written.

The triumph of the festival was the Angel of Miss Marie Brema. She sang, it is no exaggeration to say, with veritable inspiration the beautiful and tender music which Mr Elgar has put into the mouth of the Soul's guardian angel. I am almost inclined to say that it is in these pages, and in the choruses 'Be merciful, be gracious', and 'Rescue him, O Lord, in this evil hour', that the genius of Elgar shines forth with the clearest light. The underlying tenderness of the poem has been realised by the composer with the most touching art. The climax of rejoicing at the end, the realistic horror of the demons, is on the one hand powerful enough, and on the other sufficiently weird; but I fancy that a good many composers could have written these pages, whereas none that I know among living British musicians could have composed such infinitely tender and beautiful music for the phase of the poem (its essential reality) which I have particularised. I missed, however, a tone of other worldliness in the prelude to the second part which is meant to illustrate the upward flight of the soul released from its prison of flesh. Perhaps no one but a Wagner could musically illustrate it.

Mr Elgar has done well; his music is in keeping with the thought of the poem here; but it seems to me just to miss a spiritual something I know not what. This may be thought to be poor criticism, but it is all that I have to offer to account for the impression the music gave me. We certainly have not heard *The Dream of Gerontius* adequately performed. Even the orchestra (I have said enough about the chorus) was not perfect. Over and over again I thought that I saw points in the score which Dr Richter did not properly bring out. The fact is, great conductor as he is, he is by no means gifted with a subtle spirit - a fact which his conducting of the *Tristan* and *Parsifal* selections given at his concerts proves. In broadly glowing music such as that of *Die Meistersinger* he is unapproachable. But though the *Dream* was not presented to us as the composer intended, it was sufficiently well done for us to gain some kind of idea of it. Although not a great work in a conventional sense - that is to say, it makes no pretence to architectural magnificence - it is a work of genius, inasmuch as the composer has poured into it his own soul, and this is expressed in beautiful music written with beautiful art.

Musical Opinion, November 1900

A MEMORY from the CHOIR

William Bennett

Bennett's forthright views are valuable as they give a picture of the doom-laden première from the perspective of the chorus. They first appeared in The Monthly Musical Record.

Many different theories have been advanced for the failure of the chorus in the first performance of *Gerontius* at the Birmingham Festival of 1900, and many condemnatory articles have been written blaming the singers for their lack of interpretative power. One who was a chorister on that memorable occasion feels it time that he should attempt some explanation from the standpoint of the choir. First, let a few examples of the criticisms of the performance be quoted. Sir Richard Terry in his book *On Music's Borders*, published by Fisher Unwin in 1927, wrote :

> Nineteen-hundred saw the production of Elgar's *Gerontius* at the Birmingham Festival, marking a new epoch in choral work. Its disgraceful rendering by the choir showed to what depths of incompetence that self-satisfied and complacent body of once-famous singers had sunk. When the composer was obliged to tell them that they did not understand his music (which was obviously true) their friends raised a howl of indignation at the impertinence of a mere composer in telling a body of such authority as lay-clerks and soulful amateurs that they were not perfect.

The *Musical Times* after the first performance reported (November, 1900) :

> The production of *Gerontius* at the Wednesday morning performance was the great event of the Festival and the feature which will be the best remembered. Unfortunately the memories will not all be as pleasant as they should be owing to the shortcoming of the chorus. The defects may have been due to specific accidental causes. We understand that Hans Richter did not see the full score of *Gerontius* till the evening before he conducted the first orchestral rehearsal at Queen's Hall.
> Owing to the lamented death of Dr Swinnerton Heap, which occurred during the progress of the choral rehearsals for the recent Birmingham Festival, Mr Stockley kindly undertook to discharge the duties of choir-master at the recent meeting.

Now to cite Grove's *Dictionary of Music* (1927 edition) :

At its first appearance *Gerontius* seemed to miss fire. Probably Richter, in spite of his great Wagnerian experience, understood this subtle combination of voices and orchestra less thoroughly than he had grasped the orchestral style of the Enigma Variations. Certainly the Birmingham choir was puzzled by its startlingly new choral idiom.

Fourthly there are Mr Basil Maine's remarks in an article in last December's issue of the *Monthly Musical Record* :

The failure of the first performance of *Gerontius* is famous. The Birmingham chorus could not rise to the occasion, in spite of Richter's conducting and his belief in the greatness of the music.
Some say that his zeal led him to overwork the chorus, but this excuse is hardly good enough. A festival of that kind always involved arduous and concentrated preparation. A more probable reason is that the singers did not understand the music and had not developed a technique sufficient to meet its exacting demands.

First let me answer Sir Richard Terry by saying that if he had been a chorister he would have known that the reason for the failure was not an incompetent choir but an incompetent choir-master - incompetent, that is, by modern standards. Sir Richard speaks of 'lay clerks' in the choir and 'soulful' amateurs. There were no lay clerks in the choir. Such clerks as were there were from counting-houses, not cathedrals. And as for 'soulful amateurs', Birmingham does not breed them. Only twelve choristers out of 350 were 'soulful' enough to refuse the honorarium of £3 or £4 (there were two grades of choristers) granted according to a signed contract to singers who agreed to attend all rehearsals and all performances.

Grove hits the right nail on the head in its statement that 'the choir was puzzled'. It certainly was, but that is not all the story.

Mr Maine is wrong in thinking that Dr Richter overworked the choir through his zeal for the work, but he is right in saying that "they had not developed a technique sufficient to meet the exacting demands". But the choir could have developed that technique had the choir-master enjoyed any understanding of the nature of poetry and had he been a musician conversant with modern developments and in sympathy with Elgar's setting of Newman's poem - a poem which neither he (I venture to say) nor more than half a dozen of the 350 choristers had heard of prior to the festival. Not only had they never heard of it before; but even then they did not trouble to find out about it more than could be gathered from the single-voice chorus parts from which they sang.

The choral programme of the week was a very full one. It included the first performance in Birmingham of Bach's *St Matthew Passion*. Yes, the first! For although Stockley had been conductor of the Festival Choral Society, which supplied most of the members for the Triennial Festival, he had in his forty years' conductorship never attempted a work by J S Bach, his nearest approach to J S Bach being a motet by Johann Christoph Bach (J S Bach's uncle), *I wrestle and pray*. Coleridge-Taylor's *Hiawatha* was also down for its first Birmingham Festival performance, and also Parry's 12-part Psalm *De Profundis*. Dvořák's *Spectre's Bride* and Brahms's *Requiem* were also sung in addition to the usual *Messiah* and *Elijah*.

Stockley at the age of seventy or thereabout had resigned from the Festival Choral Society in 1896 and had incidentally been asked to resign the conductorship of the local orchestra by some of his leading supporters. Dr Swinnerton Heap succeeded him as conductor of the Festival Choral Society in 1896 and as choir-master to the festival of 1897. He commenced the choir-training for the 1900 festival, but he was taken ill in March and he died on 11 July [sic] 1900. The festival committee, instead of appointing a young musician acquainted with modern choral developments, chose the line of least resistance and brought Stockley forth after four years of retirement, during which I question whether he had heard any choral or orchestral music. No doubt Dr Heap's death was partly the cause of the lamentable failure of the choir training that nearly led to disaster. This story should be a warning to festival committees.

When *The Dream of Gerontius* was in rehearsal an old chorister said to me, "I call this a nightmare, not a dream." It was probably a nightmare, too, to old Mr Stockley. Another elderly chorister, when I asked him what he thought of the new oratorio, said to me, "What a queer finish! Surely it would have been better to end with something like the Hallelujah Chorus."

Newman's poem was not then available in a cheap edition, and I remember going to the Birmingham Reference Library to read the work and understand what we were striving to express. If only an able young musician with a love of poetry and the power to explain it to us had been chosen as choir-master a very different tale might have been told of the first performance.

Instead of its being over-rehearsed, as Mr Maine suggests, many of the choristers went to Stockley as the date of the festival approached to try for further help in pages that had never been learned. 'Dispossessed, aside thrust,' was one of these. The cynical utterances in the demons' chorus were bound to shock Stockley, who, when conducting Berlioz's *Faust*, would hurriedly run through the mocking fugal, 'Amen', horrified, never attempting to dramatize it.

Richter, if my memory serves me right, took only one choral rehearsal of *Gerontius*. It was his usual course to devote one evening to each work before the final morning rehearsal with the orchestra. Elgar was present that morning, and I shall never forget his look of disappointment and how he railed, especially at the tenors, when he found that even the notes were not known. As for interpretation, it had never been thought about. Stockley had been the organist at a Congregational chapel, and he was much too anti-Catholic, I imagine, to have any sympathy with Newman's poem or the Catholic Elgar's music. The choir were aware that they did not know the work and the majority sincerely regretted it. I do not hesitate to question Richter's suitability as the conductor of the first performance of *Gerontius*, fine orchestral conductor though he was. What did he know of the subject of the work? Probably nothing. No wonder the performance was a failure. The composer should have been appointed conductor.

The Monthly Musical Record, February 1933

A NEW KIND of MUSICAL ELOQUENCE

Arthur Johnstone

Arthur Johnstone (1861-1904) was born in Staffordshire, and educated at Radley and Oxford. In 1887 he studied for a year at the Cologne Conservatorium. He travelled widely on the continent and taught for a time. In 1896 he became chief music critic on the Manchester Guardian, a post he held until his early death, from complications following appendicitis. Elgar wrote to his widow : "Your dear husband was so much to us musicians". The following extracts are from a memorial volume which was published in 1905.

Birmingham Festival, 3 October, 1900

"The Dream of Gerontius" Cardinal Newman called his poem, with exquisite modesty. How that poem may stand in the estimation of those who share Cardinal Newman's point of view in regard to religious matters is perhaps an important question, but not one with which musical, or any artistic, criticism is concerned. For nothing is more certain about art than that it is subservient to a person's view of life. Artistic or æsthetic criticism must be humble, and must abstain from trespassing on the ground of faith and morals. Indirectly, indeed, æsthetics may have a bearing on these more serious subjects. For is it not written of religious doctrines, "By their fruits ye shall know them"? - and nothing else is in so complete a sense a "fruit" of a religion as a work of art arising therefrom. Nevertheless, the function of æsthetics is not to commend or blame a view of life, but rather to enquire with what eloquence, with what sincerity, with what measure of convincing power the artist expounds his ideas and communicates his feelings, whatever those ideas and feelings may be. With these reflections I find it necessary to premise my notes on Edward Elgar's new work. The reflections are rather solemn, but the new work is very solemn. It is deeply and intensely religious; it is totally unconventional, and must be discussed in an unconventional manner. First, then, let me state a point of difference from all that I have experienced in listening to other oratorios and sacred cantatas, and, I may say, all other musical works with words made by one person and music by another. The point is that *this* music, on the whole, is apt to bring home to the listener the greatness of the poem. The composer has not merely chosen from the poem such material as suited him. He has expounded the poem musically, and to the task of expounding it he has brought what may be described without inflation as the resources of modern music. We shall doubtless hear of plagiarism from *Parsifal*, and there is indeed much in the work that could not have been there but for *Parsifal*. But it is not allowable for a modern composer of religious music to be ignorant of *Parsifal*. One might as well write for orchestra in ignorance of the Berlioz orchestration as write any serious music in ignorance of the Wagnerian symbolism. Edward Elgar does nothing so affected as to ignore the development which, for good or for evil, the language of music underwent at the hands of Wagner. His orchestral prelude, however, reverts to an earlier Wagnerian type. It gives a forecast of the whole story in such wise that at the end of it the imagination has to be carried back. We have the last agony of the sick man, his death, and passage to the unseen. The symbols, though employed in the Wagnerian manner, are, nevertheless, thoroughly original, taking us into an atmosphere and a world absolutely remote from all that is Wagnerian. When the voice of Gerontius (assigned to a tenor solo) enters we are carried back to the death-bed - to the prayers of Gerontius and his companions. A series of choruses with intervening and accompanying passages for the solo voice is devoted to the King of Terrors. Here the music touches the various notes in the gamut of feeling, from the agony of terrors to serene confidence. After the parting of Gerontius, with the words "Novissima hora est," a new voice enters, that of the Priest (baritone), chanting "Proficiscere, anima Christiana." Among the supplications for the departed is a chant three times repeated, each of the two parts ending with a choral "Amen" that bears a tender echo of the mediæval 'Cantus fictus.' An extended section of chorus and semi-chorus bring the first part of the cantata to a peaceful and prayerful ending.

In the second part the soul of Gerontius is winging its way towards the celestial regions, holding colloquy with an angel. There is a Dantesque passage in which a chorus of demons is overheard by the pair - the soul and the angel. Gerontius is encouraged by the angel. Echoes of earthly voices, praying for the departed soul, are borne up from the earth, and in the end the soul of Gerontius is affectionately delivered over to Purgatory by the angel, there to await suffering indeed, but in resignation and in the assurance of salvation.

Naturally the prevalent poetic note in such a work is the mystical exaltation, now of the contrite sinner, now of the aspiring saint. The chief climax is reached, not at the end, but in the hymn of the Angels, 'Praise to the Holiest in the Height,' recurring before the departure to Purgatory. But the whole work sings "Praise to the Holiest in the Height *and in the Depth.*" A powerfully contrasting note is heard in the death-agony of Gerontius and, above all, in the chorus of demons occurring in the second part. Here a comparison with Berlioz is simply inevitable - for Edward Elgar's dramatic power admits of comparison with the great masters. His demons are much more terrible than those of Berlioz, who was a materialist in the profound sense - not, that is, in virtue of more or less shifting beliefs, but of unalterable temperament. Infinitely remote from that of Berlioz is the temperament revealed in Edward Elgar's music, which, like parts of the poem, fairly merits the epithet "Dantesque."

Lower Rhine Festival, Düsseldorf 22 May, 1902.

"Ever since the far-off times of the great madrigal composers, England has played but a modest part in the concert of the great musical powers. For the products of the musical mind it has depended almost entirely on importation, and has exported nothing but works of a lighter order." Such are the words with which the German author of the *Gerontius* programme, specially written for this Festival, introduces his subject. The economic metaphor is ingenious. It does not imply too much or justify the state of things to which it refers. Rightly or wrongly, Germany and the Continent of Europe in general did not feel that serious English music was a thing to be taken seriously, and to that fact the writer refers with ingenious delicacy, going on to say that about the turn of the century a change began to be noticeable. Everyone conversant with musical affairs knows how that change was brought about, though not everyone on our own side of the Channel cares to admit what he knows. It is in the main to Edward Elgar - a man who has done his best work living quietly in the Malvern Hills, without official position of any kind, remote from social distraction and the strife of commercialism - that the change is due. The presentation of so lengthy a work as *The Dream of Gerontius* at a Rhine Festival has a kind of significance that the English musical public would do well to consider. The programme is much more carefully selected than at our own festivals, the idea being not at all that it should contain "something for all tastes," but that it should be characteristic of musical art as it now stands, giving only the most typically excellent of newer compositions, and of older compositions only those upon which it is felt that contemporary genius had been more particularly nourished. It is not accidental that on the present occasion the names of Handel, Mendelssohn, Schumann are absent while Bach is very abundantly represented; Beethoven's name figures in connection with the most modern in feeling of all his works (the C minor Symphony), and Liszt's with his revolutionary *Faust Symphony*. Nor is it accidental that the preference is given to Strauss among German and Elgar among English composers. For those are the men who really carry the torch, and the Germans are not to be deceived in such matters.

The performance of *Gerontius* yesterday evening had a good many features of special interest. Full justice was done to the instrumental part of the work by the magnificent Festival orchestra of a hundred and twenty-seven performers. Those peculiar qualities of the imagination which make of Dr Wüllner, jun., by far the best representative of Gerontius as yet found, were once more demonstrated, and the part of the Angel was given by Miss Muriel Foster with the wonderfully beautiful and genuine voice that has long been recognised as her most remarkable gift, and with considerably greater and more expressive eloquence than any previous experience might have led one to expect from her. In the bass parts of the Priest and the Angel of Death Professor Messchaert sang with wonderful dramatic power, and the semi-chorus, seated in a line before the orchestra, acquitted themselves almost to perfection in the delicate task that they have to perform throughout the death-bed scene. I have already expressed the view that the final section of the first part, beginning with the Priest's "Proficiscere, anima Christiana," is the point at which one first becomes conscious of actual genius in the composition; but now, after further study and another complete hearing of the work, I am not quite satisfied with that statement. Perhaps at that point a good many listeners first become clearly conscious of the composer's genius. But on looking back at the extraordinary eloquence and beauty of the musical symbolism in the prelude and death-agony of Gerontius, one perceives that the *quietus* which comes to the spirit in the scene following Gerontius's death is merely a climax in a process that really begins with the first notes. The heavenly calm at the opening of the second part I realised yesterday more thoroughly than ever before. Splendid as the treatment of the hymn "Praise to the Holiest in the Height" is, the final section is not so completely adequate as the rest. The truth is that the composer there found himself in presence of a task hopelessly beyond the powers of any mortal except Bach. In the "Sanctus" heard on Sunday evening the shining circles of the heavenly choir are, as it were, made audible to the ears of mortals. Bach could only do it once, and no other composer could do it at all. Elgar gives a beautiful and grandly conceived hymn of the Church Triumphant, and with that we may well rest satisfied. He is in the main a dramatic composer, and, in those cases where he enters the domain of purely religious music, he gravitates back rather to Palestrina, with his "souls like thin flames mounting up to God," than to the greater and serener spirit of Bach.

Preliminary Article, 12 March, 1903

In subject, though not in treatment, this oratorio - the first performance of which in Manchester will be given this evening - is closely akin to the morality play *Everyman*. Gerontius is not a historical character, but a typical person, belonging to no particular age or country. He is further like Everyman in being a layman, who has lived in the world, as distinguished from the Church, and in being just a plain, well-meaning man, without very great or shining qualities. The poem on which the oratorio is founded begins, at a later stage than *Everyman*, with the death-bed scene, and does not end with the death of Gerontius's mortal part, but peers wistfully into the world beyond, and "under the similitude of a dream," tells much of what holy men have imagined about the experiences of Christian souls going to their account under the guidance of angels.

In the oratorio the utterances of Gerontius are assigned to a tenor soloist, who in the first part has to deliver the broken phrases of the sick man "near to death," and in the second the delicately restrained raptures of the soul that "feels in him an inexpressive lightness and a sense of freedom," as he gradually becomes conscious of the angelic presence that is bearing him along towards the heavenly regions. The only other soloist in the first part is the Priest (bass), who delivers the solemn "Proficiscere, anima Christiana, de hoc mundo," as the soul of Gerontius quits the body. In the second part the second and third soloists represent, one the Guiding Angel (mezzo-soprano) and the other the Angel of the Agony (bass), who, at the most solemn moment of the oratorio, is recognised by the Soul as "the same who strengthened Him, what time he knelt, lone in the garden shade bedewed with blood." The semi-chorus in the first part is the group of "assistants," or friends gathered about the dying man's bed. The function of the chorus in the first part is not defined, but it may be taken as voicing the prayers and aspirations of other faithful souls, aware of Gerontius's case and sympathising with him. In the second part the chorus is now of "angelicals," now of demons. The semi-chorus again represents the voices of friends on earth, which at one point are imagined as again becoming audible to the Soul, and also takes part in certain phases of the great hymn "Praise to the Holiest in the Height," where the vocal harmony falls into as many as twelve parts.

Those who are to hear this music to-day for the first time should beware of judging it by false standards. Let them be prepared for the fact that from beginning to end there is not a particle of anything in the least like Handel or Mendelssohn. Without the slightest intention of doing anything revolutionary, but simply following the bent of his own genius, the composer here brushes aside the conventions of oratorio very much as Wagner brushed aside the conventions of opera, and justifies himself just as thoroughly in so doing. To hear the *Gerontius* music is to become acquainted with by far the most remarkable and original personality that has arisen in musical Britain since the days of Purcell. One might trace the manifestations of that originality in the harmony, that always shows a touch both sensitive and sure, in the orchestration and interplay of chorus and semi-chorus, in the amazing sweetness and depth of feeling that sounds in the Angel (mezzo-soprano solo) music, in the force and truth of musical expression which, for the most part, extends even to elements of minor importance in the work. But for the present these broad indications must suffice, and we will only add the warning that the music is powerful, subtle, and of manifold significance, not to be judged in too great a hurry, and yielding up the best of its secrets only to those who listen repeatedly and study between.

Hallé Concerts, 13 March, 1903

Originality is disadvantageous to a composer at first in two ways. The more obvious is that listeners find the music speaking to them in an unknown or partially unknown tongue, and are displeased; and the less obvious, that players and singers cannot, as a rule, do justice to an unfamiliar style. When it is a case of winning recognition for something new and original a thoroughly adequate rendering is half the battle. Such a rendering carries with it a sense of enjoyment and satisfaction in the performers, and there is always a chance that this may to some extent communicate itself to the public; whereas in the other case the embarrassment of the performers will certainly communicate itself, and the audience attribute everything unsatisfactory to the unknown or insufficiently guaranteed composer. In Elgar's *Gerontius* the originality is strong and unmistakeable, and the performers find their technical skill severely taxed. But fortunately the composer has a clear head; he knows the technique of each instrument and he never miscalculates. Performers therefore find their task, though often difficult, is always possible and, further, that the result is always satisfactory. For Elgar has an ear; he is a man of tone, and does not care for music that looks well on paper but sounds rather muddy. These points, known to those who for some time past have taken a close interest in Elgar's work, made it possible to hope that the Manchester performance of his great oratorio would be a striking success, and perhaps even throw a new light on the merits of the composition; and it can scarcely be questioned that the experience of yesterday evening fulfilled those hopes. It was doubtless the most carefully prepared of the performances that have been given thus far in this country. Dr Richter was, for various reasons, peculiarly anxious that it should go well; Mr Wilson made up his mind some time ago that whatever conscientious work could do to secure a worthy performance should be done; the hopes and endeavours of choirmaster and conductor were seconded by the choir in an admirable spirit; and, though it seems that for some time the usual difficulties of an unfamiliar style were felt, not a trace of any such thing was to be observed in the performance, the remarkably willing and energetic style in which the choral singers had grappled with their task bearing its proper fruit in a rendering that sounded spontaneous and unembarrassed, as though the singers were sure of the notes and could give nearly all their attention to phrasing, expression, and dynamic adjustments. In the highest degree remarkable, too, was the orchestral performance. Passages of such peculiar difficulty as the rushing string figures, that represent the strains of heavenly music overheard by the Soul and the Angel as they approach the judgment-seat, came out with much greater distinctness than we have ever heard before, and we had a similar impression at many other points in the performance, which was as delicate as it was precise in detail and broad in style. But experience of all the complete performances yet given induces us to think that the difference between thorough success and ordinary half-success with this oratorio depends more on the semi-chorus than on any other point, and this is where the pre-eminence of last night's rendering, among all yet given in this country, is most unquestionable. Though not placed in front of the orchestra - as they should have been and, we hope, will be next time, - this group of twenty picked singers was really excellent. The voices blended well, and their combined tone was clearly distinguishable from the larger choir's. At the notoriously dangerous points, such as the re-entry with the 'Kyrie' after the invocation of "angels, martyrs, hermits, and holy virgins," there was no hint of embarrassment, and they played their part as a slightly more delicate choral unit with absolute success in the litany and throughout the marvellous concluding chorus of the first part, where, as the original analysis suggested, the noble pedal-point harmonies symbolise the swinging of golden censers, as the supplications of the friends and of the church rise up to the throne of God. Among the astonishingly new kinds of musical eloquence obtained in this work by the interplay of chorus and semi-chorus it is worth drawing special attention to the tenor and alto unison in the semi-chorus on p108 (we quote from the second edition). The passage is not difficult, but to realise the particular effect of tone as well as it was realised yesterday shows exquisite adjustment.

As principal soloist Mr John Coates had an enormously difficult task, which he performed about as well as was possible with the vocal material that has been assigned to him by nature. All that thorough knowledge of the part, together with high artistic intelligence, could do was done. His voice did not break on the high B♭ (p34), and he seemed to be well disposed, notwithstanding his recent illness. Though it is usually said that Elgar writes better for orchestra than for choir, and better for choir than for the solo voice, he was very finely inspired when he conceived the part of the mezzo-soprano Angel. The opening arioso,

"My work is done," is a most lovely song, to which the haunting "Alleluia" phrase forms a kind of refrain. But even this - one of the very few detachable things in the oratorio - is not the best of the Angel's music. It is surpassed by the other song, "Softly and gently, dearly ransomed Soul," where the dropping of the Soul down into the waters of Purgatory is accompanied by music of quite unearthly sweetness and tenderness. These are things which make it seem almost a shame to discuss this work in any purely technical aspect. Miss Brema made the Angel's part one of the few entirely satisfactory features of the first performance, and again yesterday her nobly expressive style did full justice to the marvellous beauty of the music. Mr. Black was vocally irreproachable in the part of the Priest who speeds the parting soul of Gerontius, and again as the Angel of the Agony in the second part.

In reference to a musical composition the word "dramatic" has sometimes to be used in a sense different from "theatrical." Thus the two great Passions by Bach - the *St Matthew* and the *St John* - both have a dramatic element so strong that at certain points the music becomes altogether dramatic. Yet no sane person ever called it theatrical, in the sense of unfit for a church. By "dramatic" in such cases one means two things - (1) having thematic material that is conceived with a certain vividness, in reference to a particular situation or mood of feeling; (2) developed according to procedure that does not sacrifice the vividness to formal or structural considerations. In this sense, then, we call Elgar's *Gerontius* a dramatic composition from beginning to end. To find fault with it for the absence of choral climax in the manner of Handel and Mendelssohn is as much out of place as it would be with Wagner's *Tannhäuser*. On the other hand, we do not agree with the criticism that *Gerontius* is Wagnerian music. In two places there is a brief and faint suggestion of *Parsifal*, first in the *sostenuto* theme for cor anglais and 'celli that enters in the fifty-second bar of the Prelude and recurs in some form at several points in the course of the work, and secondly in a recurrent phrase for strings at the entry of the recitative assigned to the Angel of the Agony - and to some extent throughout that recitative, which vaguely recalls *Parsifal*. The other elements we find to be unlike Wagner and unlike every other composer but Elgar. These elements it is convenient to classify, not according to the usual technical or formal principle, but according to a dramatic principle. One notes, in the first place, four main categories - (1) the purely human; (2) the ecclesiastical; (3) the angelic; (4) the demonic. The Prelude opens with the symbols of Judgment and Prayer. Next the 'slumber' theme enters, to be joined at the fourteenth bar by the 'Miserere.' The note of feeling contracts and sinks towards utter abasement, which reaches the lowest point in the cor anglais theme with *tremolando* accompaniment. But now the sick man's despair finds expression in a loud cry, which is answered in the majestic and ringing tones that remind him to face death hopefully. A quite new musical element enters with the Andantino theme, developed at some length, and informs the penultimate section of the noble tone-poem, which continues till a brief *reprise* of the slumber theme suggests the passing of the soul. New phases of the Judgment theme connect the Prelude with the opening recitative, and here the imagination has to be carried back, as usual after the Prelude of a dramatic composition, which as a rule epitomises a good part of the action. It is evident, then, that the Prelude is concerned only with the first two of the categories above enumerated - that is to say, with the purely human and the ecclesiastical, and not at all with the angelic or demonic. Of the angelic music the principal elements, in addition to those already mentioned, are the various phases of the great hymn "Praise to the Holiest in the Height." The extraordinary demon music would in itself offer material for an essay. Here we can only touch on a few obvious features - the upward rushing semiquaver figure in chromatic fourths, which is grotesque and rat-like; the three-part figure for strings in quavers which is first heard with the words "Tainting the hallowed air," but belongs more particularly to "in a deep hideous purring have their life"; the terrific fugato "dispossessed, thrust aside, chuck'd down"; the sinister and ominous four-note theme "To every slave and pious cheat": the *motif* of demonic pride, p83; and the sarcastic prolongation of the last word in "He'll slave for hire." The long chorus formed of these elements is a welter of infernal but most eloquent sound, the enormous technical difficulties all of which were completely mastered yesterday.

The FIRST PERFORMANCE of GERONTIUS

Mrs Richard Powell

Mrs Richard Powell is better known as Dora Penny, whom Elgar captured in the Enigma Variations as Dorabella. *In 1937, she published a book of reminiscences entitled* Edward Elgar - Memories of a Variation.[1] *This is a later piece which appeared in* The Musical Times *in 1959.*

Having heard Elgar play the music of Gerontius on the piano for hours together during the few months preceding the first performance, and having got to know a good deal of it fairly well, I was looking forward to hearing it properly performed, complete with chorus, orchestra and soloists. But it was not at all a good performance and was a dreadful disappointment. It lacked so much of what I knew was there. I could not make out what was the matter and I remember getting anxious and rather frightened, largely on account of the faulty intonation of so much of the choral singing.

Many people have asked me what happened and whether the performance was really as bad as was made out. Knowing that I was there in the Birmingham Town Hall that day, surely I could tell them what happened - and why?

I have never written about this or spoken of it in public. I really think that we all tried to forget it. But now, when nearly everyone connected with the performance, including players, singers and management, is dead, I feel it is almost a duty to set down my memory of it and explain some of the causes of the trouble.

A great many most unfortunate and tiresome things had happened. In the first place, Elgar had himself been to blame in being dilatory in getting the chorus parts corrected and returned to the printers. I am pretty firmly convinced that Elgar had not realised the difficulty the

---

[1]   Mrs Richard C Powell : *Edward Elgar - Memories of a Variation* (London, 1937)

chorus was going to have to learn this music. Choruses in those days had been brought up on Handel and Mendelssohn and this music was what one might describe as a new language. How could they master it in just a few weeks? Elgar's mind was soaked in this music of his and therefore it must have seemed natural and easy to him.

An aunt of mine (wife of Archdeacon Hodgson, of Handsworth) who was a soprano in the chorus, wrote to me soon after some of the chorus parts had been received - "How lovely this music is! but shall we *ever* learn it in time?" - and she was a fine sight-reader.

Then, in May 1900, soon after the combined rehearsals had begun, came the illness and sudden death of the beloved chorus master Dr Swinnerton Heap (who was an enthusiastic admirer of Elgar's music) and his replacement by the former chorus-master, Mr Stockley (who was not). Mr Stockley was an elderly and rather old-fashioned man; he was also a strong Protestant and was not in sympathy with either the words or the music of *Gerontius* or with its composer, and I think he must have allowed his personal views to colour his actions to some extent. Dr Heap's death was a terrible blow, and the old proverb about changing horses while crossing a stream came to mind. Apart from the sorrow we all felt, and the loss Dr Heap was to many choral societies in the Midlands, it was undoubtedly a very bad stroke of luck for Birmingham at this particular time. Dr Heap was a very able musician, a splendid chorus-trainer and a delightful personality.

Dr Hans Richter, who conducted the Festival, was at that time pretty well beyond criticism, but in my opinion, and I was not alone, even he misjudged the difficulty of the work. His mind was not intimately familiar with this new music as was the composer's, and, moreover, he was both surprised and worried to find at his first rehearsal how ill-prepared the choir was to give him what he wanted. After what was to have been the final rehearsal the work was found to be so far from ready that he was obliged to ask for an additional long rehearsal.

I heard, years afterwards, that he spent half the night after his first rehearsal pacing up and down in his hotel bedroom with the full score stuck up on the mantelpiece - learning it! Another fact that will probably astonish choral singers of today was that at all rehearsals, and at the performance too, the chorus were using single chorus-parts;

thus, the sopranos, for instance, could not see what the other sections were supposed to be singing. Of course, large choirs often use these single parts for familiar works as it saves a lot of turning over.

The lack of sympathy between Elgar and Stockley was responsible for the unfortunate fact that Elgar was not asked to attend any of the *Gerontius* rehearsals until Hans Richter took over. Elgar was then, naturally, asked to come.
All this happened nearly sixty years ago, and it is probably quite difficult for people now to realise that the music of *The Dream of Gerontius* came as something entirely new, and was like a new language for all performers, players as well as singers, to master in just a few weeks, when it really needed a whole season's work. In addition to this, there was, of course, other new music in the Festival programme to be learnt as well. The chorus was, I am told, dead tired before the Festival opened.

At the time of the 'Jubilee of *Gerontius*', in October 1950, the Birmingham City Choral and Orchestral Society kindly invited me to be present, and after a very fine performance I was fortunate enough to get in touch with an elderly tenor who had sung in the chorus in 1900, and he told me a lot of interesting things. He said that he and some of his friends in the tenor section of the chorus got together and rehearsed at home. Evidently they were very keen and enthusiastic and "they knew their parts well and made no mistakes". Far from having rehearsed at home, the basses did not know their parts properly and so, instead of being the reliable foundation to a chorus that basses usually are, they were a positive deterrent to correct singing.

Even one of the soloists, Plunket Greene, was not perfect in his part. In a place in Part 2 he came in a semitone wrong and stuck to it until the end of the piece! I heard that he was dreadfully upset and miserable afterwards. In later years I have heard the truth about that. The particular place in which he made that mistake (fig 106) is rather difficult, but, if he had not been nervous, he would not have forgotten to wait for a certain lead given by one of the wind instruments.

Talking of soloists, how odd it is to note that Edward Lloyd sang the part of Gerontius. Of course, he was at the top of the tree in those days. He had a splendid voice, and it was said that he could read or sing anything at sight correctly, but he is not one's idea of Gerontius, fine singer of Handel arias and drawing-room ballads though he was. I do not remember anything particular about his singing that day. Marie Brema, the well-known opera singer, sang the part of the Angel very well and I am told that she saved the situation in Part 2 several times. Plunket Greene, again, is hardly one's idea either of the Priest in Part I or of the Angel of the Agony in Part 2.

I shall never forget leaving the Town Hall that day after the performance. I was so disappointed and miserable; I could not help thinking of poor Elgar and the intense disappointment he must be suffering. I avoided everyone who might want to ask me how I had "enjoyed" it, and was thankful, that day, when I got home. However, there were some people in the audience who knew and understood. One was Professor Julius Buths, of Düsseldorf; Jaeger, of Novello's ('Nimrod' of the *Enigma Variations*), was escorting him and the two of them sat together. In his long letter to me, full of misery and disappointment, Jaeger told me that "directly the performance was over, Buths grasped my hand (*coram publico*) and blurted out 'ein wunderbares Werk; eins der schönsten Werke die ich kenne'." Immensely impressed by the work, he started on the translation of the words into German directly he got home. A very fine performance was given in Düsseldorf in 1902, to which the composer and his wife were invited. It was a brilliant success. I shall never forget the excitement on my next visit to the Elgars at Malvern when Mrs Elgar showed me the two huge laurel wreaths hanging up in the study ("like cartwheels," Elgar said; "what to do with them on the platform I did not know"). There were large red satin bows on each, inscribed in German. (I wondered how on earth they managed to get them home!) Mrs Elgar spoke German very well. After all these years I can fancy I hear her now; her light, high voice singing about the house - "Preis Gottes Heiligkeit in der Höh".

There was also a very musical connection of mine at the 1900 Festival, Mrs Meath Baker (wife of 'W.M.B' of the *Enigma Variations*). She and I sat together that day. She knew the music pretty well and had done a good deal of 'turning-over' for Elgar too. When it was over she said : "A very poor performance, but what a wonderful work!" What a pity a remark like that did not appear in the Press; it would have helped!

The Press accounts that followed were mostly concerned with pointing out all the mistakes, and one critic excelled himself by commiserating with Messrs Novello, "whose philanthropy had risked overloading their shelves with more useless copies". One or two of the writers actually had the penetration to see that they had been listening to something very much out of the ordinary. It makes one think that music critics, as a race, are much better at pointing out imperfections in performance than at assessing the value, or otherwise, of works that are new to them. There are many morals that could be drawn, but I think that by far the most important is that if a work is great enough it does not matter in the long run how poor the first performance is; the greatness will win through.

Far from being put off by the disappointment of the production of *Gerontius* at Birmingham in 1900, various cathedral choirs and musical societies studied and performed the work, and the beauty and value of it soon began to be realised. So the regrettable first performance was gradually forgotten.

Unfortunately, London did not hear *Gerontius* until 1903, but the West Country could not, and would not, wait. The Three Choirs Festival at Worcester in September 1902 gave it; Sheffield followed in October of the same year, and early in 1903 it was heard in Manchester, Wolverhampton and Hanley. So fine was this performance by the North Staffordshire Festival Chorus and Orchestra that they were asked to give it in Westminster Cathedral in June 1903. In the spring of 1904 *Gerontius* was heard at an Elgar Festival at Covent Garden and it won golden opinions there.

In 1957, the Elgar centenary year, *Gerontius* was performed at one of the Promenade Concerts under Sir Malcolm Sargent. I am told that the crowded audience listened spellbound throughout, and were obviously enthralled by the music. After a second or two at the end, when all performers stood motionless, the applause that followed was tremendous.

Elgar was a master of orchestration and it is often said how fine is the orchestration in *Gerontius*, but a thing that, oddly enough, is never mentioned, is the skill with which the words have been chosen from the poem and how beautifully they have been set to music. This work took Elgar a long time, but with the help of his great friend Father Knight, who had given him a copy of the poem as a wedding present in 1889, the work was done.

Finally, since it has become common practice to call *Gerontius* an oratorio, it is worth pointing out that Elgar himself was careful not to do so. On the title-page we find :

> *The Dream of Gerontius,* by Cardinal Newman, set to music for mezzo-soprano, tenor and bass soli, chorus and orchestra, by Edward Elgar

Both *The Apostles* and *The Kingdom* he called oratorios. You may be inclined to say "What's in a name?" but I suggest that it really becomes important when misapprehension leads to the making of comparisons which are quite inadmissible. The principal characteristic of oratorios is that they are episodic, and usually have words that are taken from or based on, Holy Scripture. *Gerontius* has continuous dramatic unity, and this places it, as Elgar was well aware, in a different category.

The Musical Times, February 1959

HANS RICHTER and GERONTIUS

Gareth H Lewis

Gareth Lewis (1938-1992) was a founder member of the London Branch of the Elgar Society, and as a member of the London Philharmonic Choir took part in recordings of Elgar under Boult, Handley, and Slatkin. His knowledge of choral and orchestral music was profound, and he was an expert on Welsh music. For many years Gareth was the chief record critic of the Elgar Society Journal; yet still found time to be a busy and well-loved GP.

Without a doubt, Hans Richter deserves to be remembered with the deepest gratitude for his courageous championship of Elgar's music in the years around the turn of the century - when the composer was still experiencing difficulty in arousing the enthusiasm of his fellow countrymen. In particular Richter gave superb first performances of the *Enigma Variations* and the First Symphony. It is sad therefore that to many Elgarians the name of Hans Richter calls to mind chiefly the disastrous first performance of *The Dream of Gerontius*, which he conducted at Birmingham on 3 October 1900. There are many puzzling features about Richter's part in this failure. We know that the chorus was ill-prepared and that their morale had been undermined by the sudden death the previous June of their chorus-master Swinnerton Heap. We also know that the soloists experienced difficulty both with the idiom and the vocal writing. One would have expected, however, that Richter, with his reputation for understanding new and unfamiliar music, would have grasped the essentials of the work sufficiently firmly to have been able to convey a sense of leadership and to guide the choristers to greater confidence and insight. When we look more closely at Richter's personality, however, it becomes clear that there was a deficiency in his emotional spectrum which

Richter conducts - from a contemporary postcard

put a surprisingly wide range of music outside his understanding - and it is probable that *Gerontius* came into this category.

Elgar, talking to Arnold Bax in 1901, bitterly blamed Richter for not knowing the score of *Gerontius*. This is hardly likely to have been the case. Richter's reputation as an interpreter of new music had been gained by careful and painstaking preparation of his performances. Richter had access to a copy of the full score early in September 1900 (giving sufficient time for a musician of his calibre to study it in detail) and it would seem, from Elgar's correspondence with Jaeger, that the composer and the conductor went through the work together at that time. We cannot therefore blame Richter for not having done his homework, and we must look more deeply for the reasons for the failure of *Gerontius*. Hans Richter was Hungarian by birth, having been born at Raab in 1843. His mother was an opera singer with close associations with Wagner (she sang in the first performance of *Tannhäuser*) and she arranged for the young Hans to become a chorister in Vienna at the age of ten, and for him to study both the horn and the piano. It was presumably through his mother also that he became acquainted with Wagner - in the 1860s he assisted the composer by preparing fair copies of *Meistersinger* for the printers. As Richter's conducting career became established, he naturally emerged as one of the leading champions of Wagner's music, and he was invited to conduct *The Ring* at Bayreuth in 1876. Two years later he became chief conductor of the Bayreuth Festival.

It was as a Wagner conductor that Richter began his career in Britain, sharing with the composer the conducting of a Wagner Festival at the Royal Albert Hall in 1877. From 1879 Richter was an established part of London musical life, following the launching of the first of the very successful annual series of Richter concerts. After the death of Sir Michael Costa in 1885, Richter was invited to become the musical director of the Birmingham Triennial Festival. On the face of it this was an appointment difficult to justify; Richter's reputation in this country was exclusively as an orchestral conductor. Although he had conducted opera on the Continent, he had had little involvement with large-scale choral works - the main fare at the major British festivals. He was still unfamiliar with the work of those British composers kept busy providing the festivals with their regular 'novelties' and he had no experience in the administration of such large-scale festivals. On the other hand, the Birmingham committee no doubt recognised the commercial value of capturing a young conductor with a rapidly growing international reputation. There was, of course, considerable opposition to Richter's appointment. It was felt that a British conductor would have been more suitable in view of the nature of the Festival - and in particular the appointment was seen as a personal snub to Sullivan, who was generally considered to be the conductor most suitably qualified. Sullivan expressed his own dissatisfaction to his friend, the critic Joseph Bennett, tempering his disappointment with his characteristic generosity and magnanimity : "I should certainly have considered it an honour if they had offered me the festival, whether I could have undertaken it or not. But it is not entirely selfish, for not a thought of envy or regret should I have felt if Cowen, Stanford, Barnby or Randegger had been selected. They would have done the work well ... I think it is an affront to all of us English." In general the appointment of Richter to the Birmingham Festival was considered to be yet another example of a committee of businessmen failing to understand the musical problems involved.

Things seem to have started well, however. Many years later Stanford, in an essay on the great conductors of his youth, recalled the effect Richter had at Birmingham. He wrote : "England had been, for long, in a condition of mezzo-forte in orchestral playing. The best material was there, but performances were only pretty good. To make them super-excellent as players was the work of an authoritative man such as Richter. He swept away the ridiculous hash of everlasting items from opera... He restored the orchestra to its proper balance... He signalised his tenure at Birmingham by securing Joachim to play. He knew his value, and the personal effect the great violinist would have upon all the players who came into contact with him. With that Festival mediocrity disappeared."

Undoubtedly Richter's influence on the standard of orchestral playing in this country was considerable. Stories abound of his patient coaxing of players to produce tone-colours from their instruments which were outside their previous experience. In particular, as a horn player himself, he laid great emphasis on improving the standard of tone production of horn players. He was not above stepping down amongst the orchestra in order to take the instrument from the player's hand in order to give a personal demonstration of his requirements. Stanford, on the evidence of the essay already quoted, and which was published in his collection *Interludes* in 1924, clearly held Richter in high regard - but he was by no means blind to his limitations, and it is from Stanford's picture of Richter's musical personality that we can obtain a glimpse of those blind-spots which inevitably led to the failure of the 1900 *Gerontius* performance :

> Richter was often stiff in his reading of an unfamiliar score. [He] was, and remained, a species of ideal bandmaster... for him, all music which was not German was foreign. Richter was all for straightforwardness. He hated extravagance, and even took the 'diablerie' out of Berlioz. He took everything from the standpoint of commonsense; for this reason he was strongest in what he knew best - Beethoven, Weber and the *Meistersinger*. He was not often electric [although] he had magnetism... He had an even temper, was always careful [and was] little affected by moods.

Despite this apparent equanimity, Richter was undoubtedly an authoritarian conductor of the old-fashioned type. Eugene Goossens who, as a young man in Liverpool, regularly attended Hallé concerts conducted by Richter, recalls in his autobiography *Overture and Beginners* an incident when an unfortunate cymbal player miscounted his bars in the finale of the Dvořák *New World* symphony. The resultant misplaced crash drew a glare of fury from the conductor - the full horror of which can readily be imagined by anyone who has seen a photograph of Richter's stern, imposing figure. Richter's eye remained fixed on the poor musician until the end of the movement, and at the end of the concert the man was instantly dismissed. Despite incidents like this, Richter was held in great affection by British orchestral players although Goossens goes so far as to describe him as 'a martinet'.

As far as Richter's conducting technique is concerned, Goossens gives a description which perhaps clarifies what Stanford meant by an 'ideal bandmaster':

> There is a tendency among my older colleagues to disparage his conducting powers in the light of dashier and more recent stick technique. Richter's technique was simplicity itself. He used a short, thick piece of cane with a padded grip, and indulged in few superfluous gestures... The beat was a square one, vehement, simple and best suited to classic and romantic styles. Especially in long sustained rhythmic patterns did he preserve a marvellous continuity of style.

From these accounts we can conclude that Richter was a thoroughly sound, conscientious and painstaking musician, of the highest integrity, but ultimately perhaps just a little dull and emotionally contained as an interpreter. Against this, however, must be placed his indefatigable support for new music and he clearly regarded it as his duty as an internationally respected conductor to use his position to give the works of young composers a fair hearing - whether or not he himself felt temperamentally in tune with their idiom. Goossens reminds us of his early championship of Richard Strauss "and much other fairly provocative music" and says that only French impressionism "utterly escaped him". Yet his inhibitions sometimes prevented his getting close to the works of the more mature German composers of the latter half of the nineteenth century - Stanford tells a story of Brahms leaving a concert hall in anger at Richter's treatment of the slow movement of his First Symphony.

By the time of the preparation for the *Gerontius* performance, Elgar had every reason to feel confident of Richter's ability to understand his work - after all Richter had already given two splendid performances of the *Enigma Variations. Gerontius*, however, occupies a totally different world - much further from the mainstream of European music of that time, and consequently further from Richter's safest ground. Perhaps if the preparations for the performance had been less disrupted, Richter's professional competence might have resulted in an adequate representation of the work. Under the circumstances only the inspiration that comes from total involvement could have pulled together the scattered threads. Elgar's friends shared his bitterness. The great Sheffield choral conductor, Henry Coward, not only attended the performance, but had been Elgar's guest at several of the choral rehearsals, including the one when Elgar's frustration allowed him to express his dissatisfaction with the quality of the choral singing in rather immoderate terms - succeeding only in alienating the singers still further. Coward was in no doubt that Richter should be held chiefly responsible for the failure of the Birmingham performance, and in his memoirs had this to say about the great conductor's limitations:

> Even the cleverest man has his prejudices and limitations in sympathies, outlook, and grasp of musical idiom. A striking case of limited attainment is afforded by Dr Hans Richter. He was undoubtedly a great orchestral conductor, but as a choral conductor he was quite ordinary. The worst performances of *Messiah, Faust* (Berlioz) and *Gerontius* were under his baton, and, though he was excused on grounds of his lack of sympathy with, or knowledge of, the idiom of the works, this did not make for the

musical success of a festival. He, being a German, was not criticised, whereas, for a similar result, an Englishman would have been flayed alive.

Richter's career in Britain lasted little over a further decade after *Gerontius*. The regular seasons of Richter concerts in London ceased in 1897 when Richter succeeded to the conductorship of the Hallé concerts in Manchester, following the death of Charles Hallé. Interestingly this appointment aroused just as much opposition from the English musical establishment as his appointment to the Birmingham Festival. Again it was felt that Manchester should have a British conductor - an attitude hard to justify in view of Hallé's own German origins! Richter rarely conducted orchestral concerts in London after this time, although he became a familiar conductor at Covent Garden, where he conducted several complete cycles of *The Ring*. At Manchester he gave in 1908 the first performance of Elgar's First Symphony - a completely successful occasion - thus making amends to the composer and his admirers for the Birmingham disappointment. By this time, however, Richter's health was failing, and in particular his eyesight was rapidly deteriorating to an extent that he found the reading of orchestral scores almost impossible. The following year he conducted his last Birmingham Festival and two years later terminated his association with the Manchester orchestra. He retired to Bayreuth where he remained for the last years of his life. Although the political climate after 1914 forced him to renounce the many academic and other honours awarded him during his career in Britain, Richter retained to the last an interest in the composers and other musicians whom he had encouraged through his Birmingham, Manchester and London associations. In particular he would always ask any visiting British musician about 'Unser Elgar'. Despite the war, Richter was able to get occasional letters through to his British friends, and in one of the last of these, addressed to his son-in-law, Sydney Loeb, and written only a few months before his death in 1916, Richter movingly gives us clear evidence of how much the years spent in Britain had meant to him :

Give my love to my friends and all the artists who worked with me, when you meet them. They are with me in my waking hours and in my dreams and my thoughts of them are always good and pleasurable. With thankfulness I think of the hours I spent with them. They were the happiest of my artistic life.

Based on an article in *The Elgar Society Newsletter*, January 1978

ELGAR and GERONTIUS :
the early performances

Lewis Foreman

Lewis Foreman has for many years explored the music of the early twentieth century, producing, among others, books on Percy Grainger, Havergal Brian, Edmund Rubbra and the standard biography of Sir Arnold Bax. For many years a leading librarian, he is now a full time author. A member of the Elgar Society, in the 1970s he was involved in organising several concerts at St John's, Smith Square which re-established some of Elgar's forgotten choral works, including The Black Knight, King Olaf, *and the* Coronation Ode.

A few years ago a copy of the published full score of *The Dream of Gerontius* appeared in a sale at Phillips, the auctioneers. What was particularly interesting about it was that a previous owner had written the dates of a whole string of early performances on the front flyleaf,[1] and although I failed to buy it at the sale it started a line of research trying to document the early performances, in order to understand what had been heard on each occasion, how the audience had received the music, and although no-one had recorded any of the music before Clara Butt in 1916,[2] to *try* to understand how those singers actually sounded, albeit in other repertoire. Many of the men made records but, unfortunately, only one of the women who took part in the earliest performances of *Gerontius.* This was Louise Kirkby Lunn, the contralto who sang one of the early performances of 'The Angel's Farewell' and was later associated with the full part. Also Claire Croiza who was the Angel in the first Paris *Gerontius* in May 1906.

What does survive are picture postcards of the artists, press cuttings and all manner of ephemera, and these have been used to document the early performances. I think this will show that although the first

---

[1]   A similar copy, thought to have belonged to Herbert Thompson, was once in the Music Library of Liverpool University.

[2]   Butt recorded four extracts on Columbia 7128-31 with Maurice D'Oisly as Gerontius, conducted by Sir Henry Wood, reissued on CD on CDAX 8019.

performance had significant problems, which have become something of a legend, in fact almost from the first *Gerontius* was a masterpiece recognised.

When considering the singers of a century ago, a good starting point is Andrew Black, the baritone in the first Hallé *Gerontius* in March 1903, who in 1906 recorded the 'Sword Song' from *Caractacus*.[3] I have never been very impressed with that recording, and I think it is quite a good example to illustrate our problem in trying to understand what was actually heard at the early performances of *Gerontius* : did any of these singers leave recordings, adequate enough for us to have any understanding how they really sounded in the hall? And if the recordings actually give us a good idea of the real them, could it be that they were prized for something different then from what we value today?

There is another problem too : to put ourselves in the place of the audiences of those earlier performances and try to hear the music as something startlingly new. Take for example the celebrated Tudor Davies recording of 'And King Olaf Heard the Cry' recorded by HMV in March 1923.[4] I wonder how many are familiar with the original 78 coupling: it is the aria 'God Breaketh the Battle' from Parry's oratorio *Judith*, one of the most Handelian solos Parry ever wrote. It is a tremendous sing, but if you regarded this as the acme of modern music then *Gerontius* would be quite a shock.

As we will see, Parry was intimately concerned with the problems that beset the first performance of *Gerontius* at Birmingham in October 1900, because it was not only Elgar who was affected by the performers' difficulties at that time. Parry suffered, too. As *The Times* reported the week after the Festival[5]:

In justice to the choir it should be pointed out that when they framed the programme they knew they were given a heavy task in including Bach's Passion Music, the

---

[3]   Andrew Black with orchestra, G&T 3-2324, 2485e, recorded London 1906, reissued on LP ELG 001, and on CD on CDAX 8020.

[4]   HMV D 723, the Elgar reissued on CD, CDAX 8019. The Parry has not been reissued.

[5]   *The Times*, 8 October 1900, p 9

longest task ever attempted. Then, instead of a half hour programme from Mr Coleridge Taylor, they did the whole of his *Hiawatha*. Mr Elgar's work took 35 minutes longer than they were told it would take, and putting aside the Elijah, the choir had to prepare 11 hours 40 minutes music against 9 hours 20 minutes at the previous festival.

How should the tenor taking the part of Gerontius actually sound? In a quotation[6] familiar to all Elgarians, Elgar saw him as :

a man like us and not a Priest or a Saint, but a sinner... no end of a worldly man in his life, & now brought to book. Therefore I've not filled his part with Church tunes & rubbish but a good, healthy full-blooded romantic, remembered worldliness.

The year 1899 had started out with Elgar almost ready to abandon his attempt to be a full time composer. He wrote to Nicholas Kilburn[7] on 6 January :

We have been thro' a time of much searching of heart with the result that I am going to write a little more music before going back to my teaching: it seems ludicrous to think that the position I have striven for & in a great measure attained shd be utterly & entirely useless from any practical point of view... but - to avoid breaking my dear wife's heart I am going on once more - but without the spirit - it seems a wrecked life!

Yet it proved to be an extremely busy year for him. One only has to consider anyone who suddenly catches the public imagination and becomes famous, even on the most modest scale, to experience the pressures this creates; and these are largely unnecessary pressures that dissipate energy on every kind of activity other than one's main work. 1899 was that year for Elgar, building to the immense task of writing and printing *Gerontius* in one huge eight month period of concentrated effort in 1900. Typical of the growing demands of celebrity was a part-song in honour of the Queen's eightieth birthday which "led to a summons from Windsor to hear its performance. Later that year he was again at Windsor Castle for a concert at which a number of his pieces were performed.[8]

---

6   Moore, Jerrold Northrop: *Elgar and his Publishers - Letters of a creative life. Vol 1 1885-1903* (Oxford, Clarendon Press, 1987) p 228

7   Moore, Jerrold Northrop: *Edward Elgar - letters of a lifetime* (Oxford, Clarendon Press, 1990) p 73

8   Young, Percy M: *Alice Elgar: enigma of a Victorian lady* (Dennis Dobson, 1978) p 141

Of course 1899 was at first dominated by the *Enigma Variations*, first heard on 19 June, and Elgar would have been involved in the proof reading of the piano solo version, printed copies of which were taken into Novello's warehouse as flat sheets as much as three months before the performance.[9] Several shorter pieces followed and then the *Sea Pictures*, first performed by the 27-year-old Clara Butt at Norwich, in October. Elgar's other works including *King Olaf* and the more recent *Caractacus* were also receiving performances, and engagements were being offered for him to conduct. This was a career beginning to take off.

Some material in *Gerontius* has been identified in the surviving manuscripts dating from November 1896 and April 1898,[10] but work really only started in September 1899, when Elgar was reconciled with his publisher Novello, with whom he had quarrelled over terms.

As has been stated by many commentators, Elgar had known Cardinal Newman's poem for many years,[11] but the key exercise in shaping a libretto from it was only really completed when he was faced with a deadline. *Gerontius*, or at least the composition of the music, does not seem to have been pursued with constant drive until Elgar had been set an immutable target. That target was the Birmingham Festival of 1900.

The Birmingham Festival had first sounded Elgar in November 1898 about a work for their 1900 meeting. For the whole of 1899 Elgar had found every excuse for putting off deciding what his Birmingham Festival work was to be: he was busy. But he must have been uncomfortably aware that it would have to be faced. In the event it was

---

[9]   Novello and Company Business Archive in the British Library Add MSS 69516 - 69792

[10]   Kent, Christopher: *Edward Elgar - a guide to research* (New York, Garland Publishing, 1993) pp 172-5. *See also* Robert Anderson: *Elgar in manuscript* (The British Library, 1990) p 45

[11]   "As a wedding present Elgar had received from Father Knight of St George's, a copy of Newman's Gerontius, with its original inscription by Frank Power, who had received it from [General] Gordon" - Percy M Young: *Elgar, Newman and the Dream of Gerontius* (Aldershot, Scolar Press, 1995) p 112

not until the chairman of the Birmingham Festival Committee and his wife called and bearded Elgar in his den, on New Year's Day 1900, that any decision was made.

We need to remember the chronology of the creation of *Gerontius.* Dr Percy Young published[12] such a chronology and I am grateful to him for permission to include here this expanded summary, based on his.

Table 1 - GERONTIUS: chronology of composition
(With acknowledgements to Dr Percy Young: *Elgar OM*, amended and expanded)

1900

Jan 1	"Mr & Mrs Johnstone came to lunch and arranged for E's work Birm. Fest"
Jan 2	"E. sent telegram accepting terms. Began again at former libretto"
Jan 12	"E & A to Birmingham 8.30. E to Oratory"
Mar 2	Sent 1st part of Dream of Gerontius to Novello
Mar 20	Sent 2nd set of MS Gerontius to Messrs Novello
Ap 3	Had proofs of 1st part of Gerontius
Ap 6	With Fr Blakelock to go through Dream of Gerontius
May 4	Jaeger to lunch
May 21-23	E writing hard
May 25	E very engrossed last chorus Gerontius
May 29	Very hard at last chorus
May 30	Nearly finished great chorus. A not out. Jaeger *delighted.*
June 6	E finished the Dream of Gerontius [in vocal score]. Deo gratias. Rather poorly.
June 15	End of vocal score proofs received
June 27	Full score pages 1-56 received by Jaeger
July 20	25 advance copies of vocal score received by Novello
July 23	Elgar received copies of vocal score
Aug 3	Full score completed.
Aug 9	150 proof copies of vocal parts issued
Sept 10	1500 copies (in sheets) of vocal score received by Novello warehouse
Sept 19	Last of proofs of strings returned to Jaeger
Sept 20	Elgar goes to London to finish correcting orchestral parts
Sept 22	Full score reassembled into one volume
Sept 23	Score delivered to Richter by Elgar during evening
Sept 24	Only orchestral rehearsal, and check of parts during run-through
Oct 3	Performance
Oct 3	Further 1500 copies of vocal score received by Novello in flat sheets

---

[12]   Young, Percy M: *Elgar OM - a study of a musician* (Collins, 1955) pp 88-9

It was not until well into February 1900 that Elgar was engaged on the daily intensive work, over many weeks, of actually getting the music down on paper. So, from the Birmingham Festival perspective, we have a vast project with an immutable deadline, in fact in modern parlance a project without a project manager and with the principal contractor, Elgar himself, very much an unpredictable quantity. In the end he became his own project manager - or possibly Alice Elgar did, but he did not have control over all the elements of the project.

Elgar's publisher, Novello, had made the crucial decision to print only the vocal score and chorus parts, and the strings, but not to print the remainder of the orchestral parts and not to make even a manuscript copy of the full score. They must have had significant doubts about Elgar's commission. At the previous two Birmingham Triennial Festivals the main commissioned work had only been a *succès d'estime*. In 1894 it had been George Henschel's *Stabat Mater* for which Novello had produced 1500 copies of the vocal score in 1894, with another thousand and the full score in 1895. But although these copies sold out and in 1906 they had to print a further 1000 copies of the vocal score, years later some of these were pulped, and it was never widely established as a favourite work. In 1897 the publisher of the commissioned work, Stanford's *Requiem*, had been Boosey. Having the score delivered in good time, they pushed the boat out publishing complete orchestral materials and the full score as well as the vocal score. This was a work that must have taken many years to return their investment for although it remained in the repertoire it did not enjoy frequent performance. As far as Elgar was concerned, one may guess that Novello would have regarded with most favour the frequent performances and healthy sales of vocal scores of his early work most popular at the time, *The Banner of St George*. By July 1900 this had 6500 copies in print[13] (and would go on to sell 73,500 copies by the time of the First World War). But the work they were getting was not only several times longer, but much more difficult and also of a Roman Catholic persuasion.

Elgar had to plan his work, fix on the libretto, and then compose it in vocal score, passing the manuscript to the printer as he did so, for engraving. We should also remember that engraving printing plates

---

[13]   British Library Add MS 69557

was very much a craftsman's job involving hammering metal punches into sheets of metal : and the published vocal score runs to 177 pages. Without the printed copies, or at least chorus parts, the choral rehearsals could not start. At that stage it would still have had to be orchestrated, so there would be no full score, which had to be prepared by the composer in time for the orchestral parts to be written by hand and there would then only be one score. All of this was carried out over late nineteenth century communications (although, of course, in fact with postal services in some ways more reliable than today) between Malvern, London and Birmingham.

The first 44 pages of the vocal score, as far as 'Sanctus fortis', were sent to Novello remarkably quickly - 2 March, with proofs a month later - but all was not finished until 6 June, and there were no printed copies before August. Until there were printed copies, in pre-photocopying days, there were continual problems with key personnel not having a copy to work with, including Elgar himself. Thus 25 advanced copies of the vocal score were received by Novello's warehouse as sets of flat sheets on 20 July and by 23 July Elgar had copies for his use. The choir seems to have been trained using chorus parts, 150 advanced sets of which (described as 'proofs') were received by Novello's warehouse on 9 August, with a further 50 copies of each on 20 September. The use of choral parts means that few associated with the chorus, apart from the choirmaster and the rehearsal pianist, can have had a vocal score to play through at the piano, and hence few of the performers could have had any clear conception of the whole work before the orchestral rehearsals.

The chronology of publication opposite is derived from Christopher Kent's *Guide to Research*,[14] which I have again expanded and dated in the light of the Novello Archives now in the British Library.[15]

The chorus parts and vocal score were all published in order that the first performance could take place, but the copyist of the orchestral parts, and Hans Richter the conductor at the first performance, would have used the one and only manuscript full score. A vocal score in tonic

---

[14]   Kent, *op cit,* p 173

[15]   See footnote 9

Table 2 - GERONTIUS : chronology of publication
(With acknowledgements to Christopher Kent, expanded)

1900	vocal score
	chorus parts
1901	string parts
	vocal score: German translation (J Buths)
	tonic sol-fa edition
1902	full score - English & German
	vocal parts with German words
	wind and brass parts
	full score 'Prelude & Angel's Farewell' for orchestra alone,
	or with mezzo-soprano solo ad lib
1903	organ transcription of the 'Prelude & Angel's Farewell' by Herbert
	Brewer
	full score - 'Sanctus fortis' only, in A♭
1905	vocal score - French translation
	chorus parts - French translation
1914	miniature score

sol-fa, and the German edition of the vocal score came in 1901 and one in French in 1905. In fact the foreign language editions sold very poorly. Also, that very curious edition, the full score in German published in 1914. I must say I have long wanted to hear it sung in German or French.

Various extracts were also published, not least the 'Prelude and Angel's Farewell' for either mezzo-soprano and orchestra or orchestra alone, which appeared in 1902. This signalled the journey to the work's wider acceptance. As well as studying the early performances and their reception, *Gerontius'* growing popularity may be best seen by considering the number of copies of the vocal score in print and the appearance of the other printed copies - scores, orchestral parts - which we can obtain from Novello's archives, now in the British Library, and which are listed in table 3.

The smallest print run for any Elgar score is 'Sanctus fortis', I presume the version in A flat, of which Geidel printed 12 copies on 30 June 1903.

Table 3 - GERONTIUS : printing history

Vocal score :	20/7/00	25
	10/9/00	1,500
	3/10/00	1,500
	balance 1/7/01	825
	28/7/03	2,000
	26/9/03	2,000
	12/12/03	5,000
Voice parts :	9/8/00	proof copies 150 of each
	26/9/00	further 50 copies
	30/1/01	250 each
	22/2/02	500 each
	8/4/02	500 each
Tonic sol-fa version :	11/4/02	500
	balance 1/7/02	100
	30/9/03	500
	14/11/04	500
	balance 1/7/05	250
	18/5/06	1,000
	balance 2/7/06	750
	balance 1/7/08	500
	13/2/09	1,000
	9/1/19	250
	later 4,000 between 1920 and 1939	
Vocal parts with German words :		100 of each voice
		('from Germany')
	4/1902	500 each
	balance 2/7/06	only sop/alto 150 each
	stock destroyed April 1943	
Vocal score with German words :		
	28/10/01	1,000
	balance 1/7/02	400
	balance 1/7/03	150

Presumably the plates must have been shipped from Germany, for another twelve copies were printed, in house, on 5 May 1922.

The complete full score of *The Dream of Gerontius* was supplied to stock in sheets on 13 May 1902, in a printing of 100 copies. One of these was bound up in a special binding (perhaps the presentation copy for Sheffield[16]) and the remaining balance was down to only nine by 1 July 1904. This dissemination of full scores was undoubtedly the engine that fuelled the enormous expansion of performances from 1903 onward and its acceptance into the permanent repertoire. On 21 January 1905 they had another hundred, with a total of a further 162 copies printed between the wars. However, in the case of *Gerontius* the full score appeared in a miniature study score as early as 1914 and on 27 May 1914 we find 500 copies, printed in Germany, taken into stock. This was not reprinted again until 1934 (another 500) and 1946 (250).

When it appeared as an organ transcription, made by Herbert Brewer, in 1903, the year that performances began to take off, it was also an important stepping stone in promoting the work in its early life.

~~~o~~~0~~~o~~~

The programme for Birmingham in 1900 included the works listed in table 4 :

Table 4 - Choral Works Played : Birmingham Festival, 1900

Bach:	*St Matthew Passion*
Brahms:	*German Requiem*
Byrd:	*"Mass - selections"*
Coleridge-Taylor:	*Hiawatha* complete
Cornelius:	*Die Vätergruft*
Dvořák:	*The Spectre's Bride*
Elgar:	*The Dream of Gerontius*
Handel:	*Messiah*
Handel:	*Israel in Egypt* - selections
Mendelssohn:	*Elijah*
Parry:	*De Profundis*

---

[16]   See footnote 76

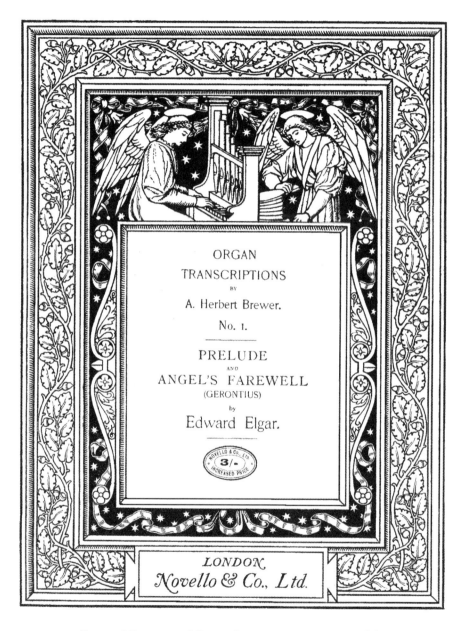

*Cover of the score of Brewer's organ transcription of the
Prelude and Angel's Farewell*

In the last analysis, it was not his conductor, Hans Richter, in whose hands Elgar's reputation now lay, but with his chorus master, who, as we have seen, had to prepare an enormous quantity of music to very high standard in an amazingly short time. A demanding schedule was made worse by the fact that the chosen chorus master, Charles Swinnerton Heap, himself a composer, caught pneumonia and died on 11 June, at the age of 53, before rehearsals for any of the programme had seriously been launched. Indeed before Elgar's music had been printed. The Birmingham committee found themselves faced with impending disaster.

There was nothing for it but to ask William Cole Stockley, the choirmaster to the Birmingham Festival from 1858 to 1894, to take over at the age of 70. In spite of his long experience, in Elgar's music he found himself faced with music whose virtuosity he did not understand, a religious sentiment with which he was profoundly out of sympathy, and far too little time to prepare all the music required, and in particular the performing material of the Elgar was still unfinished.

It was not only *Gerontius* that was to suffer. The day before *Gerontius*, two works by Parry were heard : his choral *De Profundis* and a new scena for baritone and orchestra, *The Soldier's Tent*, written for Parry's son-in-law, Harry Plunket Greene, who would be the bass soloist in *Gerontius* the next day. Parry documents all this in his diary, making clear the problems that were being experienced over *Gerontius*, and that they were at least partly responsible for problems that also occurred in the rest of the programme.

It is worth considering the character of Hans Richter at this point. In his essay 'On Some Conductors and Their Methods',[17] Stanford, who had known Richter well, and who had not only played under him but also had his own music performed by him, found Richter :

a species of ideal band-master...Richter was often stiff in his reading of an unfamiliar score ... he hated extravagance, and even took the *diablerie* out of Berlioz; but his mastery of the orchestra was as great as von Bülow's, and he had authority and instrumental knowledge to back it. He took everything from the stand point of common sense: for this reason, he was strongest in what he knew best.

---

[17] Stanford, Sir Charles V: *Interludes, Records and Reflections* (John Murray, 1922) pp 29-38

The orchestral rehearsals were held at Queen's Hall, in London, a week before the festival and Parry notes that rehearsals for *Gerontius* and excerpts from *Götterdämmerung* encroached on the time available for the rest of the programme. And at Birmingham Parry wrote in his diary[18] for 29 September:

> To rehearsal in Town Hall. Elgar's *Dream of Gerontius* gave a vast amount of trouble and kept chorus and orchestra at work till past 5.30. No use trying to get anything out of *De Profundis* with them all tired out.

The performance duly came to grief, Parry noting it was "terrible", the sopranos making their first entry a bar too soon and the whole thing being "flabby". This is a fair indicator of the problems with the whole festival - a lack of incisive singing from the choir, who seem, literally, to have been overwhelmed. One only has to listen to Parry's score[19] to appreciate the contrapuntal idiom and the complex demands on the choir.

Now, we must not focus exclusively on purely musical matters. What were the concerns of the time? What would the solid middle class audience at Birmingham have been reading in their newspapers during the Festival? One of the things we tend to forget was that it was in the middle of a general election; in those times voting was spread over several days so it was not an overnight spectacular, with high drama as the votes were declared. The results emerged cumulatively over the period of the festival. Second, the news of the war - the Boer War - after a bad start was improving. And third, the war in China was an emotive issue with news of the relief of European interests in Peking becoming public. So the mood was a nationalist one, and as West Country regiments were deeply involved, the 'Glosters' - the Gloucestershire Regiment - having emblazoned battle honours from the Boer War, not a few of the audience may well have had worries about serving sons and husbands, and a significant sprinkling might have lost nearest and dearest.

One more taste of that concert on 2 October 1900 before we consider what happened on the following morning. Parry's 9½-minute scena

[18]   Dibble, Jeremy: *C Hubert H Parry - his life and music* (Oxford, Clarendon Press, 1992) p 373

[19]   *De Profundis* was last performed, on BBC Radio 3, on 23 July 1960.

The interior of Birmingham Town Hall

The Soldier's Tent was the other novelty at Birmingham. It was a romantic, noble vision of the soldier doomed to die, an approach that could still be taken seriously by an audience for whom the realities of war would not be fully appreciated for another decade or so. When asked to present Parry as 'This Week's Composer' on Radio 3, in 1995[20], I made a point of asking that this piece be included, for although revived by Garry Humphreys in September 1986 with piano accompaniment, it had not been heard with orchestra for sixty or seventy years. It proved to be a delightful piece, the orchestration, unusually for Parry, colourful and romantic, and the piece a direct, if demanding, sing.

So we come to the first performance of *The Dream of Gerontius*, which took place in Birmingham Town Hall on the morning of Wednesday 3 October 1900. *Gerontius* formed the first half of a concert which went on to include Schubert's *Unfinished Symphony* and extended selections from Handel's *Israel in Egypt*!

---

[20]   'Composer of the Week: Parry' BBC Radio 3, 28 September 1995. Arwel Huw Morgan (bar)/BBC Concert Orchestra/Barry Wordsworth. It has since been recorded by Christopher Maltman (bar) and the BBC Scottish Symphony Orchestra, conducted by Martyn Brabbins on Hyperion CDA 67065.

Before broadcasting, recordings and today's availability of music in a centre such as London, the great triennial festivals were of an importance that is hard really to understand today. At comparatively high prices they attracted large audiences for programmes which I think *we* would probably find endurance tests. These were events which elicited wide national press coverage, and by 1900 Elgar was a sufficiently important figure to be a subject of sustained press commentary, and indeed the main focus of the reporting of the Festival.

As we have noted, the band rehearsals for the Birmingham Festival took place in London, in Queen's Hall, the week before the festival, and the rehearsal for *Gerontius* on the first day was attended by a large audience and was widely reported in the press. The rehearsal started at ten with a morning call for the orchestra only, the conductor Hans Richter being reported as having only received the full score on the previous evening. Here is the *Birmingham Post's* account[21]:

> At ten o'clock Dr Richter called the band to attention, Mr Edward Elgar took his place beside the conductor, meeting with a cordial reception, and proceedings began with the orchestral rehearsal of *The Dream of Gerontius*. The whole of the morning was devoted to reading through the band parts alone, and a wonderful piece of sight-reading it was. It was, so to speak, the final revision of the instrumental parts. Mistakes were found here and there, but they were surprisingly few. The score is most intricate, and the music extremely difficult. Apart from the errors in the copies, stoppages were few, and those mainly in regard to the matter of tempi.... Dr Richter was unremitting in attention, and seemed to know every detail of the score.... as time went on the number of listeners increased. The Lord Mayor of Birmingham and Mr Alfred H Wiggins represented the festival committee and there were many of the London critics in attendance. Shortly after two o'clock the rehearsal was resumed with the vocal principals. There was a virtual recitation from beginning to end.

Two further days of rehearsals for the remainder of the programme followed in London before the full rehearsals in Birmingham, which took place immediately before the festival. Here is *The Musical Standard*[22]:

---

[21]   From the issue of 25 September 1900

[22]   *The Musical Standard*, 29 September 1900

Undoubtedly the most interesting feature of the coming Birmingham Festival will be the production of Mr Edward Elgar's *Dream of Gerontius*.... it is clear enough that Mr Elgar has given us... the best work he has yet done. We shall be surprised indeed if at the festival the composition does not prove one of the finest achievements of British composition.

The *Standard's* writer launched into a critique of the impossible task that faced festival performers with so little rehearsal.

It is late in the day to speak of the rehearsal arrangements at Birmingham. It was stated, not officially, it is true, that both *Messiah* and *Elijah* were to be rehearsed otherwise than chorally, but we note that neither of these masterpieces figures in the printed order of rehearsals, although the selections from *Israel in Egypt* do. That is rather a pity, for no festival has yet taken place for which the fashion of giving these familiar works without full rehearsal has not had bad results - at least, if one expects perfection. But when two novelties, *The Dream of Gerontius* and the *Song of Hiawatha*, are in the programme,... all to be rehearsed with soloists, chorus within the space of a full day, an evening and a morning it is difficult to understand how time could be found for the rehearsal of familiar masterpieces.... Still, in listening to the orchestra trying over the orchestral music of *The Dream of Gerontius* and afterwards to the soloists running through their parts,... one could not help feeling strongly once again that the rehearsal arrangements at our festivals entirely prevent them taking the stand they should.... How all this is to be obtained from the single rehearsal at Birmingham, we do not understand, but rest in the placid hope that it will be all right "on the night".

One of the well-remembered stories about the Birmingham *Gerontius* is how, at the dress rehearsal, Elgar suddenly hurried to the platform and addressed (perhaps "berated" would be a better word) the choir, trying to tell them what was wrong. This not only antagonised his singers, but generated hostile press commentary. As Jerrold Northrop Moore pointed out "Richter, seeing an impossible situation, cut short his rehearsal".[23] He quotes a member of the choir, W T Edgley, who, half a century later, told the story to Dora Powell[24]:

[Elgar] was alongside Richter most of the rehearsal, prompting him and trying to explain what he required. I must record, however, that things got very chaotic and everyone worked up to a high pitch and unfortunately E E more than anyone, naturally. He seemed desperate, with whom I cannot remember, but it was not all 'the chorus'...

---

[23]   Moore, Jerrold Northrop: *Edward Elgar - a creative life* (Oxford University Press, 1984) p 330

[24]   *ibid*

The part of Gerontius at the first performance was sung by Edward Lloyd, towards the end of a long and celebrated career. He had already made his Three Choirs farewell appearances the previous month - in the Verdi *Requiem, Elijah* and the third part of *Caractacus,* and he retired at the end of the year, though he appeared on many occasions subsequently, and he lived until 1927. At the time of *Gerontius* he was 55 and was not new to Elgar premières, having sung in the first performances of both *King Olaf* and *The Light of Life.* Rosa Burley[25] was dismissive of Lloyd's contribution as we will see below, even though in fact he had quite a good press.

The mezzo was Marie Brema, who also did not find favour with Rosa Burley, though generally having the best reception of all the soloists by the papers. At 44 she was at the peak of her career as a Wagnerian singer. Having appeared at Bayreuth since 1894 she would have been known to Richter who subsequently chose her for Brunnhilde in *Götterdämmerung* in Paris in 1902.

Finally there was Harry Plunket Greene, who had become Parry's son-in law the previous year, and at 35 based his career on songs and oratorio. Parry wrote his bass parts for him from *Job* onwards, and Stanford many of his songs. Whether this qualified him to create the bass parts in *Gerontius* is difficult to decide.

Of the soloists at the first performance only Plunket Greene participated in the performances that followed over the following two or three years. However, Lloyd and Plunket Greene both made recordings of other repertoire, including some very soon after *Gerontius,* and so we can at least listen to them, and see what manner of voices they were.

But first what did Rosa Burley have to say? She[26] wrote :

---

[25]   Rosa Burley (1866-1951). In 1891 she became the headmistress of The Mount, a finishing school for girls in Malvern where Elgar called to teach violin. Elgar's daughter, Carice, became a pupil. During the decade when he was gaining recognition, she probably knew him more intimately than anyone except his wife and daughter, and she accompanied the Elgars on various holidays including the Munich Musical Festival in 1893 where they heard many of Wagner's operas.

[26]   Burley, Rosa and Frank C Carruthers: *Edward Elgar - the record of a friendship* (Barrie & Jenkins, 1972) pp 139-40

Artists from the Birmingham premiere :
(above left) Marie Brema; (above right) Edward Lloyd; (below left) Harry
Plunket Greene; (below right) Hans Richter and umbrella

Mrs Evans of Wolverhampton, a lady who actually sang in the choir and whose extreme candour makes her a valuable corroborative witness, remembers that the Wolverhampton contingent of the choir first heard of Dr Heap's death on the station platform when they were leaving for rehearsal.... so it is evident that the rehearsals had begun in good time yet the copies of *Gerontius* did not arrive till late in August.

Stockley, [the choir master], Mrs Evans describes as a pathetic figure unable to bear the strain of even standing for the long periods required. Again and again he had to rest and eat sweets to keep himself going. The rehearsals were so ruthlessly shortened that sometimes the Wolverhampton party felt resentful at having taken the twelve miles' journey for so little result. With great honesty she admits that she did not herself realize the importance of *Gerontius* till afterwards - which was not surprising.

When the day of the concert arrived we went over to Birmingham in a rather sober frame of mind,..[but]... the overture...went off so smoothly that one breathed a sigh of relief, hoping that one's anxiety had been unnecessary but when Edward Lloyd entered with what should have been the heartrending cry of the dying man it was clear that he was not only ill at ease but completely out of rapport with the means by which Edward had expressed Gerontius's spiritual struggle. Lloyd was a lyric tenor well able to sustain so straightforward a part as that of Olaf but with no understanding of anything more profound than *I'll Sing Thee Songs of Araby* into which one almost expected him to burst at any moment. Had he done so, I thought, it might have been some relief for he would at least have understood what he was doing.

Trenchant views indeed. Edward Lloyd made quite a few recordings[27] between 1904 and 1907 and among the earliest there *is* 'I'll Sing Thee Songs of Araby' from Edward Clay's 1877 cantata *Lalla Rookh*. The sound is very distant but it does give a clue to the way he sang. Perhaps more informative is his 'Prize Song' from *Meistersinger*, delivered in a ringing free style, to hear what he made of a big role. But he had not been regarded as one of the leading oratorio singers for several generations for nothing, and with oratorio in mind, his performance of 'If with all your hearts' from *Elijah*[28], recorded in 1907, is a remarkably persuasive example of his projection of line and words.

The Times' critic didn't agree[29] with Miss Burley :

---

[27]   Edward Lloyd recorded 34 sides between 1904 and 1908. See Roberto Bauer: *The new Catalogue of Historical Records 1898-1908/09* (Sidgwick & Jackson, 1947, 1972) p 287

[28]   (G&T, GC3-2801)

[29]   *The Times*, 4 October 1900, p 5

> Mr Lloyd's delivery of the tenor part was wonderfully beautiful in feeling, and must have filled the composer's ideal as it will scarcely be fulfilled again...

After criticising the choir and Richter's tempi as too slow Miss Burley moved on to the bass soloist, Plunket Greene :

> Suddenly there was the dramatic pause which follows Gerontius's death and I waited for the ringing cry of the Priest whose 'Proficiscere' should, as I knew, sound like a trumpet call. But here again there was a ridiculous anticlimax, for Plunket Greene had anything but a strong voice and was always uncertain in intonation.

Plunket Greene is reported as managing to get out of tune with the orchestra towards the end and was all too aware that he had not been as helpful to the composer as he would have wished.

Plunket Greene first recorded in London in 1902, with Schubert's song *Der Abscheid* and made his last recordings some thirty years later. The late recordings are made very close to the microphone giving a remarkable impact to the voice. But from the earlier recordings[30] it is clear that, while striking, in one respect at least Rosa Burley was correct: it was not a thunderous voice. He was however an exquisite singer of songs, not only publishing a book on vocal technique but also recording two 78s on 'The Art of Singing[31].

Finally Marie Brema of whom, unfortunately, no recording survives. Rosa Burley thought her "a goddess from Valhalla if ever there was one" and considered her "unsuited for her part" concluding[32]:

> had she made the most brilliant success of it she could not have saved a performance which had been hopelessly wrecked by the choir, whose pitiful stumblings indeed remained the outstanding impression.

What was the truth? A few years ago I attended a local performance of *Gerontius* when many of the same flaws were in evidence; in particular the Demons' Chorus was beyond them, the pitch sagged and there were

---

[30]   See 'Harry Plunket Greene - The Records' *Record Advertiser* Vol 1 no 6, Sept-Oct 1971, pp 2-4

[31]   HMV D 40149/50, recorded in 1932

[32]   Burley, *op cit*

a number of wrong entries. Yet despite these flaws one still came away with a strong impression. These intrinsic qualities of the music were certainly appreciated by many commentators in 1900 who appear to have recognised the greatness of the music but had reservations about the performance. Indeed there does not appear to have been a single adverse criticism of the *score*.

The Times in its overview of the festival on the last day attempted to assess the choir and allocate blame[33]:

> It is certain that few, if any, of the series of Birmingham Festivals have been so ill-provided in this respect; for in the matter of tone considerations of refinement have been sacrificed to the production of a great volume of sound; in that of time, the lapses have been so numerous as to force themselves upon the least attentive hearer; and in that of intelligence, it has been made clear that there is an abundance of distinctly bad readers in the chorus who must sing mainly by ear. Where an accidental occurred in an unlikely place, it was pretty certain that two adjacent semitones would be distinctly heard simultaneously, and this, though more commonly among the tenors than elsewhere, was noticed fairly often in all parts.

There is not space here to quote from a wider range of press criticism, which have been cited by several authors. Northrop Moore's *Edward Elgar - a creative life*[34] is probably the most useful for a selection of the crits, but they all sent the same message : a masterpiece recognised in spite of a less than perfect performance.

Birmingham had two immediate effects : it persuaded Sir August Manns to cancel the performance he had scheduled for 27 October at the Crystal Palace, on the grounds of choral difficulty, and it allowed Jaeger to send the German conductor Julius Buths back to Germany with the ambition of producing *Gerontius* there.[35]   At the time Elgar was despairing at what he perceived as a disaster. But his music was to establish itself as a mainstream repertoire work in a remarkably short time, though while it was doing so it must have been easy for him to believe that it would never succeed.

---

[33]   'Birmingham Musical Festival', *The Times*, 6 October 1900, p 9

[34]   Moore, *op cit*, pp 332-4

[35]   "A wonderful work; it's the most beautiful work I know" - Michael Kennedy: *Portrait of Elgar* (Oxford University Press, 1968) p 95

Performance of Extracts

However, almost immediately there were announced performances of orchestral extracts, either of the Prelude or the 'Prelude and Angel's Farewell' that he quickly extracted for either orchestra without soloist or with the mezzo-soprano taking the angel's role. Thus the Prelude was performed at a Saturday Concert at Crystal Palace on 10 November 1900, and on 16 February 1901 Elgar himself conducted Muriel Foster, who would later become so associated with the role of the Angel, in four of the *Sea Pictures* with the Bradford Permanent Orchestra in St George's Hall Bradford, preceding it with the orchestral version[36] of 'Prelude and Angel's Farewell'. He later conducted the latter at the 1901 Three Choirs at Gloucester, although the Dean had prohibited the full work owing to doctrinal objections to the libretto.

It reappeared at various concerts and Louise Kirkby Lunn sang the Angel in the version with soloist on 20 February. This was conducted by a notable future champion of the work, Henry J Wood. Jaeger remarked[37]: "Wood conducted it with loving care; spent one and a half hours on it [at rehearsal] and the result was a performance which completely put Richter's in the shade." Kirkby Lunn made recordings at about this time both for the Berliner and Gramophone & Typewriter companies, but the closing bars of her slightly later recording of 'But the Lord is mindful' from Mendelssohn's *St Paul*,[38] gives us a surprisingly vivid insight into her impact in the hall in *Gerontius*, and she undoubtedly played an important role in Wood's success with the aria, and in less than two years in the complete role.

There were also other extracts and arrangements. As early as 7 February 1901, Ivor Atkins, the young organist of Worcester Cathedral, included the Prelude in his cathedral organ recital, following it with organ transcriptions of Wagner (*Siegfried's Funeral March* and the

---

[36] Which was the first music from the work to be recorded by Elgar himself in 1917.

[37] Jacobs, Arthur: *Henry J Wood - maker of the Proms* (Methuen, 1994) p 74

[38] 'But the Lord is mindful of His own', HMV 03232

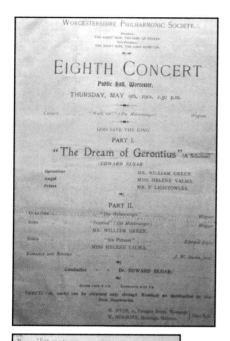

Handbills and programmes advertising early performances of excerpts from Gerontius. Above : Two 1901 performances in Worcester (left) and Bradford (right); Below : Two London performances in 1902 (left) and 1900 (right)

Prelude to *Parsifal*). In March 1901 the *Illustrated London News* reported Ethel Barns, a popular violinist of the day, playing a violin transcription billed as 'My work is done' at Steinway Hall, while a Miss Minnie Nelson programmed the 'Angel's Song' in a recital otherwise unspecified.

A figure who would later be associated with the role of the Angel is Clara Butt, and she actually participated in the 1900 Birmingham Festival, singing four of the *Sea Pictures* under Elgar's baton. It would be 1915 before Clara Butt sang in the full work, but on 1 February 1902 she made her first association with the music when she sang the 'Prelude and Angel's Farewell' under Elgar's baton at Queen's Hall. These performances of extracts immediately gave Novello the problem of extracting orchestral parts from the complete performing materials. On 3 January Elgar wrote to Jaeger :

> Private. I am hoping to do Prelude & Farewell on Feb 1: after all in London (Clara Butt) & Angel's song... Can the parts be had for that? You have strings but how about woodwind & horns - you have a double set of wood but the horns wd. (might) have to be copied for the concert.[39]

It was doubtless to resolve such practical problems that Novello printed the 'Prelude & Angel's Farewell' separately, the first part of the full score to be printed. This was engraved and printed in Germany and 100 sets of flat sheets were received on 7 August 1902, only 25 remaining on 1 July 1903.

Curiously when Busoni programmed the 'Prelude and Angel's Farewell' in the first of his celebrated concerts of new music in Berlin on 8 November 1902, that is *after* the two celebrated Düsseldorf performances of the complete work, it was greeted by an uncomprehending critic as "the most barren piece of senseless music-fabrication that has been heard for a long time",[40] reminding us how modern the piece appeared to its first audiences.

The Birmingham Festival had attracted a huge conspectus of British musicians and although Elgar did not know it at the time, several

---

[39]   Moore, *Elgar and his Publishers*, p 323

[40]   Dent, Edward J: *Ferruccio Busoni - a biography* (Eulenburg Books, 1974) p 131

determined to mount their own performances. Chief among these were Henry J Wood and Dr Henry Coward, the pioneering Sheffield chorus master. They would soon achieve it together.

Table 5 opposite gives us an overview of the sequence of early performances before we follow the story for the first three or four years.

Worcester, May 1901

Gerontius was next performed seven months later, in Worcester, with Elgar himself conducting. This was announced as "a selection" but appears to have been most of the score, though without the Demons' Chorus. William Green, an established oratorio singer of his day took the role of Gerontius with Helene Valma as the Angel and the now forgotten Mr Frederick Lightowler, an habitué of Worcester Philharmonic platforms, in the bass roles. This was the eighth concert of the Worcester Philharmonic Society's season, on Thursday 9 May 1901 at 2.30 pm. The concert was preceded - as were all Worcester Philharmonic Programmes - by the short chorus 'Wach' auf' ('Awake : bright day is drawing near') from *Die Meistersinger,* and by the National Anthem. The second half offered the Overture to *Die Meistersinger,* William Green in the 'Priestlied' from that opera - in the event not given - Elgar's *Sea Pictures* sung by Helene Valma, and ended with a *Romance and Bolero* by a member of his orchestra, J W Austin, jnr. *The Musical Times*[41] reported :

> The practicability of Dr Edward Elgar's setting of *The Dream of Gerontius* was fully demonstrated at a performance of a selection of the work given by the Worcestershire Philharmonic Society.... The Worcester amateurs sang well in tune throughout and with real devotional feeling, and the work proved to be well within the capabilities of an intelligent choir. The audience, one of the largest ever assembled in the hall, was profoundly impressed by the performance.... The concert concluded with a *Romance and Bolero* for orchestra composed by Mr J W Austin, Jnr... which was conducted by the composer, the leader of the orchestra. During its performance... Dr Elgar led the second fiddles.

The flavour of the occasion is perhaps more authentically given by the account in the *Worcester Herald*[42]:

[41]   *The Musical Times,* June 1901

[42]   11 May 1901

Table 5 - Performances of GERONTIUS: 1900 - 1904

1900

Birmingham	3 Oct	E Lloyd	M Brema	Plunket Greene	Richter

1901

Worcester	9 May	W Green	H Valma	F Lightowler	Elgar
Düsseldorf	19 Dec	L Wüllner	A Beel	W Metzmacher	Buths

1902

London*	8 May	G W Cooper			Royds
Düsseldorf	19 May	L Wüllner	M Foster	J Messchaert	Buths
Worcester	11 Sept	J Coates	M Foster	Plunket Greene	Elgar
Sheffield	2 Oct	J Coates	M Foster	Ffrangcon-Davies	Elgar

1903

Edinburgh	12 Jan	J Coates	M Foster	R Burnett	Cowen
Danzig	11 March	F Dierich	F Kisielnicki	J Staudigl	F Binder
Stirling	12 March	H Brearley	P Allen	C Tree/ J Browning	Marchant
Manchester	12 March	J Coates†	M Brema	A Black	Richter
Hanley	13 March	J Coates	M Foster	A Black	Elgar
Chicago	23 March	E Williams	J O Hannah	G Miles	T Thomas
Wolverhampton	23 March	W Green	A Lakin	C Knowles	Bantock
Liverpool	24 March	L Wüllner	M Brema	A Black	Cowen
New York	24 March	Van Hoose	Ada Crossley	J Walker	Damrosch
Birmingham	26 March	W Green	M Foster	A Black	Sinclair
New York	26 March	Van Hoose	Ada Crossley	David Bispham	Damrosch
Middlesbrough	23 April	W Green	M Foster	Ffrangcon-Davies	Elgar
Bristol	25 April	W Green	M Foster	D Price	G Riseley
Westminster Cathedral	6 June	L Wüllner	M Foster	Ffrangcon-Davies	Elgar
Hereford	10 Sept	J Coates	M Foster	Lane Wilson/ Plunket Greene	Sinclair
Darmstadt	? Oct	Oscar Noë	E Bengel/ M Obsner	A Heinemann	W de Haan
Newcastle	9 Nov	W Green	M Foster	Ffrangcon-Davies	JM Preston
Sheffield	17 Nov	Ch Saunders	M Foster	Joseph Lycett	Coward
Glasgow	24 Nov	J Coates	M Foster	Walter Harvey	J Bradley
Sydney	21 Dec	A Richards	F Gibson	R Gooud	J A Delany

1904

Queen's Hall	15 Feb	J Coates	M Brema	Ffrangcon-Davies	Fagge
Covent Garden	14 March	J Coates	Kirkby Lunn	Ffrangcon-Davies	Richter
Queen's Hall	9 April	G Elwes	'H Foster'	Ffrangcon-Davies	Weingartner

* Part I only, probably without orchestra   † Replacing Wüllner.

There was a large and fashionable audience at the Public Hall on Thursday afternoon on the occasion of the eighth concert given by the Worcestershire Philharmonic Society... Dr Elgar kept all up to their work, and not only did he keep a firm hold on the chorus and orchestra, but on the audience also. By an imperious wave of the hand he silenced untimely applause, and when the buzzing chatter and shuffling, which always fill up the interval, failed to cease when he took his stand at the conductor's desk, he called for silence, and waited with arms folded, gazing at the audience... The chorus singing was exceptionally good, whether in the subdued passages, or giving forth the bold, massive harmonies which are a striking feature of the work. At the close of the cantata, the audience were most enthusiastic, but though the applause was kept up for four or five minutes, the composer declined to bow his acknowledgement.

William Green was sufficiently well-known in his day to have made seven recordings,[43] and in the very year of this performance he cut waxes for six of these for the Gramophone & Typewriter Company. A good example is 'If With All Your Hearts' from *Elijah,* a work he sang at the Hereford Three Choirs in 1900. The voice is bright and forward, rather different from the more solid heroic quality of Lloyd. This was the sort of voice that Elgar conducted later when Steuart Wilson sang *Gerontius,* and certainly the role has an honourable history of this English quality in Parry Jones and Peter Pears.

The First Düsseldorf Performance

Popular legend has it that the two Düsseldorf performances in December 1901 and May 1902 single-handedly demonstrated the stature of *Gerontius.* As we have seen, this was not strictly true, as Sheffield and the following Manchester performance were already being planned before the music was heard in Germany. But there can be no doubt of the impact of the music at Düsseldorf, or the influence it had in both countries.

The December 1901 Düsseldorf performance was reported in the press both in England and in Germany. To the *Liverpool Daily Post* A P

---

[43]   Green's oratorio recordings included 'If with all your hearts' (from *Elijah,* G&T 2-2577) and 'Be Thou faithful' (from *St Paul,* G&T 2-2599); two popular operatic arias ('Yes, Let Me Like a Soldier Fall' from Wallace's *Maritana,* G&T 2-2600) and 'O Vision Entrancing' from Goring Thomas's *Esmeralda* G&T 2-2754) and several popular songs of the day by Braham, Leoni and Sullivan.

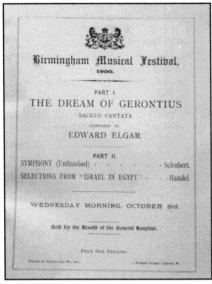

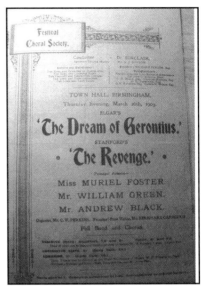

*Above : Advertisements for (left) the 1900 Birmingham première and (right)
the second (1903) Birmingham performance of* Gerontius;
Below : the programme for the 1901 Düsseldorf performance of the work

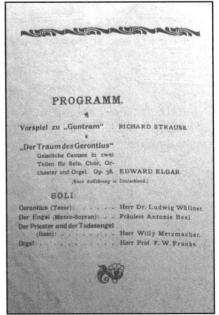

Mignot[44] wrote :

> The first performance of Dr Elgar's oratorio *The Dream of Gerontius* seems to have been the event of the musical season at Dusseldorf, and to have attracted musical notabilities from all parts of the Rhineland, than which there is no more musical part of Germany. Professor Buths, the distinguished conductor of the local Musikverein, attended the Birmingham Festival last summer, and, it seems, he conceived there and then the idea of introducing Elgar's new work to a German audience at Düsseldorf, a town in which in the days gone by a Mendelssohn, Schumann and Bruch did not hesitate to confer a similar distinction.

The soloists at Düsseldorf were Ludwig Wüllner, who would later sing the first London performance, Antonie Beel, a mezzo soprano about whom 1 can trace nothing, and Willy Metzmacher in the bass roles. How was it reported in the German press? Here are some extracts from *Die Musik* for January 1902 (specially translated by Julia Chandler) :

> Elgar arranges brilliantly and shows himself an excellent composer. The introduction is superb. The voices are thankful, adroit, free from all triviality. Elgar is at his most dramatic in the 'demons' section. He knows how to create an effect using contrasts - powerful modulations not always free from theatrical pathos alternate with parts warm with sensitivity. An imposing finale provides the remarkable work with a worthy ending. The composer witnessed an excellent performance conducted by Buths - who also translated the text into German. The choir sang wonderfully, the orchestra performed splendidly. Wüllner shone as a performer in the title role, even if he displayed a certain arbitrariness as a singer. Metzmacher sang the bass solo very well and Antonie Beel in the mezzo-soprano role of the Angel mostly pleased. Professor Francke of Cologne was exemplary on the organ. Elgar received tempestuous applause. He may consider his work a total success.

Elgar had dithered about going to Düsseldorf, and Jaeger had to go on his own because he could not afford his wife's expenses. In the end they went together.

Elgar had conducted the first British performance of Philipp Wolfrum's *Eine Weihnachts-Mysterium* for the Worcester Philharmonic on 12 December (incidentally a work which some enterprising society must promote again). The most vivid account of the proceedings was contained in a long letter that Jaeger, signing himself 'Rodnim' sent to Mrs Richard Powell, 'Dorabella' of the *Enigma Variations,* on 29

---

[44]   *Liverpool Daily Post* cutting for 1901 in the Elgar books of press cuttings at Broadheath

December. It is too long to quote complete but here are a few cameos which bring the scene to life[45]:

> We travelled to D'dorf together & had a lovely passage. Buths and a friend met us & we drove to 17 Ehrens Strasse a nice house & a comfortable one. Buths, his Frau Professor & his 2 daughters were as kind as kind could be. On Wednesday morning we went to the first orchestral rehearsal with Soloists. The orchestra of 80 odd was not like Wood's 110 for reading powers or tone, but they answered every purpose & Elgar had not very much to find fault with.... But directly Wüllner opened his mouth to sing 'Jesus, Maria, meine Stunde kam' we said that man has Brains. And by the Olympian Jove he had Brains galore. He made us sit up and realise that Elgar's intention, & what I had expected when I wrote my much maligned analysis, could be realised by an artist. I never heard such intellectual deeply felt singing. Not that W's voice is wonderful. No! But his Brains & his heart are; & they are more than mere voice in a work of such greatness as this wonderful *Gerontius*. We were delighted and moved to tears. As for dear Mrs E, you can imagine her state of seventh-heaven-beatitude, with eyebrow lifting, neck twisting, forget-me-not glances towards the invisible Heavens!... There was another Rehearsal with Chorus in the evening. The audience (admitted on payment) was quite considerable & the applause ditto.

The performance took place on the Thursday evening. The hall was reported "crammed full though it was a beastly night". Jaeger continued :

> The Hall is a fine one, and acoustically superb.... Every little detail came out beautifully & I can assure you I have not had such an elevating soul-stirring experience for years as listening under such circumstances to this wonderful music. The Chorus was perfect, there is no other word for it. The effect of the pianissimo 12-part passages sung dead in tune (throughout the work) was quite ethereal, while the fortissimo tutti thundered out with imposing force & splendid sonority. They speak of the 'Rhineland tone' among Choruses in Germany & I realised here, where the beauty of the tone lay. It is in a remarkable roundness & sweetness in the female voices & by a big sonority in the male.... The terrific Dämonen Chorus was given with perfect ease & yet with strenuous dramatic force which one could not possibly realise through studying the music on paper. Wüllner did not seem in very good voice & he made one serious blunder; but these were only as blots on a summer sun. Elgar was very nearly called after Part I, & during the long pause (20 minutes or more) he held a reception in the 'Soloisten-Zimmer' where I was told many musicians from other towns congregated to congratulate E & Buths.... In Part 2 Wüllner was great, especially in the 'Take me away'. The big Chorus 'Praise to the Holiest' which astonished the German musicians by its monumental architecture was a masterly performance & the Finale, that wonderful Finale, was another revelation to those who heard it only at

---

[45]   Powell, Mrs Richard: *Edward Elgar - memories of a variation* (Methuen & Co, 3rd ed, 1949) pp 45-9

> B'ham. Unfortunately the Angel was anything but angelically perfect. But though Elgar suffered sundry twitches & pangs when the Angel threatened to 'fall', the audience could not have realised, thanks to Buths' alertness, how dangerously near collapse the performance came once or twice through this d[amned] Angel's shortcomings.... Well at the end E was enthusiastically called, & though he had to fight his way through thronging crowds of people down the stairs & to the front, the applause & shouts were kept up until <u>at last</u> (the time seemed a small eternity) he reached the Podium. There the Chorus & Orchestra & Organ joined in a <u>Tusch</u> [a fanfare] & a large fine laurel wreath was handed to him.

The performance was widely reported in Germany, and English translations of the German reviews create a vivid picture. I am most grateful to David Mason who has translated them for their publication here :

1) *Düsseldorfer Zeitung* of 20 December 1901

Fourth Concert by the Civic Music Society

Düsseldorf, 19 December

When cherished expectations are fulfilled we feel that a good beginning has found a perfect culmination. What was predicted in our preview came to pass in every particular. On the 12th, Dr E Elgar was able to telegraph from Worcester that Philipp Wolfram's *Weihnachtsmysterium*, a masterpiece that has been duly appreciated here at home, had also made a most profound impression at its first British performance, which he had conducted, and now in the same way the telegraph has been spreading the fame of the most important British composer of the present day from Düsseldorf to all the points of the compass. The sacred cantata *The Dream of Gerontius* was an amazing and total success. The composer attended the full rehearsal on Wednesday and even here he was given an unusually warm ovation while today, at the actual performance, the end of the first part saw the impressive audience, including many foreigners, giving the most heartfelt proof of its appreciation and at the end it was indefatigable in again and again congratulating the eminent composer. The task the composer had faced was a most unusual one and for this reason alone people who may not immediately respond to the work will find it impossible to ignore its purely musical power. The subject, deeply serious as it is, has never before been treated in music in such a manner. The composer has dealt with it here not just in a new form but by making quite superlative use of his mastery of every available means of expression, means which only his most eminent predecessors had at their disposal. The overall picture which Elgar's imagination paints is an extraordinary one and it will stir the emotions of the listener to a degree never previously achieved, so extraordinarily accurate is the composer in expressing his meaning. The language of the orchestra is rich in modulation and employs all the latest methods to colour situations and produce moods. His bold brush paints the tender, the grotesque, the lovely and the terrible. The music expresses itself in a startling mixture of the strictly religious and subjectively conveyed feeling. The first can be heard in the psalm-like passages for the choirs, while the second forms the keynote of the outcries of the dying Gerontius and the consoling songs of the Angel. But there is far more besides that Elgar parades before his tensely listening audience. In a double fugue, wildly raging apostates seek to assuage and drown their misery. Contrasting with this are the resplendent choruses of angels and those for the heavenly hosts, which are often divided into 12 parts by using semi and full chorus. The fearsome language in the Chorus of Demons is contrasted with the comforting, solemnly exultant words of the heavenly hosts. However, what must be acknowledged to be of quite outstanding merit is the final chorus of part I. An impression of Handelian grandeur and wonderfully effective sonority is achieved at the words "Go in the name of Angels and Archangels", at which the twelve-part chorus is heard above a pedal point, several of which form a quite remarkable feature of the masterpiece, such as in the broad, supremely eloquent chorus in C major 'Praise to the Holiest in the height'. The chorus also has a superbly beautiful theme in A flat major in the first part at "Be merciful, be gracious" and this theme is used with particularly profound expression at the words "From all the sins that are past".

In the solos, of which a particularly large number are given to the tenor, Gerontius, it is the chromatic element which prevails. The hearer often finds himself reluctant to follow the voice and accompaniment as they slip swiftly from key to key and in the second part this produces some rather tiresome longueurs where the Soul of Gerontius carries on dialogues with the Angel in Wagnerian fashion. Yet the prelude is brilliantly atmospheric in conception. The themes of the work are woven into it with great artistry and it develops swiftly from the plaintive opening theme for the woodwind and violas in unison to a massive grandeur and anguish only to subside again into the opening theme. I have only mentioned certain details of the work which, as one becomes more closely acquainted with it, seem strikingly beautiful and unusual. Many of the English composer's colleagues from his own country and abroad were present and they acknowledged him as a great master endowed with immense erudition and great emotional empathy whose cantata had been impressive in so many ways, some of them quite new. All the parts of the work present difficulties and, as far as the orchestra and the large part it plays, the double chorus and the soloists were concerned, it was given a quite outstandingly successful performance. It was by showing the most complete devotion that Professor Buths achieved this admirable result. The chorus produced impressive power in exactly the same way as, where necessary, it took pains to produce the most delicate pianos, as it did for the voices of the earthly participants and in the chorus of the Souls in Purgatory "Lord, thou hast been our refuge". The difficulties of getting things right in the Chorus of Demons were so convincingly overcome that there was not the slightest sign of how great they in fact were, while the two great concluding choruses can undoubtedly be numbered among the finest achievements the Society has to its credit. Dr Ludwig Wüllner had been chosen to sing the part of Gerontius and his musical assurance and absorption in what he was singing were both of an equally high standard. Again and again his fine enunciation showed itself worthy of special mention. The physical and mental task was almost too demanding and he was deserving of all the more praise for successfully tackling it in that he appeared to be somewhat indisposed, which was evidently the reason for a number of adjustments. The mezzo-soprano role of the Angel had been given to Fräulein Antonie Beel from Frankfurt, who had probably thought her way into the role but whose forced, palatal production proved distracting now and again. Herr Metzmacher's concept of the Priest failed to take proper account of the situation in that he made too forceful an entry into the anxious hush of the death-chamber. He sounded better in the strange passage where he has to sing as the Angel of Death. The semi chorus which was composed of the town's best choral singers showed itself capable of producing an exceptionally beautiful sound. The orchestra required is large, even including two harps, and as it has so often proved able to in the past, it played at the height of its powers, while its effects were also greatly enhanced by the contribution of the organ. Preceding the cantata was the prelude to Richard Strauss's *Guntram*, a work whose polyphonic nature, whose harmony, whose violin tremolo to the woodwinds and whose beautiful melody can probably be looked upon as preparing the way for it. The evening passed in both a solemn and an artistic mood. Düsseldorf may take satisfaction in the fact that though this highly significant work, which was written for the Birmingham Musical Festival and was first performed there on 3 October 1900, will have started on its course through the other great German concert halls from here, the composer will always have special ties with the artistic metropolis on the Rhine.

2) *Rheinisch-Westphälische Zeitung* of 21 December 1901

Concerts

Düsseldorf, 20 Dec. **Fourth Concert by the Civic Music Society - "The Dream of Gerontius"** by **Edward Elgar.** (First performance in Germany). The name of this English composer has been little known to date even though *The Dream of Gerontius* has already taken him as far as opus 38. At Düsseldorf last year a very significant orchestral work of his, the *Variations,* made a highly successful debut. Of the present poem - by the well-known Cardinal Newman - the only translation that existed was one by Molidor but this was totally unsuitable for concert purposes so Buths himself had to produce one which, by following the English text exactly, could be fitted to the notes but which was at the same time a true and artistic reflection of the contemporary spirit of the German language. Buths has succeeded splendidly in his efforts by making use in them of Wagner's style of word and sound. When the poet called his work *The Dream of Gerontius* (he had no particular reason for choosing the name), he probably did so particularly in the light of its second part. Whereas in the first part Gerontius is dying and seeks greater strength to win through the final agony of death by professing his faith before the friends gathered round his death-bed, in the second part the world of reality is left behind and now appears to the incorporeal soul (of Gerontius), which has entered the unseen world, as simply a dream while the spiritual world, the metaphysical world, now seems a new and visible reality.

The first part consists of a highly atmospheric prelude which moulds together the main themes of the work and of the alternating pleas and prayers of Gerontius and his friends, and it ends with the priest's prayer for the dying mingled with the sounds of the funeral bell. It is someone of an indisputably religious nature who speaks to us in this part but the range of moods within which the music moves is precisely circumscribed and in the absence of any antitheses and any marked characterization it might easily be found wearisome. The second part is quite different for here, in a vividly dramatic way, the struggle between the angels of light and the demonic spirits, between the spiritual and the sensual, is acted out before the eyes of the transfigured soul. Here Elgar has produced something imperishably beautiful when he shows his particular greatness in the depiction of celestial peace and produces music whose beauty and unassuming nobility are simply ravishing. Yet he also has the power to conjure up the demonic forces in the life of the spirit with harsh characterisation, as he does in the powerful choruses for the demons, the performance of which is probably the most difficult thing a large choir could be called upon to undertake. The melodic structure, and even more so the harmony, show that Edward Elgar has been receptive to and has assimilated the enormous widening of its powers of expression that music has undergone through the work of Wagner and Liszt. At the same time he is a master of polyphonic construction who knows how to imbue his counterpoint with such genuine feeling that the listener hardly realises how skilfully interwoven the tonal strands are. Similarly, for richness and splendour of instrumental colouring, *The Dream of Gerontius* does not suffer by comparison with even the very latest orchestral works. All in all this is a work which in certain parts may suffer from a monotony of mood but which, when its finer points are appreciated, is something quite extraordinary. Today's first performance was a very considerable success. The composer, who was present but had remained hidden away among the audience at the back of the hall, was so persistently and enthusiastically applauded after both parts that he finally had to appear on the platform and from there bow to Professor Buths and the fine body of orchestral players and chorus singers to show his gratitude to them. The orchestra and chorus, who were faced with immeasurable difficulties, performed an exemplary feat for which no praise could be too great. Of the soloists, the one most deserving of mention is Dr Ludwig Wüllner (of Cologne), who performed the part of Gerontius in declamatory style with such intelligence that it was hardly ever possible to raise any objections to the character or nature of his vocal technique. The bass roles in the work (Priest and Angel of the Agony) were taken by Herr Willy Metzmacher (of Cologne), who in the first part was not fully alive to the situation and sang the prayer for the dying man with an excess of vocal power. His contribution in the second part was very fine. Fräulein Antonie Beel (of Frankfurt am Main) showed no lack of vocal security but her not very opulent and rather palatally produced voice had a hard struggle with the waves of orchestral and choral sound in which she seldom gained the upper hand and was never the victor. The organ part was played by Professor F W Francke of Cologne with the mastery he has often demonstrated before. As an introduction quite unlike it in style and mood, the new work was preceded by the prelude from Richard Strauss's opera *Guntram*, a splendidly euphonious piece of music constructed with magical skill, which the orchestra played with uncommon reverence.

3) *Düsseldorfer Volksblatt*, 22 December 1901

Fourth Concert by the Civic Music Society

"The Dream of Gerontius", poem by Cardinal Newman
composed by Edward Elgar

Düsseldorf, 20 Dec.

A memorable and epoch-making first performance. Not since the days of Liszt - and here we include Philip Wolfrum's *Weihnachtsmysterium* - has anything been created in the field of oratorio which can equal the grandeur and significance of this sacred cantata. The story delves so deeply into the religious, the metaphysical, the eternal that only biblical stories can be put forward as in any way comparable to it. It was written by one of the greatest minds England has ever produced, Cardinal Newman, and in his poem Newman has given the most exalted poetic expression to the Catholic view of life after death, of judgement, heaven, hell and purgatory (in some cases by taking over word for word prayers belonging to Catholic ritual). The thoughts and feelings of a dying man and ideas about the life of the soul after death, developed on the basis of Catholic doctrine - these in short are the subjects of Newman's poem *The Dream of Gerontius*. As we learn from the introduction, which we follow here, Newman is said to have been inspired to write the poem at the deathbed of a beloved friend. In the first part of the poem, he depicts for us the moment of just such a death. Gerontius (there was no special reason for choosing the name) feels the approach of death and asks the friends gathered at his bedside to pray for the salvation of his

Conductors of Gerontius *: (top left) Julius Buths, conductor of the Düsseldorf performances; (top right) Henry Wood, an early British champion of the work; (bottom left) Frederic Cowen; (bottom right) Felix Weingartner*

soul as his own strength is already failing. In professing his faith he is seeking extra strength to enable him to face the final agony of death. Exhausted, he sinks back on to his bed longing for the deliverance of sleep. With the words "Into thy hands, O Lord" he falls asleep. The priest has arrived and intones the "Proficiscere anima Christiana". Bells are heard tolling and the chorus of friends joins in the priest's prayers beseeching eternal rest for the departed. This scene, drawn from the real world, contrasts with the second part of the poem which describes the reception of the soul in the other world. When the poet called his work *The Dream of Gerontius*, what he probably meant, particularly in relation to the second part, was this: the real world has been left behind and its place has been taken by the imaginings of a pious soul; to the incorporeal soul which has now entered this invisible world, the real world now seems to be no more than a dream but the imagined world, the world of the spirit, now seems to be a new and visible reality. Gerontius (ie. the soul of Gerontius) awakes as from a refreshing sleep. Time and space have ceased to exist for him; what are left are his thoughts and feelings. Facing him stands the guardian angel who was his invisible companion in life. What in life was to him merely the idea of a protective love has become a being with whom he can exchange thoughts and who, as he reveals to him the wonders of the other world, is ready to lead him before the throne of the Eternal Judge. Before the gates to the judgement seat are encamped the demons and they demand the souls as their property but redeeming love and mercy await the believer. The guardian angel bears his precious charge onwards through the realms of heaven, filled with the song of the divine hosts, to the mysterious presence of the Almighty, before whose throne he stands to intercede. The soul is ready to receive its judgement; it will look into the face of the Almighty - this is rapture for it but also there is the agonizing perception that it is still in need of a purifying change and is not yet worthy of everlasting peace. The guardian angel enfolds it in his arms and bears it off to the flood that will cleanse it of sin (purgatory), into which the soul is plunged to test it. The poem closes with the angel's song of farewell, which promises that the soul will soon be received into the realms of eternal bliss.

The German translation of the poem was the work of Professor Buths, who has thus acquired for himself a sort of copyright in the work. It was no mean achievement on his part to have found a form in which the poetry could be recast in German which was suitable for musical purposes (for the piano reduction and the singers) and yet still left the German stylish and intelligible. Professor Buths, who here and there may not be entirely innocent of giving a hint of *Parsifal*, did what was best and most suitable in both these senses by rightly taking as his golden rule the principle of spoken declamation. When we see from the results of Buths' work on a modern-day translation how difficult it is to make a transposition of this kind, we may perhaps be a little fairer in our criticisms of past translators into German of operas and oratorios.

In every sense, material like this which is such a tight fusion of the highly poetical, the human and the divine, demanded from the composer an even more profound expression of the imaginative idea at the heart of it. Such deep absorption in the religious spirit could only be achieved by someone whose innermost being was rooted in the religious sentiments of Catholic dogma. As far as the technicalities of composition are concerned, what has to be borne in mind is that, although people's ideas of what the art of religious music is have been different at different times, music in the field of oratorio and the cantata has to keep pace with the art of contemporary music generally and must allow for the advancing demands that art is making. However, because of the work of Berlioz, Liszt and Wagner, the music of our own times has undergone such an enormous increase and expansion in its capacity for expression that the modern-day composer is almost faced with an embarras de richesses as far as the means of expression available to him for constructing his harmonies and melodies are concerned. Edward Elgar, whose opus 38 *The Dream of Gerontius* is, has made use of these means in his compositional practice with good sense and originality and to excellent effect. It is not, say, poor taste when he combines melodic structures from old church music with a mode of expression which seems modern but rather the spirit of the poem. There is a unity of feeling in the poem but the external form this takes is subject to fascinating changes and it is this that gives the atmosphere it creates its power and conviction. As a creator of atmosphere Elgar is supreme and here the contrapuntalist has even been able to deploy his mastery of polyphonic construction in the service of feeling and atmosphere. The first part concludes with a chorus which is divided into ten or twelve parts and develops with all the grandeur and impressiveness of the old classics above a pedal point and choruses like this, or the full and semi choruses of the angels and demons in the second part which, unrivalled though their characterisation may be, present the performers with inconceivable difficulties, are towering monuments to the art of modern-day polyphony. The listener hears the splendid multipart writing in the choruses, but in some of the solos he will also be conscious of a certain monotony of mood which even the highly artistic handling of the orchestra and the most ingeniously modulated writing for the voice cannot compensate for. Otherwise, there is in the solos a simplicity, directness and truth about the composer's melodic structures, which are as beautiful to the ear as they are deeply expressive, which go directly to the heart, and the great success which this most significant work, whose imagination and deeply felt expression cleave to a line that is not of this world, again had at yesterday's performance provides the most convincing proof of the powerful effect the work has. The composer was present and at the end of the first part and at the conclusion of the performance he was called forward. In him we have made the acquaintance of the man who is probably England's most important living composer. Professor Buths can take the credit for having given the work a masterly performance and thus for smoothing the path for it through German concert halls. So totally invigorating was the way in which he conveyed the intellectual and musical meaning of the work to the performers that the resulting interpretation was as effective as the composer could possibly have wished. The choirs, who made child's play of the formidable difficulties of the Chorus of Demons and the other choruses, some of them fugal, and the orchestra both performed with superb sound and uncommonly vivid expression. Frau Karoline Kaiser also contributed at the head of the semi chorus. Of the work's three solo roles, that of Gerontius was taken by Dr Ludwig Wüllner from Cologne, who interpreted it with a directness of expression, a warmth of feeling and a masterly intellectual meaningfulness which allowed one to ignore the inadequacy of his purely vocal resources and the sometimes highly arbitrary way in which the notes were treated. Herr Willy Metzmacher (Cologne) sang the Priest's prayer for the dying man in the first part with the fanaticism of one of Meyerbeer's Anabaptists; the *f* and *ff* in this passage simply do not call for the voice to be deployed with such power. On the other hand he dealt most musically with the song of the Angel of Death in the second part. As the Angel, Fräulein Antonie Beel (Frankfurt am Main) had difficulty in making her not particularly opulent voice heard amongst the flood of sound. The organ was once again played by Professor Francke from Cologne. The first piece played was the prelude to Richard Strauss's opera *Guntram*.

4) *Kölnische Zeitung*, 27 December 1901

Art, Science and Life

[The Dream of Gerontius], an oratorio for choir, soloists and orchestra by Edward Elgar, words by Cardinal Newman, translated into German by Julius Buths, had its first performance in

Germany under the baton of the latter as part of the fourth subscription concert by the Civic Music Society of Düsseldorf. Even though the work undoubtedly employs the very latest means of expression and is based on how music is experienced by modern-day audiences, the impression made on listeners of all proclivities was so gripping that this *Dream* will unquestionably be followed by a large number of realities in the form of performances. It is rare enough that the light of an important new work should shine forth to us from England. Of Sullivan only the immortal and comic Mikado managed to cross the Channel, leaving aside his Ivanhoe which was accorded a solemn funeral at the Berlin Hofoper. But of serious English music there have only been isolated examples of works that have beaten a path to us. A quartet by Stanford and a few instrumental works by Mackenzie are virtually all that there has been while a productive symphonic composer like Cowen is still awaiting his call outside the gates of the German Reich. When the strains of Edward Elgar's orchestral variations were first wafted to our ears two years ago at a Richter concert at London's Queen's Hall, we took the liberty of drawing the attention of German conductors to this work, in which the unusual mastery of technique and the splendid tonal colouring made it highly eligible for export. Buths was the first to take up our suggestion and he has now been joined by others. Yet in the present work Elgar plumbs even greater depths and although Newman's poem describes in poetic language the profoundly disturbing spiritual dilemmas faced by the Catholic believer, Elgar summons up the involving and expressive force required to totally resolve them by the affecting eloquence of his vocal and orchestral writing. The work as a whole is as it were a transposition on to the religious plane of Richard Strauss's *Tod und Verklärung*. The first part depicts the release of the soul from its ailing body: there are a plea and a prayer from Gerontius, a chorus and words of intercession from his friends, and a farewell from the priest. In the second part the guardian angel conducts the soul to purgatory, while imparting to it the most profound and heartfelt enlightenment and not without its being vouchsafed a promised and therefore intimidating sight of the Almighty. In both parts we find beauties of imperishable splendour such as in the chorus "Rescue him, O Lord, in this his evil hour", in the final chorus of the first part with its subtle suggestion of the tolling of bells, and in a vocal polyphony which is a modern revitalisation of the work of the old masters. The second part is of course less spirited rhythmically but the sombrely defiant demons which endeavour to deny the soul access to the pastures of heaven provide a refreshing contrast, and the final chorus of the souls in purgatory is probably the finest thing in the whole work. Elgar stands on the shoulders of a Berlioz, a Wagner, and a Liszt but, except for the need to retain a significant measure of individuality, he has freed himself from their influence. Technical skill of genuine virtuosity may perhaps still be exploited at the expense of depth of imagination but at all events he is one of the leaders of modern music. We have never heard a performance like the one in Düsseldorf and, particularly looking back on the last decade, we must proudly acknowledge the salutary way in which Professor Buths has trained the choirs and also his total absorption in art and all its works. The tenor part was taken by Dr L Wüllner with gripping expressiveness and Herr Metzmacher was an estimable singer of the bass part, while the agreeable talent of Fräulein Antonie Beel brought a substantial voice and rhythmic security to the mezzo-soprano part. The orchestra and Professor Franke at the organ could not be faulted.

Wüllner with gripping expressiveness and Herr Metzmacher was an estimable singer of the bass part, while the agreeable talent of Fräulein Antonie Beel brought a substantial voice and rhythmic security to the mezzo-soprano part. The orchestra and Professor Franke at the organ could not be faulted.

Ludwig Wüllner

We should note that there were two Wüllners. Ludwig was the singer and actor; Franz was his father, the Director of the Cologne Conservatoire and conductor of the Gürzenich Concerts. He was present at Düsseldorf and promised to consider *Gerontius* for a concert in 1902, but I cannot trace that it ever took place.

We need to consider Ludwig Wüllner, for he would sing Gerontius again on two further key occasions, the second Düsseldorf performance at the Lower Rhine Festival in May 1902, and then in London at Westminster Cathedral in June 1903. He preceded his London performance by singing the role at the Liverpool première in March 1903. He was widely admired by English music lovers, including Elgar himself.

Wüllner was born in 1858 and started out with an academic career in German philology. Family reservations stopped him following his desired stage career and so he studied music, but on the death of his grandmother he auditioned for the Duke of Meiningen and was engaged as a leading man and character actor. He took part in the Meiningen company's final tours and left in 1895 with the title of 'Ducal Court Actor'. We follow the story according to the 1900 edition of Spemann's *Das Goldene Buch der Musik*. I am again most grateful to David Mason for this translation :

After a short and extraordinarily successful career giving dramatic readings, in 1896 Wüllner began to appear as a singer. This venture was all the more remarkable in that he was by no means generously endowed vocally. However, the admirable determination which had helped the actor to overcome a natural speech impediment also helped him to make up to some degree for his lack of vocal endowment. By sheer hard work, he managed to wring the utmost possible melodiousness and flexibility from his voice, and what he is lacking in pure beauty of tone he makes up for in artistic intelligence. He is helped in this not only by the force of his strong-willed personality but also by the mastery he has in the handling of words. To convey his intuitive musical and poetic feelings, Wüllner uses first and foremost the language and it is by this very means that he is able to convey such powerful suggestions to the listener. In this way he has become the representative of a new German trend in the singing of lieder and other songs. His singing of German folksongs is unrivalled and his concerts, which at first were only sparsely attended, are attracting larger and larger audiences. Wüllner continues to give occasional dramatic readings. His Manfred [Byron] is a significant and unique achievement.

*Wullner, with and
without moustache!*

I illustrate Wüllner with postcards of him with and without his moustache. It is probable that he was not clean-shaven at Düsseldorf. Though reference to the illustrations in Franz Ludwig's book[46] shows him thus in 1898 and 1900, *The Musical Times* in 1902 shows a moustached figure. Wüllner was widely admired as a lieder singer, and the reception given to his recital at St James Hall in Piccadilly on 20 March 1903 is an additional clue to his success in *Gerontius*[47]:

> ... a notable event... His musical and powerful tenor voice and keen dramatic perception were advantageously displayed in an admirable selection of songs...

Edward F Kravitt[48] quotes a review by E F Taubert from the *Berliner Post* which vividly evokes what audiences saw, as well as heard :

---

[46] Ludwig, Franz: *Ludwig Wüllner - sein leben und seine kunst* (Leipzig, Erich Weibezah Verlag, 1931). I examined the copy in the Library of Congress.

[47] *Musical Times*, April 1903, p 249

[48] Kravitt, Edward F: *The Lied - mirror of late romanticism* (New Haven and London: Yale University Press, 1996) p 60

There is nothing of consequence to mention about his voice with respect to its quality, but his treatment of text is so full of life, so richly endowed, so saturated with his unique perception that as soon as the singer opens his lips one is at once spiritually gripped by him. Every fibre of his being appears to take part with complete devotion to the subject and content of the poem that he sings. The singer follows the music inwardly even when his voice is silent [during instrumental passages]. His bearing is always composed. But this composure seems to be externally forced because, from his heaving breast, his facial pantomime - his raising and lowering of his brow - the listener can feel the performer's excitement very intensively.

Wüllner certainly delivered the text clearly. He came from that tradition of crisp enunciation, pronouncing "the individual consonants, such as 'k' in the word 'gehenkt'("hanged")[in August Strindberg's *Ein Werb*], so that they formed an image of complete barbarism".[49] Yet curiously enough the critics who praised him, in both the United States and Europe, called Wüllner "the singer without a voice".[50]

At once exciting and frustrating to any study of Wüllner is that he made a number of recordings, but only of dramatic *readings*. Thus we have his speaking voice but only briefly and in passing do we hear him singing. Wüllner's recordings are in a now dated histrionic style. An example is Goethe's *Der Konig in Thule*[51] - "A king there was in Thule, was faithful unto death, to whom his lady, dying, a golden goblet gave." - which was made during the First World War. Later, Wüllner recorded von Schillings' *Das Hexenlied* with orchestra,[52] again giving an idea of the voice when projected against an orchestral tapestry, albeit thirty years after *Gerontius*. What do they tell us? Well, it is true that there is often no connection between the register of a speaking voice and singing, but I think it suggests a personality and an approach.

Elgar, in his letter to Novello[53] after the second Düsseldorf

---

[49]   *ibid*, p 54

[50]   *ibid*, p 59

[51]   Issued in 1915. Grammophon 041028 (single sided); 65086 (double sided)

[52]   Recorded by Wüllner with the Berlin Philharmonic Orchestra conducted by Max von Schillings on Grammophon 35000/2, now reissued on Preiser MONO 90294. Earlier, he had made a now forgotten acoustic recording on Odeon R 80113/18, which I have not heard.

[53]   Moore, *Elgar and his Publishers*, op cit, p 320

performance, called Wüllner :

> *...splendid -* not in voice - but intelligence, *genius -* he carried everyone away & made Gerontius a real personage - we never had a singer in England with so much brain - even here he is exceptional.

For Felix Weingartner "Ludwig Wüllner was the 'master of the art of interpretation'. Wüllner 'reflects his deep inner agitation not only upon his face but also upon those of his listeners'. Brahms, Gerhardt and Culp... agreed that Wüllner was the most expressive and thus the most modern interpreter of lieder... The stimulus of the moment was so important to Wüllner... [he] might suddenly perform a lied that was not on the program[me]." [54]

There is one further clue : Wüllner's recording of von Schillings's orchestral melodrama *Das Hexenlied*, noted above, made in 1933 - when Wüllner was almost seventy-five. "The intensity of Wüllner's reading is astonishing. His emotions range from the calm to the violent, even hysterical." [55] It is certainly histrionic. In his recording Wüllner actually sings in some passages - or rather when excited unconsciously moves into *parlando,* using elevated speech at moments of high emotion. One can imagine that the technique, even if only an element of his style, when applied to *Gerontius* would have made for a very emotional, un-British, effect. In fact it may have been this aspect of his performance which generated a number of hostile British criticisms of his performance at the first London *Gerontius* in 1903 (see below). Yet when Wüllner sang the solo at Liverpool on 24 March 1903, possibly his first outing with the English text, it was reported[56] that :

> His phrasing was a delight; his intonation perfect; his method something of a revelation, whilst his finely sympathetic embodiment was peculiarly rich in that spirit of imaginativeness to be found in the work itself.

I think we also need to remember that Wüllner sang 'Sanctus fortis' transposed down, and as the first Düsseldorf performance was immediately followed by the chores leading to the publication of the full score, Elgar must have taken it very seriously to propose publishing

---

[54]   Kravitt, *op cit,* p 192

[55]   *ibid*

[56]   *Musical Times,* April 1903, p 261

the alternative key version, in A flat, as an appendix. So, in fact, when John Coates, and later Gervase Elwes, came on the scene, they benefited from the contrast, 'Sanctus fortis' gaining in their hands a degree of brilliance that may not have been apparent in these early hearings.

Before coming to the enormous razzmatazz attached to the second Düsseldorf performance, we should remember perhaps the least publicised performance of *Gerontius*, which was the London performance of Part I given by 'Miss Holland's Choir', probably only with piano or organ accompaniment,[57] on 8 May 1902 at St Andrew's Hall. This appears to have attracted no press coverage in an age when almost every event received enormous coverage, perhaps suggesting it was an entirely amateur initiative.

The Second Düsseldorf Performance

The next performance of *Gerontius* was the most celebrated early one : the second at Düsseldorf, on 19 May 1902. This time it was given in the presence of Richard Strauss; and Elgar arrived in Düsseldorf on 17 May. By then rehearsals for the Worcester Three Choirs performance in the coming September were already well under way, and Ivor Atkins, in charge of rehearsals at Worcester, in only his second festival as cathedral organist, was unable to join him there, but Elgar and Jaeger later gave him detailed accounts, of which he left notes. I think we can do no better than take these from Wulstan Atkins's book[58]:

> There were banquets each evening, and the English party were lavishly entertained, Strauss going out of his way with Buths to ensure their comfort. For the performance of *The Dream of Gerontius* on 19 May, the organ was again played by Professor F W Francke of Cologne. There was an orchestra of 127 players: 42 violins, 16 violas, 12 cellos, 10 double basses, 6 flutes...

---

[57]   This would have been before the publication of the orchestral full score and parts, and the only set would have been in Germany for the Düsseldorf performance or with those working on engraving and printing it.

[58]   Atkins, E Wulstan: *The Elgar-Atkins Friendship* (Newton Abbot: David & Charles, 1984) p 74

There are some flights of fancy here : some of the woodwind can't be right -

Richard Strauss

oboe d'amour, 6 cor anglais, clarinet, 4 bass clarinets, bassoon, 4 contra bassoons, 8 horns, 6 trumpets. The chorus of 490 singers, which included members of the Düsseldorf Society who had sung in the previous performance, included 169 sopranos, 169 altos, 56 tenors and 96 basses. The semi-chorus was again placed behind the soloists and in front of the orchestra. Dr Ludwig Wüllner repeated his 1901 success as Gerontius, and Johannes Messchaert of Wiesbaden rendered the parts of the Priest and the Angel of the Agony with great dignity and understanding, but it was Muriel Foster, with her impressive and moving performance as the Angel who was the great sensation at this festival. Buths directed a superb, brilliant and deeply moving performance, which was cheered to the echo, with Elgar once again making repeated appearances on the platform. Again he was presented with a large laurel wreath, which for long afterwards adorned a wall in his study.

It was at the Grand Festival Supper at the Town Hall in Düsseldorf, before all the performers and many eminent visiting musicians, that Richard Strauss made his now celebrated toast[59]:

I raise my glass to the welfare and success of the first English Progressivist, Meister Edward Elgar, and of the young progressive school of English Composers.

The English party included Jaeger, Alfred Rodewald, Alfred Kalisch, Vernon Blackburn, Arthur Johnstone, Henry J Wood and "two or three Lancashire enthusiasts, among whom was the late R G W Howson, of the Morecambe Festival".[60] Arthur Johnstone, music critic of the

---

[59]   Scholes, Percy A: *The Mirror of Music 1844-1944.* (Novello and Oxford University Press, 1947) Vol 1, p 123

[60]   "Düsseldorf & Morecambe Reminiscences" (From a Correspondent), *Manchester Guardian,* 2 June 1927

Manchester Guardian was bi-lingual in German and English, and it was he who replied in German for the English party. "Elgar was lionised in the approved fashion, and I recall an excited admirer gripping the shy composer's hand and telling him that 'the orchestra was his instrument'. Buths, the recogniser of his genius, stood quietly by enjoying the enthusiasm which his discernment had generated. Twice in company with the late Arthur Johnstone I was privileged to share the homely hospitality of the Buths family to Dr (as he then was) and Mrs Elgar, the second being a family lunch party. As the party broke up I recall the scene as composer and champion rose from the table and, in true Rhinelander fashion, embraced each other. Never can I forget the light of pride shining in Lady Elgar's eyes."[61]

It is the Angel we need to note at this performance. In Muriel Foster, then only 24, Elgar had found his ideal interpreter. She also sang in the Düsseldorf *B minor Mass* before *Gerontius* and seemed poised for a big career. In 1906 she was in the première of *The Kingdom*. But after her marriage that year she sang much less and a serious illness took her away from oratorio singing, though she later sang in the première of *The Music Makers,* and was long associated with Elgar. She never recorded so we have to content ourselves with her postcard portrait. Sir Henry Wood remarked in his autobiography[62]:

> A richer, warmer mezzo-soprano voice I have rarely heard, and her musicianship was of the highest. I am quite sure that Elgar conceived all his mezzo-soprano parts in Gerontius and later oratorios with Muriel Foster in mind. I do know that no other mezzo-soprano or contralto ever extracted a word of praise from him over their interpretation of his parts.

The account in the *Niederrheinische Volkszeitung* for 20 May 1902 (again translation by David Mason) conveys a vivid picture of the occasion.

The 79th Lower Rhine Music Festival
Second day Düsseldorf, 19 May

On the second day the general picture was much the same as on the first: outside a grey, cold rainy sky discouraged the casual visitor to the festival while inside there were the yawning gaps left by

---

[61]   *ibid*

[62]   Wood, Sir Henry: *My Life of Music* (Gollancz, 1938) p 214

the many unfilled seats in the body of the hall and the gallery. Nor was the public in a particularly enthusiastic mood, probably because the programme, enticing though it may have been to the musician, offered too little fare of a kind easily digestible by festival-goers generally. It would have been better if, after Bach's *Mass in B Minor*, the second day had not presented two works so difficult to come to grips with as Cardinal Newman's religious poem *The Dream of Gerontius* to music by Edward Elgar, and Liszt's *Faust Symphony*. But who can blame the organiser of the festival, our civic Musikdirektor Julius Buths, who this season performed *The Dream of Gerontius* for the first time in Germany, for wanting to present the work to guests coming to the festival from far and wide, like a proud mother wanting to show off her newborn baby, so that a path can be smoothed for it through Germany's concert halls as expeditiously as possible? And what a splendid work the cantata is.

The critic must have been the same as his paper's reviewer of the previous Düsseldorf performance, for he then quoted much of the text already quoted.[63] He then went on :

> Professor Buths - who is also the German translator of Newman's poem - gave the work a consummately beautiful second performance which in many respects was even better than the first in Düsseldorf (about which Elgar and the British music critics who were present sent enthusiastic reports to England at the time). Both the choirs, who made child's play of the formidable difficulties of the Chorus of Demons and the other polyphonic and fugal choruses, and the orchestra performed with superb sound and uncommonly vivid expression. Of the work's three solo roles, that of Gerontius was taken by Dr Ludwig Wüllner from Cologne, who interpreted it with a forthright expressiveness and a masterful intellectual meaningfulness which allowed one to overlook the inadequacy of his purely vocal resources and the sometimes highly arbitrary way in which the notes were treated. The Priest's prayer for the dying man was sung expressively, with the correct sentiment, and in fine style by Professor Messchaert of Wiesbaden, who yesterday gave a most effective performance of the bass part in Bach's *Mass*. The songs of the Angel were quite splendidly sung by Fräulein Muriel Foster, before whose lovely voice and technically accomplished singing in the Mass yesterday even Frau Noordewier-Reddingius in the less prominent soprano part paled, even though her middle register seemed to be more affected by the bronchial trouble she was suffering from today than it did yesterday. The organ was again played by Professor Francke from Cologne.
>
> After the interval, the second work and the final one of the evening was Liszt's great *Faust Symphony*. It is several years since this work of genius, which is one of the towering monuments of 19th century music and one of the peaks in the development of the symphonic style since Beethoven, was last performed by Professor Buths. On this occasion it was performed by the Festival's honorary conductor, Kapellmeister Richard Strauss.

We may see vividly the practical problems attendant on moving from manuscript to printed copy by a few quotations from Elgar's correspondence, published in Jerrold Northrop Moore's two-volume edition of Elgar's letters to his publisher.

---

[63]   See pp23 and 24. For a translation of the full text, see the *Elgar Society Journal* Vol 10 No 6 Nov 1998 pp363-4

In August 1901 Jaeger wrote to Elgar asking him to bring the full score of *Gerontius* when he came to London for rehearsals. In his reply Elgar remarked, "It's difficult to get it to rail or post".[64] At that time Elgar was working on the proofs of the German edition of the vocal score of *Gerontius* which appears to have been completely re-engraved for the German edition.

After the first Düsseldorf performance of *Gerontius*, Novello must have realised the impossibility of continuing with manuscript copies of the key performing materials, and in a postscript to a letter of 24 December 1901 Alfred Littleton indicated that Novello "are ordering the full score and wind parts of *Gerontius* to be engraved".[65] From this decision came the work's later success. On 29 December Elgar wrote to Jaeger, "I *must* see the score... and, as we have not time, or rather time before our departure is too short to allow Neitzel to send it *here*, I am asking him to send it to 1 Berners St whence you can send it to me in Malvern : of course I'll try to call at Berners St on my way thro' London but trains may not allow it".[66]

13 Jan 1902
My dear Elgar
...The Score of Gerontius has at last turned up - at Geidels! [ie. Novello's engravers in Leipzig] I wired for it last Saturday & it came this mg. I have sent it on to you today, *carriage paid*.[67]

24 Jan 1902
... I hope I can have a proof of the score *to keep* as it comes out from Geidel - please, dear one! arrange this because I shall be wanting to refer to it so often - for the revision of the parts as well : G can easily pull two or three proofs : nicht wahr?[68]

We need to note Novello's attempts to develop the European (that is, German) market for British choral music, which despite the high point of *Gerontius*, failed to take off.

---

64   Moore, *op cit*, p 300

65   *op cit*, p 321

66   *ibid.*

67   *op cit*, p 324

68   *op cit*, p 330

Many full scores from J F Barnett's *The Ancient Mariner (Der Alte Matrose)* in 1869 onward were published in bilingual editions, English and German. The full score of *The Dream of Gerontius (Der Traum des Gerontius)* was certainly published thus in 1902. However, in the case of Novello's three big hits with the choral market at home - Parry's *Blest Pair of Sirens*, Stanford's *The Revenge* and Coleridge-Taylor's *Hiawatha's Wedding Feast*, separate German language editions were issued, which from their dates seem intended to capitalise on the success of *Gerontius* in Germany, but in the event all were failures. Additionally the Parry was also issued in Italian and *Gerontius* in French. The editions[69] were as follows:

Parry :   Holde Sirenen 13/3/03 :   500
                 balance 1/7/03 :   194;
         also chorus parts 500 of each, 250 of each later destroyed

Stanford :   The Revenge :   issued 1697 less 347 returned

Coleridge-Taylor : Hiawatha's Hochzeit 11/7/02 : 1000
                   balance 1/7/08868; sheet stock destroyed April 1943.

Only *Gerontius* was successful, and even that was only briefly, and after a stupendous impact over a very few years it quickly faded. It shows what was lost with the demise of the Anglo-German culture in which music publishing operated before the First World War.

Gerontius Finally Arrives in 1902

Novello had now printed all that was needed for performances, and so more than one could be prepared at a time. The full score was published in the summer of 1902, as were the remaining orchestral parts, and inspection copies could be sent to prospective conductors all over Europe, indeed the world. Henry Wood, for instance, insisted on having his own personal copy as a condition of programming it, which he now did at Sheffield. Thus in the remainder of 1902 there would be English performances at Worcester in September, with a new Gerontius, John Coates, with Muriel Foster and Plunket Greene, and

---

[69]   BL Add MS 69559

Four performers who came to be closely associated with Gerontius :
*Above : John Coates (left) and Muriel Foster;
Below : Louise Kirkby Lunn (left) and Gervase Elwes*

in Sheffield in October conducted by Elgar himself. The Sheffield Festival also saw the first performance of the *Coronation Ode* which had been delayed by the King's illness and the postponement of the Coronation.

The decision to programme *Gerontius* at Sheffield was taken soon after the reports of the first Düsseldorf performance began to appear in the newspapers. The *Daily Telegraph* reported as early as 14 February 1902 :

> A change has been made in the programme of the Sheffield Festival with a view to the insertion of Dr Elgar's *Dream of Gerontius* to which a successful performance in Germany has redirected attention.

At Worcester, Elgar experienced his first exposure to the doctrinal problems that would cause him considerable worry in the promotion of the work at the Three Choirs over the next few years. Wulstan Atkins has emphasised the general goodwill felt towards Elgar's music[70]:

> the Invocation to the Blessed Virgin Mary and the saints in the poem, although in accordance with Roman Catholic doctrine, were contrary to the Thirty-nine Articles of the Church of England. Atkins therefore had informal discussions with Canon T L Claughton (the Chairman of the festival executive committee) and with the Dean, Dr R W Forrest. All were anxious for the performance to take place in the cathedral and for a solution to be found. It was clear that the Litany of Saints would have to be omitted, and alterations or omissions made in the references to the Blessed Virgin Mary.

There was also the Cardinal Newman copyright to be resolved, and when Elgar agreed to pursue this, choral rehearsals had already started. However by the time he had to leave for Düsseldorf for the second German performance he still had not taken action. Already the proofs of the programme book were to hand, which had been set with omissions rather than changes, as agreed with Bishop Gore. In the event it was Atkins who called on Father Neville at the Birmingham Oratory, an interview of which he left a verbatim account:[71]

> I spoke of my own feeling for the poem and pointed out that no word would be changed. 'No,' he said, 'there must be no alteration'. I then produced the proofs of the

---

[70]   Atkins, *op cit*, p 70

[71]   *op cit*, p 73

poem as it was to appear in word books. He looked at the opening line where the word 'Maria' had been omitted and indicated by dotted lines - 'Jesu,... I am near to death'. He went carefully through the poem, I at his side... At the end he put the proofs into my hands with the words, 'In that form I give my consent...'

As seems to have been the case with most festival performances of major choral works when London orchestral players were to be employed, there was to be a rehearsal for soloists and band in London, and this had been set to start on 2 September, Elgar having taken the choral rehearsal in Worcester the previous evening. It was over the rehearsals that the solo line-up changed, at the time seeming a disaster but in the event one of those lucky changes that found two principals who would have a significant impact on the future progress of the work, and become inseparably associated with it. William Green had to bow out on finding himself double booked for the rehearsal. This gave Elgar considerable worry, writing "I will not say a word to W Green - it is really absurd to think Gerontius can be whistled through like a well-known work..."[72]

The tenor John Coates, then little-known, was available and at the age of 37 his assumption of the role of Gerontius became the turning point of his career. Coates had only changed from singing baritone parts a year or two earlier, in which guise he sang in musical comedy. As a tenor he moved into operatic roles and also later sang the lead in Elgar's *The Apostles* and *The Kingdom* as well as singing the role of Gerontius many times. His earliest records date from 1907 including 'Lohengrin's Narration' and 'Farewell', and 'Celeste Aida' and, in 1915, Elgar's *In the Dawn*. These give us an idea of the timbre of the voice when he first performed Gerontius, while much later two scenas from Holbrooke's *Bronwen* recorded in 1929 give a flavour of his dramatic delivery and pacing of an extended scene.[73]

To compound the difficulties, Marie Brema who was to sing the Angel now fell ill and also had to withdraw. Although both Green and Brema would sing their roles again, it provided the opportunity for Muriel

---

[72]   *op cit*, p 84

[73]   See *The Record Advertiser* Vol II, no 3 (March-April 1972) pp 2-7 for a Coates discography. The Lohengrin arias are on G&T 02108/9, *In the Dawn*, HMV 02584, reissued on the Elgar Society LP ELG 001, and *Bronwen* is reissued on CD on Symposium SYMCD 1130.

Foster to step into the role, and like Green and Coates she effectively replaced Brema as the first choice Angel for years afterwards. It was, of course, a triumph, and the cathedral was packed, Northrop Moore[74] telling us that the attendance was 3130, though the *Musical Times* noted that "the tremendous strain of the work told upon them somewhat at the end".[75]

In the remaining years before the War, *Gerontius* would be heard seven times more at the Three Choirs - in 1903, 1906 and 1912 at Hereford, in 1905 and 1908 at Worcester; and 1910 and 1913 at Gloucester, where Dean Spence-Jones held out longest against its Catholicism, and even in 1910 insisted on the 'Protestantized' version.[76] At Hereford, Sinclair, perhaps taking his cue from Marchant at Stirling, started the tradition of having two bass soloists, so notably embraced by Sir Malcolm Sargent in his first complete recording in 1945.

We now reach the Sheffield Festival performance on 2 October 1902, just one day short of two years after the first performance. This marked the final acceptance of the stature of the work, self-evident to all present.

> Dr Coward noted the failure of an historic festival choir... Birmingham failed, Sheffield must succeed. Sheffield did succeed. The composer at last heard his conception realised. He had attended a choral rehearsal prior to the Festival and was amazed at the finish and colour of the singing. In connection with the singing of the Demons' chorus, which, under the trainer's teaching, had become a hard snarling, unmusical orgy of "despairing, cursing rage," the composer said to the chorus: "You are just right; you cannot overdo that expression".[77]

This was certainly the impression left with the blind organist Alfred Hollins[78]:

---

[74]   Moore, *op cit*, p 375

[75]   *Musical Times*, October 1902

[76]   Boden, Anthony: *Three Choirs - a history of the festival* (Stroud: Alan Sutton, 1992) pp 148, 267

[77]   Rodgers, J A: *Dr Henry Coward - the pioneer chorus master* (John Lane, the Bodley Head, 1911) pp 33-4

[78]   Hollins, Alfred: *A Blind Musician looks back - an autobiography* (Edinburgh and London: W Blackwood & Sons, 1936) p 268

Six notable choral trainers : (above left) Arthur Fagge of London;
(above right) James Whewall of the North Staffordshire Festival Chorus;
(below left) Henry Coward of Sheffield; (below right) the organists-cum-choir-
masters of the Three Choirs, (from left to right) Atkins, Sinclair and Brewer

It was as great a success as the performance at Birmingham had been a failure. I shall never forget the realistic effect of the demons' chorus; the snarling was terrifying... In the Sheffield rendering I lost much of the musical detail of the chorus of demons, but the effect was infinitely more realistic.

This was a time when Sheffield - along with most other major cities - was very conscious of its civic dignity, and so Elgar's presentation of a copy of the printed full score to the Sheffield Free Library as a "token of sincere gratitude and friendship"[79] must have been a matter of considerable local pride.

The Gerontius and Angel from Worcester were now joined by David Ffrangcon-Davies in the bass parts. This really established *Gerontius* with the British public, and until a nervous breakdown only five years later ended his public singing career, it forged a link between Ffrangcon-Davies and Elgar. Perhaps these performances were particularly important as springboards for the most prestigious performances in 1903, which was the final breakthrough as far as the reputation of the music was concerned. It was

a huge success: just as at Worcester, the demand for seats was greater than any other festival event.[80]

Performances in 1903

In Britain there were performances in Sheffield, Stirling, Manchester, Hanley, Wolverhampton, Liverpool, Birmingham, Middlesbrough, Bristol, at the Three Choirs at Hereford, and at long last in London at the newly built Westminster Cathedral. There were also performances in Europe at Danzig and Darmstadt and very probably in many other centres. Certainly in 1902 in the euphoria of Düsseldorf, performances were promised at Cologne, Aix-la-Chapelle, Heidelberg, Breslau, Liege and Utrecht.

The Dream of Gerontius was established after its two celebrated performances in Düsseldorf in 1901 and 1902, and it is interesting to

---

[79]   Mackerness, E D: *Somewhere Further North - a history of music in Sheffield* (Sheffield: J W Northend, 1974) p 99

[80]   Moore, *op cit*, p 375

see Novello attempting to back this up with copies sent 'On sale', which I take to mean 'sale or return':

Table 6 - GERONTIUS :
Copies Sent on Sale

20 Becker of Breslau
20 Hainanen of Breslau
10 Cohmerill(?) of Vienna
20 Doblinger of Vienna
25 Gutmann of Vienna
20 Rose of Vienna
20 Robittschek of Vienna
20 Schmiddl & Co of Vienna

Yet we find 336 copies of the German edition were consigned to 'basement rack' on 5 June 1912. So the total number of copies issued must be under 1,000.

We might take special note of seven of these performances; those at Hanley and Manchester, Bantock's performance at Wolverhampton, the London première, the two first American performances, and the Sydney performance. Much of this was crowded into March, which saw nine performances, six in the UK and three overseas, by when Elgar was deeply involved in the headlong crisis attendant on writing *The Apostles* in time for the Birmingham Festival at the beginning of October.

In Edinburgh in January, conducted by the composer Frederic Cowen, it achieved good notices and further established John Coates and Muriel Foster in their roles. There followed in Danzig on 11 March what may have been the first overseas performance since Düsseldorf in May 1902. Reporting to the *Musical Times*,[81] Dr Carl Fuchs rated it :

... an artistic achievement of the first rank, chiefly on the part of the conductor, Herr Fritz Binder, but also of the chorus (that of the Sing-Akademie) and the orchestra. The excellent soloists, Frl. Frida Kisielnicki, Herr Fr. Dierich and Herr Joseph Staudigl, rounded off and completed a performance which was received with enthusiasm...

---

[81]   April 1903, p 247

Mentioning civic pride as a driving impulse in the Sheffield performance reminds us of the involvement of various crack northern choirs in the final establishment of Elgar's masterpiece. Reginald Nettel has reminded us[82] of the strong sense of rivalry engendered by the competitive choral festival movement largely in the north. These provided highly trained bodies of singers anxious to outdo their neighbours :

> Elgar received a deputation from the Potteries asking him if he would be prepared to conduct a performance of *The Dream of Gerontius* in Hanley. The proposed arrangements, moreover, were such as would gladden any composer's heart. Elgar was to be consulted about the choice of soloists, he was to choose the members of the orchestra himself, and he was offered a chorus that had just achieved a record by winning the premier award of the Welsh National Eisteddfod two years in succession... Few of the singers had any doctrinal sympathy with Cardinal Newman's faith. Being mainly recruited from the northern end of the Potteries, the chorus comprised a good proportion of Methodists, but that in no way damped their ardour for Elgar's music. Indeed the performance went far to justify Mr Ernest Newman's theory that music is a direct transmitter of spiritual feeling, transcending the quibbles of theology.[83]

The driving force behind this performance, by the North Staffordshire Choral Society, was Havergal Brian, but the architect of its success was their choirmaster James Whewall.[84]

In fact there was a near clash with Richter's first performance since Birmingham, to be given in Manchester, and the one at Hanley which Elgar conducted himself. At Manchester Richter took great care with the performance,[85] but although scheduled for 5 March it had to be postponed for a week when John Coates fell ill. It thus took place the

---

[82]   Nettel, Reginald: *Music in the Five Towns - a study of the social influence of music in an industrial district* (Oxford University Press, 1944); *North Staffordshire Music - a social experiment* (Rickmansworth: Triad Press, 1977)

[83]   Nettel, *Music in the Five Towns*, op cit, pp 89-90

[84]   Bury, David: 'Elgar and James Whewall - a study of the North Staffordshire Choral Society', *Elgar Society Journal*, Vol 2 No 3, September 1981, pp 10-16

[85]   Fifield, Christopher: *True Artist and True Friend - a biography of Hans Richter* (Oxford: Clarendon Press, 1993) p 360

night before Elgar's own performance at Hanley, in which many of the Hallé Orchestra were to participate. Richter must have been chagrined when Elgar's dress rehearsal in the Victoria Hall, Hanley, clashed with his performance, meaning that Elgar was not there to witness his champion from the Birmingham Festival finally triumph. The *Musical Times* reported[86]:

> Nothing, it may safely be said, in the way of a musical performance in Manchester has ever been better prepared than the rendering of Elgar's *Gerontius*... The orchestral parts were, I believe, considerably better done than ever before - and having heard two German renderings, as well as the original production at Birmingham and the repetitions at Worcester and Sheffield, I may perhaps be allowed to express an opinion on the point. The chorus and semi-chorus showed themselves completely at home in the music; Mr Coates gave his highly expressive interpretation of Gerontius's tenor solos; Miss Brema sang in the Angel's part with her customary power; and Mr Black gave the utterances of the Priest and the Angel of the Agony in unexceptional style. The impression created by the performance was altogether extraordinary, most of the vast audience remaining till some time after the end to applaud the conductor, principals, and, in fact, everyone connected with the performance.

Richter would go on to give a total of ten performances of *Gerontius*.[87]

The Hanley performance followed the next day and it seems probable that many people attended both. The local paper felt "without exaggeration the singing of the Choir was the finest which has yet been heard in the work".[88] Elgar would not forget what they had done for him. After Hanley Elgar wrote to express his thanks[89]:

> I was delighted, and, I will add, deeply impressed by their performance. I have rarely heard such finished, musicianly singing, and have never had less trouble to get my exact reading - often a difficulty with one [orchestral] rehearsal. This was made easy for me by the splendid training of Mr Whewall and by the alert, attentive, and friendly attitude of the chorus. The tone is magnificent - silvery, yet solid, well-balanced, and sonorous, and the attack fine. The infinitesimal trifles, not shortcomings, which did occur, were caused by want of more time in rehearsal with the orchestra. I place the chorus in the highest rank, and I thank the members for giving me the opportunity of hearing a performance of my work almost flawless.

---

[86]   *Musical Times*, April 1903, p 262

[87]   Fifield, *op cit*, p 504

[88]   Bury, David: 'Elgar and James Whewall...', *op cit*, p 14

[89]   Nettel, *op cit*, p 91

At the time this was important for Elgar, but it soon achieved a wider significance as the North Staffordshire District Choral Society were chosen, at Elgar's insistence, to sing in the London première in Westminster Cathedral in June.

Before then, the performance trained and conducted by Granville Bantock had been a notable one. The concert closed the Wolverhampton Festival Choral Society's 35th season, at Agricultural Hall, Wolverhampton. Bantock started his programme with Tchaikovsky's Sixth Symphony, thus presenting the two leading novelties of the day in the one concert, and it was certainly very much a new music concert. The *Midland Evening News* reported[90] that the society

> had been busy preparing for the performance for some months past, and Mr Granville Bantock, who has special advantages in relation to its interpretation, had done everything possible to ensure a performance worthy of the work itself, and of the reputation of the Wolverhampton Society.

Reviewers noted the "magnificent" contribution of the orchestra, and highlighted Henry Lyell Tayler, principal violin, who would later become celebrated in his own right as the conductor of the Brighton Municipal Orchestra.

Bantock only had one soloist of national reputation, in William Green as Gerontius. The *Wolverhampton Express & Echo*[91] wrote :

> Mr Green's robust style seemed a trifle too much so in the earlier portions - one could hardly conceive a dying man being quite so lusty. Afterwards he subdued himself more in keeping with the idea of a disembodied spirit, and sang with great beauty and effect... Mr Green, however, is a singer of whom we have such a high opinion that we expect very much from him, more than we quite obtained on Monday. For Miss [Alice] Lakin's singing as the Angel, however, we can have nothing but praise. It was beautiful in quality, and reverent in expression. Any attempt at display in such a part would be fatal, and Miss Lakin sang with perfect taste in this respect. Mr Charles Knowles's great voice and sincere style left nothing to be desired.

---

[90]   *Midland Evening News*, 24 March 1903. Cutting in Bantock Collection, Worcester Record Office

[91]   24 March 1903. Worcester Record Office

Mr William Green

The critic of the *Wolverhampton Daily Gazette* put a slightly different spin on it; clearly Alice Lakin was not as bold in her presentation as her colleagues in theirs[92]:

[92]   24 March 1903. Worcester Record Office

Mr William Green sang grandly, as usual; Mr Charles Knowles was in every way excellent, and Miss Lakin proved herself thoroughly adequate to a part which is intellectually as well as vocally exacting.

How far this same critic was exercising poetic licence when he quoted Elgar as shaking his head deprecatingly at the end and saying; "It was too perfect: it was too perfect!" as he walked away slowly and sadly, it is difficult to judge.

Performances outside Europe began to take place, and the first productions in Chicago, New York, and Sydney provided a notable test of the music's prospects in the longer term. They also provided the choral forces in those places with a considerable technical challenge.

The American première took place in Chicago on 23 March 1903, quickly followed by New York on 26 March. In Chicago the concert was given by the Apollo Music Club conducted by Harrison M Wild, a notable pioneer of turn of the century choral works. In the programme of their concert on 9 February 1903 the forthcoming performance of *Gerontius* was announced as "one of the foremost musical works of the present generation and has awakened wide enthusiasm among musicians in England and throughout Europe. It contains some of the most marvellous orchestral and choral effects that have ever been conceived. Musicians who have heard it compare it with Wagner's *Parsifal.*"[93]

The scrapbook of the Apollo Society is held by the Chicago Historical Society. Unfortunately owing to the very deteriorated and very brittle state of the paper on to which the cuttings[94] were originally pasted, it is likely that this will not long survive. The following extenso quotations paint a vivid picture of how the music was received.

---

[93]   The Chicago Public Library provided me with a copy of the programme for the concert.

[94]   The cuttings themselves are in rather better condition but as in the case of some photograph albums of that period as the pages crumble they are likely to take the cuttings with them unless restoration takes place very soon. It is beyond photocopying. I had to transcribe the cuttings in longhand.

THIRTY-FIRST SEASON
ONE HUNDRED AND SIXTY FIRST
CONCERT

Apollo Musical Club

PRESENTING

The Dream of Gerontius
Elgar

SOLOISTS

MRS. JENNY OSBORN HANNAH, *Soprano*
MR. EVAN WILLIAMS,   *Tenor*
MR. GWILYM MILES, *Baritone*

THE CHICAGO ORCHESTRA

MR. WM. MIDDELSCHULTE, *Organist*
MR. ARTHUR DUNHAM, *Rehearsal Accompanist*

MR. HARRISON M. WILD, *Conductor*

THE AUDITORIUM
MONDAY EVENING, MARCH TWENTY-THIRD
NINETEEN HUNDRED AND THREE

*The Weber Grand is used at the
Apollo Club Rehearsals*

The US premiere of the work : the choir (below); the title page of the programme (left); the conductor, Harrison M Wild (above) and the three soloists, Jeannie Osborn Hannah (mezzo), Evan Williams (tenor) and Gwilym Miles (baritone)

Mrs. Jenny Osborn Hannah

Mr. Evan Williams

Mr. Gwilym Miles

Inter Ocram [*Chicago*] 24/3/1903

'THE DREAM OF GERONTIUS'

First American Performance of Cantata Given by Apollo Club

A noteworthy occasion in music the country over last night was the first performance in America of Edward Elgar's musical setting of Cardinal Newman's poem *The Dream of Gerontius*...

The scene in the theatre was little short of inspiring. An audience of over 4,000 filled almost every seat back of the parquet to the last row of the family circle. On the stage stood the conductor, Harrison M Wild, facing an orchestra and chorus of over 400 persons, one of the largest gatherings on the Auditorium stage. The Chicago orchestra, assisted by several outsiders, occupied the center, with the three soloists in front and a small portion of the chorus to one side.

Back of the orchestra sat the gigantic chorus with the kettle drums, the trombone players, and the other brass instruments wedged in between the front rows of the altos and sopranos. On both sides were the men in solid rank far back almost to the rear wall. Their rows of black set off the light dresses of the women. It was a striking, picturesque sight, impressing the eye - as the words and music later impressed the ear - with the dignity, solemnity, and power of the occasion.

And the music! An orchestra of 100 pieces, in which the composer had skilfully utilized drums and brass to produce the utmost wealth of sound; the grand organ - the loudest and most voluminous organ in the world - pealing forth its droning double bass and its pealing treble like a dozen church bells on Easter morning...

Musically considered the evening was not above criticism. But it should be remembered that the task attempted last night was perhaps more difficult than any ever before undertaken by the Apollo club. Elgar's music bristled with technical difficulties... William Middelschulte, organist, was, as always, above criticism.

[Chicago] Daily News 24/3/1903

Edward Elgar's *Dream of Gerontius*, presented last evening, came as the crowning work not only of this season but of the years of previous endeavour of the Apollo Music club. This great choral composition, neither oratorio nor cantata, which was given last night in the Auditorium for the first time in Chicago, is such a departure from the timeworn form of the sacred musical drama that its presentation was in the nature of a revelation. Modern composers with the exception of the Englishman and the American have not expended much time on the oratorio and its ilk, contending that this class of music is losing its popularity; its range is too narrow for modern ideas - and, in fact, that the oratorio is about to become extinct, to put the matter bluntly.

The Dream of Gerontius, however, introduces new and great possibilities along this line of composition. The orchestral work becomes the prominent feature as in the Wagnerian dramas, the leit-motif is the keynote to its construction and the choral work is divided and subdivided... The tenor has a monopoly of the solo work, which was unfortunate last evening because of the indisposition of Evan Williams, to whom was assigned the leading role. Mr Williams was suffering from a cold of such severity as to cause wonderment that he could proceed with his difficult task and have any voice left. He held bravely through, however, with no apparent nervousness, delivering the 'Sanctus fortis' with its involved tempo and dramatic requirements in a manner that convinced as to his capability under more propitious circumstances. Mrs Jeannie

Osborn Hannah, who is well equipped both vocally and interpretatively for oratorio, was, as usual, successful with the soprano solos - which lie rather low, by the way. As for Gwilym Miles, his magnificent barytone [*sic*] rolling forth was never more grateful than when it sounded the chant of the priest with clear enunciation and resonant volume after muffled and half-lost tones of the tenor...

Harrison Wild was most successful with the orchestra and the chorus, the latter rising with fine enthusiasm in the Demon chorus...

[*Chicago*] *Record Herald* 24/3/1903

The Dream of Gerontius lies in the tonality of *Everyman*. Several centuries before Cardinal Newman put pen to paper the Dutch monk who wrote the old morality play sounded the keynote - the chord of human agony and unfaltering faith - which dominates the later work. But the poem, with its luxuriant musical garb, differs as widely from the primitive, Gregorian quality of the play as do the Cardinal's rich vestments from the monk's severe garb. At the fundamental notes the resemblance stops; the monk halts at the gate of the unknown, the cardinal goes on and follows the soul of Gerontius even past the final judgement.

Thematically, harmonically and orchestrally, Elgar's oratorio, founded on Cardinal Newman's poem, which was presented at the Auditorium last evening by the Apollo Musical Club, shows the influence of Wagner. The use of the leit-motiv, with various metamorphoses; the surprising and daring harmonic progressives [*sic*]; the remarkable orchestration; the treatment of the vocal passages - especially in the second part - prove that the composer has sat at the feet of the master of Baireuth [*sic*].

Elgar has, however, outstripped Wagner, Berlioz, Richard Strauss and all other original writers in his demands on the orchestra, and the listener feels at the close that he has heard the work of one who is undoubtedly the greatest composer England has produced since the days of Purcell at least. That it is a masterly work cannot be doubted.

With regard to devotional fervour and spiritual exaltation, the opening chorus, the 'Kyrie', sung by friends at the deathbed, was one of the most effective features of an evening of music that was a delight from beginning to end. A chorus of French horns in the distance could hardly have surpassed the mellow softness of the singers' tones. It was a tone, too, that by its living, fervent quality fairly searched out the heard strings and made them vibrate in sympathy with the pain of those who watched the final agony.

With the opening of the second section, which is devoted to the Soul's flight, the composer faces the difficult task of representing the silence of infinite space through the medium of an enormous sound-producing organism. It is not hard for the imagination to accept the music for what it is supposed to represent, for the interweaving of the instrumental parts gives a peculiar effect.

Following this soon came the high lights of the work, and the colours are laid on with a daring hand. The orchestral representation of the demons is striking and the choruses with their double fugues and augmented intervals are extremely difficult. When the soul of Gerontius is taken into the divine presence there is a passage where the composer has written: 'For one moment must every instrument exert its fullest force.' This chord comes suddenly, out of silence, and the effect is appalling.

It was a herculean task that confronted Mr Wild, the conductor, but both he and the singers succeeded admirably. It is current rumour among musicians that Elgar himself almost gave up the attempt to do what Mr Wild succeeded in accomplishing. At the first performance in Birmingham the final rehearsal was a dismal failure, and Elgar, it is said, came close to not presenting his work.

Evan Williams, the tenor soloist who represented Gerontius, sang unevenly. His tone was sometimes of pure quality and again defective. His low notes were almost gone and several passages were cut out for his benefit. Gwilym Miles, barytone [*sic*], has a resonant voice of great volume that is always even and musical. Mrs Jenny Osborn Hannah fully sustained her reputation as a soprano of unusually high class.

W L Hubbard wrote in the *Chicago Tribune* :

The first performance in America of Edward Elgar's *The Dream of Gerontius* took place last evening at the Auditorium, under conditions that were both propitious and gratifying. The Apollo club, under the leadership of Harrison M Wild, was in exceptionally fine form; the Chicago orchestra, after more thorough preparation than is, as a rule, possible for an oratorio performance, played the intensely difficult score with a technical finish and a beauty worthy of the splendid organization's high standing; the solo parts were in competent hands, and - what was especially gratifying - the audience was of a size that left no unoccupied space in the great hall, and that gave assurance that the giving of a new work does not of necessity mean financial loss. It was an evening important in the music annals of the country, and it is subject for congratulation to all concerned that no untoward condition marred its success.[95]

Having read these various reports of the performance, the account in *The Musical Leader and Concert Goer* suggests that there were considerable problems with the performance, concluding "the choral part of it (always judging by the results obtained) seems to be distinguished chiefly for monotony. Never once was there a suggestion of life or spirit." The biggest bombshell was left for the end, where the writer reports : "never was there a colder, more unenthusiastic audience gathered for an 'Apollo' concert. The work fell flat, and petered out at the finish without so much as a hand raised to applaud."[96] In the light of the other accounts can this be true? It would be interesting to trace corroborating evidence in diaries, letters or autobiographies of those present.

In fact, the *Musical Times*[97] published one such report, but an account in glowing terms. It underlined the emerging nationalist phenomenon, that once the place of *Gerontius* had been established in the British press, it was no longer acceptable to report it in negative terms.

---

[95] Hubbard, W L : "Dream of Gerontius" *Chicago Tribune* 24 March 1903 p 5

[96] "Production of Elgar's 'Dream of Gerontius' at Apollo Club" *The Musical Leader and Concert Goer* April 1903 p 13

[97] *Musical Times* May 1903 p 311

The first performance in America of Dr Elgar's *Dream of Gerontius* was given by the Apollo Musical Club of Chicago, on March 23, with every indication of success. The President of the Club, Mr Clarence P Van Inwegen, in a private letter to an English friend, thus refers to the event:-
'I thought you would be interested in learning how *The Dream of Gerontius* was received by a representative American audience... We had more than four thousand people present - hardly a vacant seat in the vast auditorium. It was an audience made up of musical people of the city and for a hundred miles around Chicago, some enthusiasts coming five hundred miles to hear the work presented by the Apollo Club.
Speaking from my own standpoint it was the greatest and most satisfactory concert the Club has ever given. The work was studied on-and-off for upwards of five months, and though it was not given so well as it will be next season (for we are to repeat it), it was a great triumph. All through the first part you could literally have heard a pin drop, and so intense was the feeling that many sat as in a trance.

In that same Chicago Historical Society file there is preserved the typescript memoirs of the conductor of *Gerontius*, Harrison M Wild. These were later published in many instalments in *The Music News* during 1929. As a guide to choral conductors seeking repertoire this is a wonderful record of enterprise, and a number of works that are named and were then successful are now totally forgotten. There is also the typescript of a thesis history of the Apollo Music Club which lists the works first produced in Chicago by the Club. Other Elgar performances included *The Light of Life* (30 November 1903), *The Apostles* (23 April 1906), and *Caractacus* (4 March 1912).[98] Looking at the programme for the first of these I was delighted to find it in a double bill with *King Olaf* until, on looking more closely, I discovered that this was not Elgar's *King Olaf*, but the Danish-born American composer Carl Busch whose *King Olaf* was one of a succession of cantatas written in the 1890s.

In his memoirs Harrison Wild highlighted the difficulties he had with *Gerontius*.

We had rehearsed it several months, when I was requested by the president to give it up. 'It was too difficult and the audience wouldn't receive it.' But we did give it, and the audience did receive it. I didn't get, and couldn't get the club to do for me as I wished in the Demon chorus. I wanted a thin, harsh, nasal tone, but the idea prevailed, I guess, that to sing in such manner was beneath the dignity of the Apollo.

---

[98] Hilton : *History of the Apollo Club of Chicago*. Thesis p 91 (Carbon copy in Apollo Club papers, Historical Society of Chicago]

Along came the Sheffield chorus[99]; that body sang with just that snarl and the effect was startling.[100] Then the Apollo gave in, and in our second performance my wish was carried out.[101]

In New York the performance took place on Thursday 26 March, but in fact the work had been heard two nights previously, on Tuesday 24 March when the performers gave a "special invitation rehearsal" of the work "for the benefit of the public school teachers, who are concerned with the teaching of music and many of whom are unable to hear the best concerts."[102] The performers on this occasion were identical to those of the public concert two days later, except that David Bispham was unable to take the bass roles which were taken by the local soloist Julian Walker.

The conductor, Frank Damrosch, reported to the *Musical Times* :

> *The Dream of Gerontius* has been heard in New York, and has made a deep impression. No work of recent years has created such profound interest, both during its preparation and at the performance, and the general sentiment is one of joy and gratitude that at last there has appeared a composer who has original ideas and is able to express them sincerely in his own way and language.

The New York papers wrote at considerable length about the performance, *The Sun* giving the concert 12 column inches the next morning and two days later in its Sunday edition two complete columns, writing in eulogistic terms. The Sunday edition of *The New York Times* gave a similarly lengthy treatment. These and other accounts deserve to be reprinted but there is not space to do so here. As Richard Aldrich wrote in his piece *"The Dream of Gerontius* does indeed show a vital power, a soaring imagination, a fervour of religious

---

[99]   On 24 April 1911 conducted by Elgar himself

[100]   For the story of the tour of the Sheffield Musical Union during 1911 see *Round the World on Wings of Song* by Sir Henry Coward, (Sheffield, J W Northend, 1933). The account of the visit to Chicago is on pp 65-70.

[101]   Wild, Harrison : 'History of the Apollo Club of Chicago', *The Musical News [Chicago]* 3 May 1929 p 30 [Cutting in the Apollo Club papers, Historical Society of Chicago]

[102]   'Invitation Rehearsal of *The Dream of Gerontius', The New York Times* 25 March 1903

exultation, a dramatic impulse, a command of the resources of choral and orchestral writing that put it far above any other piece of music brought forth in England for generations."[103] In a letter to Elgar, W H Bowes, writing on the letterhead of Royal Exchange Assurance, New York, reported : "At the end of Part one there was tumultuous applause and at the end of Part II the thousands filed out almost in silence - This speaks for itself".[104]

When we come to the Sydney Town Hall performance, on 21 December 1903, *The Sydney Morning Herald* critic was inclined not to be impressed, and it is difficult to decide how good the performance may have been. However, a clue to the local musical climate and the critic's sensibilities may be found in his preference for Spohr's *The Last Judgment* which had been given in St Andrews Cathedral - next door to the Town Hall - the previous Sunday.[105]

A debt of gratitude is certainly owed by the entire musical community to Mr J A Delany,[106] the choir of St Mary's Cathedral, and the hundreds of singers associated in last night's performance for their enthusiasm and enterprise in producing Edward Elgar's new oratorio, *The Dream of Gerontius*. The complex character of the new work, with its choruses that occur in eight and sometimes in 12 parts, must have involved the most arduous rehearsal for the attainment of such accurate results as those yielded last night.
The oratorio itself is devotional but gloomy, and in spite of some melodious phrases the solo music must be summed up as ungrateful. Wagner's influence is shown in the employment of motives, of which Dr Jaeger, in his analytical notes to the book of the words, enumerates more than thirty. The importance of the instrumentation, which is paramount, should also be noted. Regarding the work

[103]   Aldrich, Richard : "Elgar and the English Oratorio", *The New York Times* 29 March 1903.

[104]   Original pasted in Elgar cuttings books, Elgar Birthplace, Broadheath

[105]   I am most grateful to Max Keogh of Sydney for researching Australian newspapers and reminding me of the local geography.

[106]   John Albert Delany (1852-1907). Delany had been born in London and accompanied his parents to Australia when a small child. He enjoyed a varied musical career focused on the demands of organist and choirmaster in Roman Catholic churches, but including playing violin in theatre orchestras, conducting and opera. He composed a *Captain Cook Cantata*. His *Mass in A* of 1892, clearly influenced by Gounod, has been recorded on CD (Walsingham Classics WAL 8010-2CD) by St Mary's Cathedral Choir/ Jubilee Choir/ Sydney Conservatorium Choir & Chorale/ Jubilee Orchestra/ David Russell.

as a whole, it must be pronounced dull. Hence, once more, our gratitude to Mr Delany and the orchestral forces so ably led by Mr Rivers Allpress. But for their art-enthusiasm, the first performance in Australia of Elgar's oratorio might have been delayed for years, and in that case we should all have been 'bursting in ignorance' of a work which the great body of English writers have trumpeted forth as likely to rival the immortal efforts of Handel. In the meantime we shall adventure the prediction that the London press will gradually withdraw from this untenable position. The new oratorio, composed for the Birmingham Festival of October, 1900, and rendered last year [ie June 1903] at the Roman Catholic Cathedral, Westminster, by a choir from North Staffordshire has not yet been produced by a London choral society, nor will it be performed in that way until March, 1904. This delay might not have meant anything. After hearing the work, the conclusion to be drawn is that it meant a great deal.

At this far remove from the centre of action, conjectures can but be of a hazardous character, yet it should be reasonable from the course of events to suppose that Dr Elgar is not only a musician of undeniable talents, but also a smart business man. Reference has already been made to a masterly analysis of the oratorio by the eminent musical critic Dr Jaeger. It is erudite, amazingly detailed and of immense length. Also it has to be added that it is from the pen of a writer who is intoxicated with admiration for Dr Elgar. Either because he was commissioned to make this analysis, or for pure love of art and hard work, Dr Jaeger prepared this pamphlet in such good time that it was ready for distribution at the Birmingham Festival already mentioned. That is to say, the entire audience, including all the journalists had this amazing eulogy of Dr Elgar's oratorio placed before them as a guide to the work. The question which must always remain unanswered for a few years is this - 'Had this fact any influence upon the press opinion of the hour, and in that way upon the public opinion of the day?' Because Jaeger's talent must not be underrated. His analyses have long been celebrated, and very properly so. What is more is that it is so complete and shows such a minute study of the music (from the viewpoint of a rapturously enthusiastic Elgarite), that after reading it is impossible to write a line about the work without trespassing upon the ground it covers.

Before leaving this subject, which is important also because many who were present last night left the hall with the book in their possession, it may be useful to quote one of many instances in which the voice of honest commonsense is forced to protest against the finely-worded comments of the eminent but too partial Jaeger. It is at the point where Gerontius dies, and the 'Miserere' theme (p 19) 'vanishes into space, its last chord unresolved, the prayer unfinished, as the immortal soul of Gerontius takes its flight to God.' Then follows the bass solo of the Priest, and we are instructed (p 29) 'As the sunshine suddenly flooding an erstwhile darkened sick room is welcomed when the patient is well, so the bright, sonorous chords, which announce and support the Priest's words 'Proficiscere, anima Christiana,' are welcomed.' Not at all. Pure, authoritative, misleading Jaegerism. Whatever the chords are the whole effect of the solo is inky-black, 'a darkness that may be felt,' a gloomy piece of declamation which possesses some element of grandeur, indeed, but taken as a whole is so frightfully lugubrious as to be almost ugly. And the new oratorio is flooded most gloriously with 'sunshine' of this kind! Similarly, there is a learned note on p 45 concerning the bass solo of the Angel of the Agony, to the effect that the composer shows 'an exquisite effect in spite of a flagrant violation of the rules against consecutive fifths, and proving once more that a master of his art can step boldly outside the pale of restricting rules to produce the intrinsically beautiful.' 'But no,' cries the reader, who has an ear for melody, and the courage of his opinions, 'this is not beautiful. I know little of your consecutive fifths, and care less, but I do know when an aria is uncouth and inexpressive from a vocal standpoint, and I am listening to such an aria now. The "intrinsically beautiful" is just exactly what I do not find.' Very few readers will dare to say this, unfortunately, because they cannot help seeing that the writer of the Notes is a learned musician, and it does not occur to them that he may also be a violent partisan. This at any rate is the only conclusion that we can come to after listening most carefully to the new oratorio. Just as Berlioz's *Faust* and Braham's [*sic*] *Song of Destiny* when first produced here but a few years ago exceeded in emotional power and beauty all that we had dared anticipate, so equally do we find *The Dream of Gerontius* clever and learned, but very rarely inspired and in no wise exciting to the emotions.

Taking this view of the new oratorio, that it will ultimately be catalogued with a vast number of other works which have been similarly praised in their day and subsequently forgotten, a detailed commentary of any length becomes superfluous. By far the finest part of the work is the orchestration, and the prelude, which opens with the impressive 'Judgement' theme and includes many other of the 'motives' subsequently employed, is an imaginative and attractive piece of music. The general tenor of Cardinal Newman's poem is lyrical, however, and as the great author never intended it to be adapted to oratorio purposes he had no object in affording dramatic contrast. Nevertheless, at the moment of dissolution the horrified anguish of the Soul gives occasion for an imposing orchestral ensemble, in which the demoniac element transitionly prevails, and attention is arrested at the end of the first part, where there is some of the finest music in the work for a four-part semi-chorus and eight-part chorus. Mr Delany had the singers perfectly in hand all through, and the pianissimo close, during which the first violins were heard in high harmonic descending passages, possessed an ethereal charm which aroused enthusiasm. At this point the conductor was rewarded with a laurel wreath and floral harp.

Chorus and orchestra, the former with an especially weird 'ha-ha-ha', also triumphed over the difficulties of the colossal 'demon ensemble'. 'We are approaching a cloud [sic] of demons and hear their distant howls (p 29). A scene of great power, remarkable boldness, and wild grandeur commences and holds us in its grip.' Thus Jaeger. But does it? Or is it merely clever and superior pantomime music? Does it, for example, as a pure piece of 'theatricalism', come anywhere near the final movement (in the Hall of the Mountain Troll) of Grieg's *Peer Gynt* suite? Let someone other than Jaeger give answer! One other triumph of the united forces must be mentioned, namely the Choir of Angelicals in the tremendous setting of Newman's own unrivalled hymn, 'Praise to the Holiest in the Height'. The composer touches greatness at this point, and is genuinely inspired by the majesty of his theme. The interpretation was magnificent, and after the sudden silence which follows the *fff* close the enthusiasm was so insistent that the whole had to be repeated. Unfortunately two or three really fine pieces of music will not redeem a dull work.

The solo music had the effect of considerably raising Miss Florence Gibson, a young light contralto, in the public estimation. Her mezzo soprano part of the Angel had been admirably studied, and the solo, 'My Work is Done' with its many gracious phrases, and the elevated beauty of the 'Alleluia' passage proved effective. To this part also fell the solo, 'Softly and Gently' charmingly orchestrated, and rendered with tenderness by the singer. Mr A R Richards may be congratulated upon his sureness in the tenor music. But - was there a tune in it anywhere, anyway? It is possible, to enjoy Bach's Passion music, and yet to find oneself asking such questions as these as do the Philistines when listening to Elgar. Mr Reginald Gooud had some moments of grandeur and of gloom in the dual role of the Priest and the Angel of the Agony.

This interesting performance of a new and much-talked-of work by one of the foremost English musicians of the day was in commemoration of the Sacerdotal golden jubilee of his Eminence Cardinal Moran, who was present, and during the evening cordially congratulated Mr Delany upon the success achieved.

Already a Gerontius tradition was beginning to develop. It is interesting that David Bispham, the baritone in Damrosch's New York première, had been present in Birmingham in 1900, where he had been heard both in the Brahms' *German Requiem* and William Byrd's Five Part Mass. At New York Ada Crossley sang the Angel, but Ellison van Hoose as Gerontius is a name not remembered by us today. Ronald Taylor has reminded us that van Hoose lived from 1868 to 1936 and enjoyed a distinguished career. "After early lessons in New York he went to Europe, where he studied with Jean de Reske in Paris, and with Antonio Cotogni in Rome. His early career was operatic - his debut in Philadelphia was a *Tannhäuser*. He came to England and studied with Sir Henry Wood, working on the concert platform and in oratorio".[107] After *Gerontius*, he toured the USA with Melba and later with Marcella Sembrich. He made a handful of records, all now rare. Taylor reports "having heard two of them in recent times, I can report that the voice comes over as a strong and well-trained tenor".[108] H E Krehbiel reported the performance of *Gerontius* as making "the most profound impression of any novelty of the last fifteen years."[109] Bispham later made a reputation for recitations in the Wüllner mould.[110]

However, after sixteen performances, the complete work still had not reached London. There were four performances which established it in the capital. The first was at Westminster Cathedral on 6 June 1903 with Wüllner, Foster and Ffrangcon Davies conducted by Elgar himself. This performance was all the more remarkable in that it took place in the middle of the Richard Strauss Festival held at St James's Hall from 3-9 June at which Mengelberg and the composer presented Strauss's then complete works almost in their entirety.

The Cathedral was not completely finished and had not been consecrated when the performance took place. While it was undoubtedly a *succès d'estime*, a great new Catholic work performed in the new Catholic cathedral, the acoustic was not kind for a first performance in London.

---

[107]   *The Elgar Society Journal*, Vol 11, no 1, (March, 1999) p 64

[108]   *ibid*

[109]   "Music in America", *Musical Times,* May 1903 p 329

[110]   Kravitt, op cit, p 96. For photographs of Bispham's dramatic reading see Kravitt's p 56.

David Bury has recounted the story[111] of this performance, with particular reference to Wüllner. From this it is clear that Wüllner's engagement was engineered by the promoter of the performance, Hugo Görlitz, his agent in the UK. Wüllner was not universally admired by the English critics, *The Monthly Musical Record* finding the "unattractive quality of his voice and unsatisfactory vocalization made his performance anything but a thing of beauty."

Later, in 1904, Arthur Fagge appears to have secured the first Queen's Hall performance on 15 February, soon followed by two others, more prestigious: the Elgar Festival at Covent Garden in March, and the performance conducted by Weingartner at Queen's Hall in April.

This is the point where another exponent of the role of Gerontius comes on the scene and deserves special mention, despite not recording the part. This was Gervase Elwes who first sang the role of Gerontius under Weingartner on 9 April 1904. It was a great success and by his own estimation he sang it again three times in 1904, five in 1905 and seven in 1906. In all during the sixteen years remaining to him he sang Gerontius a hundred and eighteen times. Winefride Elwes in her book *Gervase Elwes - the story of his life* records how they attended Wüllner's London performance in Westminster Cathedral.[112]

> Wüllner was a fine singer, rather of the operatic type, but to our way of thinking he was too eager to emphasise the dramatic aspect of the part, even to the point of being theatrical. Moreover, Newman's verse inevitably suffered from being delivered in a strong German accent.

She records that "Gervase realised our most soaring hopes" and she quotes this letter from the critic Robin Legge[113]:

> I cannot help writing to say how enormously you impressed me by the tremendous conviction and sincerity of your performance in *Gerontius* this afternoon.... I shall not forget it: it has earmarked *Gerontius* for me.

---

[111]   Bury, David: 'Ludwig Wüllner and the Westminster *Gerontius*', *Elgar Society Journal*, Vol 2, No 1, January 1981, pp 8-13, reproduced here in the following article (pp 237-244)

[112]   Elwes, W and R: *Gervase Elwes - the story of his life* (London: Grayson & Grayson, 1935) p 138

[113]   *ibid*

There is a mystery about this performance. The mezzo soloist is listed in the programme as 'Harriet Foster', surely a misprint for Muriel Foster, and yet in her book Winefride Elwes refers to her as 'Mrs Harriet Foster'. I am grateful to David Bury for pointing out that there were two Foster sisters, twins and both singers. Whether Hilda Foster could have been chosen by Elgar for so prestigious a performance seems extremely unlikely, and Winefride Elwes is not exactly celebrated for her accuracy elsewhere in her book.[114]

After a first half consisting of the whole of *Gerontius* it is remarkable to a late-twentieth century listener to discover that it was only the first half. It was followed by Beethoven's *Choral Symphony*! You certainly got value for money in those days.

Can we in any way recall how Elwes gave the part? His singing in other repertoire certainly gives us some clues. A good example is his recording of Sir George Henschel's *Morning Hymn* recorded in 1912.[115] Later, in 1916, Clara Butt promoted a week-long season of *Gerontius* at Queen's Hall conducted by Elgar himself in aid of war charities. "Mr Gervase Elwes (Gerontius), who is able to infuse into his voice a singular poignancy and awe-stricken feeling".[116]

Performances of *The Dream of Gerontius* now proliferated and it entered the permanent repertoire of choral societies, and the nation's musical consciousness. However, its appeal has remained an international one, and it is appropriate to end with a cutting from the first Paris performance.[117] This took place on 25 May 1906, with the celebrated French mezzo-soprano Claire Croiza as the Angel. Croiza was another young exponent of the part, being only 23 at the time, having made her debut the previous year. You will probably best remember her on disc as Genevieve in the letter scene from *Pelleas*, recorded many years later.

---

[114]   See also: Bury, David: *Elgar and the Two Mezzos* (Thames Publishing, 1984). The two mezzos are Foster and Brema.

[115]   Henschel's *Morning Hymn*, HMV B 322, was reissued in Volume Two of *The Record of Singing*, EMI RLS 743, side seventeen.

[116]   "A Remarkable Musical Event", *Musical Times*, June 1916, p 296

[117]   *Musica*, Juillet 1906, p 112

112   MUSICA

Le «SONGE de GÉRONTIUS»

Par les soins de la Société des Grandes Auditions Musicales de France, dont Mme la comtesse Greffulhe est présidente, a été exécuté, pour la première fois en France, le 25 mai, au Palais du Trocadéro, le Songe de Gérontius, oratorio en deux parties, poème du cardinal Newman (traduction française de M. d'Offoël), musique de Sir Edward Elgar. On attendait avec curiosité cette œuvre du plus illustre représentant de la jeune école musicale anglaise; cette attente n'a point été déçue.

Dans un argument qui fut écrit sur le Songe de Gérontius, il est dit ce qui suit :

« Le poème chrétien du Songe de Gérontius a été inspiré au cardinal Newman par un douloureux événement de sa vie : la perte d'un ami qu'il assista à son chevet de mourant.

« Gérontius, agonisant, entouré de ses amis, cherche dans leurs visages douloureusement affectueux et dans la suprême affirmation de sa croyance, le courage nécessaire pour la dernière lutte, la force de combattre l'ultime assaut des puissances démoniaques, et surtout le réconfort dans sa douleur extrême.

« Soudain, le calme s'est fait en lui; une voix angélique vient de retentir, appelant son âme au ciel, et voici que nous suivons cette âme dans son mystique voyage. Alors commence à proprement parler le rêve de Gérontius, rêve de l'au-delà, vie ineffable des âmes pures et libres dans un monde lumineux et paisible, immatériel et subtil, qu'il nous faut entrevoir suivant la tradition de la foi catholique. A cette merveilleuse vision de la vie des âmes, le cardinal Newman s'est élevé avec l'élan intense d'un sincère et enthousiaste croyant, et l'imagination d'un vrai poète lui en a révélé toutes les splendeurs.

« L'auteur, pourtant, voulait mieux encore; sans doute comprit-il que dans la vision de ce monde idéal, la parole seule n'avait pas assez de puissance, et que toujours elle gardait un sens trop précis, trop limité, surtout dans l'évocation d'un monde mystérieux et infini. La musique seule avait le pouvoir de nous faire entrevoir cette sphère mystique : génie ailé, à l'envolée puissante, elle pouvait nous emporter loin des réalités de la terre, dans ce monde invisible des âmes heureuses et libres. Le cardinal Newman proposa donc son manuscrit à plusieurs musiciens dont aucun n'osa accepter une tâche aussi difficile.

« En 1886, lors d'une visite de Dvorak, le cardinal lui montra le

LE CARDINAL ANGLAIS NEWMAN
Librettiste de l'oratorio : Le Songe de Gérontius

poème, lui fit aussi part de ses désirs et crut bien que le compositeur tchèque allait enfin les réaliser. Celui-ci, en effet, promit d'examiner le sujet en détail, mais ne donna pas de suite à la chose. Enfin, en 1892, Elgar prit à son tour connaissance du manuscrit qui, dès la première lecture, l'enthousiasma; il vit aussitôt tout le merveilleux parti qu'il pourrait en tirer; toutefois, avant de se mettre à l'œuvre, il voulait s'en pénétrer tout entier, se l'assimiler complètement, et, à cet effet, l'étudia pendant des années. Au fur et à mesure que le poème se gravait plus profondément dans son esprit, il lui apparaissait de plus en plus clairement dans sa nouvelle lumière, dans son atmosphère idéale, évidemment inhérente à l'œuvre primitive, mais à laquelle la musique seule pouvait donner tout l'éclat, toute la vie, toute la vibrante intensité. A cette existence profonde et cachée, Elgar allait enfin donner son libre essor par la puissance magique et libératrice de la musique, et en 1900 eut lieu, au festival de Birmingham, et sous la direction de Hans Richter, la première exécution du Songe de Gérontius dans sa double conception poétique et musicale, telle que le cardinal Newman l'avait souhaitée. »

Le Songe de Gérontius ne laisse point de rappeler Mort et Transfiguration de Richard Strauss; mais il faut bien dire que l'œuvre du grand compositeur allemand a, plus que celle de M. Edward Elgar, d'espace, de nombre et d'intensité.

Ce que l'on pourrait reprocher à cette dernière œuvre, c'est un peu de raideur... disons : britannique, puisque l'auteur est anglais; et, çà et là, y contrastant avec trop de soudaineté, des mièvreries qui ne conviennent guère à la gravité du sujet traité. Mais une grande noblesse remplit cet oratorio; la ligne mélodique y est souvent haute et pure; l'orchestration en est solide; les voix y sont traitées avec franchise et vigueur. L'opposition des chœurs d'anges et des chœurs de démons est vraiment saisissant. Le Songe de Gérontius méritait que la Société des Grandes Auditions de France sacrifiât pour nous la faire connaître; on doit l'en louer grandement.

Il faut louer aussi, et sans réserve, l'interprétation soigneuse, fouillée, intense, que M. Chevillard, dirigeant son orchestre, nous a donnée; les chœurs, en nombre considérable, furent parfaits; et M. César Galeotti fit preuve, à l'orgue, d'un jeu excellent. Tous éloges sont dus aussi à MM. Plamondon (Gérontius), à M. Frolich (l'Ange de l'agonie) et à Mlle Croiza, débutante (l'Ange).

Au résumé, une glorieuse manifestation à l'actif de la Société des Grandes Auditions musicales de France, à celui de Mme la comtesse Greffulhe, à qui les arts doivent beaucoup. Il suffit de rappeler les représentations de Béatrice et Bénédict, de Berlioz, à l'Odéon; et plus tard les Troyens à Carthage du même compositeur, représentations mémorables au cours desquelles débuta la célèbre Marie Delna; les auditions d'œuvres de modernes compositeurs français; les mémorables représentations, à Orange, de Jules César, de Méfistofèle, et, à nouveau, des Troyens à Carthage, et le récent Festival Beethoven. C'est là le meilleur apostolat.

FÉLICIEN GRÉTRY.

LE GRAND MUSICIEN ANGLAIS SIR EDWARD ELGAR
compositeur de l'oratorio : Le Songe de Gérontius

WESTMINSTER CATHEDRAL

AMBROSDEN AVENUE, VICTORIA STREET, S.W.

(By Gracious Permission of H.E. CARDINAL VAUGHAN).

Saturday Afternoon, June 6, 1903, at 3.

FIRST PERFORMANCE IN LONDON

OF

Che Dream of Gerontius

(EDWARD ELGAR)

Under the Sole Management of Mr. HUGO GÖRLITZ
(119, New Bond Street, London. W.).

Tenor - - - Dr. LUDWIG WÜLLNER

Mezzo-Soprano - Miss MURIEL FOSTER

Bass - - - Mr. FFRANGCON DAVIES

AND

Chorus of the North Staffordshire District Choral Society

(Conductor—Mr. J. WHEWALL)

FULL ORCHESTRA

Conductor - Dr. EDWARD ELGAR.

Organist—Mr. R. R. TERRY.

The net proceeds will be for the Benefit of the Cathedral Choir Schools.

PRICE ONE SHILLING.

NOVELLO AND COMPANY LIMITED, PRINTERS, LONDON.

8

LUDWIG WULLNER and the WESTMINSTER 'GERONTIUS'

by David Bury

David Bury is a member of the Elgar Society's London branch, having served for many years as the branch's Secretary and having recently completed a term of office on the Society's national Council.

The full story of the belated first London performance of *The Dream of Gerontius* has not yet been told - but it is a fascinating one. It took place on Saturday, 6 June 1903, in John Francis Bentley's new, unconsecrated, and incomplete Cathedral at Westminster, and involved heated disputes over numerous issues, varying from the propriety of Edward VII's entering a Catholic place of worship (in the end he did not), to whether Alice Elgar`s ticket should be paid for.

Elgar was, of course, in the thick of it all. He got his own way over the positioning of the choir, the choice of contralto, and wording of publicity handbills; all of which involved Görlitz, the long-suffering impresario who had guaranteed the performance to the tune of £1,000, in additional expenses. When the famous Amsterdam Orchestra withdrew from the performance six weeks before the event, Elgar badgered Görlitz continually about the personnel and strength of the hastily improvised replacement. Richard Terry, the Cathedral organist, was compelled to abandon his intention of interpolating a performance of his edition of Tallis's *Lamentations* into the programme - "squashed" as Lady Edmund Talbot put it.

Melba, it is true, got the better of Elgar when it became necessary to rearrange rehearsals to accommodate those members of the orchestra who were committed to her 5 June concert, - "Melba is not willing to oblige anyone by a change." Stanford's pessimism regarding the Cathedral acoustic, so justified in the event, left Elgar irritated but ineffectual in his famous letter to Littleton of Novello on 20 April.

On the day itself confusion reigned over whether or not applause was appropriate, and Elgar found it difficult to commence the second part because of the hubbub of the fashionable audience, who had paid as much as 5 guineas for their seats. In the end he had recourse to the expedient of requesting the bass, Ffrangcon Davies, to quit his seat and speak to the ushers. The whole was played out against the background of the imminent death of Cardinal Vaughan, who had received the Last Sacrament in March, and whose Requiem, just over a fortnight later, was to be the next great Cathedral event. But perhaps most interesting of all was the role of Dr. Ludwig Wüllner.

Wüllner was born at Münster, Westphalia, on 19 August 1858, the son of the noted conductor and composer Franz Wüllner (1832-1902), who was, in turn, Munich court Kapellmeister, Director of the Dresden Conservatory, and Head of the Cologne Conservatory. Despite his parentage Ludwig faced family opposition to a theatrical or musical career. He took a doctor's degree in philology after studying at the Universities of Munich, Berlin, and Strasbourg, and became a lecturer in the Münster Academy. It was only after his grandmother's death that he turned to the stage, at Meiningen in 1889, and not until 1896 that he graduated from actor, via reciter, to singer. This step caused considerable surprise because of his many vocal shortcomings, including, according to Spemann in his "Das goldene Buch der Musik" (1900), a "speech impediment from birth". But the dramatic intensity of his performances compensated for his limited vocal means. Otto Klemperer recalled the deep impression Wüllner made on him at about this time in *Tannhaüser*, while, in England, the *Staffordshire Sentinel* summed it up when it noted that Wüllner "wouldn't secure many engagements from people who believe that melody should be the beginning and ending of all efforts", but that "Dr. Wüllner is the Irving of singers".

Elgar first came across Wüllner at the famous Düsseldorf performances of *Gerontius* in 1901 and 1902. Elgar and Jaeger were captivated. "Directly Wüllner opened his mouth to sing 'Jesus, Maria meine Stunde kom', we said 'that man has brains'... He made us sit up and realize that Elgar's intention could be realised by an artist. I never heard such intellectual deeply-felt singing. Not that W's voice is wonderful. No: But his brains and his head are", wrote Jaeger to Dora Penny. While Elgar wrote to Novello's about the first Düsseldorf performance, "Dr. Ludwig Wüllner was splendid, not in voice but intelligence, genius. (He carried everyone away and made Gerontius a real personage.) We never had a singer in England with so much brain."

The driving force behind the notion of a performance of *Gerontius* at Westminster Cathedral, in aid of the endowment of the Cathedral Choir, was Lady Edmund Talbot, sister-in-law of the Duke of Norfolk. Alice Stuart Wortley put Lady Edmund in touch with Elgar in a letter of 14 March 1903. The suggestion found Elgar at his most receptive, - "I am quite in sympathy with the plan...the North Staffordshire Choral Society knows the work well. It is a very fine chorus and sang *Gerontius* under my direction on Friday last... Mr. Coates, however, must be Gerontius". (On Friday, 13 March, Elgar had conducted the highly successful Hanley performance. He was brimming with confidence and determined to have the same choir and soloists, Muriel Foster, David Ffrangcon Davies and John Coates.)

However, once the organisation of the event was placed in the hands of the impresario Hugo Görlitz, [sole agent for Wüllner whose British début was just about to be launched), it became inevitable that Wüllner, not Coates, would be the preferred tenor. Elgar, with his enthusiastic memories of Düsseldorf, had no objection. Indeed, even before the Westminster performance was mooted, Elgar had agreed to attend the singer's recital début at St. James's Hall. By 31 March, Wüllner had been engaged, and before April was out Elgar and Jaeger were corresponding about the necessity of transposing the "Sanctus Fortis" for his benefit.

Meanwhile, Wüllner,"the most renowned lieder singer of the present day", duly made his English début on 20 March. Elgar, however, "rather lumbagoish", had taken to his bed. Alice's diary for the 19th records that Dr Earl "would not let E. go to London next day". So Elgar missed the recital, which was favourably reviewed.

"In Dr Wüllner we have undoubtedly a master...(his) voice has little or no beauty of tone. At times its quality conjures up visions of Beckmesser. But for musical intelligence, for beauty of interpretation...and for clearness of enunciation...for in a word the complete triumph of the musical mind over such matters as a rather unmusical voice, his equal has not been heard on a London concert platform since the days of Julius Stockhausen", reported *The Times*.

Further recitals followed at St. James's Hall and Queen's Hall in May, but of more interest and significance was his performance of *Gerontius* in Liverpool on 24 March. Elgar was not present, and he affected not to read the critics, but even if he remained unaware of press misgivings - "the embarrassment inseparable from singing in an unfamiliar language...much embarrassed by the high notes" (*Manchester Guardian*); "too vehement in his declamation" (*Liverpool Courier*); "did not commend himself to his audience by his voice" (*Liverpool Mercury*); - Elgar received a personal hint from the conductor himself, Frederic Cowen, who wrote: "Just a line to tell you that we had a really excellent performance last night in Liverpool. The only thing was that Wüllner's English was rather unsatisfactory ".

In the circumstances Wüllner was perhaps unwise to eschew the rehearsal on the morning of the Westminster performance - the only one with the choir, whose members, at their own expense, travelled by special train from the Potteries in the small hours of 6 June. "Dr. Wüllner will not attend the rehearsal on Saturday morning...[he] will rehearse his part on Friday afternoon, or will do without rehearsal altogether", Görlitz informed Elgar bluntly at a low point in their correspondence. His place was taken by Mr. John Harrison "the new English tenor", a protégé of Görlitz whose career the impresario was assiduously attempting to further. However, Wüllner not only attended Friday afternoon's rehearsal, but also lunched with the Elgars at Schuster's house, 22 Old Queen Street, where Edward and Alice were staying as guests, having travelled from Malvern the previous day. Alice's diary records her impression of a "charming and wonderful personality."

For Alice Elgar the great day itself was, of course, a triumph. "Dressed in haste. There came to lunch Lady Edmund Talbot, Lord Northampton, Lord Shaftesbury, Mr. Cary (i.e. Gervase) Elwes and Lady Winefride, the Stuart Wortleys. Then the Cathedral - most beautiful. Glorious afternoon and vast audience. E. conducted splendidly. Chorus very beautiful. Wüllner finer than anyone".

Alice's view of the performance, and in particular the soloist, was not widely shared. Certainly *The Sunday Times* thought that, with due allowance made, his enunciation "was remarkably distinct and clear", and *The Daily Chronicle* was disturbed "only occasionally" by his pronunciation. Predictably, too, the Catholic weekly *The Tablet* enthused about the tenor, as about everything, uniquely discerning "great vocal beauty" in a Wüllner performance.

But led by J R Fuller-Maitland of *The Times*, a pupil of Stanford and no friend of Elgar (though his article on Elgar in the second edition of Grove, which he edited, is full and pretty fair), the main body of critics destroyed Wüllner's performance. Fuller-Maitland observed that among "the many imperfections...at the words 'Take me away' only one vowel was pronounced as it would be by an Englishman. *The Standard* disliked the "Teutonic twang which is undesirable in works of sacred character", while *The Westminster Gazette*, singling out Wüllner as the sole factor operating against success, was reminded of the Prima Donna who referred affectionately to her spouse as her 'horse pond'. Both Rosa Burley and Lady Winefride Elwes made similar observations. The latter, who imagined very mistakenly that she was attending only the second English performance of the work in which her husband was to have such great success, found that "Newman's verse inevitably suffered through being delivered in a strong German accent", while Rosa Burley considered that "Wüllner produced horrible distortions of our vowel sounds which seriously endangered the gravity of the proceedings", and in general judged it "a sad disappointment".

Indeed the professional critics soon turned to the wider matters of Wüllner's vocal limitations and melodramatic approach. The *Monthly Musical Record* found the "unattractive quality of his voice and unsatisfactory vocalization made his performance anything but a thing of beauty". In *The Pall Mall Gazette* the singer was "considerably exaggerated", and in *The Globe* though "intensely dramatic - the effort was too obvious". *The Referee* felt the performance "bordered on exaggeration" and *The Westminster Gazette* described the performance as "overdone" with liberties being taken with the tempo "profoundly unsatisfactory". The *Daily News* and *The Times* were particularly scathing. The former dismissed Wüllner's efforts as "mere ranting", and added the sarcasm, "personally I have some liking for definiteness of pitch". Lady Winefride Elwes described Wüllner as a fine singer, "rather of the operatic type, but to our way of thinking...too eager to emphasise the dramatic aspect of the part, even to the point of being theatrical".

Fuller-Maitland, however, alone found the performance insufficiently dramatic on top of all its other shortcomings. "The whole, from beginning to end was sung without alteration of tone quality, nor was anything particularly expressed excepting only the weakness of the

Boards round Westminster Cathedral in 1903 testify to the fact that it was still unfinished. However, they also carried posters for the first London performance of Gerontius. The wording is very similar to that in the programme (repro-duced in David Bury's article) and it is interesting to see that the concert promoter, Hugo Gorlitz, who was also Wullner's agent, showed the name of the tenor soloist in bigger print than that of the composer!

dying man. In the fine litany the tenor solo should surely be audible through the chorus; it was not, and there was no suggestion of any contrast between the man in his bodily agony and the disembodied spirit in its new surroundings". Wüllner's vocal defects and the transposition of the "Sanctus Fortis" were not compensated for by any intellectuality of interpretation or intensity of realization, which attributes were on this occasion "hardly perceptible".

It seems certain that, for one or two critics, the dissatisfaction with Wüllner was an expression of a wider chauvinism. "Next time ...he (Elgar) will do well to secure the services of a native tenor", observed *The Westminster Gazette*, and *The Telegraph* observed that "it seemed strange to engage a foreign artist...since we possessed an English artist (Coates) who had proved so fine an exponent". Fuller-Maitland made the generalisation that "In Oratorio the English...are easily the superiors of foreign singers", and indeed went on to attribute the very survival of *Gerontius* to "the lavish praise that was bestowed on it by Herr Richard Strauss...no doubt, speaking with an authority based on an exhaustive knowledge of the whole of British music". The upshot of Strauss's remarkable tribute was, thought Fuller-Maitland, that "many who would not venture to express a favourable opinion of anything English on their own account have the satisfaction of feeling that they have the right to admire what has been so warmly praised in Germany". Hence it was that *Gerontius* had become "a prime favourite", whereas previously "there was no reason to doubt whether the oratorio would not meet the fate of many better works and be put straightway on the shelf. To this doom it seemed, indeed, for some time to have been consigned". In conclusion he said: "Still, Londoners have now heard the work, and as two more performances in different surroundings are spoken of, it will not be allowed to share the oblivion which is the lot of so much of the best English music". This seems to indicate a lack of awareness of events outside London, and indeed England, in the previous two years.

Thus it was that Wüllner provided a catalyst for wider controversy. Elgar made typical reply. In a letter of thanks to the choir, he observed that "The whole of the work was splendidly done...Several critics who have been brought up to regard a mere shouting machine as an ideal English chorus have naturally something absurd to say, but the real judges were more than satisfied and so was I". Published in *The*

Staffordshire Sentinel, this opinion, recalls R W Shipp, was much resented by the London writers. Already, a week before the Gerontius performance, Elgar had written his well-known letter to Canon Gorton referring to "the sleepy London press" and containing his assertion "that the living centre of music in Great Britain is not London, but somewhere farther North". This, too, was now published in the July issue of *The Musical Times* with the somewhat rhetorical question - 'What will the musical critics of the "sleepy London press" say to this?'

It is difficult, however, to disagree that the Westminster performance was not a very happy one. After this fresh *Gerontius* setback, when London next heard the work on 15 February 1904, John Coates re-emerged in the title role.

Part Four

The
Intervening Years

A REMARKABLE MUSICAL EVENT
Six Consecutive Performances of *The Dream of Gerontius* and New Music by Elgar

Clara Butt gave the first performance in October 1899 of Elgar's Sea Pictures, *the work immediately preceding* Gerontius *in Elgar's oeuvre. This has led some people to believe that he wrote the part of the Angel with her in mind, as she was one of the soloists engaged by the Birmingham Committee - she sang four of the* Sea Pictures *under Elgar's baton the evening before the* Gerontius *première. We know that she was present the following morning; and a few months later she was one of a group of nine leading musicians interviewed for the* Strand Magazine *who were all asked the question, 'What is the greatest achievement in music?' Her reply is fascinating. "Courage is generally required to recognise the greatest achievement in contemporary work, and Miss Clara Butt has certainly shown this quality in her reply to my question. 'Of all the later works', declares the eminent singer, 'Edward Elgar's* The Dream of Gerontius *shows the highest art and genius, in my opinion'". Yet surprisingly enough, she did not sing in* Gerontius *until 1915, though she then made up for lost time; for as well as the unique set of performances described below, she made four single-sided Columbia discs of excerpts from* Gerontius *with Maurice D'Oisly as the tenor soloist, conducted by Henry Wood. (These were the first ever recordings of the work, preceding Elgar's own version of the Prelude and Angel's Farewell in 1917.)*

As preparation for the London 'run', there had been performances in Leeds on 3 May, and Bradford on 4 May; the performers were the same, except the Hallé Orchestra replaced the LSO. The former concert saw the première of the two extracts from The Spirit of England. *Alice wrote in her diary: "The Concert was magnificent. Enormous audience & orch. Very good & chorus perfect. E. conducted superbly". At Bradford "Very fine performance in evening, immense audience". The first London concert was four days later. "Enormous crowd at Queen's Hall, people not able to get seats - performance wonderful. E. conducting most masterly. New works made profound impression, A.Nicholls' 'We will remember them' never to be forgotten. The semi-chorus perfect in Gerontius, the opening Kyrie breathed out pp in perfect time. most beautiful". 9 May: "The enormous audience continued on Tuesday evg. & everything was even more perfect". 10 May: "This afternoon was even more beautiful - & performance still more perfect - Enormous audience. King & Queen present. King seemed very fidgety & un-King like in demeanour... [He] was said to be much affected by 'For the Fallen' but Gerontius was evidently too long for him". 11 May: "The evening performance most beautiful & perfect... This was a specially beautiful evening". 12 May: "Another superb performance". 13 May: "The last day of this very memorable week & a most perfect performance. Each time seemed more beautiful than the last. It is probably unprecedented that for a whole week, one composer's work shd. be repeated every day. D.G. that it has happened for E. Enormous audience each time & it seemed as if there wd. be just as great crowds if the works were repeated for another week". The following review appeared without by-line in the* Musical Times *in June 1916.*

A contemporary journal advertisement for the four recordings of excerpts from Gerontius made by Clara Butt, Maurice D'Oisly and Henry Wood. Note that a donation from the sale of each record was made to the Red Cross.

The most remarkable enterprise undertaken in this country since the War began was carried out with complete and wonderful success at Queen's Hall during the week that ended on 13 May. Six performances on consecutive days were given of *The Dream of Gerontius* and two sections, 'To Women', and 'For the Fallen' of Elgar's new work, born of the agony and pride of the War, which in its entirety will be called *The Spirit of England*. The consummation of the scheme was a triumph of optimism and of organisation. The finest musical resources available in this country were brought together - the Leeds Choral Union, trained to perfection by Dr Coward, the London Symphony Orchestra, and soloists of the front rank - and all welded into a unity by the composer from whose brain and soul the music had emanated. Verily, in this instance it was the 'ever womanly' that beckoned us on, for to Madame Clara Butt must be accorded the credit of the initiation of the scheme, and animated by a profound belief in the uplifting character of the music to be performed, her strong personality and determination provided the chief driving force in its successful accomplishment. Then, so far as gathering audiences was concerned, there was the leverage that the proceeds of the performances were to be devoted to Red Cross Funds. Distinguished patronage was secured, including that of their Majesties The King and Queen, who attended on 10 May, and of Queen Alexandra, who attended on 13 May.

Although *The Dream of Gerontius* makes its deepest impression in a cathedral, it may be said of these performances that never before has the work been given so adequately. At the first of the concerts the technical and interpretative standard of execution was very high, but later, as orchestra, choir, and soloists were more and more sympathetically unified, the ease, fluency, and plasticity of the performance were striking. The soloists were Mr Gervase Elwes (Gerontius), who is able to infuse into his voice a singular poignancy and awe-stricken feeling; Madame Clara Butt (the Angel), who sang with much warmth; Mr Herbert Brown (the Priest), who sang with unusual sonority and breadth, and Mr Charles Mott (the Angel of the Agony), who sang with all the fervour of his strong temperament. On this occasion the Angelicals were a special semi-chorus of singers brought from Yorkshire with the choir and trained by Dr Coward, and not as it was somewhere stated, by Madame Butt.[1] The grouping of the soloists was novel: Madame Butt, the Angelicals, and Mr Mott being together, towards the back of the orchestra; Mr Elwes and Mr Brown being in front, near the conductor. Some of the choral effects were sublime. The Demons' Chorus was a wonderful exhibition of choral technique and intensity of expression, and it was not too realistic.

The settings of Mr Laurence Binyon's poems, 'To Women' and 'For the Fallen', were... both... very finely performed, and created a deep impression. The touching tenderness of the words of 'To Women' is very intimately brought out in Elgar's chaste and beautiful setting. But 'For the Fallen' was found even more searchingly expressive. It was heard by many with tears and emotion born of the poignancy of the words and the wonderful appeal of the music. Surely this solemn inspiration of poet and composer is our nearest approach we have by way of a British Requiem for our fallen soldiers and sailors! It deserves to be performed wherever there are resources to do it justice.

The solos were sung by Miss Agnes Nicholls, who sang very finely, and Mr John Booth, who also rose to the demands of the music.

We are glad to hear that the funds of the Red Cross will derive substantial benefit [£2707 net; plus £2600 from "other activities" of Madame Butt, presumably including proceeds from the two Yorkshire performances of *Gerontius*].

The Musical Times, 1 June 1916, p 296

---

[1]   There was clarification and correction of this in the next issue: "The semi-chorus consisted of sixteen choralists (four of each part), all members of the Leeds Choral Union, and trained by Dr Coward, and the Angelicals were a separate body of twelve professional singers (six sopranos and six contraltos) selected by Madame Butt in London, and rehearsed by Madame Butt and Sir Edward Elgar. This body also took part in the performances that were given at Leeds and Bradford."

I GO to MASS

A J Sheldon

A J Sheldon (1874-1931) succeeded Ernest Newman as critic of the Birmingham Daily Post *in 1919. He was active in the promotion of the Birmingham Grand Opera Society. Prior to this he had written for the* Manchester Courier. *Under the pseudonym 'Schaunard' he wrote an occasional column 'Stray Musings' in* Musical Opinion. *This article (under his own name) was the first of ten articles on Elgar which appeared in* Musical Opinion, *and which were later published as a book in 1931, this being the first chapter.*

Literally, - it was not to Mass I went : spiritually, - it is the feeling which comes over me whenever I listen to *The Dream of Gerontius*. I am not of the way of thinking which sends people to Mass; rather am I a heretic on the points of belief which find expression therein. But music is an Icarus which carries us within the glow of many suns. Its wings subside and we fall to earth: though however often we fall we are ever ready to make the flight again. When our fibres, mental and physical, thrill to music, we come to find ourselves living for its exaltations. And though I have rarely missed a season since the early years of its life without hearing *The Dream of Gerontius*, and through circumstances may be said nearly to know it inside out, I know before each new hearing that I am not going to be disappointed unless an evil fortune attends the work in performance.

Ordinarily the beauty of music newly heard comes to one in a sort of instantaneous revelation. One sits in the concert room taking in the music as a whole, with sensitive feelers acutely stirred, and the soul filled with what may be in the music for it. Had I first heard *The Dream of Gerontius* in this way, I do not doubt I should have been drawn as intimately within its spell as came to pass in after years. It did not so befall, however, and though I knew the music in a way such as can hardly come through hearing it in the concert room, nine years were to lapse before the opportunity came to hear it, as they say, from the front and in the way most of us acquire our knowledge of music. Still, there can have been nothing unique in that circumstance. There must be many like myself whose first acquaintance with Elgar's oratorio was made through the study of a chorus part. You cannot learn much about a piece of music with no more than a chorus part to help you; and the natural thing to do is to procure a score at the earliest possible moment, even if you do not sing from it. You do not do that, however, unless you feel certain you are going to like the music, and the laying out of a few shillings happens to be of no great matter to your purse. As it happened, the natural thing to do, though it was done in the end, was postponed for a time. And as a result there came what seems a special joy in the recollection : a slow and gradual assembling of the details of the music, so that what had here and there seemed incomprehensible and indeed angular according to the standards of the time became meaningful and beautiful in a way whose newness was itself a source of fascination.

It was not so much Gerontius in the throes of death as Gerontius alive beyond "the busy beat of time" which won me. Indeed, a sense of something unmanly about his manner of facing what to him must have loomed ahead as a transfiguration rather than a dissolution comes over me to this day when I listen to the music : my grudge on this score, nevertheless, lies against Cardinal Newman rather than against Elgar. When, in rehearsing, the work took shape, and a sort of run through could be ventured on, the first part was always left behind with a sense of relief. Nor did I altogether like the way the demons were disposed of. There must be a case, surely, for "the mind bold and independent, the purpose free." Why should it not have the ascendant? But the colloquy between the Angel and the Soul came in after days to provide an intoxication which dispelled any questioning on that score. For a time, however, it was the angelic choruses which took me out of myself, and I think most of all the music of the pages which in the vocal score are numbered 104 to 107. One phrase hereabouts I came to listen to in a sort of agony of ravishment. The distant singing of the Choir of Angelicals has faded away; and the Soul, guided by the Angel, has passed the gate and is within the House of Judgment. The sound of the holy singing now comes upon them "like the rushing of the wind" :

> Glory to Him, who evermore
> By truth and justice reigns;
> Who tears the soul from out its case,
> And burns away its stains.

The voices swell and then subside on the last line of the verse. The Angel tells Gerontius of his "approaching agony ;" but while the Angel speaks, the last two lines of the verse are elongated by the tenors and contraltos of the semi-chorus, until the contraltos are left alone to sing softly this phrase : -

And   burns   a - way its   stains!

On paper the melodic phrase conveys little : but coming where it does, on a pedal F, and with harp-like chords above it, and on the contralto voice where it is at its most liquid and full, it seemed an ineffable expression of the exceeding loveliness of the Agony which is to come. If genius declares itself in little things as well as in great, this alone, one felt thus early, told of genius in Elgar.

The day came when rehearsing was put aside, and what had been built up was put to the test of performance. Of Elgar's orchestration of this music I had not heard a note; of the solo music, little more had been heard beyond such leads as were sung by the chorus-master, though these had been found wondrously winning. The Gerontius, I feel certain, was John Coates; the Angel I know without doubt was Muriel Foster; the identity of the bass singer I cannot at all remember. The conductor was Richter. The prelude overwhelmed me, though as much through the stab of pain in its opening phrases as through the majesty of the middle section, which draws on the "Go forth" chorus at the end of the first part of the oratorio. The intensity of feeling, united with a sort of mystical exaltation which I still feel, nevertheless, curiously limited and almost "precious" in its application, had its way with me. Most of all, it was the orchestration of which I was conscious; and in particular the sumptuous web of sound in the "Go forth" chorus. The choir to which I belonged had a poor singer in its ranks that night, for it seemed more natural to listen than to sing. It is a good thing to sit in the body of a hall while a complex choral and orchestral ensemble is being woven; it is, indeed, the only way in which to get the true hang of the music. But there is a special delight in being in the midst of it all, in being within the flame that is ascending, rather than outside it.

The interval over, there came that sweet and ethereal opening for the strings alone, which is so little, and yet means so much in an imaginative way. The sense of lightness, of the Nothingness which is an ecstasy, has surely never been so perfectly evoked in music as Elgar has done here, and in the succeeding dialogue between the Angel and the Soul. There was sufficient common ground of conviction between Elgar and myself hereabouts to draw me at once within his vision. Once within it, there was no help for me; there could be no going back to earth. And so, after the Angel's song had completed my conversion, it was inevitable that one, at least, among the Demons should be a poor-hearted fellow at pleading his cause. Enslavement became complete with the development of the "Praise to the Holiest" chorus, for though its choral phrases had been nearly memorised through frequent hearings at rehearsal, its orchestral setting was being savoured for the first time.

The verses from "O Loving wisdom of our God" seemed like a rosary of devout recollections, and when the chorus proceeded to move along to its stupendous climax, it was the spirit rather than any voice in me which moved along with it. No choir, for sure, had ever a feebler member in its ranks when the time of need was at hand. The Angel of the Agony sang his hymn of invocation - a solo which, with the few bars succeeding, brings the dramatic climax of the work - and one could there and then have enrolled oneself among those of Elgar's persuasion in the field of religious belief. It is still for me, after about a couple of score hearings of the oratorio from the auditorium, the finest solo in the work. Following this solo, it will be remembered, Gerontius goes before his Judge. What effect this passage had on me at the time is not remembered. If it now is found disappointing it may be that anything of which man is capable in relation to that moment must inevitably disappoint. Most of us will be agreed that what Elgar has done with it is a monument rather to discretion than to genius. For the rest, the solo for the Soul, "Take me away," and the ensemble in which the Angel sings, "Softly and gently, dearly ransomed soul," do not fail today, as they did not fail on that first hearing to round off the work beautifully and convincingly. In the latter is another instance of the composer's feeling for the contralto voice, and its range of colour. How lovely is the fall of the voice at the words "O'er the penal waters, as they roll," and at a similar point in the succeeding verse!

The winds that blow through musical genius come not only from the four quarters of feeling but from many points between. Some find no vent through Elgar. He has written no love music, in the sense in which

Wagner at one pole and Berlioz at the opposite can be said to have written love music. But if Elgar has never been erotically moved, he has been moved in more ways than one. Three winds, at least, blow through his music; and for an understanding of the full man and his message, it is needful to take all three into account. For the moment we need only concern ourselves with the wind that blows through *The Dream of Gerontius* : for one wind, and one only, moved the composer to the creation of that work. So intense is the concentration on a single idea that the music as a whole treads on the borderland of the neurotic. It could hardly be otherwise : no milk-and-water approach to Cardinal Newman's poem could do more than splutter round about it. None but a passionate believer in the ideas which there find expression could have given us the music of Elgar, even were his musical genius equal to Elgar's. There is sufficient kinship between its theme and the theme of Strauss's *Death and Transfiguration* to justify a comparison between the two works. Strauss's picture of the dying man holds its own with Elgar's in every graphic way; moreover, its conciseness can be regarded as a merit. But who will allege that in the Transfiguration section of Strauss's poem we get any sense of transfiguration at all? Granting all the assistance derived from Newman's poem, is there not an imaginative reach in Elgar's music infinitely beyond what is to be found in Strauss's? Beside the English master's vision, Strauss's is a puny affair. The composer of *Death and Transfiguration* does little more than erect a stone over the grave with a suitable inscription : the strength of Strauss does not lie in any ability to suggest the infinite.

That in any estimate of ultimate values certain limitations in the scale of the thought and feeling which find expression in *The Dream of Gerontius* must be taken into account is to be admitted. The great things in art have the quality of universality in them. That is why Franck must be accounted a peg or two below Beethoven, and Tchaikovsky below Brahms. It is why one feels Elgar more in line with Francis Thompson than with Shelley or Shakespeare.

The music of *The Dream of Gerontius* is an intoxication, and it is possible for us to understand the point of view which shies at accepting it. To any but the clear-headed in a world of visionary imaginings, it might even be dangerous music. One must be able alike to surrender and to cut oneself free. But there is much other music, from Wagner to Scriabin, which demands from us a like power. In this life we are safer with the citizens of earth, who sit peering out into infinity, than we are with those who try to persuade us that they have dwelt in heaven. There are many heavens but only one earth.

Yet this intensity of vision, which in Elgar's music to Newman's poem springs from intensity of belief, is a virtue in relation to the task attempted. We can never now think of the poem without thinking also of the music. Hardly any music so glows with the heat of passionate conviction; hardly any music so convinces us of the sincerity of the feeling within it. Byrd and Palestrina are no less sincere in a like cause; but *The Dream of Gerontius* is a trumpet of conviction, in comparison with which their ecstasies are hardly more than flute-like. It is music of the type which makes converts : it might be termed a great revivalist hymn. For our purpose it is one of the keys to the psychology we meet with in Elgar's music. There are others, but it is possibly the most important of all. *The Dream of Gerontius* comes very near to being an epitome of the man Elgar, just as it also comes very near to being an epitome of the musician Elgar. It will help us later towards an appreciation not only of the oratorios which succeeded it, but considerably also towards an understanding of certain features in the music of the symphonies, the concertos and the works for chamber combinations. For the moment, one pays tribute to it as a great work in its kind, and possibly the most emotionally intense expression of religious feeling in all music.

Musical Opinion, December 1925, p 261

A RE-EVALUATION after THIRTY-FIVE YEARS

Harvey Grace

Harvey Grace (1874-1944) was an experienced organist, culminating in the post at Chichester Cathedral 1931-38. He was also a prolific author, adjudicator, lecturer and choir-trainer; and he edited The Musical Times *from 1918 to his death, contributing articles under his own name and the pseudonym 'Feste'.*

Saint-Saëns, on returning to France after a visit as composer-conductor to the Birmingham Festival of 1879, wrote a shrewd comment on the English oratorio habit. The causes, he said, are not entirely musical :

> England has been sometimes Catholic, sometimes Protestant; in reality, she could not be Protestant like the Germanic race, nor Catholic like the Latin races. England is Biblical, and the Old Testament holds in her religion a place almost equal to that which it holds in the Jewish religion. This explains the intensity of success of works such as 'Israel in Egypt', 'Elijah', 'Solomon', the subjects of which will never have for the publics of the Continent the interest they have for the English.

There was something in this, but less than Saint-Saëns thought. He overlooked two important facts : oratorios have always been concerned mainly with Biblical stories; and the great majority of early examples were written in Italy and Germany. Thus, there was an Italian *Samson* two hundred years before Handel's; an Italian *St Paul* three hundred years before Mendelssohn's; and so on.

However, the best comment on Saint-Saëns' dictum is the fact that the oratorio now established in England as second only to *Messiah* is non-Biblical and uncompromisingly Catholic.

The greatness of *The Dream of Gerontius* is shown not only by its appeal today, after the test of over thirty years, but by the completeness with which it overcame two formidable obstacles that stood in the way of its immediate success. First, there was the sectarian difficulty, concerning which little need be said today. It is easy to understand that choralists brought up on the Biblical oratorios of Handel and

Mendelssohn and a few later examples of the ethical type experienced discomfort when faced with *Gerontius* (discomfort which here and there developed into antagonism, and even a cry - or at least a murmur - of 'No Popery'. One famous musician dismissed the work with the remark, 'It stinks of incense!') Today the general public accepts *Gerontius* as it accepts the old morality *Everyman* - ie, as a work of art in which the theological implications matter little or nothing in comparison with its beauty, sincerity, and human appeal.

The other obstacle was the technical and interpretative difficulty of the choral writing. The story of its inadequate first performance need not be retold, especially as various explanations were put forward. No doubt there were a number of contributory causes, but the failure of the chorus has never been seriously disputed. Yet it was easier to blame the singers at the time than it is today, when experience has proved that *Gerontius* is still among the most exacting tasks that even the best-equipped choirs can undertake. And there is significance in the fact that the demands of the work led to what was known as 'the new choralism', which was 'new' chiefly in that it developed subtleties and effects that were not called for by the Handelian oratorio - they would, indeed, have been foreign to the style of oratorios in general. The difficulties of *Gerontius* on the interpretative side were due to an entirely new element - 'the strange combination of mystical, diabolical, and ecstatical elements which run through the whole oratorio'.[1]

It is a generally accepted principle in criticism that a composer comes up for re-evaluation every thirty years or so - a natural process, because, dating from a composer's death, each generation necessarily makes up its own mind about his work. To a considerable extent a large-scale composition undergoes a similar judgment. No doubt many listeners who, as performers or hearers, have been familiar with *Gerontius* since its production, have during the past year or two been comparing their present with their past impressions.

Here I may be allowed to become personal. Last year I found myself in a small group of musicians who were discussing the work from this point of view. We were unanimous in feeling some loss of grip during the passages of dialogue between the Angel and the Soul; the choice of

---

[1]　　Sir Henry Coward in *Choral Technique and Interpretation*

3/4 time for the long song of Gerontius beginning 'Sanctus fortis' seemed more than ever to be a risk that was not always escaped (of all measures, 3/4 and 6/8 are apt to induce monotony or triteness - sometimes both); and the Demons' Chorus was still - perhaps inevitably - unconvincing.

On the credit side there was no falling-off - an increase rather. We were as aware as ever of what Ernest Walker calls 'the sort of entrancing unearthly charm' of the songs of the Angel; and the familiar spell was cast by the Introduction to Part II - surely unique as a representation in sound of stillness and remoteness. The beauty of the kyrie and 'Be merciful' had lost none of its searching quality. The mastery shown in the gradual approach to the chorus 'Praise to the Holiest', and the entry of the tutti (on a six-four chord - a fine stroke) was as overwhelming as ever. And so on, from one well-remembered page to another. There had been nothing like this in English music before, and familiarity had not staled it. Recent years have seen the production of many choral works that astonish by their ingenuity and novelty of effect; but is there one that has revealed so much of sheer beauty?

The Demons' Chorus having been mentioned, the problem set by this portion of the text calls for a few words. If Elgar has failed here, he has done so in good company. Has anybody yet succeeded in a musical portrayal of the infernal? Franck's feeble melodramatic Satan in *The Beatitudes* has been too readily ascribed to his saintly disposition; perhaps a truer explanation is to be found in his fatal preoccupation with the third-rate opera of his day. If any composer could have risen - or descended - to the occasion, surely Berlioz was the man. Yet are the infernal choruses in *Faust* really and truly horrific? True, Berlioz evidently realised the absurdity of infernal beings singing in the vernacular, for he invented a language for the purpose. *His* demons, instead of singing French as Elgar's sing English, burst forth with 'Has! Irimiru karabrao! Tradi oun Marexil fir tru dinxé burrudixe Fory my Dinkorlitz', etc; which seems to suggest a tribe of fallen Romanies. But the music itself is bald, whereas Elgar's is full of interest and vitality. The question of tone-colour comes in, too. It has been said that the Demons in *Gerontius* sound like a meeting of excited churchwardens; and undoubtedly choralists as a rule are content to depend on normal tone-colour. Berlioz foresaw this difficulty, and directs that his devils are to sing 'in snarling tones'. Sir Henry Coward, in the book quoted above, suggests various ways in which the Elgar chorus can be made convincing - nasal tone especially. I once heard a famous Yorkshire choir sing the Demons' Chorus splendidly, with all the aids that vivid tone-colour and dramatic contrast could give; but I was interested rather than thrilled. The fact seems to be that a derisory tone is more convincing in a solo singer than in a crowd, and there still remains the crucial difficulty of the words. Had Elgar discarded his text at this point and fallen back on the orchestra alone the result would have been realistic beyond anything that can be achieved by a chorus. For it is one of the functions of music to step in at the point where (owing to their definiteness and inescapable associations) words fail. Moreover, Elgar did not need the coming of the dance-band saxophonist to make him aware of the grisly, grotesque, and half-human sounds of which wind - and especially wood-wind - instruments are capable. Let it be granted, however, that as a piece of writing the Demons' Chorus is in the virtuoso class, and its adequate performance never fails to be at least arresting.

But one's last thought of *Gerontius* is of its beauty and human feeling. Not for nothing did the poem take possession of the composer for ten years before he put pen to paper. And, despite the splendid things that were still to come from him, few will question the truth of the words he wrote at the end of the score : 'This is the best of me. - Edward Elgar'.

The Listener, 6 November 1935, p 837

GENIUS, ORIGINAL and FINAL

Neville Cardus

Sir Neville Cardus (1889-1975) was for many years the music critic of the Manchester Guardian, *as well as being its chief writer on cricket. Though he lacked formal education in music, he was nonetheless an informed and perceptive observer with a wonderful way with words. Cardus was always a passionate Elgarian, ever since, at the age of 19, he had attended the première of the First Symphony at the Free Trade Hall. There is a chapter on Elgar in his book* Ten Composers *(1945), which was expanded in 1958 as* A Composer's Eleven.

The people who go to the Hallé Concerts only to hear fashionable soloists stayed at home last night, so that the rest of us were able to listen in peace to one of the most beautiful performances of Elgar's masterpiece which a long memory can recall.... Every artist who contributed to this deeply moving experience may well be proud of his share in it. Dr Malcolm Sargent has done nothing more compelling than this. There were small errors.... Now and again there was a want of distance; of disembodied rapture, in the sighing of the semi-chorus, the Angelicals; and the violins failed to give purity to the high Es during the ecstasy of 'O gen'rous love'. But, taking all in all, the choir sang with affecting eloquence and always musically; each part was expressive as though the vocalists had gone well beyond the ordinary procedure of the concert platform and were perfectly "translated".... Dr Sargent achieved an ideal balance between choir and soloists; there was no hint of strain, little forcing of effects beyond the ends intended by Elgar. It was a performance which went far to make the work Dr Sargent's own amongst contemporary conductors....

The work itself sounded as great as ever it did, in spite of occasional flaws which, as Brahms might say, any fool could see. The air 'Go forth' is possibly vulgar - at any rate it seems so when blared out by the brass in the prelude. But it is not more vulgar than the notorious chorus of the Knights of the Grail in *Parsifal*; and we do not think the less of *Parsifal* because of that. The debt which Elgar owed to *Parsifal* has been commented upon often enough by the enthusiastic hunters-down of the obvious. The echo of the agonized cry of Amfortas may be heard by all as early in the work as in the prelude. At one point only does Elgar fail completely and that is in the Demons' Chorus. Strauss, in a letter to Hofmannsthal, confesses that he cannot find the right music for Joseph (in the *Joseph Legend*) because there is no strain of piety in his family. Elgar could be pious or devout with the best of them; but he did not understand Satanism. His devils are even more gentlemanly than Milton's Lucifer is noble. The Hallé Chorus were not to blame if the demonic laughter had less of irony in it than any laughter (ironic) heard night by night in the House of Commons. Satanic music is rare; the art scarcely lends itself to the expression of irony, which is an intellectual matter. Only Liszt has come close to putting into music the sinister colour and accent of Satanism. *Gerontius* is great exactly where it had to be great; the demonic elements in the argument are episodic and not essential. Elgar in *Gerontius* is not less vivid than Strauss is in *Tod und Verklärung* in suggesting the dreadful sense of man's dissolution, "this emptying out of each constituent". But also, in the Chorus of the Angelicals, he lets us feel the white paradisal light - Strauss failed here and gave us only a Teuton Christmas-card view of heaven. The contrasted drama and "transfiguration" in *Gerontius*, the almost macabre portrayal of the "faltering breath", the "chill of heart", of the opening of Part I; and the quiet, timeless, radiant intensity of the opening of Part II - here, surely, are some of the most vividly and individually "seen" pages in the whole world of imaginative music. The lovely swaying figures of the muted violins create in a flash the changed scene, the changed state and plane; I know nothing in music more moving in its simple beauty of statement than Elgar's use of the reiterated notes at the words "I went to sleep", followed by the inspired rise to the F natural on the word "strange" at the phrase "a strange refreshment".

Not half enough has been written of Elgar's style of recitative in *Gerontius*; it seems to me to solve instinctively the old problem - how to find the proper element that divides a full lyricism or song from the prosaic levels of declamation. Could a lovelier 'via media' be discovered than the speech-song of Elgar's when Gerontius says : "I hear no more the busy beat of time"? If this is not genius, original and final, then I do not know what genius in music means. Why have Germany and France neglected *Gerontius*, Germany especially? The work was given in Düsseldorf in 1902; the performance made history. If a German or an Austrian, a Czech or a Bashi-bazouk, had composed *Gerontius*, the whole world by now would have admitted its qualities. On the point of current discussion of "freeing melody from harmony", what of Elgar's recitative writing in *Gerontius* - has Mahler surpassed it? As I say, it is easy to point to the defects in *Gerontius* - to the occasional hints of a too familiar melody, and what not. The flaws in *Gerontius* are those of greatness; the power of beauty is, to use the old language, inspired.

Manchester Guardian, 10 February 1939

The GREATNESS of GERONTIUS

F Bonavia

Ferruccio Bonavia (1877-1950) was born and educated in Italy, but in 1898 came to this country where he joined the Hallé Orchestra as a violinist. In 1908 he left to give himself to composition and criticism, first on the Manchester Guardian *and from 1920* The Daily Telegraph. *He wrote the articles on Elgar in A L Bacharach's* Lives of the Great Composers *(Penguin, 1935), and in* The Symphony *(Penguin, 1949, ed. Ralph Hill).*

It is certain that in that vast audience which attended the first performance of *The Dream of Gerontius* there was not a single individual who thought that the work would in a short time take its place amongst the finest oratorios of all time. Richter, having accurately gauged the difficulties of the new idiom, had insisted on long and exhausting rehearsals, with the result that during the actual performance the tired Birmingham Festival choir, losing touch with the orchestra, dropped a good half tone. Plunket Greene, who sang the part of the Priest, did not know whether to fall in with the singers or with the players. The first part ended thus with everybody's nerves on edge while Richter paced up and down the artists' room refusing to speak. The second part went better but anything like impartial appraisement was out of the question in that tense atmosphere. The audience was bewildered and disappointed. The critics felt baffled and some of them, unable to make anything of the score, attacked the libretto which was said to 'stink of incense' - a remark remembered now for its ineptness and not for its originality since only a few years before a German critic had discovered that Richard Strauss' *Death and Transfiguration* reeked of hospital wards. That comment brought forth a pertinent rejoinder : "The function of aesthetics is not to commend or blame a view of life but rather to enquire with what eloquence, with what sincerity, with what measure of convincing power, the artist expounds those ideas and feelings".

Thus wrote the one critic who then divined something of the greatness of the new oratorio, Arthur Johnstone. Even he however was not entirely happy in his estimate. A staunch Wagnerian and a champion of Liszt, Johnstone saw Wagnerian influences where there were none, and though deprecating a possible charge of plagiarism asserted that much in the work could not have been written but for the precedent of *Parsifal*. The article he then wrote for *The Manchester Guardian*, however, concluded with the statement that the composer's temperament as revealed by the music, like parts of the poem, deserved the epithet 'Dantesque'.

We who now have the advantage of knowing the whole of Elgar's work may say that if he could be 'Dantesque' in *The Dream of Gerontius* he could also be 'Kiplingesque' in *Land of Hope and Glory* and the true-born romantic in the concertos. But the definition fits both the music and the text of *Gerontius*. Elgar's choruses and semi-choruses have the mystic exaltation characteristic of the singers in the *Divine Comedy*, as his demons have all the fierceness of Dante's fiends. The connection between that epic and the text of *Gerontius* is less close but, as far as it goes, perfectly clear.

Gerontius on his death-bed tormented by pain and terror reminds us inevitably of Dante who, setting out on his pilgrimage, is attacked by the lion and the she-wolf and feels anguish so sharp that 'death is not more bitter'. Virgil rescues him and during the journey through hell and purgatory aids and comforts the poet. In *Gerontius* it is an angel who fulfils a similar office and explains the meaning of all the soul hears and feels on his way to Judgment. It is not too fanciful to see also a connection between the thoughts of earthly affections that make sharper the pain of Dante's sufferers and the voices that, reciting the 'subvenite', reach Gerontius from the world he has left. There is possibly also an analogy between the glad song Gerontius hears when about to enter the House of Judgment and the hymn of praise that shakes the mountain of purgatory when one of its penitents ascends to heaven. But as an Englishman Cardinal Newman knew *The Pilgrim's Progress* and *Everyman* even better than he knew the *Divine Comedy*. His Gerontius is no poet or philosopher but a plain man who at the end of his journey tries vainly to cast his accounts. Soundness or unsoundness of theology does not concern us.

The profound sincerity and convincing power of Elgar's setting, clarifying and amplifying, giving new breadth to the text, have placed *The Dream of Gerontius* by the side of *Messiah* as the most eloquent and most moving of oratorios far outdistancing the brilliant but somewhat superficial *Elijah* once considered *Messiah*'s only peer and rival. The reason for this re-assessment of values is not far to seek. *Elijah*, for all its many and considerable musical excellences, lacks the spiritual qualities of *Messiah* and *Gerontius*. Like Liszt in his Dante Symphony, Mendelssohn is concerned with externals. True, sincere mysticism, the passionate longing of the soul for perfection, a pose with Liszt, was entirely foreign to Mendelssohn. He had found perfection of a kind in his art; he asks for nothing more. Mysticism provides links with Dante and with Wagner who touched upon it at first tentatively in *Tannhäuser* and then with riper art in *Parsifal*. That is one aspect of the oratorio that an audience which knew only the *Enigma Variations* could not easily have grasped.

The Dream of Gerontius has now won praise from all responsible critics. Johnstone delighted in its unconventionality and found its demons much more terrible than those of Berlioz. Others have exalted the skill of a composer whose symphonic genius enabled him to discover new and lovely combinations of orchestral tone and the cunning division of the choristers into chorus and semi-chorus. These attributes, however, dependent mainly on fertility of imagination and technical ability, do not constitute a final proof of greatness. Time is apt to overshadow all that is but skill and ingenuity. A more reliable criterion is offered by the theme itself, which Elgar presents in a way that is as profound as it is realistic. The passing of Gerontius is grim and no romantic euthanasia; it leads not to Beatrice but to the unknown; it is death that the materialist must find as mysterious as the believer, death that overtakes saint and sinner, Cordelia and Cressida. Moreover the words of the poem often do not invite, and almost repel, musical setting, either because they possess a rhythm of their own that can only with difficulty be brought within the narrower compass of musical rhythm or because their philosophical purport chills the lyrical vein. With this in our mind we can better appreciate the strength of wing that was needed to turn metaphysics into a great work of art. There can be no doubt that this *Gerontius* was conceived by Elgar, in Carlyle's words, when the whole heart of him was 'rapt into the true passion of melody'.

This seems to me a more decisive consideration than the originality of the setting, which is yet far from negligible. *Gerontius* was said to constitute as radical an innovation in oratorio as Wagner's musical drama did in opera - which is true since in the oratorio, as in Wagner's operas, the conventional divisions into arias, choruses and ensemble-piece no longer obtain. But the importance of such concessions to the rational temper of the times can easily be exaggerated. *Messiah* still moves us profoundly in spite of its wholehearted acceptance of the conventionalities of its day. The greatness of *Gerontius* is in its profound sincerity rather than in its originality, in the beauty and truth of the emotion rather than in the material skill with which heavenly rapture and hellish vision are portrayed. We are told that when the people of Verona met Dante in the streets of their town they pointed to him saying : 'There goes the man who has been to hell'. After listening to *Gerontius* we are apt to think that Elgar too has passed through the dark valley before his time - and beyond as far as human thought or human imagination can reach.

The Listener, 22 April 1943, p 493

The ILLUSTRATED GERONTIUS

Ma - ri - a   I am near to death, and thou, thou art call - ing me.

That mas-ter-ful ne - ga-tion and col - lapse of all that makes me man!

A strange   re - fresh-ment: for I feel in   me an in- ex-press-ive light-ness

I hear no more the bu____ - sy beat of time

A un -i -form and gen- tle pressure tells me I am not self- moving,but borne forward on my way

Dear An - gel, say, Why have I now no fear at meet - ing him?

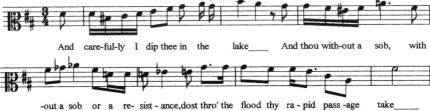

And care-ful-ly I dip thee in the lake____ And thou with-out a sob, with

-out a sob or a re- sist - ance,dost thro' the flood thy ra - pid pass -age take____

Part Five

The
Recorded Legacy

A PERSONAL VIEW on the RECORDED LEGACY

Walter J Essex

Walter Essex is a trained singer, and is one of the founder members of the Southern Branch of the Elgar Society. He was the Branch's first Chairman, a post from which he has recently retired.

I remember vividly my first encounter with *The Dream of Gerontius*. It was the summer of 1963. I used to visit my local record library in Coventry every week, invariably taking home a diet of Gilbert and Sullivan, Tchaikovsky and certain Verdi operas. On the occasion in question, I decided to be adventurous and took home Wagner's *Die Meistersinger* (all six discs of it!) and *The Dream of Gerontius*. The Wagner I found very boring (a judgement long since thoroughly revised!), but that may have been because I was completely bowled over by what I heard of the Elgar. I remember it was Sargent's 1955 recording that I had taken home, the only one available at the time, and whilst my rapture at this performance has been somewhat modified over the years, it remains a very special item in my current collection for what it did both to me and for me at that time.

With anything that remains a focal point for devotion, one is always in danger of losing a sense of objectivity. With regard to *Gerontius* I admit that I quite fail to be objective about the work; it is too deep-rooted in my spirit for that. However, with recordings I find that I can bring a level of objectivity to it, but inevitably personal taste plays a considerable part and I do not necessarily expect everyone to agree with my views.

In the *Elgar Society Journal*, when greeting the recording of *Gerontius* under Vernon Handley, the Society Chairman, Andrew Neill wrote of "a work which has now been recorded more times than Elgarians have any right to expect". With twelve different versions (not all currently available as I write) as well as the excerpts conducted by Elgar himself, one can only agree. Among these recordings there are many fine performances: from soloists, choirs, orchestras and conductors; but

A magazine advertisement for the 1955 Sargent recording of Gerontius which led to the author's discovery of the work

these "fine performances" do not always coincide within the same recording. To my mind, the *Gerontius* recording with the perfect synthesis of forces has yet to be made, and in this I perhaps strive for an improbable perfection.

I do accept that we all hear voices differently, and with the soloists, at least, there can be wide divergences of opinion. Within my own immediate Elgarian circle, several people will each come up with a different *Gerontius* recording from which they could not be parted, or which they would have to take with them to that mythical "desert island". For myself, I could not be parted from any of them; each performance has at least one element I could not be without.

* * *

In all the recordings of *Gerontius*, the playing of the Prelude gives notice of the style of performance which is to follow, which is not to suggest that the Prelude is detached from the rest of the work: it is a vital ingredient of the whole. At the very opening, as with Wagner's *Parsifal*, the listener immediately enters a unique sound world, and I look for the way a conductor recreates this "sound world" in terms of orchestral textures, dynamics and tempi. In both of his recordings, Sargent indicates that it is the dramatic rather than the spiritual nature of the work which will predominate. There are some oddly perfunctory sections in both performances (a criticism that can be levelled at Sargent's interpretation overall, particularly in the 1955 recording). In 1945 the 'Go forth' theme moves briskly, yet retains much warmth. By 1955 this same section lacks momentum; there is no forward flow, and the tempi throughout the Prelude are pulled about rather too roughly. Britten, as might be expected from a supreme opera composer, unfolds the full drama of the work in a quite thrilling performance of the Prelude. He takes a few liberties with the score, not only here but throughout, but there is an unerring rightness about it when he does, given his intense interpretation. An example is at eight bars after fig 9 and again at fig 10 where Elgar indicates a total silence on the bar line - a moment's pause to gather strength. Britten allows the timpani roll to continue across the bar line each time, thus momentarily assuming the spotlight. Unauthentic it may be, but it is undeniably spine-tingling!

Gibson is disappointing in the Prelude, many of the contrasts in both tempi and dynamics going for nothing. Handley, conversely, is very attentive to the dynamic shading, without giving any hint of calculation. His transition to the 'Go forth' theme at fig 12 is probably the smoothest of all, and he conjures up a real shiver down the spine just before fig 17 with the *fp* on woodwind and tam-tam as it introduces the 'Sleep' theme.

In both of his recordings, Barbirolli establishes his dramatic viewpoint in the Prelude. He makes the most of every contrast and maintains a forward propulsion, avoiding all temptation to linger. The live 1957 Rome performance perhaps catches him in a more inspired mood than in 1965, although the Symphony Orchestra of Rome Radio seems unhappy at times, with some raw string tone at the great climaxes. Both Rattle and Hickox blend the dramatic and spiritual in an almost ideal way. The very opening of the Prelude with Rattle and the CBSO is the most sheerly beautiful of all. When I first heard this performance, its kinship to the opening of *Parsifal* became immediately obvious. Both openings, in their transparency and colouring, establish the spiritual feel of what is to follow. With Rattle the opening *pp* and the *ppp* at fig 2 really are just that. However, given the very wide dynamic range afforded to this recording, the great climaxes make for uncomfortable domestic listening when the volume control is adjusted to be able to acknowledge the very quietest moments.

Wide dynamic range is also a problem with the latest recording to be issued, that under David Hill on Naxos (1997). In fact it is probably appropriate to state at this stage that the engineering of this recording is its greatest drawback. The soloists suffer most, seemingly recorded in a separate, drier acoustic. However, the orchestra undeniably comes off best, and with the Bournemouth Symphony Orchestra in very fine form, the woodwind in particular being very characterful, Hill directs a fine Prelude, linking and moulding its distinctive sections into a satisfying whole.

Boult is very much in a dimension of his own. Certainly there is drama in his Prelude, but it is the spiritual resonances which impinge on one's consciousness. Even the magnificent 'Go forth' theme, for once, is not brazen, but manages to convey a measure of gentleness and restraint - a real nobility of spirit. Throughout, Boult is not one to linger and keeps up the forward momentum of the piece... which is more than can be said for Svetlanov! His recording, on the Russian Melodiya label, is an oddity amongst all these recordings. It was a performance recorded *live* in Moscow in April 1983 with British soloists and choir, and Russian orchestra. Svetlanov's reading of the Prelude is idiosyncratic, to say the least. Both opening and ending are very slow; there is little sensitivity to the changing tempi, creating an overall blandness. The somewhat bronchially afflicted audience mars some of the quieter moments.

Elgar's audience at the Royal Albert Hall in February 1927 was similarly afflicted - some should clearly have been at home in bed! - and Elgar himself proclaimed the test pressings of the recording of the Prelude "a sad disaster". However, thanks to the tenacity of Jerrold Northrop Moore, we have this recording. Inevitably, there is something special about Elgar's own conducting of the Prelude. Is the intensity I feel when listening to this account real or imagined? Am I simply in awe of the presence of the composer himself? Again, objectivity fails to register as one submits to the overwhelming majesty of the performance.

And so, our conductors have laid down their credentials and little that follows should take the listener by surprise. None of them is let down by his orchestra. Even Barbirolli's Rome orchestra has some fine moments; in any case, with the recording quality rather unfocused, it would be unfair to make a negative judgement. However, if I were to choose amongst the orchestras for sheer brilliance, Rattle's CBSO and Handley's RLPO really do stand out for body of string tone, unanimity of woodwind blending, and all sections displaying a virtuosic command of the score. The score itself is hugely detailed in both dynamics and tempi; again and again, both Rattle and Handley prove the composer's eloquence in their adherence to these markings, although, paradoxically, neither is slavish in his approach.

* * *

Gerontius makes tremendous demands on the choir(s) and there is not one choir amongst these recordings which does not rise to the challenge, even if full satisfaction is not always achieved. The two big set pieces - the 'Demons' Chorus' and 'Praise to the Holiest' may be bench-marks by which any choir is judged in this work, but there is much else in the score which taxes its full resources.

Both of Sargent's recordings use the Huddersfield Choral Society. In 1945 the choir displays great depth of tone, with altos and tenors particularly striking. The latter are quite superb in the 'Demons' Chorus', and this section shows the power and vitality of the whole choir. Sargent's beautifully shaped account of 'Praise to the Holiest' raises the hair on the back of the neck. By 1955 the HCS has lost some of its bloom, the tone often sounding pinched. In the 'Go forth' section at the end of Part I, the choir sounds stodgy and there is some suspect soprano intonation. Even 'Praise to the Holiest' fails to lift off. The HCS re-appear, in combination with the Royal Liverpool Philharmonic Choir under Vernon Handley, and very fine they are. The 'Demons' Chorus' is a *tour de force*. It is sung *straight*, ie. no leering characterisation, but is rhythmically taut and exciting. Throughout, the tone is full-bodied and the semi-chorus sopranos are truly ethereal. Only in the closing pages of 'Praise to the Holiest' is there a slight feeling of running out of steam.

Barbirolli (1965) certainly presses his combined choirs to play up the drama of the Demons. The sneering and leering are vividly characterised, but at the expense of tone - very edgy at climaxes - and rhythmic precision. Elsewhere, the choirs acquit themselves well and satisfy this listener at least. Barbirolli's Rome choir (1957) sometimes has difficulty with the English vowel sounds, but otherwise diction is the least troublesome aspect. There is a forthright honesty about much of the singing, and they master Barbirolli's variations in tempi in 'Praise to the Holiest' magnificently, but ultimately it is the unyielding tone of the choir that wearies the ear. The sopranos, particularly, lack an essential purity of sound.

Under Britten, the London Symphony Chorus sounds undernourished at the great climaxes, although in the quieter moments there are some ravishing sounds; for example, 'Be merciful, be gracious' (fig 35), where Britten provides a tempo steadier than is usual, but to great effect. Where Britten really scores is in his inspired use of the choir of King's College, Cambridge for the semi-chorus. The section in Part II which leads up to the main statement of 'Praise to the Holiest' (figs 60-68) is stunning, the choral sound being truly of another world.

Britten also manages, in this section, to convey the necessary forward momentum of Gerontius's soul moving 'with extremest speed' to its judgement.

Gibson's SNO Chorus offers good, forthright singing, but little subtlety. Occasionally the sopranos are edgy at the top of their range, and the tenors ragged. Gibson's sometimes hard-pressed speeds may be responsible for some lack of unanimity of tone. There is a great warmth of sound in Boult's combined London Philharmonic Choir and John Alldis Choir. This registers immediately in the 'Kyrie' (fig 29) and 'Holy Mary, pray for him' (fig 30) sections. The choirs sound particularly beautiful in the double-chorus section at the end of Part I (fig 75): 'Go forth on thy course'. The **pp** and **ppp** markings are observed without any loss of intonation and the soprano top B is etched in ethereally. The 'Demons' Chorus' is very impressive both in its choral sound and in the power of the orchestra, although ultimately real drama is lacking. 'Praise to the Holiest' does not move along as one might wish, Boult's tempi not entirely in keeping with the score, but there is an undoubted grandeur in the reading. The choirs respond with some glorious singing and achieve a real sense of repose at the section beginning 'O gen'rous love' (two bars after fig 80).

The London Symphony Chorus's contribution to the Svetlanov recording is uneven, but given the conductor's eccentric tempi this may not be surprising. The 'Kyrie' and the ensuing 'Holy Mary, pray for him' sound very stodgy. 'Be merciful', taken very fast, is edgy with almost an air of impatience about it - quite wrong for the feeling behind the words! However, the 'Demons' Chorus', again very fast, has a real thrill about it. Part way into 'Praise to the Holiest' I closed my score and simply listened. I stopped worrying about the tempi; the choir, singing superbly, simply followed Svetlanov and it all seemed of a piece. It felt right! A stunning account. Recording the work in studio conditions some five years later, the LSC seem much happier and the singing is uniformly excellent throughout. There are moments when I feel it is not quite big enough in sound to encompass the huge climaxes (as with Britten), but there is an energy and a sense of drama when needed, and no thinning out of tone in the quieter passages.

Hill's combined choirs are backwardly placed and they do not always make the effect they undoubtedly would in a better engineered recording. The first entry of the semi-chorus, 'Kyrie eleison' (fig 29), is well nigh inaudible, even at a high volume setting. This is surely not Elgar's intention, even though it is marked **ppp**. The semi-chorus is treated similarly throughout the recording. However, the choirs do provide thrilling singing, as in the rhythmically biting 'Demons' Chorus', and finely-textured tone in quieter passages.

If I leave Rattle's CBSO Choir until last, it is because I feel that, in conjunction with its conductor, it approaches the ideal. It does not sound as large a body of singers as in other recordings, but there is a richness of tone throughout the dynamic range. (It also sounds a youthful choir!) If I were to choose just one example to display the merits of this choir and conductor, I would choose the section 'Be merciful, be gracious' (fig 35). At the beginning the tenors sing 'Be merciful' (**mf**), joined by the altos in the same register on 'Be gracious' (**pp**). At fig 38 it is the basses (**mf**), joined by the tenors (**p**), who have these phrases. The seamless *legato* and precise observance of the dynamics make these ecstatic moments. On the words 'Lord, deliver him' there is a unanimous rhythmic precision which I find matched only by Boult's choirs. These are also matched by Rattle's at fig 75, 'Go forth on thy course', at the end of Part I. The clarity of texture and secure intonation, in a section which can too often sound pinched and undernourished, almost takes one's breath away. This choir's precision is used to great effect in the 'Demons' Chorus' where, incidentally, there is a real difference between the slurred 'Ha! ha!'s and those marked *staccato* **sfz**. 'Praise to the Holiest' is a sumptuous piece of choral singing. Rattle's tempi toward the end might not accord exactly with the score, but the ending brings an exhilaration matched only by Sargent (1945) and - yes! - Elgar himself. If there is a drawback with the CBSO Chorus, it is the rather distant placing of it within the overall sound spectrum. I feel this is a miscalculation on the part of EMI's engineers (though not as damaging as with Hill's choirs on Naxos), but it cannot diminish my sheer joy in listening to this choir.

* * *

For many people, I am sure, the casting of the principal singers is a major factor in any recording of *Gerontius*. With regard to Gerontius himself, what sort of voice does one expect? In Part I he is a man near to death, burdened by the weariness of pain. This must be conveyed by any interpreter, as well as the fear and dread; and yet he must rise to the heroic challenge of 'Sanctus fortis' in Part I and 'Take me away' in Part II. Inevitably, it is a difficult part to bring off in all its facets.

There is a richness of interpreters in recorded performances. However, before examining the complete recordings, I must go back to Elgar's own recorded extracts. There is too little of Steuart Wilson on the Royal Albert Hall account to make any real judgement, although the tone, in what we hear, has a heroic ring to it. There is a little more of Tudor Davies in the Hereford extracts (and how tantalisingly brief they are!). Here we have a wealth of open, Italianate tone and operatic full-bloodedness which would seem to have the composer's blessing. Elgar himself said that he saw Gerontius as "a man like us, a sinner, a repentant one of course, but still no end of a worldly man in his life"; his music, therefore, was no "church tunes and rubbish, but a good, healthy, full-blooded romantic, remembered worldliness". That would seem to point to the Tudor Davies approach, and I have to admit it is the approach I personally prefer. In the complete recordings only two interpreters measure up to this (Arthur Davies and Jon Vickers), which is not to say that the others are not equally valid.

Only one interpretation would I willingly discard; regretfully it is that by Robert Tear. I say "regretfully" for Tear is an artist I much admire, but on his recorded showing at least, he is not a Gerontius. His singing is forthright and honest, but no more. The varied dynamics go for little; more often than not his singing is unrelentingly loud. His opening in Part I is effortful (perhaps not inappropriately so!). 'Sanctus fortis' begins **ff** rather than the marked **mf** and so leaves no room for expansion. (Few of the tenors actually observe this; those who do show that Elgar really knew what he was about!) However, Tear is not helped in this section by Gibson's very fast tempo which robs the piece of any dignity. In much of the colloquy with the Angel in Part II Tear is unbearably hectoring. No, this is not a performance to be comfortable with.

Richard Lewis has assumed the part twice on these recordings, with Sargent in 1955 and with Barbirolli in 1965. The later recording displays a certain loss of bloom on the voice in the intervening years, and a beat in the upper register has developed. However, in both recordings his is a riveting interpretation. At the opening he is utterly believable as a man on his death-bed, employing a 'drained' tone which, however, opens up magnificently when required. Particularly in the later recording, there is real exhaustion expressed in the words 'I can no more' (two bars after fig 57), yet there is no holding back from the high B in the phrase 'in thine *own* agony' (two bars before fig 63), thrillingly delivered. The natural speech rhythms in the opening section of Part II are a joy. 'Take me away' finds Lewis stretched in both recordings, with some lumpy phrasing, but overall his performances are heartfelt and truly cherishable.

Peter Pears (with Britten) is completely credible in his characterisation. In Part I one can really empathise with the anguish of Gerontius, and his verbal articulation in his exchanges with the Angel in Part II is mercurial. However, although his is a voice I much admire, it is not one I can really love. It is neither lyrical (at this stage in his career) nor heroic, and it is the latter qualities that he is lacking for a fully rounded portrayal. The climactic passages in 'Sanctus fortis' and the attack on 'Take me away' are really not for him, but for much else in the score I am thankful that he recorded the part.

John Mitchinson's recorded Gerontius (with Rattle) has not met with universal approval, the undeniable beat in his voice troubling some listeners. Certainly in live performance I have found him less constrained and with a much freer tone. He has the full vocal resources to do the part justice, from the hushed opening to Part I to the demands of 'Sanctus fortis'. There are some magical moments, such as his colouring of the word 'bewilderment' (fig 34), and the lovely head tones at the reprise of 'Sanctus fortis' (fig 53) which expand seamlessly into full voice. There is real fear in the voice as he conjures up the Demons in his mind (fig 58-61), and there is real heartbreak in 'Take me away', without becoming maudlin. This is a vital portrayal which goes right to the heart of the character.

Perhaps the most sheerly beautiful assumption (vocally) of the role of Gerontius is that by Anthony Rolfe Johnson (under Handley). A voice of much lighter means than Mitchinson's, he, too, has the resources to meet all the vocal demands, but I have the overriding impression of blandness in his reading. Yes, the opening is exquisitely sung, but there is no real anguish. Where Mitchinson (and Pears) conjured up horror at the vision of the Demons in Part I, with Rolfe Johnson the feeling is almost casual. The opening of Part II finds him at his best : 'I went to sleep' (fig 4) is a *real* awakening and Elgar's *parlando* markings are observed to wonderful effect. But when we reach 'Take me away' there is no real emotion, just good, clean singing.

Arthur Davies appears as Gerontius twice on these recordings. When I first heard his performance with Hickox I was bowled over by the sheer generosity of voice in the part. Here, at last, was a tenor to match his namesake, Tudor Davies. There are many places in the score where one simply wants sumptuous tenor tone to match the passion in the music, eg. in Part II : 'But hark! A grand mysterious harmony...' (fig 71), and Davies provides this in abundance. His is a thrilling performance *per se*, but characterisation is not consistent. With Svetlanov, five years earlier, and caught "on the wing", as it were, in a live performance, the voice is even more free in tone, but there is a tendency to lachrymose delivery and much use of the glottal stop, presumably for dramatic effect. 'Sanctus fortis' is taken at a very hectic pace by Svetlanov, leaving Davies no room for dynamic shading (and probably the cause of some doubtful verbal juggling!). 'Take me away' is probably even more exciting than with Hickox and is given a forward momentum by the conductor whereby the singer can express the heartbreak without becoming sentimental.

William Kendall (with Hill) cannot compare with Davies in vocal splendour; in fact, it would seem to me that his voice is a size too small to encompass the full range of the part. In the openings to both Part I and Part II he seems almost ideal, but the bigger moments stretch him uncomfortably. That having been said, the weary resignation in his smaller-scale 'Take me away' convinces me almost as much as the heroic outpourings of bigger-voiced tenors! At times the tone seems shallow, and a lack of bite on consonants robs the text of vitality - but both of these faults could be the result of the poor balance of this Naxos recording, as mentioned earlier, and perhaps judgement on Mr Kendall should be reserved.

Boult's casting of Nicolai Gedda as Gerontius caused a few ripples back in 1976. This much-admired and versatile tenor had previously recorded *Elijah* (in English) and *Messiah*, thus giving notice that the English oratorio *tradition* was not alien to him. I was excited by his performance at that time, probably because he opened my eyes to the full operatic potential of the role, having been so used to Richard Lewis as the norm. I am not sure that that excitement has remained. I say "not sure" because it is a performance about which I am constantly changing my mind. Currently, I find it a heart-warming, sometimes thrilling re-creation of the role, but set beside the two interpreters yet to be discussed, it is not fully satisfying. Gedda's English is almost wholly idiomatic, only the occasional too-open vowel, as in 'manhood' and 'veneration' betraying his non-native background. In Part I and the latter part of Part II he is almost perfect, characterising vividly and scrupulous over dynamics. Only in the exchanges with the Angel in Part II does he appear a little brash, the tone consistently open and bright and, consequently, tiring on the ear.

The final two interpreters of Gerontius are Heddle Nash and Jon Vickers. No serious lover of *The Dream of Gerontius* should be without either performance. They are very different interpretations, yet each reaches the very heart of both music and character as no others. The voices themselves are quite different in timbre, Nash essentially a lyric tenor, Vickers a dramatic tenor, though this is over-simplifying the matter. Both singers command attention from their first utterances, both for beauty of voice and for interpretative powers. Both conjure up a picture of a man *in extremis*. Both produce beautiful head tones at 'That I am going, that I am no more' (one bar after fig 25). Both begin 'Sanctus fortis' *mf* and observe the *semplice e dolce* at fig 44. Both... but no. I could go on pin-pointing so many places in the score where Elgar's detailed markings really do tell in these interpretations. If I might choose just one more highlight for each: at fig 53, the *pp* reprise of 'Sanctus fortis', Vickers also observes the *piangendo* and produces an ethereal head voice which he then gradually mixes with full chest voice as the music expands - all seamless and creating a heart-stopping moment; Nash's 'Novissima hora est' (fig 66) is the most moving and most beautiful of all, and the ensuing phrases, up to when Gerontius expires at fig 68, make me really believe that he is 'wearied' and at the end of all that he can bear. No words can do full justice to these interpretations; they demand to be heard. If, under threat of rack and thumbscrew, I was forced to choose between these two singers, I think it would have to be Vickers for the sheer thrill and open-hearted generosity of his tenor voice.

* * *

The casting of the Angel has been particularly successful in *Gerontius* recordings. Of the ten mezzos/contraltos, only one, I feel, fails to bring some insight or special quality to the part. However, what is your view of an angel? It is definitely regarded as male in Newman's poem; but the voice here is that of a mezzo-soprano or contralto. There are, of course, no real problems with this, especially given Cherubino, Oktavian *et al.* But there is a danger that the singer might sound matronly - or perhaps I should say motherly - which gives quite the wrong effect. If I include Helen Watts, Alfreda Hodgson, Marjorie Thomas, Gladys Ripley and Constance Shacklock in this category, this is not to denigrate them, for they all give quite lovely performances; but if one wants something a little more self-effacing of femininity, one must look to Yvonne Minton, Felicity Palmer, Catherine Wyn-Rogers or Dame Janet Baker. I should perhaps also include Sarah Fryer in the latter group, but hers is, I am afraid, the one Angel which fails to make its mark. She has a voice which seems, as yet, unfinished, and was certainly not ready to have her interpretation committed to permanence. There are isolated moments which are quite lovely, but overall her tone lacks individuality and her delivery of the text is bland. It must be said that she is not aided by Hill in the 'Farewell'; he takes this section very slowly indeed and it threatens to grind to a halt! This creates a maudlin effect, which is quite wrong.

Margaret Balfour, Elgar's Angel, has a voice which moves me very much. There is not much to judge her by, but enough to wish there were more! Her 'Farewell' is sung with gorgeous, velvety tone. The timbre of the voice is of a type which is rarely heard these days. Amongst the complete recordings, Gladys Ripley and Constance Shacklock come nearest in style. Ripley (Sargent 1945) is consistently warm and comforting, a voice one feels almost able to wrap around one to keep out cold winter draughts! One of my personal testing points for any Angel is the launching of the duet beginning 'A presage falls upon thee' (fig 26), and here Gladys Ripley is radiant and the blending of her voice with that of Heddle Nash is matched for sheer beauty only by Janet Baker and Richard Lewis (Barbirolli 1965). Constance Shacklock, in Barbirolli's 1957 Rome performance, has some wayward intonation to begin with, but settles to give a satisfying performance overall. There is something deeply affecting about her characterisation - something indefinable. At the words 'And I will come and wake thee on the morrow' (in the 'Farewell', three bars before fig 134) there is a smile in the voice which lifts the spirit; after all, the message is full of hope and promise. A wondrous moment.

Marjorie Thomas (Sargent 1955) is a generally sensitive Angel, but surprisingly bland in places and fails to move me. However, her rendering of the 'Farewell', poised and beautiful, redeems much. Alfreda Hodgson is the one cherishable ingredient of the Gibson performance which I simply could not be without. Her opening 'Angel's Song' is a trifle edgy, but thereafter there is one glorious moment after another. Her utterance of 'Yes, for one moment thou shalt see thy Lord - one moment' (two bars before fig 56) never fails to bring a lump to my throat, not only for the tonal quality of the voice, but for the intensity of meaning she brings to this phrase. She is consistently responsive to the text and secure in all the extremes of the role. Thus, her build-up to 'Praise to the Holiest' with its climactic A is ecstatic and exciting; her final words, 'Brother dear', sung *dolcissimo* as marked, are truly melting. This is a jewel of a performance in a less than lustrous setting.

Helen Watts, for Boult, is not as vocally resplendent as other recorded Angels, yet she gives a fascinating account of the role, constantly alert to verbal nuance, not least in her exchanges with Gedda's Gerontius. Her account of the *stigmata*, beginning at fig 58, 'There was a mortal who is now above...', aided by Boult's eerily brilliant accompaniment, represents the height of her art. Catherine Wyn-Rogers, for Handley, does not have the warmth of tone which I find to be a prerequisite for an ideal Angel. To be fair, much of what she does is very good, even though I feel that the recording does not do her justice. (I *know* it doesn't, having heard her on more than one occasion in live performance!) She simply does not sound at ease for much of the time, and a rather neutral quality predominates. However, at the section 'Thy judgement now is near...' (fig 102), she conjures up a real frisson of mystery, of spirituality, of drama - she sings beautifully - and all is forgiven!

Felicity Palmer appears with Hickox and also on the *live* Svetlanov recording, partnering Arthur Davies on both occasions. Hers is a voice which arouses much controversy in Elgar recordings, and it seems to me that it is a voice which either you can take or you cannot. I can! There is little to choose between the performances although the *live* occasion engenders more electricity between Palmer and Davies. The duet is particularly lovely, beautifully blended. Miss Palmer brings her considerable dramatic gifts to bear on the stigmata passage in both recordings; but under Svetlanov her 'Farewell' has a radiance which is missing with Hickox. The phrase, marked *dolcissimo*, 'Shall tend and nurse thee as thou liest' (two bars after fig 131) shows her at her most melting.

Yvonne Minton's Angel is one of the glories of the Britten recording. The opening 'Angel's Song' immediately marks her out as an Angel of special qualities. Her last 'Alleluia' (one bar after fig 15), sung **pp**, would melt the stoniest heart, as would 'You cannot now cherish a wish which ought not to be wished' (four bars after fig.20). With a fine sensitivity to words, combined with dark, honeyed tone, Yvonne Minton shines throughout the work. Even Britten's brisk pace for the 'Farewell' (thus avoiding any hint of sentimentality) cannot rob her of poise or dignity.

Dame Janet Baker has recorded the role of the Angel twice : with Barbirolli (1965) and Rattle. More than twenty years separate the recordings, but both bring huge rewards. There is no denying that the voice is far fresher in 1965 where Dame Janet delivers a very dramatic reading of the role, no doubt spurred on by Barbirolli. The interpretation has softened and deepened by 1986, but it is to the earlier recording I turn again and again. As when discussing the Gerontius of Nash and of Vickers, words cannot adequately do justice to the sheer thrill of Dame Janet's performances, but a few examples must be given. As with Yvonne Minton, the poise on the last section of the 'Angel's Song' is exquisite with Barbirolli; with Rattle it remains very beautiful and there is even an added warmth. 'You cannot now cherish a wish...' in the 1965 recording is one of those phrases that simply lives on in the mind - totally unforgettable. Staying with 1965, the launching of the duet, 'A presage falls upon thee' is simply glorious and, as already implied, with Richard Lewis an ideal blend is achieved. With John Mitchinson (Rattle) this section lacks a sense of repose. Only Dame Janet Baker, in both recordings, can match Alfreda Hodgson in the section 'Yes, for one moment thou shalt see thy Lord - one moment'. With Dame Janet I hear it with tears pricking my eyes. Throughout her exchanges with Mitchinson's Gerontius, she achieves a stillness not always in evidence under Barbirolli. And so I could go on. If you want to judge for yourself, I would ask you to listen to the

'Farewell' in the Barbirolli recording. This is glorious singing by any standard, and with some heart-stopping moments, eg. 'I poise thee, and I lower thee, and hold thee' (figs 128-129). This is surely at the peak of Dame Janet Baker's art.

***

At the end of Part I we first hear the bass, or baritone, soloist in the role of the Priest. He intones 'Proficiscere, anima Christiana!' - 'Go forth upon thy journey, Christian soul!' This is the magnificent piece which brings Part I to an incandescent close. Our soloist is heard again in the Angel of the Agony's grave utterances in Part II. Much has been said and written as to the need for *two* different voices in these parts : a baritone for the Priest and a bass for the Angel of the Agony. Certainly the high tessitura of the Priest's music would seem to call for a baritone, whilst the Angel of the Agony ideally needs a true bass to bring the necessary weight to the part.

In Elgar's recorded extracts we have the second half (with chorus) of the Priest's part, and the whole of the Angel of the Agony's solo as sung by Herbert Heyner, and again the whole of the Angel of the Agony's solo as sung by Horace Stevens at Hereford. Heyner would seem to have the vocal means to encompass both parts and his Angel of the Agony is certainly very dramatic. But it is to Horace Stevens that I constantly turn in this piece. There is, perhaps, too much used of snatched breath for dramatic effect, but the voice is just right; he instils both authority and awe. Elgar's accompaniment sends shivers down the spine. This is probably the most moving account on disc.

Sargent's 1945 recording is the only one to make use of two singers in the parts of the Priest and the Angel of the Agony. This may well have been the right idea, but is badly let down by Dennis Noble's Priest. I fail to understand the almost universal approval for this performance. In his contribution to the volume *Elgar Studies*, Michael Kennedy, in discussing Elgar interpreters, writes : "Dennis Noble's 'Proficiscere' has a clarion quality all too often missing". Unfortunately, I cannot share his enthusiasm. I find Noble's tone dry and uningratiating; he brings a laboured treatment of individual notes rather than smooth phrasing; there is a total lack of warmth. Elgar's detailed dynamic markings are largely ignored. The worst fault concerns the long notes (six crotchet beats) on the second syllable of both 'mundo' and 'world' : they are cut to just two crotchet beats, leaving gaping holes in the texture of the music, the effect of the underlying changing harmonies being quite lost. Indeed, throughout this section long notes are often cut short, even his very last note at the end of Part I. No, I cannot endorse the good opinion of this performance. In the same recording Norman Walker is the Angel of the Agony. As a performance it is good and solid, but lacking in real imagination.

The Priest is a figure of authority, yet is present to bring comfort to the dying Gerontius - a sympathetic figure. Both aspects are there in Elgar's music : a commanding beginning; then a softening and warmth on the word 'God' in the phrase 'Go in the name of God' (fig 70); a *diminuendo* on the words 'who bled for thee', and again on the words 'Holy Spirit', where notes and dynamics indicate a caressing of the words. The Australian John Cameron (Sargent 1955) is a lightweight baritone who shows ease in the upper reaches of the music. He is exemplary in his adherence to the score's markings and his tonal colouring encompasses the full range of Elgar's expectations. Above all, there is great beauty of tone. His voice lacks the required weight for the Angel of the Agony, although it is a beautiful performance which is, unfortunately, not matched by Sargent's rather pedestrian reading of the section.

A singer who really does fulfil the above-mentioned requirements for the Priest, as well as having the *gravitas* for the Angel of the Agony, is Boult's Robert Lloyd, to my mind the most successful singer on disc to combine these roles. As the Priest, Lloyd has the power and authority for the opening - also great dignity. He observes all the dynamics quite scrupulously, softening his tone beautifully where required, to astonishing effect. He manages the high tessitura well. Occasionally the long phrases are broken, but the overall magnificence remains - and he shows that those long-held notes really count for something! Boult gives a very measured account of this section, in accord with his intensely spiritual overview of the work. There is no undue haste in easing the soul of Gerontius out of this world. This performance is quite special. Lloyd's Angel of the Agony is equally magnificent. There is a huge ruggedness and a sense of anguish which is truly contained; he achieves a real **pp** in his handling of the wide dynamic range; there is warmth which is not contrived. The only blot occurs when he splits the phrase 'glorious/home' when the orchestra swells in a sensuous arc, but it is a small price to pay for such a moving account.

Matthew Best (with Hill) comes near to Lloyd's achievement. His Priest has authority and power, if not subtlety. His Angel of the Agony inspires real awe, much helped here by Hill, who keeps the section moving forward. In both parts he is short-breathed, resulting in some choppy phrasing, but his performances are thrilling in the best sense. Kim Borg (Barbirolli 1965) has had a rough ride from critics over the years, mainly due to his unidiomatic English, but he gives a beautiful account of the Priest - very warm and sympathetic, and it is a lovely sound. As the Angel of the Agony, the phrasing is a little choppy and he needed to get hold of the consonants more firmly, but it is by no means a bad performance.

Gwynne Howell (with Hickox), a singer I admire deeply, is sorely tested by the high, repeated notes of the Priest and there is some less than secure intonation. As the Angel of the Agony he exudes power, if not subtlety. I do not feel that he has done himself full justice in this recording. Benjamin Luxon's Priest (for Gibson) is much too hectoring; his 'Go!' sounds like a rather cross schoolmaster shouting "Get out!" to a troublesome pupil. Hardly the tones for a deathbed! His Angel of the Agony is sung with a fine *legato* (in spite of the inherent vibrato in his voice, which worries me not), but he is too overt, almost too expressive when restraint is needed; the drama should be internalised, the anguish felt rather than thrust full in the face!

Norman Bailey (Svetlanov) reminds us what a cruelly exposed first entry it is for the Priest, coming *cold* to it in live performance. Bailey makes a very rough beginning, but he quickly settles to give a moving account of the music, although some of the phrasing lacks ideal smoothness. Elgar wanted a voice of a Wotan for the Angel of the Agony and in Bailey we have a favourite interpreter of Wagner's god. His singing here is very satisfying. The weight of tone is right and the long-breathed phrasing is helped by Svetlanov's relatively brisk tempo. Marian Nowakowski (Barbirolli, Rome 1957), a much underrated singer in his time, manages the first entry of the Priest in a live context much better than Bailey. He brings a full, rich tone to the Priest and is not troubled by the tessitura. His Angel of the Agony is just as satisfying, if a little generalised, but there is a disfiguring moment at fig

113 on the phrase 'where they shall ever gaze on Thee'; Nowakowski uses an upward *portamento* on the second syllable of 'ever', followed by a large breath before attacking the word 'gaze'. Not a comfortable moment.

Handley's Michael George is prodigious in his breath control; as both Priest and Angel of the Agony there is seamless phrasing. As the Priest this, together with the controlled approach to dynamics, makes him a comforting figure. His Angel of the Agony opens with a curiously muffled quality of voice on the high Ds and Es, but he gives a satisfying account of the solo, without achieving the fully searing quality which one finds with Robert Lloyd and Horace Stevens. John Shirley-Quirk appears for both Britten and Rattle and, like Michael George, he has tremendous breath control, achieving long, beautifully-shaped phrasing. His dark-hued baritone fully encompasses both roles. Inevitably, the voice is fresher in his earlier recording with Britten, but ultimately I would choose the performance under Rattle to represent this singer. His Priest has command and warmth in equal measure and his Angel of the Agony is filled with anguish and awe. In this latter part, he really does observe the **pp** *teneramente* and **p** *dolce* to spine-tingling effect. Rattle's accompaniment here achieves the right proportion of fear and comfort.

* * *

For the sake of completeness, there is another recording which I ought to mention, albeit in video format. The performance, under Andrew Davis at St Paul's Cathedral in November 1997, was broadcast *live* on BBC television, and is now available commercially. Inevitably, the sound quality cannot compare with digital sound on CD (at least not on my equipment!), but the performance itself transcends all sonic limitations. Catherine Wyn-Rogers, as the Angel, gives a performance which completely effaces that on her recording with Vernon Handley. With Davis she is as complete an Angel as any other, including Dame Janet Baker; she is deeply moving and the voice is in lustrous form. Alastair Miles, as Priest and Angel of the Agony, gives the finest performances of these roles in any recorded format. The voice is rich and pliable, easily encompassing Elgar's requirements, and despatching them with a depth of feeling rarely so fully encountered. Philip Langridge's Gerontius must be the finest assumption of the role currently before the public. He is fully alert to verbal nuance, inflecting the text with mercurial changes of tone colour. The interpretation is very contained (perhaps too internalised?), but the voice opens out when required, to thrilling effect. I have long hoped that there might be a recording of *Gerontius* from Andrew Davis. This performance displays a complete understanding of the score on Davis's part. He serves the spiritual and dramatic aspects of the score with equal skill and affection. Despite the tricky acoustics of St Paul's Cathedral, Davis is well served by the BBC Symphony Orchestra and Chorus (and the sound engineers!) This is a truly inspired and inspiring performance which no true Elgarian should be without.

* * *

Going through all these recordings within a relatively short space of time has not wearied the ear of the work; rather it has enriched and energised it and left me wishing for more. There are always artists who one hoped would have recorded the work, or one hopes might yet do so, but one must not be greedy! We are lucky indeed to have so many recordings to choose amongst. I would not be presumptuous in recommending a recording outright - and nothing I have written is going to influence firm adherents to particular recordings or performers - but in introducing the work to an acquaintance for whom it was his first experience of Gerontius, I settled for the performance under Handley as a good all-round presentation in modern sound.

Which recording do I turn to most frequently for sheer pleasure? That is easy: always Barbirolli's 1965 reading. However in my "desert island" mood I conjure up my own personal ideal : Barbirolli, Vickers, Baker(1965), Lloyd, CBSO and CBSO Chorus. Mind you, it could so easily be : Rattle, Nash, Hodgson... See? The permutations are endless!

***

The author's personal assessment of the performances of the individual artists, conductor, choir and orchestra in each of the recordings reviewed in this article appears in the facing table. This should be read in conjunction with the discography that follows to determine the identities of the performers in each recording.

Recording	Conductor	Choir	Orchestra	Mezzo	Tenor	Baritone/ Bass
Sargent (1945)	***	****	***	***	*****	*/**
Sargent (1955)	**	**	***	*	****	***
Barbirolli (1957)	*****	*	**	***	*****	***
Barbirolli (1965)	****	***	***	*****	****	***
Britten	****	***	****	****	***	*****
Boult	***	****	***	***	***	******
Gibson	**	**	***	*****	*	**
Svetlanov	**	***	*****	***	****	***
Rattle	*****	*****	*****	****	****	****
Hickox	****	*****	****	***	****	**
Handley	****	****	****	***	***	***
Hill	***	****	****	*	**	****
Davis (video)	*****	****	*****	****	****	*****

Rating :   ***** Excellent;   **** Very good;   *** Good;   ** Disappointing;   * Poor.

A GERONTIUS DISCOGRAPHY

compiled by John Knowles

The following table lists all commercial recordings of Gerontius known to have been issued. The list includes early recordings that, reflecting the limitations of the technology of the time, were originally offered for sale as a series of separate 78rpm records, and more recent recordings of excerpts from the work including arrangements for other instrumental combinations, mainly brass band.

For each recording, the table gives :

- the (approximate) year the recording was made;

- the artists appearing;

- the label and number of the original issue(s) with an indication of the format to which each number relates, followed by all subsequent re-issue(s) of the complete recording. Finally, details are given of any excerpts taken from the original recording and issued separately;

- for those wishing to read more about a particular recording, a final column gives the publication date of the issue of *Gramophone* magazine in which the record was reviewed.

The format of each issue is represented by the following abbreviations :

78	12" 78rpm record
AC	audio-cassette
AR	reel-to-reel audio tape
CD	audio compact disc
EP	7" 45rpm record
LP	12" 33rpm record
VHS	VHS-standard videotape

Year	Mezzo/Tenor/Bass-Baritone(s)/ Choir/Orchestra/Conductor Excerpt :	Record Label and Number	Format	Review Date

Recordings of the Complete Work

Year	Mezzo/Tenor/Bass-Baritone(s)/ Choir/Orchestra/Conductor	Record Label and Number	Format	Review Date
1945	Gladys Ripley/Heddle Nash/Dennis	HMV C3435/46	78	6/45
	Noble/Norman Walker/Huddersfield	HMV C7611/22	78	
	Choral Society/Liverpool Philharmonic	HMV RLS 709	LP	4/75
	Orchestra/Malcolm Sargent	Testament SBT 2025	CD	2/94
	Sanctus fortis :	EMI CDM763370-2	CD	4/90
		EMI EG763370-4	AC	4/90
	Jesu by that shudd'ring dread :	Dutton CDLX 7021	CD	12/96
1955	Marjorie Thomas/Richard Lewis/	Columbia 33CX1247/8	LP	5/55
	John Cameron/Huddersfield Choral	WRC T 658/9	LP	
	Society/Liverpool Philharmonic	WRC TT 658/9	AR	2/68
	Orchestra/Malcolm Sargent	EMI CHS 763376-2	CD	6/90
	Praise to the holiest :	Columbia SEL1709	EP	6/64
	Go in the name/Angel's Farewell :	Columbia SEL1710	EP	8/64
	Go in the name :	HMV HQM1115	LP	12/67
1965	Janet Baker/Richard Lewis/Kim Borg/	HMV ALP 2101/2	LP	10/65
	Ambrosian Singers/Hallé & Sheffield	HMV ASD 648/9	LP	
	Choirs/Hallé Orchestra/John Barbirolli	HMV SLS 770	LP	
		EMI CMS 763185-2	CD	12/89
	Angel's Farewell :	HMV SLS796	LP	10/70
		HMV YKM 5013	LP	6/75
		HMV TC-EXES5013	AC	6/75
		HMV SLS5101	AC	12/77
	Praise to the holiest :	HMV SEOM7	LP	4/71
		HMV TC-MCS 14	AC	4/71
		CFP CFP4548	LP	
		CFP TC-CFP4548	AC	
		CFP CD-CFP4548	CD	
	Go in the name :	HMV SEOM11	LP	8/72

Year	Mezzo/Tenor/Bass-Baritone(s)/ Choir/Orchestra/Conductor Excerpt :	Record Label and Number	Format	Review Date
1957	Constance Shacklock/Jon Vickers/ Marian Nowkowski/Orch Sinfonia e coro di Roma della RAI/John Barbirolli[1]	Arkadia CDHP 584	CD	
1971	Yvonne Minton/Peter Pears/John Shirley-Quirk/Choir of King's College, Cambridge/London Symphony Chorus/London Symphony Orchestra/Benjamin Britten	Decca SET 525/6 Decca 421 381-4 Decca 421 381-2 Decca 448 170-2	LP AC CD CD	6/72 8/88 5/89 1/96,3/96
	Sanctus fortis :	Decca 5BB 119/20	LP	6/72
	Praise to the holiest :	Decca SPA576 Decca KCSP576 Decca 430094-2 Decca 430094-4 Decca 444387-2 Decca 444387-4	LP AC CD AC CD AC	11/80 11/80 6/91 6/91 8/95 8/95
1975	Helen Watts/Nicolai Gedda/Robert Lloyd/ John Alldis Choir/London Philharmonic Choir/New Philharmonia Orchestra/Adrian Boult	HMV SLS 987 HMV TC-SLS 987 EMI CDS 747208-2 EMI CMS 566540-2	LP AC CD CD	5/76 1/87 1/99
1976	Alfreda Hodgson/Robert Tear/ Benjamin Luxon/ Scottish National Chorus/Scottish National Orchestra/ Alexander Gibson	CRD CRD 1026/7 CRD CRDC 4026/7 CRD CRD 3326/7	LP AC CD	3/77 1/87
1983	Felicity Palmer/Arthur Davies/Norman Bailey/London Sympony Chorus/ USSR State Symphony Orchestra/ Yevgeni Svetlanov[2]	Melodiya C 10 23075 004	LP	

[1]   Recorded at a concert in Rome on 20 November 1967
[2]   Recorded on 21 April 1983 at a concert in the Great Hall of the
Moscow Conservatoire

Year	Mezzo/Tenor/Bass-Baritone(s)/ Choir/Orchestra/Conductor Excerpt :	Record Label and Number	Format	Review Date
1987	Janet Baker/John Mitchinson/John	EMI EX 749549-1	LP	1/88
	Shirley-Quirk/City of Birmingham	EMI EX 749549-4	AC	3/88
	Symphony Orchestra and	EMI CDS 749549-2	CD	
	Chorus/Simon Rattle			
	Thy judgment now is near :	EMI CDZ767755-2	CD	
		EMI TC767755-2	AC	
		EMI CDRATT1	CD	
		EMI TCRATT1	AC	
	Angel's farewell :	EMI WHS569245-2	CD	
1988	Felicity Palmer/Arthur Davies/Gwynne	Chandos DBRD 2014	LP	2/89
	Howell/London Symphony	Chandos DBTD 2014	AC	5/89
	Chorus/LSO/Richard Hickox	Chandos CHAN 8641/2	CD	
1993	Catherine Wyn-Rogers/Anthony Rolfe	EMI TC-EMXD 2500	AC	
	Johnson/Michael George/Huddersfield	EMI CD-EMXD 2500	CD	10/93
	Cho. Soc./Royal Liv Phil	EMI HMV 572758-2	CD	
	Choir/RLPO/Vernon Handley			
1997	Sarah Fryer/William Kendall/Matthew	Naxos 8.553885/6	CD	8/97
	Best/Waynflete Singers/Bournemouth			
	S Chorus/Bournemouth SO/David Hill			
1997	Catherine Wyn-Rogers/Philip Lang-	NVC Arts Warner MusicVision		
	ridge/Alastair Miles/BBC Symphony	3984-22351-3	VHS	2/99
	Chorus/BBC SO/Andrew Davis			

Historical Recordings

1916	Clara Butt/Maurice D'Oisly/Chorus/			
	New Queen's Hall Orchestra/Henry			
	Wood			
	My work is done (11-14 & 22-28) :	Columbia 7128	78	
		Columbia 7308	78	
		Columbia 75005	78	
	I see not those false spirits (55-63) :	Columbia 7129	78	
		Columbia 7308	78	
		Columbia 75006	78	

Year	Mezzo/Tenor/Bass-Baritone(s)/ Choir/Orchestra/Conductor Excerpt :	Record Label and Number	Format	Review Date
	We have now pass'd the gate (67-75) :	Columbia 7130	78	
		Columbia 7309	78	
		Columbia 75007	78	
	Softly and gently (126-end) :	Columbia 7131	78	
		Columbia 7309	78	
		Columbia 75008	78	
	All four excerpts :	Elgar Soc CDAX 8019	CD	8/97
1924	Edith Furmedge/Dan Jones/David Brazell/Chorus/Royal Symphony Orchestra/Joseph Batten			
	(start-9)/(9-21) :	Edison Bell VF 591	78	10/24
	(21-30)/(30-40) (32-33 is cut) :	Edison Bell VF 592	78	10/24
	(40-46 & 53-58)/(68-76) :	Edison Bell VF 593	78	10/24
	(3-11)/(11-22) :	Edison Bell VF 594	78	10/24
	(22-31)/(31 -55) :	Edison Bell VF 595	78	10/24
	(55-56 & 71-75)/ (75-88 & 74-75 in place of 88-9) :	Edison Bell VF 596	78	10/24
	(105 -113)/(116-125) :	Edison Bell VF 597	78	10/24
	(125-132)/(132-end) :	Edison Bell VF 598	78	10/24
	All :	Adlonni AH8	AC	
1927	Margaret Balfour/Steuart Wilson/Herbert Heyner/Royal Choral Society/Royal Albert Hall Orchestra/Edward Elgar			
	Praise to the holiest (60-84) :	HMV D1242	78	6/27
	Go in the name (72-end)/ Softly and gently (130-end) :	HMV D1243	78	6/27
	Go in the Name (72-end) :	HMV HLM7009	LP	5/72
	All below except Prelude :	HMV RLS713	LP	2/75
	Prelude/Kyrie Eleison (29-33)/Rescue him(63-68)/Go in the name (72-end)/	Pearl OPAL810	LP	6/83
		Pearl OPAL CD9810	CD	6/83
	Praise to the holiest (60-84/84-101)/ Jesu by that shudd'ring dread (106-114)/ Take me away (124-130)/ Come back O Lord (130-end) :	EMI CDS754560-2	CD	6/92

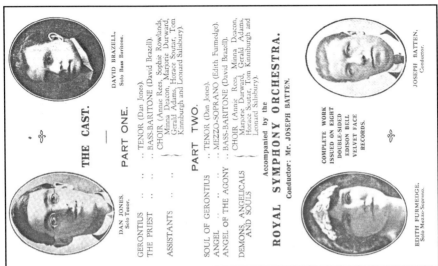

Contemporary advertisements for the 1924 Batten recording of Gerontius. Although the complete set of records covered only some two thirds of the work, it was advertised as a 'complete recording', with the excerpts being denoted by cue numbers rather than by the first line of each excerpt.

Year	Mezzo/Tenor/Bass-Baritone(s)/ Choir/Orchestra/Conductor Excerpt :	Record Label and Number	Format	Review Date
1927	Margaret Balfour/Tudor Davies/Horace Stevens/Three Choirs Festival Chorus/ London Symphony Orchestra/Edward Elgar			
	Jesu by that shudd'ring dread (106-113)/ Take me away (124-130) :	HMV D1348	78	2/28
	So pray for me (28-35)/ O Jesu help (60-68) :	HMV D1350	78	2/28
	Jesu by that shudd'ring dread (106-113) :	HMV HLM7009	LP	5/72
	All of above four excerpts :	HMV RLS708	LP	12/72
		WRC SH175	LP	8/73
		EMI CDS754560-2	CD	6/92

Miscellaneous Excerpts and Arrangements

a. **Prelude and Angel's Farewell :**

Year				
1917	Symphony Orchestra/Edward Elgar (abridged)	HMV 2-0775	78	
		HMV D181	78	
		Pearl GEM 111	LP	4/70
		Pearl EWE 1	LP	
		Pearl GEMM CDS9951/5	CD	9/92
	(*arr Brewer*)			
1976	Donald Hunt (organ)	RCA LRL25120	LP	5/76

a. **Prelude :**

Year				
1927	BBC Symphony Orch/Adrian Boult	HMV DB2194	78	6/34
		HMV ED291092-1	LP	2/87
		HMV ED291092-4	AC	
		EMI CDH763134-2	CD	12/90
		VAI VAIA 1067	CD	
		Beulah 3PD 15	CD	
1991	Brighouse & Rastrick Band/ Geoffrey Brand	Harlequin HAR1124MC	AC	

Year	Mezzo/Tenor/Bass-Baritone(s)/ Choir/Orchestra/Conductor Excerpt :	Record Label and Number	Format	Review Date
a.	**Prelude (continued) :**			
	(arr Ball)			
1970	Brighouse and Rastrick,CWS, Fairey's, Foden's and GUS Bands/Ball	Pye GSGL10470	LP	3/71
1974	Rochdale Band/Ashcroft	Decca SB316	LP	1/75
1984	Desford Colliery, Dowty and Foden OTS Band/Howard Snell	Polyphonic EHS002D Polyphonic CEHS002D	LP AC	
b.	**Kyrie Eleison :**			
1920	Sheffield Choir (with piano accompaniment)/Henry Coward	HMV C 977	78	
c.	**My work is done :**			
1944	Kathleen Ferrier/Gerald Moore (piano)	HMV HLM 7145	LP	12/78
		Elgar Society		
		CDAX 8019	CD	8/97
		APR APR 5544	CD	9/97
d.	**Praise to the holiest :**			
c1974	York Celebration Choir/Warburton	Decca ECS 2159	LP	
e.	**Angel's farewell :**			
	(arr Ball)			
1976	Virtuosi Brass Band/Maurice Handford	VR 7507	LP	9/76
	(arr. Brewer)			
1998	Christopher Herrick (organ)	Hyperion CDA 67060	CD	

The NIGHTMARE of GERONTIUS
The Story Behind A Famous Recording

Carl Newton

Carl Newton is a member of the London Branch of the Elgar Society, and has also sat on the Society's General Committee (now Council). He is the Society's official Archivist.

That the 1945 Sargent-Nash issue of The Dream of Gerontius is a milestone in the history of recording is a commonplace of Elgar commentary. The acclamation commenced with issue and has continued ever since[1] :

> one of the most important happenings in the history of recorded music.

> ... has yet to be equalled on record.

Certain assumptions have also been made about the participants and organisers:

> For the choral part the Huddersfield Choral Society was the obvious first choice... and for that reason the first choice for conductor was Dr Malcolm Sargent.[2]

> His Masters Voice and the British Council combined resources to present Elgar's Dream of Gerontius... They could not have chosen better. Gerontius...must memorably have gathered and shaped the mood of the hour... the Huddersfield Choir closed up their depleted ranks and set to work with a team of recording engineers headed by Walter Legge. The chosen conductor was Malcolm Sargent...[3]

---

[1]   The first quote is from *The Gramophone*, June 1945 issue announcing HMV C 3435/46; the second from Knowles, J., *Elgar's Interpreters on Record*, (Thames: London, 2nd ed., 1985), p 20

[2]   W McNaught in *The Musical Times* vol 86, Novello : London, 1945, p 208.

[3]   Notes by J N Moore to the 1975 reissue on LP (RLS 709) reprinted in 1993 with the Testament CD remake (SBT 2025). The second quote (next page) is from the latter, with additional notes by A Blyth.

Perhaps the wartime community spirit entered into the hearts of the Huddersfield singers...

These comments from different writers are representative of the received views of the last fifty years but the archives reveal that the outcome was largely a matter of coincidence. Only by chance was the performance attuned to the 'mood of the hour.' It had been two years in gestation and had been postponed several times. Sargent was not the conductor originally chosen but a relatively late arrival and a minority candidate. Three of the soloists were second, if not third, choices for their roles (one of them signed the contract only four days before the recording date). The Huddersfield singers were not the 'obvious first choice' and it was not only community spirit which infused them, but just as likely anger at the slights that they believed they had received, for their 'depletion' was by order, not circumstance. And Legge and HMV had little to do with the final outcome, the former having played a highly ambiguous and disruptive role throughout, and the latter having made minimal commitment to the entire project.

The extraordinary story is revealed in the archives at the Public Record Office, the British Council and the BBC Written Archives. Much of it now seems to be of the nature of those Ealing comedies with which, indeed, it was a near contemporary. If amusement is our main reaction to this saga of intrigue and incompetence, there are more serious implications in what it tells us of attitudes to Elgar and British music and the cultural politics and social mores of the time. Some reputations are dented, some enhanced, and there are one or two unsung heroes and heroines who deserve to emerge from the shadows.

The British Council was set up in 1934 with the express role of combatting Fascist cultural propaganda. In typically British fashion no programme was clearly set out by which this laudable aim might be achieved. The Council operated mainly through specialist departments with the policy decisions being based on the recommendations of advisory committees, each dealing with a branch of the arts and sciences or with education. The committees were serviced by Council staff but consisted essentially of the 'great and good' from the appropriate disciplines. The Treasury provided basic funding but commercial type activities were permissible, provided they covered their costs, or nearly so. Major items of expenditure required Finance

Committee approval, but otherwise the advisory committees seem to have been left very much to their own devices. It does not require much perceptiveness to guess what would happen if a group of distinguished, articulate, and self-opinionated persons were provided with access to public funds.

One of the first committees to be set up was the Music Advisory Committee. By 1942 the Chairman was Ernest Makower, with Pamela Henn-Collins, Director of the Council's Music Department, as Secretary. Ernest Samuel Makower was a businessman who had sponsored a series of concerts at the London Museum, of which he was a Trustee, in 1929-32. The other members were: the composer, Arthur Bliss; the critics and musicologists Ernest Dent and Henry Cope Colles; Lesley Boosey of the music publishers; Myra Hess, then in the midst of the fame of her National Gallery concerts; academics Jack Westrup and Victor Hely-Hutchinson; Adrian Boult; Phillip Godlee; and Lord Glentanar. Godlee was a Manchester textile manufacturer who was Chairman of the Hallé Society and Treasurer of the Royal Manchester College of Music. It was he who was instrumental in bringing Barbirolli back from the USA. Thomas Coats, 2nd Baron Glentanar, seems to have been the statutory Scotsman. A member of the famous textile family of Paisley, he lived at Aboyne and never attended a meeting. A somewhat mixed team with which to challenge the formidable Dr Goebbels.

Bliss, it should be noted, was also at this time Director of Music at the BBC, a post he had held from July 1941. He was to give this up on 31 March 1944 when an interregnum occurred during which Boult acted in the capacity. Hely-Hutchinson then took over as official appointee in September 1944. Colles died on 25 March 1943 and was replaced on the Committee by William Walton. These changes have some bearing on what follows.

It was in 1942 that the idea of subsidising recordings was first mooted. The evidence suggests that this was entirely the idea of Walter Legge, who was not a member of the Committee. He proposed on behalf of his employers, HMV, that the Council should go 50/50 on the costs and guarantee HMV a sale of 500 copies. Each recording was supposed to cost £1,000 to produce, but it was anticipated that the publishers of the recorded music would contribute. The idea was discussed at the meeting of 10 February 1942 and the Committee then turned to the thorny problem of what should be recorded. Miss Henn-Collins recommended that the records should be of major 'modern' (undefined) British works and madrigals.[4] Madrigals and lute music, indeed, became something of an obsession with the Committee. Objections were immediately raised on the grounds that this ignored young composers (?because they did not write major works). It would cause professional jealousy among living composers and was not in accord with the Council's mission. The latter was indeed a valid point and it will be seen that this remained throughout a largely unresolved issue.

By April the Council had agreed Legge's terms but insisted, understandably, that there should be a return to the taxpayer in the form of a 6% royalty, publishers of the works recorded receiving 4%. It also made the interesting condition that the BBC orchestras should always be used and that, to avoid rehearsal costs, the chosen works should always be broadcast. The first work proposed was Walton's *Belshazzar's Feast* to be followed by Parry's *Blest Pair of Sirens* and Ireland's Second Violin Sonata. As the Finance Committee would only allow a budget of £1,500 for the recordings this was as far as the programme for the first year could go. By now, however, the Committee members had the bit well and truly between their teeth.

A whole string of works was put forward, argued over, rejected, taken up again and discarded a second time. This process continued with great vigour, and not much positive outcome, until the meeting of 13 April 1943, when *Gerontius* was first added to the, by now, much bruised list. Unfortunately we do not know who made the proposal. It had some strange bedfellows, being linked with Rawsthorne's Piano Concerto, Rubbra's Third Symphony and Britten's *Les Illuminations*. These were all relatively recent works compared to the Elgar, and by composers two generations younger. Also, significantly, they were less than half the length of *Gerontius* and much easier and less costly to produce. The really critical meeting was held on 11 May. According to the minutes, "after long and exhaustive discussion" it was decided to record for the 1943-4 programme Bax's Third Symphony and Vaughan Williams' *Flos Campi*. However it was agreed that if any funds were left

---

[4]   British Council Archives MIN 35.

there might be room for *Gerontius*.[5] In this rather back-handed and unenthusiastic fashion the Council, at least officially, paved the way for "one of the most important happenings in the history of recorded music."

The attendance at this critical meeting should be noted. In addition to the Chairman and Secretary only Bliss, Boosey, Hely-Hutchinson and Westrup attended. One is entitled to suspect that some of the absences were diplomatic. There is no doubt that the decision was contentious, for a variety of reasons. In the files at the Public Record Office there is a remarkable letter from Makower to Henn-Collins. It reveals that she had expressed concerns arising from the attitude of some of the members about the wisdom of proceeding with the Elgar. In the course of the letter he states that the proposed recording:

is one of long term policy with the object of presenting to other countries the best of modern compositions and such great British classics as have not been recorded owing to the fact that they have not a commercial value.

Having made such a breathtakingly casual extension of the Council's objectives, Makower went on to say:

The Dream of Gerontius is perhaps the greatest work... of what may be termed... modern British composition. It has special appeal in Roman Catholic countries and the fact of the great cost involved should be no deterrent.[6]

The Council subsidy, he goes on, is to enable it to record works commercial companies would find unprofitable. Anyway, Elgar, Bax, and Vaughan Williams are 'older generation' composers. The confusions behind this letter need not be commented on. Bax would certainly have been surprised to find that he belonged to the same generation as Elgar, particularly as he had recently been invited to a Huddersfield concert as a representative of the younger generation of composers. At this date he was 59!

---

5   British Council Archives MIN 36. In the event *Flos Campi* was not included in the programme and this may be the reason why funds were available for *Gerontius*.

6   Public Record Office(PRO) BW2/178 (24 May 1943).

The news that the Council was to support a complete recording of *Gerontius* seems to have spread rapidly and it was bombarded with suggestions as to performers. This was probably the result of an inspired leak by Legge (perhaps through Boult). There are letters to Legge on the same file asking him, politely, to keep his mouth shut. They seem to have had little effect.

Someone realised that the Elgar Trustees should be informed. A letter was sent to Carice Elgar Blake, then at Woodend, Broadheath, asking for her approval to the recording and telling her that the performers would be chosen by listening 'blind' to various recordings. This appears to have been a device to avoid entering into discussion with Carice, as no one had suggested this curious proceeding. Another letter went to Novello, publishers of *The Dream of Gerontius*, asking for a contribution. The reply was decisive. Novello's funds were reserved for works needing them.[7] Rebuffed in no uncertain manner the Committee put aside further consideration of the project for the moment. Nevertheless by the summer of 1943 Pamela Henn-Collins must have thought that her troubles in this respect were at an end. They were just beginning.

It will not have escaped notice from the above account that, despite what had been said to Carice, no steps had been taken to find the necessary forces to make the recording. Nor was there any real idea, therefore, of the likely costs. There seems to have been a vague assumption that the BBC would provide the orchestra and Boult would conduct, not so much because of his connection with Elgar as that he was on the spot and a member of the Committee. The Huddersfield Choral Society had been mentioned as possible participants. Matters drifted on for more than a year before any positive steps were taken.

The assiduous Legge was clearly leaking like a sieve about the project. On 26 June 1944 Kenneth Wright, BBC Deputy Director of Music, wrote to Henn-Collins to say that he had picked up rumours, but that the BBC Symphony would not be available for the recording until the spring of 1945 when:

---

[7]   *loc. cit.* (7 June 1943).

...as a matter of practical convenience it could be linked with Sir Adrian's performance on Good Friday of the work, but this would be in Bedford with the Luton Choral Society...[8]

The BBC had, apparently, earmarked Heddle Nash for the title role for this performance. This seems to be the first indication that he might be involved in the recording and his ultimate inclusion was therefore, at least in part, a matter of chance rather than any special affinity he might be supposed to have with the role. It is also important to remember the original constraints regarding the use of performers. According to Wright, Boult was pressing the claims of the Luton singers and hints that he (Boult) had an aversion to Huddersfield - whether to the town or its choir is unclear. By this time the realities of budgets had begun to impinge and much of the subsequent discussion was coloured by the need to come up with the most economical solution. That this made nonsense of the original decision to do *Gerontius* anyway no one seems to have noticed. Not everyone was in favour of economy. From his northern fastness, Lord Glentanar now made his only contribution on 10 July, writing to urge that no expense be spared.[9] This might be thought an odd sentiment for someone charged with the use of public funds during a major war.

Matters were reaching an *impasse*. On 13 July 1944 Makower sent a telegram to every member of the Committee calling an emergency meeting at his country house near Henley. The wording was stark:

Dream Problems- Committee Unable To Choose Conductor, Orchestra or Choir.[10]

There is evidence, however, that a short-list existed. Pencilled on the Wright letter of 26 June is a set of names that had presumably been given to him or his assistant over the telephone. The list is intriguing : Nash, Ferrier/Ripley, Tom Williams, Walker, Boult/Wood. Wright reported to his superior that the Council choice was for Nash, Ferrier, Williams as the Priest, and Walker as the Angel of the Agony. It was agreed that the idea of having two basses was "a break with tradition"

---

8   BBC Written Archives WAC R 46/74/1.

9   PRO BW2/178.

10   *loc. cit.*

but the proposal met with the approval of Steuart Wilson.[11] Wilson, a former notable singer of Gerontius himself, was at this time the BBC Overseas Music Director and a person who might be supposed to have good knowledge of foreign tastes. Tantalisingly, Wright refers to the 'person' making the recommendation for two basses without disclosing their name.

Prompted by receipt of the dramatic telegram, two major musical figures now entered the lists. Arthur Bliss loosed off a broadside to the, by now, increasingly unhappy Henn-Collins on 15 July:

> I was lukewarm about the recording - not to say cold. Elgar is sufficiently well known anyway and recording the *Dream of Gerontius* will not add to his admirers. Novellos tell me they could not believe that recording *Gerontius* at this late date will materially add to performances abroad. It would be like a Franco-Belgian Council deciding now to record Cesar Franck's Beatitudes.[12]

Bliss's own preferences were for Dowland's Lute Music, Byrd's *Great Service* and Delius's *Song of the High Hills,*

> ...or coming to what I personally consider our first aim, the spreading of living composers' music.

It need hardly be said that there was nothing in the Council's charter or stated objectives that justified the latter assertion. Could it be co-incidence that Bliss was himself a living composer?

Two days later William Walton made his contribution in characteristically no-nonsense style:

> [*Gerontius*] should be done as soon as possible with Malcolm Sargent, the Liverpool Philharmonic and the Huddersfield Choir...I think the fact of having the Huddersfield Choir outweighs everyt[hing] that might be said for Adrian Boult with the BBC Orc[hestra] and the Luton Choir.[13]

---

[11] BBC Written Archives *loc. cit.* It is important to stress, in view of some comments which have been made, that the idea was entirely that of the British Council, prompted perhaps by the BBC. Neither Legge nor Sargent had anything to do with it.

[12] PRO BW2/178.

[13] *loc.cit.* 17 July 1944.

It should be said that Walton was undoubtedly influenced by the fact that the same forces had just produced a highly acclaimed recording, also Council subsidised, of his own *Belshazzar's Feast*.[14] Having chosen the winning team so far as the supporting roles were concerned, Walton then recommended Robert Easton and Roy Henderson as the bass soloists. He did, however admit that he knew very little about singers.

The crisis meeting took place on 25 July. Eleven days previously the BBC dropped a bombshell. The Secretary General of the British Council, A J White, had written to William Haley, Director General of the BBC to ask, formally, for the use of the BBC Symphony Orchestra and Boult. White had been contacted by 'a Mr Nicholls' (Basil Nichols, Controller Programmes). The file note to this conversation records that Nichols had declared that the BBC:

> ...did not really think that the orchestral aspect formed such an outstanding part of the music as to justify them in releasing their orchestra.[15]

A memo which Wright sent to Boult on 11 July states that Miss Henn-Collins and Miss Wingate (*sic* but more likely Whinyates, who succeeded Henn-Collins) from the British Council have been shown a film of the *Gerontius* performance at Bedford. Wright and Steuart Wilson acted as their hosts. The verdict was that the Luton Choir "frequently lacked the attack and bite the work demands". Neither Wright nor Wilson believed that the Luton would make "an adequate substitute for the Huddersfield for a really first class recording". However they did not express their doubts to the Council's representatives.[16] Boult replied to Wright:

---

[14]   Edwards, R A : *And The Glory* (Wm Maney : Leeds n.d.) p 108. The recording was made in January 1943. This work also draws attention (p 110) to Henn-Collins being invited to be present at a special play-back of this recording in Huddersfield. There is only a passing reference to the *Gerontius*; Mr Edwards tells me that the Society did not even have a copy of the recording in their archives.

[15]   PRO BW2/178.

[16]   BBC Written Archives *loc.cit.* This is an intriguing reference. If a film with sound track had been made of an entire performance, by definition it, and *not* the Sargent/Nash would be the first-ever complete recording of the work. Certainly Wright's memo implies this, but the possibility that some sort of recording had been made is discussed later in the text.

...I feel more and more strongly that we should be most unwise from the policy point of view as well as absolutely wrong morally to take a narrow view about sending the Orchestra up to Huddersfield if the British Council plump for Malcolm... I think Mrs Elgar Blake would come down pretty heavily on our side..[17]

Boult, despite the fact that he was by now Acting Director of Music, clearly failed to make any impression on the BBC or did not seek to make one. Moreover no one had consulted Carice for over a year. It is not clear which 'side' Boult imagined he was promoting.

The Music Advisory Committee therefore met in a situation of total disarray over the project on 25 July. It is interesting that Legge was an invitee at this meeting. The news regarding the BBC bombshell was reported and in consequence it was decided, with some reluctance, to ask Sargent, the Liverpool Philharmonic and the Huddersfield Choral Society to participate. To what extent this was the result of Makower rail-roading the Committee in the light of Walton's firm views cannot now be determined.

As soloists the Committee agreed that Nash should sing Gerontius and Walker The Priest. The initial choice for Angel fell on Kathleen Ferrier with Gladys Ripley as reserve. A decision on the fourth soloist (there was no suggestion there should only be three) and their role was left to Westrup and Legge, who were also to make the final choice between Ferrier and Ripley.[18] That Legge was not even a member seems to have been disregarded. It soon became obvious that he was pursuing his own agenda.

On the file is a manuscript letter from Pamela Henn-Collins to Makower dated 6 September 1944. It contains some remarkable information about the machinations now in full progress:

Though he pretends to have done so, Walter Legge has not yet asked for formal approval of the decision taken at the Committee meeting. He is quietly determined to make us change our minds on the strength of the Elgar 2nd Symphony recording he has just made with Boult.[19]

---

[17] *loc.cit* Boult to Wright (14 July 1944).

[18] British Council Archives MIN 36.

[19] PRO BW2/178. The recording mentioned was DB 6190/5, issued in January 1945.

She then goes on to produce a polling list of the members, indicating their preferences for conductor. Only Walton, Boosey and Makower were for Sargent, all the rest wanted Boult, except Bliss, who was against doing any Elgar at all.

> The decision is a fearful responsibility and if Walter - who is very pally with Boult - can really make him do what he wants we may be wrong in choosing Malcolm and passing over the name the world expects... I think it possible Walter has been too clever for us.[20]

In a despairing *cri de coeur* to Leslie Boosey of the same date, the unfortunate secretary confessed that she heartily wished that Elgar had never written *The Dream of Gerontius.*

By the 22nd of that month Legge was publicly professing to have accepted the Committee decision totally. The value to be placed on such protestations is demonstrated by the fact that in the same letter in which he states this he goes on to praise Boult's performance of the Elgar Second Symphony. He also disparages the Liverpool orchestra:

> Holst has broken with it and David Wise's promotion means the second violins are very weak.[21]

This is a strange statement in view of the fact that several writers have expressed the opinion that the Liverpool was at this time one of the strongest orchestras in Britain.[22] Legge announced in the same letter that 1 to 10 January 1945 had been chosen as the dates for recording. Once again it seemed as if the project was through into open water. Enter the Huddersfield Choral Society.

---

[20]   *loc. cit.*

[21]   *loc. cit.* Henry Holst, Danish-born former Leader of the Berlin Philharmonic and Leader of the Liverpool Philharmonic Orchestra 1931-1944.

[22]   See for example Reid, C : *Malcolm Sargent* (Hamish Hamilton : London, 1968) p 290 which draws attention to the fact that the Liverpool was in a particularly favourable situation to recruit outstanding players. Reference should also be made to Schwarzkopf, E : *On And Off The Record* (Faber & Faber : London, 1982) p 92 where Legge states that he was placing his own candidates in the Liverpool at this time, in anticipation of recruiting them for his proposed Philharmonia Orchestra.

The Society was approached formally, for the first time since the whole affair had begun, on 18 October 1944 by letter to Frank Netherwood its President. Intriguingly the letter states that neither orchestra nor soloists had yet been decided. It goes on:

> *The Dream of Gerontius* is perhaps the greatest English choral work there is and it is of the utmost importance that the recording of it should be the best that human endeavour can produce.[23]

Because of this fact the Council and HMV (in effect Legge) claimed the right to decide which members of the choir should actually take part.

Had it been announced that no Yorkshireman would in future be picked for the England Test Team the outrage of the White Rose County could not have been more forcefully expressed. Netherwood replied in no uncertain terms that: a) The Huddersfield was not at the beck and call of the British Council and the Society could not consider recording before April 1945 at the earliest; and b) the Society and no one else would select the choir. He also pointed out that as *Gerontius* was a well-loved work in Huddersfield *all* the members would expect to sing in it.[24] Henn-Collins wrote to Legge on 14 November reporting this. To overcome Netherwood's objection she made the amazing proposal that Legge should put the weaker singers at the back:

> ...where they would be out of range of the microphones.[25]

She also revealed that Thomas Russell, Chairman of the London Philharmonic, had been approached for the use of that orchestra. Russell, however, was too practised a hand. He realised that the recording was essentially a commercial venture and that his orchestra should therefore be paid proper royalties for their services. Legge had no intention of allowing any diminution of HMV profits and told Henn-Collins to refuse Russell's request.

---

[23]   PRO BW2/178 (Henn-Collins to Netherwood).

[24]   *loc. cit.*(Netherwood to Henn-Collins 25/10/44 and 4/11/44).He probably overstates the case. If the choir were enthusiasts for *Gerontius* the Huddersfield public was not. When next performed there (in 1947) only £4/15/- [£4-75p] was taken in ticket sales.

[25]   *loc.cit.* (Henn-Collins to Legge 14/11/44).

He also announced that Sargent had decreed that only 100 voices would be needed in the choir. There is no proof that this was the case. Indeed the evidence of the Choral Society archives leads to the supposition that it may have originated from Legge himself. The *Belshazzar's Feast* record had been made with only 100 singers after a meeting between Netherwood and Legge.[26] No doubt the latter assumed that the same arrangement would apply again, but he seems to have forgotten that, whereas *Belshazzar* had been recorded in Liverpool, *Gerontius* was to be on the Choral Society's home ground. Moreover there was no question of the choir being in a depleted state on account of the exigences of war. In the 1944-5 season the Society had 347 singing members of whom only 16 were On His Majesty's Service.[27] It should also be said that the Huddersfield was not an obvious choice for the work as their practical knowledge of it must have been minimal. They had performed it only three times in 17 years.

No decision had yet been made about the fourth soloist. By now it seems to have been assumed that Walker would sing the Angel of the Agony. It was Henn-Collins who suggested that Dennis Noble should be invited to sing that role. (In fact he sang The Priest and Walker The Angel). It also emerged that Legge had omitted to tell Nash and Ripley, probably deliberately, that the Council was involved! He had also written privately to Sargent telling him that he (Sargent) was free to choose the orchestra. This was clearly untrue. It required a face to face meeting between Legge, Sargent and Henn-Collins to put this straight on 1 February 1945, only eight weeks before the recording, rescheduled as a result of Huddersfield insistence, was due to take place. At this stage Pamela Henn-Collins, no doubt feeling the strain, departed for South America and did not return until after the event.[28]

---

[26]   West Yorkshire Archives Service (Kirklees) KC 200 1/1/11. (Huddersfield Choral Society Executive Minutes 4/12/42).

[27]   West Yorkshire Archives Service (Kirklees) KC 200 3/8. (Huddersfield Choral Society Annual Report for 1944-5).

[28]   She was subjected to further propaganda before she left as is revealed by a letter from Ann Chapman, Sargent's personal secretary, referring to her attendance by invitation at a Sargent performance of *Gerontius*. (PRO BW2/137).

Her place was taken by her deputy, Evelyn Donald, who was to suffer some of the problems experienced by her superior. The Huddersfield people were still seething at their treatment at the hands of upstart southerners and were on the warpath again. First they requested a further postponement of the sessions (refused). Then they raised a demand that Herbert Bardgett's name must appear on the record label (reluctantly agreed). Finally they demanded to know precisely how much they were going to be paid before they would agree to participate.[29]

At the last minute Carice Elgar Blake was remembered. She was invited to attend the sessions only in March. The lateness of the invitation made it difficult for her to find accommodation. The 'George', the main hotel in Huddersfield, was booked up by people connected with the recording. In the end she had to commute from Halifax to the sessions in Huddersfield Town Hall.

In view of the nature of the story it could be expected that a last minute crisis would arise. It did. On 5 March the Secretary of the Liverpool Philharmonic wrote refusing their participation on the grounds that the terms offered would result in their losing money. Frenzied last minute negotiation resulted in a compromise, but the final event in the saga did not take place until 4 April when Noble signed the contract to sing four days later. One wonders if it was only then that he was told what part he was to perform!

The recording itself is, as they say, history. It received instant plaudits from the musical press and a leader in the *Huddersfield Daily Examiner*.[30] Complimentary copies were sent to Carice Elgar Blake, Birmingham Oratory, and Toscanini. Special playings (on the new high fidelity equipment) were organised by the Council at its provincial offices.

If the recording is history the balance sheet is not, until now. In truth the enterprise was a financial disaster for the Council and the taxpayer.

---

[29] PRO BW2/178 Crawshaw to Donald (27 February 1945). David Crawshaw JP was Secretary of the Choral Society.

[30] Issue of 14 April 1945.

The fees paid to the participants were:-

Sargent	£240
Nash/Ripley	£125
Walker/Noble	£30
Choir	£300
Leader	£5
Principals	£3
Orchestra each member	£2/10/- (£2.50)

In addition expenses appear to have been paid to choir members (£1 each) and there were costs related to the hire of Huddersfield Town Hall. The total outlay on the recording was £3,606. As no contribution had been made by Novello the Council received the full 10% royalty. The initial selling price was three guineas for the 12-record set. The recording stayed in the catalogues until 1955. In those ten years it sold a maximum of 3,000 copies, probably many fewer, as the exact figure cannot be calculated because of price changes over the period.[31] HMV did include it in their special catalogue of recordings made between 1939 and 1945, ostensibly produced for the benefit of members of the Armed Forces. Despite a short write-up of the work no reference is made to the fact that this was the first complete recording. The royalty received by the Council left it with a loss of £2,562. (A multiple of about 25 is needed to translate this into money of today). This is the largest loss, in real terms, ever made by the Council on a subsidised work. HMV, on the other hand, received over £9,000 for virtually zero outlay.[32] Legge had done his work well.

There is a curious tailpiece. On 28 October 1945 Carice wrote to Miss Seymour Whinyates (Henn-Collins' successor as Director of the Music Department) implying that Evelyn Donald had suggested donating the proceeds from the sales to the Elgar Birthplace.[33] On the face of it this

---

[31]   This should be compared with the 83,000 copies sold of Sargent's 1946 recording of *Messiah*. (Reid *op.cit.* p 345). The Council sponsored recording of *Belshazzar's Feast* sold 4,750 copies in the UK and 356 abroad, (PRO BW80/1).

[32]   British Council Archives MIN 39 (Report on subsidised recordings 24/10/69).

[33]   PRO BW2/178.

was preposterous, but there is a memo on file from Donald to Kennedy Cooke, the Council's Director of Production which contains the statement:

> Efforts are being made by the Elgar Birthplace trustees to raise funds for gathering material together for the birthplace...as a shrine to Elgar. It is expected to become an attraction to tourists.[34]

Rather more modestly than Carice had implied, she suggests a 1% donation from royalties. A quick and decisive negative reply was received, rightly pointing out that this would be an unauthorised diversion of public funds. As a final twist to the story Donald reveals that she had suggested the holding of an Elgar Festival in order to raise money for the Birthplace. It would thus appear that it was from the Council, not Adrian Boult, that the idea originated from which subsequent Elgar Malvern Festivals sprang.

What questions are raised by this extraordinary and, sometimes, comic tale? The first and most obvious is - why *Gerontius*?

The small number of persons who remembered the objectives of the British Council seemed to believe, with Makower, that the work would be good propaganda in Roman Catholic countries. There are two problems with this view. It is debatable to what extent *Gerontius* is a strictly Catholic work and it is certainly not of a kind which would have been instantly acceptable in a traditionalist Catholic nation. In this context Tallis's *Spem In Alium* or even Byrd's *Great Service*, both suggested at some stage, would surely have been more immediately assimilable. The second problem relates to the realities of the situation. In 1943 Portugal was the only Catholic country in Europe not under Fascist control. It would have been impossible to have used the recording anywhere where it might be supposed to matter. True, the neutral Catholic nations outside Europe might have received it, but even they were few and far between in 1943. Remembering that even in England *Gerontius* had been criticised on religious grounds, it would surely have been more sensible to choose a less provocative work with wider appeal. Moreover, at precisely the time the Committee were deciding, by default, to do *Gerontius* the Warsaw Ghetto Rising was being bloodily crushed. Perhaps *Polonia* might have been a better expression of solidarity with our Allies.

---

[34]   *loc. cit.* Donald to Kennedy Cooke (15 July 1946)

It would certainly have been cheaper and easier to produce. It is strange that, setting aside the points made above, the Committee paid no heed to the evidence which was being fed back by British Council representatives overseas. In 1942 Sargent had made a Scandinavian tour which had been an outstanding success, particularly as it was in direct comparison with a similar tour undertaken by Furtwangler and the Berlin Philharmonic. Reports indicate that the Elgar works which received specially favourable response were *Enigma Variations* and Introduction and Allegro for Strings.[35] These would have been excellent choices with wide appeal at the time. True, no complete commercially available recording of *The Dream of Gerontius* existed then, but this aspect was not mentioned at any time in the discussions and producing such should not have been the primary objective. The overseas promotion of existing Elgar recordings might well have been seen as more relevant and having more impact. The Committee used public funds in a laudable, but essentially self-serving, project.

This leads to the conclusion that the Committee, and presumably the British musical establishment generally, either did not see Elgar as a powerful enough weapon in a propaganda war or were not interested in such a war at all. Their opponents were not so inhibited. Hitler himself had made a direct challenge on 9 November 1939 when he referred to Beethoven as single-handedly achieving more than all English composers put together.[36] The extent of Hitler's knowledge of English composers is uncertain. What is not is that there was a major Nazi drive to promote Beethoven, Wagner and Bruckner. Even minor works by Beethoven were resurrected. Ironically on 11 April 1945, while the Huddersfield sessions were in progress, a concert of music by what Prof Dennis has called "the three honoured members of the Nazi Valhalla", was held in the already besieged Berlin.[37] Yet no one doubted then, or does now, that Beethoven, Wagner, and Bruckner are cultural world citizens. Producing *Gerontius* so laboriously, and in this manner, unfortunately helped to condemn Elgar to be seen for another

---

[35]   PRO   BW2/137 (Report on Sargent's Scandinavian Tour) See also Scholes, P A : *The Mirror of Music* (Novello and OUP : London, 1947), p 897.

[36]   Dennis, D B : *Beethoven in German Politics, 1870-1989* (Yale University Press : London, 1996) p 167.

[37]   *ibid.* p 173.

generation as an English provincial musician, producing works of Victorian religiosity for home consumption. A great opportunity was missed and the poor sales demonstrate that, despite any artistic quality, it did not make a breakthrough for Elgar, as indeed Bliss and Novello had, for their own reasons, predicted.

This brings us to the roles played by the respective participants. Whatever he may afterwards have claimed, for example in his autobiography,[38] Bliss emerges as virulently anti-Elgar. Given that he was for much of the critical time their Director of Music, it cannot be believed that the BBC would state that the orchestral part was insignificant without consulting him, even more so as he was a member of the group proposing the recording in the first place. His contemptuous comparison of Elgar with Cesar Franck speaks volumes. Was this revenge for Elgar's criticism of him in his youth?[39]

If it was not Bliss who denied the orchestral significance of *Gerontius* the suspicion must fall on Boult. Indeed, despite his subsequent reputation as an Elgarian, Boult is someone whose actions are hard to follow. While appearing to approve the project he also contrived to be very subdued in his support for it. His attendance at the Committee was erratic, understandably given the nature of his commitments, but at no point does he seem to have made a decisive intervention, as did Walton, to ensure success. Having urged that the Luton choir should be involved he seems to have been glad of an escape clause. His letter to Wright is strange. Why was it a moral issue to send the BBC Symphony to Huddersfield? Was Boult temperamentally or religiously out of sympathy with *Gerontius*? Did he believe that association with it would not further his reputation? It may be significant that he made only one recording of it in his career and that 30 years after the events recounted here. It is also relevant to draw attention to his preface to the notes for his 1969 recording of *The Kingdom*, expressing his view that that work was far superior to *Gerontius*.[40] There is one other intriguing possibility. The BBC made a number of 'unofficial' recordings during the war for purposes which are now obscure. These were 'half

---

[38]   Bliss, A : *As I Remember* (Thames : London, 1989) pp 93-4.

[39]   *ibid.*

[40]   EMI (HMV) Angel Series SAN 244/245.

published in a somewhat shame-faced manner in 1947. *Gerontius* was not among them, although three Elgar recordings were (none listed in Knowles' *Elgar's Interpreters On Record*). As the work was broadcast every Easter by the BBC it would have been very easy to make a recording. Boult would have known this but for obvious reasons would have had to remain silent.

If Boult was low-key the same certainly cannot be said for Legge. Legge had joined HMV in 1927, his first job being to write record labels and notes.[41] Elgar criticised him for inaccuracies in notes to *Beau Brummel*. From this he worked himself up to supervising sessions and editing the HMV house magazine. He wrote to Elgar on 4 August 1932 to ask if he could interview him on whether there really was a Third Symphony.[42] Unfortunately this meeting does not seem to have taken place. His next approach was on 19 September 1933, through Gaisberg, who asked Elgar if Legge could have tea with him, as he is "a great admirer of your music".[43] This was surely hyperbole as Legge never showed any special interest in Elgar's music at any time in his career, being mainly concerned with lieder, opera and instrumentalists.[44] We do not seem to have any evidence if he actually made the proposed visit.

By this time HMV had merged with Columbia to form EMI. The reason was the disastrous effects of the Depression on the recording industry; HMV profits had, indeed, virtually disappeared. On the outbreak of war Legge had secured appointment as Music Director of the Entertainments National Services Association(ENSA), but this was

[41]   A useful summary of Legge's early career is given in Pettitt, S J : *Philharmonia Orchestra* (Robert Hale : London, 1985) pp 17ff. See also Schwarzkopf, E, *op.cit.*

[42]   Letter published in Moore, J N : *Elgar On Record* (OUP : London, 1974) pp 180-1.

[43]   *ibid.* p 217.

[44]   Legge later claimed that he admired Elgar but could not get anyone interested in playing him because of critical objection to his music. (Schwarzkopf *op.cit.* p 105). This statement, appearing as it does considerably *ex post facto* and in an obviously laudatory work, must be treated with some caution.

obviously not going to be a permanent job. The situation was not much better in 1942 when Legge enters our story. By then he was the only remaining record producer in the company and clearly had to justify his existence. Since recording foreign artists was practically impossible then, he targeted the BBC Symphony Orchestra as a source of work. It was clearly in his interest to try and ensure that Boult and the BBC did as much as possible. This is surely the reason for his strong campaign on their behalf over *Gerontius* and also for his entrepreneurial proposal to the British Council in early 1942. By the spring of 1944 he was in a particularly difficult situation. His high-handed methods had angered many people in ENSA and there was a move afoot to get him dismissed. Association with a high profile project was to his benefit and he must have found the Council's reserve about premature publicity especially galling.[45] One feels that if the work had been *Pop Goes The Weasel* Legge would not have worried, provided he was able to get his name on the label and maximise HMV profits.

We are left with the intriguing question - who suggested *Gerontius*? The only candidates who seem reasonable are Colles and Walton. We have no way of determining the answer but most of the other members are ruled out, either by the evidence of the archives, or by what we know of their views from other sources. Colles was an assiduous attender and may have made the original suggestion but it was Walton who played a decisive role, despite having become a member only just before the critical meeting of 13 April 1943. He was obviously a powerful pro-Elgar influence. It may be significant that on 21 December 1942, in a newspaper interview while rehearsing the Huddersfield Chorus for the *Belshazzar's Feast* recording, he said :

I have unbounded admiration for Elgar... There's no other English composer to touch him... He's becoming bigger all the time...[46]

---

[45]   Schwarzkopf, *op.cit.* reveals (pp 255-6) the extent of the decline in recording. The selective list in this work notes ten recordings for 1941, three in 1942, none in 1943 and one in 1944. Moreover no reference is made to any connection with the British Council, or any of their recordings, and, perhaps most remarkably, no reference is made to Legge's involvement with Gerontius. This curious reticence, it must be said, Legge shares with Boult and Bliss, and one can only speculate on the reasons.

[46]   Quoted in Kennedy, M : *Portrait of Walton* (OUP : Oxford, 1989) p 38.

The cover of The Gramophone *magazine for June 1945,
announcing the release of the new British Council-sponsored recording*

Whoever made the suggestion the recording, however distinguished artistically, and even more historically, was put together in a remarkably 'hand-to-mouth' fashion and the result was more good luck than judgement or planning. The performers, no doubt, gave of their best on the day, but it was the persistence of Ernest Makower, the indefatigable Pamela Henn-Collins and her Deputy, Evelyn Donald, which brought it all to fruition against a positive sea of difficulties. They, perhaps more than anyone else in the sorry saga, had the right to say, as Elgar himself, "this was the best of me."

Note On Sources

There are two series of minutes of the British Council Music Advisory Committee. The approved and signed series is still in the custody of the Council, but the Public Record Office has an unsigned series (PRO BW 80) which includes agendas and some presented papers. I have used the signed series as the definitive copy and refer to them in the above text, but the PRO series has been used for additional data.

The DREAM of GERONTIUS - a PERSONAL NOTE

John Barbirolli

Sir John Barbirolli (1899-1970) is one of this century's best-loved conductors. Born in London of Italian parents, he came to prominence in the 1920s and made the first recording of Elgar's Introduction & Allegro for Strings *in 1927. He was chief conductor of the Hallé Orchestra from 1943, and always included a great deal of Elgar in his programmes. These notes accompanied his recording of* Gerontius *in 1965, only the third complete recording, and the first in stereo.*

"Figlio mio, questo e un capolavoro sublime." With these words Pope Pius XII raised me to my feet, after I had knelt before him to receive his blessing and thanks for a performance of the first part of *The Dream of Gerontius* given at his summer residence of Castel Gandolfo, by the Choir of Our Lady of Dublin, and three distinguished British soloists.

The treasured memory of these noble and sensitively appreciative words is made all the more poignant when we remember that barely ten days were to elapse before His Holiness was to pass from this world, and that this was the last "live" music he was to hear. I have often wondered what the feelings of Newman and Elgar would be if they could know that the last music he heard had been Elgar's setting of Newman's words "Go forth upon thy journey, Christian soul".

But as I recall this, other memories crowd in, and I will go back to one of the earliest of these. Not long after leaving the army in 1919, as a regular deputy with the London Symphony Orchestra, I had the great good fortune (at the last desk of cellos) to take part in the first post-war Festival of the Three Choirs, held at Worcester in 1920. The Three Choirs Festival in those days, when Worcester was still a lovely country town, with Elgar's father's music shop still standing, could, I think, well be described as Elgar's Bayreuth.

For a young man who loved Elgar's music, it was wonderful to see the great man, radiantly happy amongst his friends in the Cathedral precincts; more wonderful still to play the *Dream* under his direction, with that great and noble artist Gervase Elwes singing the Soul. I remember that Elgar conducted from memory (the antithesis of Vaughan Williams, who always averred that he could never remember a note of his own music) and although he could not be called a great conductor by the highest professional technical standards, it was extraordinary how he could make you feel exactly what he wanted if you were in sympathy with him.

Now I come to the days when at last I had to study the work in detail for the preparation of my own first performance. I began to realise for the first time the great delicacy, imagination and subtlety of much of the scoring. (Alas, this is often obscured by lack of sufficient preparation. It is a work which has that dreaded reputation "Everybody knows it" so that one rehearsal, or at most two, is deemed sufficient.) Amongst the many performances I have now conducted, of course some of the most poignantly beautiful memories must be those in which the beloved Kathleen Ferrier took part, including the very last one she was to sing - at the Edinburgh Festival of 1950 with the Hallé Orchestra and Choir. There was an almost prophetic beauty of utterance in her singing of "My work is done, my task is o'er". The next milestone for me was the opportunity afforded me, through the enthusiasm and indefatigable efforts of Sir Ashley Clarke (then British Ambassador in Rome) to give the first performance in Italy - incredible though this may seem - in the centenary year of Elgar's birth, with the magnificent collaboration of the orchestra and chorus of the RAI in Rome. Never shall I forget the look of joyful surprise and enthusiasm on the faces of orchestra and chorus at the first rehearsal, when the wonders of the work unfolded themselves. Incidentally, since Italian and English are mother tongues to me, the very voluble comments on the work did not escape me.

Such was the great impression created by this performance and broadcast, that the next year I was invited, with the Choir of Our Lady of Dublin, to the "Sagra Umbra" (Sacred Music Festival of the Umbrian Province) to give performances of the *Dream* and also the *Messiah*, in Perugia, in the lovely old Morlacchi Theatre there; this time with the splendid orchestra of the Maggio Fiorentine.

The Dream of Gerontius has strong links with the Hallé Orchestra. Its first performance, at the Birmingham Festival on 3 October 1900, was conducted by my great predecessor, Hans Richter, who had taken over the Hallé a year before. Although that performance was a disaster, due to many causes, one of which undoubtedly was Richter's underestimation of its difficulties, Elgar did not blame the conductor. Richter however blamed himself, and he did not conduct it again until he had had ample time to prepare it and to rehearse the choir fully. On 12 March 1903, Manchester heard the work for the first time. A critic of the day who was also one of Elgar's earliest champions, Arthur Johnstone, had attended every performance of *Gerontius* including the two in Germany, and he declared this second attempt of Richter's to be the finest of all. It is particularly interesting to read that Richter attached great importance to the quality and balance of the semi-chorus. Those of you who may one day be listening to these records will, I hope, feel that I share this musical wisdom of my great predecessor.

In *fine*, it is a work exulting and exalted, written as only lasting masterpieces can be, in a constant white heat of inspiration. In this wise, it is very instructive and amusing to recall W H Reed's charming remembrance of a remark made to him by Elgar as they came out of Lincoln Cathedral after a performance of the *Dream*. "Billy, I believe there is a lot of stuff called double counterpoint, or whatever they call it, in that." Of course, that is the right way round to write "that stuff", when it comes out of the bones and tissue of the music and is not imposed on it from a species of cerebral hangover.

I am profoundly grateful to EMI for granting me the privilege of recording, with such loyal and sensitive colleagues, this great work which I love so deeply.

Part Six

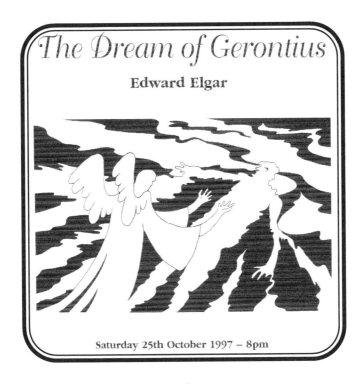

Performing
Gerontius Today

ELGAR'S ADVICE to
NICHOLAS KILBURN and GREGORY HAST

On 6 October 1902 Elgar's friend Nicholas Kilburn wrote to him with some queries regarding the performance of The Dream of Gerontius. *Elgar was busy at the time but eventually sent his answers at the end of December.*

KILBURN:

Ha,   ha!   Ha!   ha!

Page 85 of Vocal Score
What is meant by the Bind [ie. slur] over the first-Bar, as compared with the Second? In pronouncing the Ha!ha! it is hardly possible to make the notes smooth. Do you wish a strong accent gliding into a much weaker, in the first-Bar?

ELGAR:
1st bar   Ha'a (no aspirate to 2nd) *but two distinct syllables* [:] this *throws up* the horrible *Ha!Ha!* in the next bar

KILBURN:
Page 84, 85 &c   The derisive Ha! ha! &c
Am I right that a sardonic flavour rather than absolute accuracy as to the notes, is what you wish? Some of my men-choristers have indulged in this kind of expression, in a limited way [-] leaving the notes to take [care] of themselves, (or to the accompanist) & the effect *seemed to me true & good.*
Of course it could easily be overdone, & I have chaffed them rather than shut them up. All the same I wd. like to know what you have to say.

This applies chiefly to

and the like.

ELGAR:
Dear friend : as long as you think the effect *true* it will be all right - I did not want accuracy but *idea* - only the variations, as you say, must not be overdone.

KILBURN:

Ha!   ha!

Page 88
I take it, the vowel is to be repeated, staccato. I mean, there is nothing special here.

ELGAR:
Yes. Vowel sound repeated but not the aspirate

KILBURN: Page 36 Chant - Semi-chorus, 'Noe from the waters' &c
The words are, I take it, to be chanted in regular way, & that you have no special method. No sh't pause after 'Noe' &c

ELGAR:
Yes a short 'comma' after Noe (& the other names) & then go on steadily

KILBURN:
Page 137
I assume you continue to beat 3 Beats during the accel: molto, & then, at Page 138, [fig] 96 you beat 1 to end of movement.

ELGAR:
No begin *one* in a bar at 95 p 137
A difficult point is the *stringendo* two bars before 75 p 112[:] at 75 two in a bar.

KILBURN:
As regards the *Semi*-chor.
I will be glad if you will allow me to add 2 or 3 to Each Part. The singers are of course *not* professional & I feel sure I can get you a more satisfactory rendering with a few more added to the 18 which you specify. Kindly let me know about this.

ELGAR:
This I leave to you to do the best you can - & I shall be satisfied.

In November 1928 Elgar was due to conduct Gerontius *in Eastbourne. The choir there was being trained by Gregory Hast, an old friend of Elgar's and a former tenor soloist at the Three Choirs, who wrote to the composer asking about the semi-chorus. The differences between Elgar's reply[1] and his remarks to Kilburn a quarter of a century before will be noted. Elgar wrote :*

I think twelve in the Semichorus will be ample & will allow for any absentees - eight are really enough; please choose *very* 'simple' voices without the slightest vibrato.

As to the position of the Chorus; it is necessary for the *Semi-Chorus* to be able to get their pitch from the *orch*: (bar before 29 & the Chorus-tenors *must* be in a position to hear the Semi-chorus at 30; there have been disaster[s] from a neglect of this simple precaution.

¹   Moore, Jerrold Northrop: *Edward Elgar - Letters of a Lifetime* (Clarendon Press, 1990) p 414

INTERPRETING GERONTIUS
Personal memories of Elgar in rehearsal

Edgar Day

Edgar Day (1891-1983) was assistant organist of Worcester Cathedral for fifty years from 1912 to 1962. As accompanist of the Festival Choral Society he worked with many musical giants apart from Elgar, including Holst, Vaughan Williams, Parry, Saint-Saëns and Kodaly. His church music, especially his liturgical settings, is highly regarded by many.
The following article first appeared in The Musical Times, *June 1969, pp 607-8; the ensuing correspondence in the August, October and November issues that year. Sadly, the copy of the vocal score is now missing from Liverpool University Library.*

As chorus accompanist to the Worcester Festival Choral Society for 50 years, I had the great privilege of accompanying *The Dream of Gerontius* many times under Elgar's direction. I have very vivid recollections of this; the points he used to stress remaining firmly fixed in my memory.

Few composers have taken more trouble with expression marks in their music, or indicated their intentions more clearly and meticulously, than Elgar. On one occasion, at a chorus rehearsal of *Gerontius*, he stopped the singers and said, "If you will only observe the expression marks in the copy carefully, that is all I want".

I should like to draw attention to a few passages in the score on which Sir Edward always laid special emphasis, and where the marking is seldom strictly adhered to. At figure 30 in Part I each voice in turn sings the phrase "Holy Mary, pray for him", which begins *piano* with a *crescendo* to the word "Mary" and drops suddenly to *pianissimo* for the words "pray for him", enabling the next entry to be heard easily. It was this sudden *pianissimo* upon which Sir Edward always laid special stress. While on the subject of *pianissimo* singing we may turn to Part II, figure 80 ("O gen'rous love"), where the orchestra begins a long *ppp* pedal passage lasting to figure 83; the chorus drops to *pp* at seven bars after 80. Sir Edward could never get this section soft enough to satisfy him. As I bring back to mind many performances conducted by him, and in which I sang bass in the chorus - always an inspiring experience - I recall vividly a picture of his frowning and making frantic efforts to quieten both orchestra and chorus in this section.

Another small but important point is at figure 6 in Part II, where the oboe gives place to the more ethereal tone of the muted viola on a sustained C which seems to create an "audible stillness". Sir Edward always liked this note thoroughly established before the soloist sang "How still it is!" The pause over the note is marked "(*lunga*)" in the full score, but not in the vocal score, which may possibly account for the soloist frequently not waiting long enough.

I now come to a very important bar in the score - the bar before 61 in Part II - the beginning of 'Praise to the Holiest'. The marking here is often apt to be overlooked or misinterpreted; thereby nullifying the effect. The orchestra is marked *piano* at the beginning of the bar, with a rapid *crescendo* and *diminuendo* within the first two beats, and should be down to *piano* by the third beat; whereas the voices start the bar *piano*, but should not reach the climax of their *crescendo* until the third beat, thus producing two great waves of sound, the poetic meaning of which is described in the following quotation from an essay in *Elgar Centenary Sketches* by Mrs Dora M Powell, the 'Dorabella' of the *Enigma Variations:*

> Another most wonderful memory is of the day at Birchwood near Malvern in 1899 when I heard 'Praise to the Holiest' for the first time. When Elgar had finished playing that particular section in Part II of *Gerontius*, again I did not know what to say and I sat silent. At last I think I murmured "How perfectly wonderful". But he said nothing - his mind was far away, on the music and what the orchestra would be sounding like. He got out a pipe and lighted it. Then he turned to me - "How does that strike you?" Just imagine being asked such a thing! What could I say? Then, something came back into my mind : I had noticed the peculiar way in which the music had seemed to go *piano* and then *forte* again, not quite in accord with the words; so, greatly daring, I ventured : "It makes me think of great doors opening and shutting". Elgar turned round and faced me and, for a moment, I wondered if I had said something dreadful. "Does it?" he said. "That is exactly what I mean".

Unfortunately, this effect is seldom attained; partly, I think, because the chorus, hearing the orchestra making their *crescendo,* make theirs simultaneously, instead of waiting until the orchestra have made their *diminuendo.* The same effect is asked for in the bar before 69.

And now a few remarks on speeds. In Part I Elgar invariably kept very close to the metronome marks throughout, with just one exception. He took the chorus 'Be merciful', starting at fig 35, considerably faster than crotchet = 54; 66 would be nearer the mark. In Part II he never took the Introduction as slowly as marked (crotchet = 48); his speed was usually round about 60.

One night, after he had been taking the Worcester chorus through the work in the Chapter House, he said to me : "You know, I have marked the first part of the Demons' Chorus too fast. It is much better and clearer a bit slower". And from then onwards his speed for 'Lowborn clods' was noticeably slower than crotchet = 120 - about 112-16. He always made an *allargando* at the end of the bar before the fugue subject at 35 and beat out each of the two quaver chords on the fourth beat with all the emphasis he could muster. Later on, in the 'Ha has', he didn't worry about accuracy of notes in the chorus. He told them that the orchestra would play the notes and asked them to make the most demoniacal sounds of which they were capable.

In the chorus 'Praise to the Holiest' he always made a very distinct break at the end of the bar before figure 88. Apart from this, he deviated very little from the metronome marks throughout the chorus and, indeed, to the end of the work.

There remains one more vivid memory to record. In 1928 the Worcester Festival Choral Society gave a performance of the work in the Cathedral and Sir Ivor Atkins asked Sir Edward to conduct it; but he said that he would rather like to listen, for a change; so Sir Ivor conducted. The performance took place under the tower, a position near enough to the Cathedral organ for it to be used for the organ part. Sir Ivor and I went very carefully through the part beforehand, and it was agreed that I should use plenty of organ in the great passage (the 'grand mysterious harmony') from 72 to 73 in Part II, and actually bring on the Full Organ for the fifth bar before 73. This I did, and at the end of the performance as I was wondering what the composer's reaction would be, I heard (with some trepidation) his footsteps on the organ loft stairs.

As soon as I saw his face, I knew that what I had done had met with his approval; I have seldom seen him look so pleased. After thanking me, he said : "I haven't heard the organ part like that since I heard it a few years ago at Cologne. I always intended the organ to be prominent in that passage, but most English organists do not seem to bother much about it". As far as I remember, those were his very words.

In the foregoing I have recorded, as faithfully as I could, my recollections of Elgar's conducting of *Gerontius*; and it will be seen that, if a performance of the work which would have satisfied him is to be attained, the greatest concentration and attention to the smallest detail are demanded by all concerned.

———————

Mr Edgar Day's enlightening article on Elgar and *Gerontius* has set me musing on far-off performances at the Norwich Festival, the Three Choirs and elsewhere. I agree with him that most singers of the title-role have tended to shorten the pause before 'How still it is!'

I was too young to note this point when I heard Gervase Elwes at Norwich (indeed Julia Culp and Herbert Brown, the two other soloists, left clearer impressions on my memory of that very early performance). John Coates, I feel sure, gave the pause its full value. His was the interpretation which I always found the most satisfactory of all, although for sheer beauty of tone and naturalness of diction, Heddle Nash's was memorable.

Mr Day's remarks on Elgar's speeds are illuminating and they agree with my own impressions, especially as regards the opening of Part II. May I express the hope that Mr Day has some notes to publish on Elgar's direction of some of his other works, especially of *The Kingdom*?

Basil Maine, Cromer

In his letter on Elgar and *Gerontius* Mr Basil Maine expresses the hope that I have some notes to publish on Elgar's direction of some of his other works, especially of *The Kingdom*. I am afraid I haven't any notes on these works, but on looking through the music again, my chief impression is that Elgar invariably kept very closely to his markings.

I remember, however, one exception to this in *The Kingdom* : the passage from rehearsal number 69 to 76 he always took decidedly faster than marked. Another small point is worth recording. He was always very particular that the chorus should sing the fourth bar after 37 exactly as marked - *pp* and with no expression whatever in contrast to the same phrase two bars earlier. In the remainder of the work, and throughout *The Apostles*, my conviction is that he adhered fairly strictly to the markings, and seldom deviated far from them.

I am interested and gratified to know that Mr Maine's impressions of performances of *Gerontius* under Elgar are so similar to my own.

Edgar Day, Worcester

As a footnote to recent correspondence on Elgar and *Gerontius* your readers may be interested in the following curiosity. Written on to blank pages in an old Novello vocal score of *Gerontius* in our library, are details of 72 performances of the work, beginning with Richter's first performance, on 3 October 1900, and ending with one by the Leeds Philharmonic Society under Bairstow, on 3 April 1940. In addition to the names of singers and conductors, the timing of each part has been painstakingly recorded. The first performance, as might be expected, was slower than the average : Part I - 42½', Part II - 64'. Those of Elgar himself seem to have been very consistent. For example, his first performance, at the Worcester Festival, 11 September 1902, is : I - 38½' (with short cut); II - 61½'; his final one, at the Hereford Festival, 5 September 1933, a few months before his death : I - 38'; II - 60½'. A performance with the Huddersfield Choral Society on 2 November 1917 (36' and 55½') was an unusually fast sprint.

The slowest performances are those by Sinclair (eg. Hereford Festival, 11 September, 1906 : 44' and 66'); the nimblest by far was under the baton of M Sargent (Bradford Festival, 23 March 1928 : 34' and 53'). We have no record of who this meticulous clock-watcher was, but all in all he appears to have sat or sung through over 70 performances of the work. However much its vital statistics may have waxed or waned, *Gerontius* kept its shape very well.

Trevor Hold, Dept of Music, University of Liverpool

I believe I know the identity of Trevor Hold's "meticulous clock-watcher". All the evidence of his letter, covering *Gerontius* performances at the Three Choirs Festival and in the West Riding of Yorkshire, points to the owner as Dr Herbert Thompson, for 50 years the distinguished music critic of *The Yorkshire Post* (1886-1945).

Thompson timed everything; and I have before me, as I write, his famous (and equally meticulous) book of timings of orchestral performances. The neat and detailed calligraphy is microscopic, like that of the Brontë sisters. But oratorios are not included : the timing of these he indicated on the fly-leaves of the copies themselves (as he also did on his pocket scores).

All Thompson's music was bequeathed to the University of Leeds, which in 1925 conferred on him the honorary degree of D Litt. How the *Gerontius* score got to Liverpool I cannot think. But these timings had a practical use. Before the 1950 Leeds Festival I was rung up by the then secretary, John Shaw, and asked the timing of a Schubert Mass. His scornful reception of my confused, and indeed incompetent, reply convinced me that, at least in John Shaw's opinion, Thompson's successor on *The Yorkshire Post* was a nincompoop.

Ernest Bradbury, Leeds

GERONTIUS in ISTANBUL
1 July 1997

by Ann and John Kelly

Ann and John Kelly are both active members of the London Branch of the Elgar Society, where Ann has recently completed a term as a committee member and John continues to serve as Treasurer.

The International Istanbul Music Festival is now in its twenty-fifth year and in 1997 ran for three weeks from 15 June to 8 July. It was in 1973 on the 50th anniversary of the foundation of the Republic of Turkey that a first Festival of Arts took place, under the leadership of Dr Neyat Eczacibasi, but such was the success of subsequent events relating to the visual arts, and jazz, that those now have their own separate festivals at other times.

This year the list of visiting orchestras and musicians was outstanding, and the fact that the festival organisers were prepared amongst other major concerts to fly out and meet hotel costs for the BBC Symphony Orchestra, Chorus, and soloists for three nights speaks volumes for the support given by the authorities and sponsors in Turkey.

A performance of Elgar's Dream of *Gerontius* in Istanbul had long been a cherished hope of the General Director of the Istanbul Foundation for Culture and Arts, Melih Fereli, particularly since 1985, when he himself had sung with the Philharmonia Chorus in a performance at the Royal Festival Hall under Svetlanov. This year's performance had in fact been six years in the planning.

The venue for the concert was the Aya Irini Kilise/Haggia Eirene Museum (The Church of the Divine Peace), pictured opposite, which is in the first courtyard of the Topkapi Palace. The location is the oldest site of Christian worship in Istanbul, and the present building is at least the third church to stand there, having been built in AD 537. It was never converted to a mosque and, following the conversion to

Aya Irini Kilise/ Haggia Eirene Museum (The Church of the Divine Peace) in Istanbul, venue for the performance of Gerontius *reviewed here*

Islam, became a military arsenal until the 19th century. On the founding of the Republic in 1924 it was designated a museum, but is only open occasionally, as when used during the International Music Festival. Internally most of the mosaics have fallen off, leaving a long brick central nave headed by a huge dome. A large iconic cross, edged in black, set with a background of gold, is the one mosaic which remains in the semi-circular apse, and which faced the audience behind chorus and orchestra. The church contains no other images. On either side of the long nave and at the rear there is a spacious gallery. In the past the clergy would have sat on the bank of seats, five in number, in the apse, and this was where the chorus of a hundred or so voices were tightly packed for *The Dream of Gerontius*, and again on the following night for an electric performance of Walton's *Belshazzar's Feast*. This choral closeness and the acoustic in Haggia Eirene, when it became full, treated the audiences of a thousand on each of the occasions we attended to marvellous sound.

When we had first heard of the forthcoming performance of *Gerontius* in Istanbul, which was to be the first ever rendering of this strongly Catholic work in an Islamic country, we had some concerns and wondered if only an 'expurgated' version might be allowed, for had not Elgar's masterpiece even suffered such a fate in 1902 at Worcester at the hands of the Anglican clergy? We need not have feared, however, for the work was given in its entirety, and we were treated to a fine rendering by the BBC Orchestra and Chorus who were all on top form, aware and excited by the unique occasion. The choral sound was pure and well balanced, with Newman's words clearly enunciated for the foreign audience; whilst, despite the heat, the orchestra and instruments matched the demands of the evening.

There were, however, some collateral eccentricities. The worst of these was the unusually varied and exaggerated tempi demanded by Leonard Slatkin, who conducted without a stick. Part I was universally slow and, whilst in Part II there was more variety, extremes were introduced. The Demon's Chorus must have broken all speed records, and the finale threatened never to be one.

The American tenor John Aler had a strong voice and sang well, albeit with occasional heavy vibrato, and chose the higher options where the score allowed. But these listeners were left with the conclusion that he has still to enter into the role of *Gerontius* spiritually. The contrast with his Angel, Jean Rigby, could not have been more marked, for she was at her best vocally (when will she be asked to record *Gerontius*?) and by interpreting her 'task' operatically with minute but clear 'body language', especially facially, she added greatly to an appreciation and understanding by the mixed audience. This consisted mainly of Turks, in western style dress, and some tourists.

Alan Opie was the one bass, stationed for both roles centre stage behind the orchestra and just in front of the choir. This ploy seemed meaningless and, whatever its intent, failed visually and, despite Opie's strong voice, orally for certain sections of the audience.

The performance survived an early potential disaster. At the beginning of bar 2, a pigeon relieved itself from 100 feet above the conductor. Its load narrowly missed him, but caught a cello in the front desk. Quick cleaning of her instrument by the lady cellist concerned was required at the first convenient break. (By the following evening, a lesson had been learned and a long sheet of black material had been stretched across the church from the side balconies to protect the conductor and soloists.)

One remembers, too, the lurch forward with a loud stamping of his left foot by the conductor in that silence just before the climactic chord when Gerontius glimpses his God. This spoilt that special moment and really was not required to stir this fine orchestra into their fortissimo.

Despite these peccadillos, it was a stirring performance and occasion and at the end of the concert the audience rapturously showed its appreciation with many standing. As Jean Rigby said later, it really had been like singing in heaven.

On the following evening we sat next to a Turkish lady who spoke little English, but she managed to communicate that the BBC Orchestra is "the best in the world", and that she listens to it on short wave radio via the Overseas Service of the BBC whenever she can! She had enjoyed the Elgar immensely, and we wondered if she would be in the audience again a few days later when La Scala Philharmonic Orchestra under Muti would play *In the South*.

We stayed at the Pera Palace Hotel in Istanbul, built in 1892, and noted now for its nostalgia of the times when the Orient Express used to house all its passengers there. Over the years many famous persons have stayed, and brass plates on bedroom doors record their visits. Elgar stayed here for four nights during his Mediterranean cruise in 1905, although his diary notes indicate that his usual love of dogs was modified on that occasion. "In the night the most fearful noise by the dogs - a sound I never dreamt possible - like 40,000 dogs - they were just under the window. This terrible noise came on about 1.30". The postcard which he sent to Carice from 'Constantinople', now to be seen in the book *Dear Carice*, published from archives at the Birthplace Museum, interestingly shows a Turk surrounded by eight dogs. The printing refers to a Souvenir of 'Les chiens des rues', and Elgar writes, "I love these poor wows". (Incidentally, the book is incorrect where it refers to Elgar's brother Frank as being his companion on that trip. 'Frank' is, of course, Frank Schuster.)

The Pera Palace Hotel (overleaf, here seen by night) employs a part-time archivist, who did not know of Elgar's visit, as many of their old records have been lost. The Hotel was most interested when we told them, and when we showed them the narrative from Pauline Collett's book *An Elgar Travelogue*. This was kindly faxed to us by startled fellow Elgar Society member David Bury, who was woken one morning with a telephone call from Istanbul. As the number of the room in which Elgar stayed cannot be ascertained, a brass plate on a door will not be possible, but the hotel has readily agreed to accept a small montage noting Elgar's stay, to be affixed in the foyer.

The Pera Palace Hotel, Istanbul,
where Elgar stayed for four nights in 1905

GERONTIUS in BUDAPEST

Alan Tongue

Alan Tongue is an Elgar Society member who, when he is not conducting Elgar in unusual places, lives in Cambridge, England

It was a trip to Buenos Aires in 1991 that gave me a sense of direction : at a sumptuous champagne reception in the circle foyer of the Teatro Colón after conducting the Argentinian première of *Belshazzar's Feast* I had been surrounded by Argentinians eager to talk about British culture. Since then I have seized upon any chance to take the best of British music around the world, and Hungary and Romania are now my home from home. Let the Budapest Opera repetiteur and composer Jenö Pertis take up the story :

This wasn't Alan Tongue's first visit to Budapest. For a long time in the Hungarian music world he has been known as the 'ambassador' of English music. Since he began this work in 1993, the members of the BM Duna orchestra have been especially grateful for his regular contributions to the 'English evenings' (Elgar, Holst, Vaughan Williams, Britten, etc) and for giving audiences these musical treats, of which many traditional promoters are unaware. So that's how The Dream of Gerontius *was performed - in partnership with his good friends, the Duna Orchestra.*

It was an unforgettable experience. Despite the fact that this piece is virtually unknown in Hungary, the church was packed. The essence of the piece and its deeper meanings were clearly shown by Alan and it is thanks to his one-week expert training that the performance worked so magically. It was marvellous that the soloists, choir and orchestra could relate to this piece so quickly, especially as it was previously unknown to them. They performed it with such spirit and enthusiasm that the audience was quite carried away. It greatly helped in the understanding of the piece that the translation of the script was available to the audience. We appreciate Alan Tongue's wide knowledge of this piece and his commitment to popularising Elgar's works. We can truly say that the performances of The Dream of Gerontius *were the climax of the English Evenings."*

As an example of how seriously they take their music in Budapest I was given all the rehearsals I had requested : two with orchestra, one with soloists and orchestra, one with choir and orchestra, and one full rehearsal. The soloists, from the Hungarian State Opera, were well prepared before we started piano rehearsals in the beautiful Opera House. The choir had been taught the notes well by their own chorus master, and I spent two evenings working with this choir of 130 voices - 80 of them from the Hungarian State Choir, a fully professional choir! Working with them in their own ideal rehearsal room, one could hear the amount of detail in Elgar's choral writing, incvitably somewhat lost in church performance with orchestra. The participants all sensed that we were taking a lot of care over our two performances, and I received an impression of performers who had fallen in love with the work and just wanted to give of their best. There was a real commitment from our company of 200, and I continually got feedback about how much they liked the work. I have noticed that one great thing about Elgar is how well he travels : there is never any sense that there is something strange about his music ("strange" is a word once used in Romania to describe the music of *The Planets* to me!) and he seems to fit into the continental Romantic tradition very easily.

Tardy László, Director of Music at the Matyas Templom, wrote this account, which he entitled 'The Return of the Boomerang'. *"At the end of the last century a magnificent artist arrived in the UK from Hungary; Hans Richter, the son of Antal Richter, who was church music director at the cathedral of Györ, in western Hungary. Richter espoused Elgar's works and the two artists became close friends. Elgar's* The Dream of Gerontius, *first conducted by Richter, arrived in Hungary a hundred years later, when it was performed in Budapest. The Danube Symphony Orchestra, the State Choir of Hungary, the Oratorio Choir of Budapest and soloists Timothy Bentch (Gerontius), Márta Lukin (Angel) and Rácz István (Priest and Angel of the Agony) worked hard during the rehearsals with the conductor Alan Tongue, from Cambridge. The performance took place in the Parish Church at Bakáts Square in Ferencváros, where a wonderful music festival is held every summer.*

"Right at the beginning of the concert, we could recognise that it would be a magnificent musical event. The audience, who filled the church completely, were given the Hungarian translation of the words by Cardinal Newman. Everybody was full of expectation. The first sounds of the orchestral introduction revealed an unknown musical greatness : a composition which is deeply English, full of power and honesty, gentle and varied. We could feel that music take us to the depths of the human soul. The conductor Alan Tongue was able to make a magnificent balance between the large orchestra and the double choir on the one hand, and the soloists on the other. Not only the dramatic parts fascinated the listeners, but the fine expression of the transformation of Gerontius and the beautifully formed dialogues between his soul and the angel. The big applause at the end of the concert was a great honour not only to the composer, soloists, choir and orchestra, but for the magnificent work done by the conductor Alan Tongue."

We made a five-minute break for the soloists after Part I : no applause broke the atmosphere, the emotion was tangible. After Part II there was an ovation, followed by a stream of visitors into the sacristy to talk to me - including a distant relative of Newman and many local concert-goers asking when the next Elgar work was scheduled. By the second performance, three nights later, word had spread, and the church was packed to the walls, many standing. Again, after the performance the message I kept hearing was "Why have we been deprived of this beautiful music for so long?"...

AFTER 100 YEARS

Michael Kennedy

Michael Kennedy needs no introduction. The author of what many regard as the definitive biography of Elgar[1] as well as biographies on Barbirolli and Boult, he has pursued a successful career in journalism in which he became Northern Editor of the Daily Telegraph *and, since 1989, Chief Music Critic of the* Sunday Telegraph. *He is a Vice-President of the Elgar Society and the Patron of the Society's North-West branch.*

Call me pedantic, if you like, although I maintain that I am merely accurate in insisting that the first performance of *The Dream of Gerontius* on 3 October 1900 was given in the last year of the Nineteenth Century. But the point is immaterial since there is no doubt that the work itself belonged in spirit to the new century and was to have a profound effect on British music written thereafter. As with so much that is Elgarian, there is a paradox here. The music is a masterly amalgam of 19th century influences, Wagner, Berlioz, Gounod and Liszt among them, and of some even earlier (Handel). Yet, famously, Richard Strauss, seven years younger than Elgar but as much a son of the 19th century, saluted *Gerontius* in Düsseldorf in 1902 as the work of "the first English progressivist composer". So the arch-modernist of the day, as he was then regarded, recognised a fellow-spirit. I wonder what impressed him most? The similarity of the opening to that of his own *Tod und Verklärung* (and of both to *Parsifal*)? Or, more likely, the dissonances and original treatment of the chorus in the Demons' episode? Strauss had no time for the Christian religion. "What's a saint? ...a bundle of bones which fools adore" would appeal far more than "Praise to the Holiest in the Height" to the man who thought John the Baptist was a clown.

Perhaps of more significance than Strauss's admiration - which led to a firm friendship - was the immediate influence the work had on young British composers. We may hear this in Sir John McEwen's *Hymn on the Morning of Christ's Nativity*, composed between 1901 and 1905,

---

[1]   Michael Kennedy - *Portrait of Elgar* (Oxford University Press, 1968)

but never performed until it was recorded in 1998. The music comes as a revelation of McEwen's stature as a composer, hitherto unrecognised, and of the powerful and immediate impact of Elgar's blend of choral and orchestral writing. Perhaps the single most revolutionary aspect of *Gerontius* was its form. Elgar did not want it to be classified by Novello under Sacred Cantatas and reluctantly agreed to its listing under Oratorios. One can see the justice of his belief that "there's no word invented yet to describe it". His abolition of the formal recitative-and-aria lay-out of oratorios and his replacement of it by a seamless quasi-operatic format lit the way for his contemporaries perhaps seeking a similar path away from the conventional. Certainly Parry's post-1900 choral works acknowledged the example of *Gerontius*. William Alwyn made a very shrewd assessment when he called *Gerontius* a "passion play". The first post-*Gerontius* masterpiece to remain in the repertory which was acknowledged by its composer to be musically influenced by Elgar's work is Vaughan Williams's *A Sea Symphony* (1903-09). He identified the very passages where the influence was strongest - "in the opening pages of the finale" - and in that same finale he adapted Elgar's invention of the semi-chorus. But, oddly enough, part of the influence of *Gerontius* has been the determination of later composers *not* to be influenced by it. This is in itself a tribute to its stature and to its inimitability. Even Elgar himself in *The Apostles* and *The Kingdom* shied away from direct competition. Walton's *Belshazzar's Feast* of 1931 may have an Elgarian pomp-and-circumstance aspect, but it in no way follows in the wake of *Gerontius*. Britten's *War Requiem* of 1962 adapts the layers of choral sound which are what make the *finale* of *Gerontius* an unforgettable experience. Tippett's *A Child of Our Time* (1939-41) reverts to a Bach-like structure, but comes nearer than either Walton or Britten to a *Gerontius*-like treatment of narration. *Gerontius* remains essentially a poem set to music.

On the whole, then, after the passage of a century, *The Dream of Gerontius* stands alone as an isolated expression of one man's genius, a landmark, a turning-point, and a source from which other tributaries have flowed as entirely separate streams. In British music-making it stands secure, regarded as almost as much of a choral institution as *Messiah*. If it is taken for granted, that is a calamitous mistake. Richter under-estimated its difficulties at the Birmingham first performance and woe betide any conductor who makes the same mistake, for those difficulties have grown no less, although of course today's singers are used to much more difficult works and also have a much broader knowledge of music than their great-grandparents of 1900, to most of whom Monteverdi, Vivaldi and others would only have been names in a dictionary. There are, of course, still people who cannot abide the work, but one usually finds that their allergy is to Cardinal Newman's poem rather than to Elgar's music.

Lewis Foreman, elsewhere in this volume, has covered the history of early performances of *Gerontius*, extraordinarily widespread and demonstrating the interest in Elgar of continental conductors, not only Richter, who by 1900 was almost an adopted Englishman, but also Fritz Volbach, Felix Weingartner and Julius Buths. The falling-away of interest after the First World War extended to British music in general where Germany and Austria were concerned, but there has been a revival of interest since 1945. Even so, performances abroad of *Gerontius*, although increasing, are rare events compared with those of, say, the *Enigma Variations*. America has always been cool towards it in spite of efforts by Sir John Barbirolli and others (but it is amazing to be reminded that it was heard in Chicago and New York before it was first heard in London in 1903). Illness prevented Barbirolli conducting a Berlin Philharmonic performance and one may perhaps hope that Sir Simon Rattle will re-awaken German ears to what their pre-1914 forebears heard in Elgar.

The tremendous surge of interest in "performance practice" in the past decade and more has resulted in some fascinating musical insights. What began as performance on original or period reproduction instruments of the music of the 16th, 17th and 18th centuries has been extended to embrace 19th and early 20th century works. Superb recordings have been made of the music of Schubert, Berlioz, Brahms and Verdi - among others - using the type of instruments and size of orchestra which the listeners to the first performance would have heard. Sir John Eliot Gardiner's recording of Verdi's *Requiem* was an ear-opener for this listener, revealing startling aspects of a familiar work which had been obscured by the incursion of modern instruments and styles of interpretation. So it is time, surely, for the next recording of *The Dream of Gerontius* to be made with the instruments pertaining to October 1900. We have those treasured extracts from Elgar's own 1920s performances to instruct conductors in how he wanted this music to "go" - on the whole, much more dramatically than the "holy" kind of performance we often hear.

Which brings me to the solo parts in *Gerontius*. For most of its existence, the work has been fortunate in attracting interpreters who for many years remained closely identified with it. The first Gerontius, Edward Lloyd, was on the point of retirement and, so far as I know, never sang the part again. But Marie Brema, the first Angel, and Harry Plunket Greene sang in the bowdlerised Worcester performance under Elgar in 1902 and Brema sang in Richter's Manchester performances (like the bass in these performances, Andrew Black, she was teaching there). Soon, however, she was displaced by Muriel Foster, who sang at the second Düsseldorf performance in 1902 and often thereafter until her career was cut short by illness. The German tenor Ludwig Wüllner sang Gerontius at both Düsseldorf performances and at the first London performance in 1903. But then two English tenors made the title-role their own for the best part of 25 years. Gervase Elwes (who died in 1921) sang it "like a saint", according to Barbirolli. Too like a saint for Elgar, his daughter told me. He preferred the more robust, indeed more operatic, interpretation of John Coates. Nearer to Elwes was Steuart Wilson. And after him came Heddle Nash, Parry Jones, Ronald Dowd and pre-eminently Richard Lewis. After Muriel Foster, the great Angel interpreters were Clara Butt (who Elgar is said to have wanted for the first performance), Muriel Brunskill, Phyllis Lett, Astra Desmond, Gladys Ripley, Kathleen Ferrier and Janet Baker. Among the outstanding singers of the bass roles of Priest and Angel of the Agony (and what would one not have given to hear Richard Mayr in the 1905 Vienna première?) were Horace Stevens, Harold Williams, David Franklin, Norman Walker - and after them a succession of basses suggesting that no single individual was an automatic choice. The same thing has happened, in my view, with Gerontius and the Angel. Since Lewis, there has been no authoritative Gerontius, a tenor to whom everyone would turn first in casting the role. Some good tenors have sung it, but none has become inextricably identified with it in the public mind. After Janet Baker, the same is true of the Angel. The bass part, of course, has found probably its greatest interpreter in Bryn Terfel.

It sometimes seems to me, when I listen to *Gerontius* performances today, that singers have lost the key to this music. They sing it, but they do not live it. Is it because of a decline in religious observance? Such a theory is, I believe, nonsense. Even if every singer in the land today was to be discovered to be an atheist, it has not affected the way they sing Mozart's, Verdi's and Fauré's *Requiems* and any number of other sacred works you like to name. No, it is *Gerontius* that seems to me to present difficulties to them and I wonder if it is because the singers one has admired in the past all either worked with Elgar or with conductors who knew him and knew the Elgar style of performance and how to create the *Gerontius* atmosphere. That has been lost and nothing yet has replaced it. There is a danger, after a hundred years, that *The Dream of Gerontius* is becoming just another choral work instead of a very special musical and spiritual experience, akin to *Parsifal* in its demands on performers and audiences to surrender to its spell. I hope these are pessimistic views, but I set them down as perhaps worth consideration.

A UNIVERSAL WELCOME
An Annex of Recent Performances

Gerontius is alive and well and will be performed tonight in .... well, it could be just about anywhere, such is the near universal acceptance the work has now gained. Notable performances at festivals such as the annual Henry Wood Promenade Concerts and a video recording of a 1997 performance in St Paul's Cathedral, London may create an impression that the work is the preserve of the large Anglican cathedrals and concert halls of Britain - surprising in itself considering Elgar's choice of a subject that might be expected to restrict its appeal to devotional Catholic audiences. Yet a quick perusal of the accompanying list reveals a work which can command three consecutive nights in major American concert halls yet remains within the reach of amateur choirs and scratch orchestras appearing in schools and sports halls of the quieter provincial towns where any performance of serious music is a keenly anticipated event. The BBC chose the work to commemorate its seventy-fifth anniversary with the 1997 St Paul's Cathedral performance. But, in similar vein, the work was also the choice of the choir of the University of Newcastle, New South Wales to commemorate its fortieth anniversary one month earlier. This is a work with which to celebrate not so much a belief in the afterlife, but in life itself!

Admittedly, performances to non-English speaking audiences remain few. But, even setting aside the pioneering work of conductors such as Leonard Slatkin in Istanbul and Alan Tongue in Eastern Europe, there have been recent, wholly native performances in Prague, Amsterdam, Copenhagen, Lille, Cologne and Mainz (not all of which appear in the list). Germany, having immediately welcomed this work, continues to do so.

The names of artists who appeared in memorable early performances live on, but there are other, current performers as closely associated with the work whom historical perspective may treat as kindly. Only Jean Rigby can challenge the claims of Catherine Wyn Rogers to be the archetypal Angel, while Arthur Davies has dominated the role of Gerontius in the recent past; Anthony Rolfe Johnson and John Mitchinson compete for an honourable if distant second. Competition among the basses is tougher: the names of Matthew Best, Alan Opie, Stephen Roberts and Alastair Miles all recur frequently, although this author is not alone in considering the stunning entry of Willard White on the first night of the 1991 season of Promenade Concerts as among the most outstanding of all performances. And while the list includes many conductors of international repute, it is unsurprisingly the established Elgarians who predominate - Donald Hunt, Christopher Robinson, David Willcocks, Andrew Davis and, above all, Society President Richard Hickox. But this emphasis on the famous must not detract from the many superlative performances from amateur choirs - choirs such as the Philomusica of Gloucestershire and Worcestershire under the baton of the late James Cowley, whose rendition at Cheltenham Town Hall on 1 June 1997 was limited only by the acoustics of the venue.

Much is made of the immediate success of the First Symphony, leading to nearly one hundred performances in the twelve months following its première. If we discount pyrotechnically accompanied performances of the first *Pomp and Circumstance* March, most would predict the *Enigma Variations* or the Cello Concerto as the most frequently performed of Elgar's major works. Yet the concert diary that appears in the ELGAR SOCIETY JOURNAL and more recently on the Society's website (http://www.elgar.org), and from which the accompanying list has been compiled, shows that, from its unpromising start, *Gerontius* now regularly out-performs both works. We readily acknowledge that the diary captures only a small if growing proportion of performances. With at least six independent performances within the space of eight days in March 1999, and eighteen performances already on record for the first six months of 1999, who can deny *Gerontius* its place alongside the First Symphony in the 100+ club. The Dream Lives On!

———————————

Date Venue	Choir/Orchestra/Conductor Soloists
1995	
10 March Westminster Cathedral, London	BBC SO and Chorus/Andrew Davis Jean Rigby/Dennis O'Neill/Alastair Miles
18 March Leisure Centre, Wilmslow, Cheshire	Wilmslow Orch
29 April St. George's Hall, Liverpool	Liverpool Welsh Choral Union/Williams
14 May Highfields School, Matlock, Derbyshire	Highfields School Choir/Derbyshire Singers/Chesterfield Philharmonic Choir/Derbyshire Sinfonia/Clark Catherine Wyn-Rogers/A Thompson/A Holland
30 September Town Hall, Cheltenham	Oriel Singers/Burford Singers/Oxford SO/Brian Etheridge Margaret McDonald/Justin Lavender/Stephen Roberts
7 October The Heath, Crawley, Sussex	Weald Choir of Crawley/Guildford PO/Finney J Koc/Neil Jenkins/A Kubrick
28 October Anglican Cathedral, Liverpool	NFMS Choirs/RLPO/Tracey J Lawton/P Walker/C Underwood
1996	
11 February Royal Albert Hall, London	Royal Choral Soc/RPO/Charles Mackerras Jean Rigby/John Tomlinson
23 March Stopsley Baptist Church, Luton	Luton Choral Soc/Chiltern SO/Julian Mann Jenny Higgins/Bonaventura Bottone/Andrew Dale Forbes
23 March St. Peter Ad Vincula Church, Coggeshall, Essex	St Cecilia Choral Soc/Essex Chamber Orch/Jonathan del Mar
11 May De Montfort Hall, Leicester	Leicester Philharmonic Choir/Bardi Orch/Constantine Catherine Wyn-Rogers/J G Hall/G Hargreaves
11 May Cathedral, Wells, Somerset	Wells Cathedral Oratorio Soc/Wells Sinfonia/Crosland Catherine Denley/Andrew Murgatroyd/Quentin Hayes
18 May Town Hall, Leeds	Leeds Philharmonic Choir/Hallé Orch/Richard Hickox Jean Rigby/Arthur Davies/R Hayward
14 June Staatstheater, Mainz, Germany	Local choirs/conductor Peter Erckens
22 June Fairfield Hall, Croydon, Surrey	Croydon Festival Choir/Lambeth SO/Christopher Fifield A Gunson/Martyn Hill/G Hargreaves
14 July Royal Albert Hall, London	"Gerontius from scratch"/ Robert Tear (conductor)

24 August Cathedral, Worcester	Worcester Festival Chorus/BBC PO/Donald Hunt Sally Burgess/Arthur Davies/Laurence Albert
20 September Barbican Hall, London	London Symphony Chorus/Bournemeouth SO/Richard Hickox Jean Rigby/Arthur Davies/P Coleman-Wright
3 November Royal Festival Hall, London	Philharmonia Chorus/Philharmonia Orch/Leonard Slatkin Catherine Wyn-Rogers/J Lavender/Anthony Michaels-Moore
13 November Poole Arts Centre, Poole, Dorset	Waynflete Singers/Bournemouth SO & Choir/David Hill Sarah Fryer/William Kendall/Matthew Best
16 November Symphony Hall, Birmingham	City of Birmingham SO & Chorus/Christopher Robinson Catherine Wyn-Rogers/Anthony Rolfe Johnson/MatthewBest

1997

15 March Cathedral, Brentwood	Brentwood Cathedral Singers/Chigwell School Choir/Chigwellian Choral Soc/Loyola Prep School Choir/Helios Orch/Chaplin S Self/N Sherwood/D Taylor
11 May Parish Church, Stroud	Philomusica of Gloucester and Worcester/James Cowley Diana Walkley/David Parsons
23 May Clifton RC Cathedral, Bristol	Bath Festival Chorus/Richard Hickox Catherine Wyn-Rogers/Arthur Davies/Alan Opie
24 May St Nicholas' Church, Newbury	London Symph Chorus/City of London Sinfonia/Richard Hickox Catherine Wyn-Rogers/Arthur Davies/Alan Opie
1 June Town Hall, Cheltenham	Dean Close School Choir/Philomusica of Gloucester & Worcester/James Cowley Diana Walkley/John Mitchinson/E Chetcuti/David Parsons
27 June Church of St. Michael and All Saints, Watford, Herts	Pearsall Singers/Paragon Singers of Bath/ Watford Chamber Ensemble/Martin Bird Brenda Southorn/Derrick Phoenix/David Ireson/Roderick Williams
1 July Hagia Eieni Museum, Istanbul	BBCSO & Chorus/LeonardSlatkin Jean Rigby/John Aler/Alan Opie
12 July St. Albans Abbey, St Albans, Herts	St. Albans Bach Choir/City of London Sinfonia/Christopher Robinson Jean Rigby/A Thompson/Matthew Best
9 & 11 August Sydney Opera House, Australia	The Sydney Philharmonic Choirs/Edo de Waart Sarah Connelly/Glenn Winslade/Peter Sidhom
25 October Univ of Newcastle, NSW, Australia	Newcastle University Choir and Orch/Peter Brock Irene Waugh/Gregory Massingham/Michael Lewis
15 November St. Mary's Church, Bury St Edmunds, Suffolk	St. Edmundsbury Bach Choir and Orch/Harrison Oxley S Fulgoni/James Oxley/P O'Reilly
22 November St. Margaret's Church, Ilkley, Yorks	Ilkley and Otley Choral Soc/Orch/Alan Horsey

26 November St. Paul's Cathedral, London	BBC SO & Chorus/Andrew Davis Catherine Wyn-Rogers/Philip Langridge/Alastair Miles
29 November Town Hall, Cheltenham	Cheltenham Bach Choir/Oriel Singers/Forest PO/Brian Kay Sarah Walker/Martyn Hill/Michael George

1998

7 March Civic Hall, Guildford	Guildford PO & Choir/Jeremy Backhouse
18 March Westminster Cathedral, London	Monteverdi Choir/Philharmonia Orch/J E Gardiner Catherine Robbin/William Kendall/Alastair Miles
20 March Copenhagen, Denmark	Choir/Danish Radio SO/Schonwandt Ann Murray/Dennis O'Neill/Haywood
21 March Corn Exchange, Bedford	Bedford Choral Soc and SO/Smith
24 March Royal Albert Hall, London	St Barts Hospital Choral Soc/Royal PO/ Matthew Best
2 April Thame Sports and Arts Centre, Thame, Bucks	Lord Williams' Festival Choir and Orch/Robert Webb Aileen Sim
4 April Town Hall, Stockport, Cheshire	Barnby Choir/Gatley Choral Soc/Macclesfield Oriana Soc/King Edward Music Soc Choir/Stockport Symphony Orch/English Williamson/English/Caddy
1 May Town Hall, Wellington, New Zealand	Orpheus Choir of Wellington/New Zealand Symphony Orch/Walsh Payne/Martyn Hill/Macann
14 & 17 May Bridgewater Hall, Manchester	Hallé Choir and Orch/Hughes Ann Murray/Robert Tear/Alastair Miles
20 May National Cathedral, Washington DC, USA	Washington National Cathedral Choral Soc/ Woodley Ensemble/David Willcocks Judith Malafronte/Stanford Olsen/Phillip Collister
31 May New Elgar Hall, Malvern, Worcs	Malvern Festival Chorus and SO/Rory Boyle Kate McCarney/John MitchinsonJeremy White
2 June Royal Festival Hall, London	Bach Choir/Bournemouth SO/David Hill Jean Rigby/A Thompson/David Wilson-Johnson
4 July Cathedral, Winchester, Hants	Bach Choir/Bournemouth SO/David Hill Jean Rigby/William Kendall/Matthew Best
21 November Town Hall, Oxford	Oxford Harmonic Soc/Stowe Opera Orch
21 November City Hall, Glasgow	Serenata Singers/Glasgow Orch Soc/Marco Romano

22 November Town Hall, Hamilton, Strathclyde	Serenata Singers/Glasgow Orch Soc/Marco Romano
13 December Barbican Hall, London	London Symphony Chorus and Orch/Colin Davis Sara Mingardo/Robert Dean Smith/Jonathan Summers

1999

27 February Colston Hall, Bristol	Clifton Cathedral Singers/Chew Valley Choral Society/ University of West of England SO & Chorus/Martin Freke Catherine Wyn-Rogers/Neil Jenkins/Lynton Black
20 March Cathedral, Derby	Derby Bach Choir/John York Skinner Emily Bauer Jones/John Mitchinson/Mark Wildman
20 March St Botolph's Ch, Colchester, Essex	St Botolph's Music Soc Barbara Windsor
24 March Philharmonic Hall, Liverpool	Royal Liverpool Phil Orch & Chorus/Gerard Schwarz Penelope Walker/Arthur Davies/Stephen Roberts
27 March Town Hall, Kidderminster, Worcs	Kidderminster Choral Society Choir/Elgar Sinfonia/Geoffrey Weaver Yvonne Howard/Lynton Atkinson/Eddie Wade
27 March Assembly Hall, Walthamstow, Essex	Selwyn Singers/Aurelian Ensemble/South West Essex Choir/Stefan Reid Sarah Pring/Christopher Lemming/Brindley Sherrat
27 March Parish Church, Bromley, Kent	Bromley Singers
8 May Christchurch Priory, Christchurch, Dorset	Grange Choral Soc/Tim Hooper Neil Jenkins
15 May Brentwood International Centre, Brentwood, Essex	Hutton and Shenfield Choral Society/Southend Bach Choir/ Aurelian Ensemble/Gerald Bates Gordon Christie
6 June Royal Festival Hall, London	London Symph Chorus/Philharmonia Orch/Richard Hickox Pamela Helen Stephen/Anthony Rolfe Johnson/Bryn Terfel
25/26 June Bakáts Tér Church, Budapest, Hungary	Hungarian National & Budapest Choirs/BM Duna Szimfonikus/Alan Tongue Lukin Márta/Timothy Bentch/Rácz István
10 July Cathedral, Chichester	Chichester Singers/Southern Pro Musica/Jonathan Willcocks
7-8 October Lille, France	Orch Nationale de Lille/Richard Cooke (orchestral excerpts)
10 October Warwick Arts Centre, Coventry	Midland Festival Chor/Cavendish Singers/RLPO/Malcolm Goldring Sarah Walker/Arthur Davies/Laurence Albert
17 October Victoria Hall, Hanley, Staffs	North Staffordshire Festival Chorus/RLPO/Donald Hunt Sally Burgess/Arthur Davies/Laurence Albert

28 October   Northern England Festival Chorus/John Bethell
St George's Church, New York, USA   Yvonne Howard/David Robinson/Gregory Gardner

2000

22 January   RSNO & Chorus/Richard Hickox
Royal Concert Hall, Glasgow   Pamela Helen Stephen/Philip Langridge/Stephen Roberts

23 January   RSNO & Chorus/Richard Hickox
Festival Theatre, Edinburgh   Pamela Helen Stephen/Philip Langridge/Stephen Roberts

27-29 January   San Francisco Symphony Orch & Chorus/Donald Runnicles
San Francisco, USA   Jennifer Larmore/Thomas Moser/Eric Halfvarson

3 February   Jysk Akademisk Kor/Aarhus Studiekor/Den Jyske Operas Kor/Aarhus SO/
Aarhus, Denmark   James Loughran/Barbara Hölzl/Nigel Robson/Timothy Mirfin

3 March   McGill Symphony Orchestra and Choir/Iwan Edwards
Montreal, Quebec   Zoë Tarshis/Aaron Estes/Joshua Hopkins

3-5 March   Kansas City Symphony Orchestra/Lawrence Leighton Smith
Kansas City, USA

4 March   Sacramento Choral Society/Donald Kendrick
Sacramento, California,USA

4 March   Univ Surrey Roehampton Choir/Barnet Choral Society/
The Abbey, St Albans, Herts   Harrow Young Musicians Choir/Colin Durrant

5 March   Hartford Chorale & SO/Henley Denmead
Hartford Courant Arts Center, Hartford, Conn, USA

11 March   Edinburgh Bach Choir/Dundee Choral Union/Scottish Sinfonia/Neil Mantle
Assembly Rooms, George Street, Edinburgh   Colette Ruddy/Mark Wilde/Andrew Foster

12 March   Edinburgh Bach Choir/Dundee Choral Union/Scottish Sinfonia/Neil Mantle
Caird Hall, Dundee, Tayside   Colette Ruddy/Mark Wilde/Andrew Foster

15 March   University of York Choir/English Northern Phil Orch/Peter Seymour
The Minster, York, Yorkshire   Yvonne Seymour/Adrian Thompson/Glenville Hargreaves

18 March   Gloucester Choral Society/English Symphony Orchestra/David Briggs
Cathedral, Gloucester   Louise Winter/Anthony Rolfe Johnson/Graeme Broadbent

19 March   Perth Choral Society
City Hall, Perth, Scotland

25 March   Festival Chorus/Rutland Sinfonia/Barry Collett
RC Cathedral, Northampton   Rose Bellingham/Peter Wedd/Simon Theobald

25 March   Nottingham Harmonic Society Choir/Orchestra da Camera/Neil Page
Royal Concert Hall, Nottingham   Margaret McDonald/Adrian Thompson/Jeremy White

25 March   Senior Choir Bryn Mawr Presbyterian Church/Jeffrey Brillhart
Presbyterian Church, Bryn Mawr, Pennsylvania, USA   Suzanne DuPlantis/David Price

29 March   Hitchin Girls School Choir and Orch/NHGS members/Paul Adrian Rooke
St Mary's Church, Hitchin, Herts   Louise Hemmings/Andrew Catling/Roderick McPhee

1 April   Ashtead Choral Soc/City of London Chamber Players/Paul Dodds
Dorking Halls, Dorking, Surrey   Margaret McDonald/Robert Johnston/Jeremy White

8 April   St Michael's Singers/Chichester Singers/Bluecoat School Choir/Orch da Camera/
Cathedral, Coventry   Paul Leddington Wright/Jean Rigby/Charles Clarke/Paul Whelan

8 April   Lincoln and Grimsby Choral Societies and Symphony Orchestras/Neville Turner/
Cathedral, Lincoln   Lincoln Chorale/Kathryn Turpin/Robert Tear/Jonathan Gunthorpe

22 April   Huddersfield Choral Society/English Northern Philharmonia/Martyn Brabbins
Bridgewater Hall, Manchester   Catherine Wyn-Rogers/Arthur Davies/Peter Sidhom

6 May   Fleet and District Choral Soc/Surrey Heath Choral Soc/
Cathedral, Guildford   Bracknell Choral Soc/Chantry Singers

20 May   Thornbury Choral Society and Orchestra/Robert Chadwick
Marlwood School, Alveston, Gloucs   Margaret Small/Paul Baddeley/Stephen Faulkes

21 May   Penrith Singers
St Andrew's Church, Penrith, Cumbria   Margaret Watt/Paul Rendall/Alan Roscoe

3 June   Chester Choral Soc
Cathedral, Chester

10 June   Truro Choral Soc/Michael Edwards
Cathedral, Truro, Cornwall   Heather Shipp/Henry Moss/Michael Pearce

17 June   Epsom Choral Society/Robin Kimber
St Martin's Church, Epsom, Surrey

25 June - National Day of Singing   The Really Big Chorus/Sir David Willcocks
Royal Albert Hall, London   Christine Rice/Robert Tear/Roland Wood

15 July   Sheffield Chorale/Chorale Symphony Orchestra/James Kirkwood
City Hall, Sheffield, South Yorkshire   Margaret MacDonald/Hugh Priday/Mark Wildman

25 August   Three Choirs Festival Chorus/Bournemouth SO/Richard Hickox
Cathedral, Hereford   Catherine Wyn-Rogers/Anthony Rolfe Johnson

1 October   New Century Chorus/London Philharmonic Orchestra/John Cotterill
Royal Albert Hall, London   Catherine Wyn-Rogers/Arthur Davies/John Shirley-Quirk

3 October   City of Birmingham SO and Choir/Sir Simon Rattle
Symphony Hall, Birmingham   Sophie von Otter/Ian Bostridge/John Tomlinson

25 November   Birmingham Festival Chorus/Birmingham Phil Orch/Jeremy Patterson
The Oratory, Birmingham   Cantabile/Sally Bruce-Payne/Mark Padmore/Alan Fairs

2001

8-10 March   Michelle DeYoung/Anthony Dean Griffey/John Relyea
Avery Fisher Hall, New York   Westminster Symph Choir/New York Phil/Sir Colin Davis

Index

References to photographs are given in *italics*. Musical works are listed under the name of their composer. Except for London, urban geographical entries appear under the name of the town or city in which they are located (eg 'King's College Chapel' appears under 'Cambridge').

The Elgar Society was formed in 1951 with the objective of promoting interest in the composer and his music. With a number of significant achievements to its credit, the Society is now the largest UK-based composer appreciation society with ten regional branches in Britain and about 10% of its membership resident outside the UK. In 1997 the Society launched its own Internet website (http://www.elgar.org) with the aim of spreading knowledge of Elgar around the world and, in the process, attracting a greater international membership. This was followed in 1999 by Elgar Enterprises, the trading arm of the Society, whose purpose is to raise funds for the Society's charitable projects through the sale of books, CDs, CD-ROMs and other material about the composer and his music which also further the Society's charitable aims.

All enquiries about membership should be addressed to :

David Morris, 2 Marriotts Close, Haddenham, Aylesbury, Bucks, England HP17 8BT.
Telephone : +44 1844 299239
Fax : +44 1844 290742
E-mail : DavidMorris@bigfoot.com

On-line and postal membership application forms can be found on the website at:

'http://www.elgar.org/5memform.htm'

The Elgar Foundation was established in 1973. Its objectives include supporting the Elgar Birthplace, the cottage in which Elgar was born in Lower Broadheath, some three miles west of the city of Worcester. The Birthplace now houses a collection of memorabilia associated with the composer. It is open to the public throughout most of the year on every day of the week except Wednesdays.
For further information, telephone +44 1905 333224.